# AI-Driven Cybersecurity Techniques, Systems, and Resilience

Bahaa Eddine Elbaghazaoui
https://orcid.org/0000-0002-3206-5162
*Sultan Moulay Slimane University, Morocco*

Khalid Benabbes
https://orcid.org/0009-0001-4780-8790
*University of Moulay Ismail, Morocco*

Tarik El Moudden
https://orcid.org/0000-0002-6963-6686
*Ibn Tofail University, Morocco*

IGI Global
Scientific Publishing
Publishing Tomorrow's Research Today

| | |
|---|---|
| Vice President of Editorial | Melissa Wagner |
| Director of Acquisitions | Mikaela Felty |
| Director of Book Development | Jocelynn Hessler |
| Production Manager | Mike Brehm |
| Cover Design | Jose Rosado |

Published in the United States of America by
IGI Global Scientific Publishing
701 East Chocolate Avenue
Hershey, PA, 17033, USA
Tel: 717-533-8845 | Fax: 717-533-7115
Website: https://www.igi-global.com E-mail: cust@igi-global.com



Library of Congress Cataloging-in-Publication Data

LCCN: 2026035945 (CIP Data Pending)
ISBN13: 9798260034651
Isbn13Softcover: 9798260034668
EISBN13: 9798260034675

British Cataloguing in Publication Data
A Cataloguing in Publication record for this book is available from the British Library.

# Table of Contents

# Detailed Table of Contents



The rapid growth of digital infrastructure and internet-connected devices has increased the risk of malware attacks in modern networks. Traditional signature-based detection methods are reactive and cannot effectively detect advanced threats like code obfuscation, metamorphism, or zero-day attacks. This has led to the use of intelligent techniques such as deep learning for malware detection. Deep learning models can learn complex patterns from large datasets. This approach combines static analysis (from binary data) and dynamic analysis (from system calls). Convolutional Neural Networks (CNN) are used to identify patterns in binary files, while Long Short-Term Memory (LSTM) networks analyze sequences of system calls. Research shows that hybrid CNN-LSTM models improve detection accuracy and perform better than traditional methods



With the rapid expansion of Internet of Things and Industrial IoT systems, maintaining strong cybersecurity has become a critical concern. Industrial networks are highly vulnerable due to complex architectures, real-time processing demands, and continuous data flow. This chapter presents a hybrid intrusion detection system (IDS) for IoT-enabled industrial environments, combining Deep Convolutional Neural Networks (DCNN) and Bidirectional Long Short-Term Memory (BiLSTM) models. The framework utilizes DCNN for spatial feature extraction and BiLSTM for capturing temporal dependencies in network traffic, enabling effective detection of both known and unknown cyber threats. The model is evaluated on a real-world

IIoT dataset, including scenarios such as Electric Vehicle Supply Equipment (EVSE). Experimental results show high performance, achieving 99.88% accuracy in binary classification and 99.50% in multiclass classification across eighteen attack types, demonstrating its reliability and scalability.

**Chapter 3**



*Rajani Mahesh Yemul, Walchand Institute of Technology, Solapur, India*
*Shubham Suresh Vyavahare, Walchand Institute of Technology, Solapur, India*
*Virupakshappa Patil, Sharnbasva University, India*
*Mahesh Satyanarayan Yemul, Sinhgad Business School, Solapur University, India*

Phishing remains a critical cybersecurity threat, exploiting human vulnerabilities via sophisticated imitation to steal data. Traditional detection systems struggle against zero-day, dynamic phishing URLs. This chapter proposes an advanced Artificial Intelligence-based phishing detection framework leveraging machine learning classifiers trained on a comprehensive suite of lexical, statistical, and host-based features. Features like domain length and entropy are extracted to train Random Forest, Support Vector Machines, and Gradient Boosting classifiers. Experimental evaluation on a balanced dataset of 50,000 URLs demonstrates that the Gradient Boosting model achieves a detection accuracy of 96.00% and an F1-score of 0.955. Ultimately, the authors propose this framework not merely as a standalone classifier, but as a foundational perception module for agentic cyber defense systems, enabling autonomous, real-time threat mitigation within enterprise infrastructures.

Smart transportation systems are easier to watch and make decisions about now that they have artificial intelligence in them. However, this has also made them much less secure, especially against hidden backdoor attacks. During training these attacks add poisoned samples with trigger patterns, which makes models produce outputs that the attacker controls when the trigger is present, but they still work normally on clean data. This research examines backdoor vulnerabilities in AI driven smart highway monitoring systems utilizing a traffic sign dataset. A trigger is added to a small part of the training data and then the data is given a new label for the target class. We trained an EfficientNet-B0 model on both clean and poisoned data, and then we test it using clean accuracy and attack success rate (ASR).The results shows a high clean accuracy of 99.84% and an ASR of 99.52%, which shows how stealthy and effective backdoor attacks can be. The results indicate that we need strong ways to find and protect against threats to make sure that AI is safe and reliable.



The Internet of Things (IoT) technology has evolved at a fast pace and transformed industries, healthcare, and city infrastructure positively. Due to the increased pace, cybersecurity is not necessarily the capacity to prevent harmful attacks. The significant issues of IoT security that are discussed in the paper include diversity of devices, supply chain risks and lack of computing resources. It reviews the most important elements of a holistic IoT security plan, including device, network, cloud, and application layers. The paper also examines known cybersecurity standards

The growing reliance on digital technologies, artificial intelligence (AI), and interconnected systems has expanded the cybersecurity threat landscape. While AI enhances automation and threat detection, it also introduces new vulnerabilities requiring advanced expertise. Simultaneously, organizations face a shortage of cybersecurity professionals, widening the gap between security needs and available skills. This paper examines the link between cybersecurity skills demand and the development of AI-driven secure information systems. It identifies key technical and transversal competencies, including AI security, data protection, and automated threat detection, along with essential security practices.To address these challenges, a holistic framework is proposed, integrating human expertise, AI capabilities, governance policies, and technical safeguards. This approach aligns workforce competencies with AI-driven security mechanisms to strengthen resilience, improve risk management, and support secure digital transformation.

The rapid digital transformation of education has accelerated the adoption of artificial intelligence (AI), cloud computing, and smart learning platforms, enabling personalized and adaptive learning experiences. However, this evolution has also increased exposure to cybersecurity threats, making educational institutions prime targets due to the sensitivity and volume of data they handle. This chapter examines key cybersecurity challenges in AI-driven educational environments, including threats such as phishing, ransomware, and data breaches, as well as vulnerabilities related to human behavior and system weaknesses. It proposes a comprehensive approach combining governance, technical safeguards, and user awareness. The chapter also highlights the role of machine learning in enhancing threat detection, predictive security, and automated responses, emphasizing the need for proactive and adaptive cybersecurity strategies.

# Preface

## INTRODUCTION

The rapid evolution of artificial intelligence has fundamentally transformed the cybersecurity landscape. As digital ecosystems become increasingly interconnected and data-driven, cyber threats have grown in sophistication, scale, and persistence. Traditional security mechanisms, which often rely on predefined signatures, static rules, and manual intervention, are no longer sufficient to address the dynamic nature of modern cyberattacks. Artificial intelligence has emerged as a transformative force, enabling intelligent threat detection, predictive analytics, automated response, and resilient security architectures capable of adapting to continuously evolving attack vectors.

*AI-Driven Cybersecurity Techniques, Systems, and Resilience* presents a comprehensive exploration of the methods, technologies, and frameworks that are shaping the next generation of intelligent cybersecurity. Bringing together contributions from researchers across multiple disciplines and regions, this volume examines how advances in machine learning, deep learning, explainable artificial intelligence, intelligent automation, and resilient system design are redefining the protection of digital infrastructures. The book also recognizes that while AI offers unprecedented capabilities for strengthening cyber defense, it simultaneously introduces new security risks, ethical concerns, and governance challenges that must be addressed through responsible design and implementation.

The chapters in this volume span a wide range of contemporary cybersecurity topics, from AI-powered intrusion detection and malware classification to phishing detection, interpretable machine learning, adversarial attacks against AI systems, IoT security, educational network protection, cybersecurity workforce development, and intelligent security for smart learning environments. Together, these contributions illustrate how artificial intelligence is enabling more adaptive, scalable, and proactive security solutions while emphasizing the importance of transparency, resilience, and human oversight.

A central message emerging from this collection is that cybersecurity resilience depends on the integration of intelligent technologies with sound governance, robust engineering practices, and continuous human expertise. AI should not be viewed solely as an automated replacement for traditional security operations, but as a strategic capability that augments human decision-making, accelerates threat response, and strengthens organizational resilience. At the same time, securing AI systems themselves has become an equally important research challenge, requiring innovative approaches to defend against adversarial manipulation, data poisoning, model backdoors, and other emerging threats.

The contributors provide both theoretical perspectives and practical methodologies, presenting state-of-the-art research alongside frameworks that can inform future academic investigation and industrial implementation. Collectively, the chapters demonstrate the growing convergence of artificial intelligence, cybersecurity engineering, risk management, and digital resilience in protecting critical infrastructures and emerging intelligent systems.

## CHAPTER OVERVIEW

1. Presents a deep learning approach to malware detection by combining convolutional neural networks with long short-term memory networks to analyze both binary features and system call sequences, improving the detection of sophisticated and previously unseen malware.
2. Introduces a hybrid intrusion detection framework for Internet of Things and industrial environments that integrates deep learning techniques with feature extraction and temporal analysis to accurately identify both known and emerging cyber threats.
3. Examines artificial intelligence–based phishing website detection using multiple machine learning techniques, demonstrating how intelligent feature extraction and classification can support accurate, real-time identification of malicious websites and strengthen automated cyber defense.
4. Investigates the growing importance of interpretable machine learning for cyber threat detection, highlighting methods that improve transparency, trustworthiness, and explainability while maintaining high predictive performance in security-critical environments.
5. Examines hidden backdoor attacks targeting AI-enabled smart highway monitoring systems, demonstrating the effectiveness of data poisoning techniques

and emphasizing the need for resilient detection methods to safeguard intelligent transportation infrastructures.

6. Reviews cybersecurity frameworks and risk mitigation strategies for Internet of Things ecosystems, addressing device security, network protection, regulatory standards, zero-trust architectures, secure development practices, and emerging technologies supporting resilient IoT environments.
7. Proposes a hybrid anomaly detection framework designed for university Bring Your Own Device (BYOD) networks by combining signature-based detection with ensemble machine learning techniques to improve threat detection while reducing false positives.
8. Explores the relationship between cybersecurity workforce development and AI-driven secure information systems, presenting a holistic framework that integrates technical expertise, governance, human capabilities, and intelligent security technologies to enhance organizational resilience.
9. Concludes by examining cybersecurity challenges in AI-driven smart education environments, presenting integrated governance, technical safeguards, user awareness strategies, and machine learning–based security mechanisms for protecting modern digital learning ecosystems.

## CONCLUSION

Artificial intelligence is reshaping every dimension of cybersecurity, from threat intelligence and intrusion detection to resilient infrastructure protection and digital trust. As organizations continue to embrace intelligent systems, the need for adaptive, explainable, and secure AI-driven solutions will only become more critical. It is our hope that this volume serves as a valuable resource for researchers, practitioners, educators, policymakers, and graduate students seeking to understand both the opportunities and the challenges of AI-enabled cybersecurity. By bringing together diverse perspectives and innovative research, this book aims to contribute to the advancement of secure, trustworthy, and resilient digital ecosystems for the future.

**Bahaa Eddine Elbaghazaoui**
*Sultan Moulay Slimane University, Morocco*

**Khalid Benabbes**
*University of Moulay Ismail, Morocco*

**Tarik El Moudden**
*Ibn Tofail University, Morocco*

Chapter 1

# Deep Learning-Based Malware Detection and Classification Using CNN and LSTM on System Call and Binary Features

**N. Sathwik Krishna**
http://orcid.org/0009-0004-0019-8253
*Sahyadri College of Engineering and Management, India*

**K. Alakananda**
http://orcid.org/0000-0002-4892-4902
*Sahyadri College of Engineering and Management, India*

## ABSTRACT

*The rapid growth of digital infrastructure and internet-connected devices has increased the risk of malware attacks in modern networks. Traditional signature-based detection methods are reactive and cannot effectively detect advanced threats like code obfuscation, metamorphism, or zero-day attacks. This has led to the use of intelligent techniques such as deep learning for malware detection. Deep learning models can learn complex patterns from large datasets. This approach combines static analysis (from binary data) and dynamic analysis (from system calls). Convolutional Neural Networks (CNN) are used to identify patterns in binary files, while Long Short-Term Memory (LSTM) networks analyze sequences of system calls. Research shows that hybrid CNN-LSTM models improve detection accuracy and perform better than traditional methods*

DOI: 10.4018/979-8-2600-3465-1.ch001

# 1 INTRODUCTION

Significant changes in the functioning of modern society have developed due to the rapid development of digital technologies. Computing systems, in particular, have grown from standalone systems in the past few decades to highly interconnected platforms that facilitate communication, automation, data analysis, and decision-making in almost all sectors of society. Computing devices, networks, cloud computing, and large-scale IoT systems have become an integral part of life, making information interchange efficient, real-time monitoring, and intelligent control of complex systems, thereby improving productivity, accessibility, and quality of service in healthcare, finance, transportation, education, automation, and many other areas.

Even though these advancements in computing systems have improved the quality of life in many ways, the increased use of these platforms has led to a significant increase in security concerns. With more devices connecting to the internet, there is a consequent increase in attack surface for attackers. Some computer systems and information networks are negatively affected by multiple types of security threats; however, malware is among the most significant examples of a security threat. Malware, or malicious software, can include a variety of computer programs that are designed to cause harm to a computer system's operation, to obtain an enterprise's confidential business or personal data, to damage the enterprise's computer assets, or to gain unauthorized access to an enterprise's computer systems. Malware attacks can result in businesses suffering from losses due to downtime, expose companies to the risk of being involved in data breaches, may disrupt systems and can cause the public to lose confidence in the enterprise that is the target of an attack, which underscores the compelling need for us to recognize the importance of both detecting and preventing malware.

The number of malware attacks is on the rise and they are now more complicated and sophisticated than ever before. Unlike the older type of malware, which was simple and identified easily, the modern generation is more advanced, which makes it difficult to track or identify because of using several techniques like obfuscation, encryption, polymorphism and metamorphism. The new generation of malware supports several forms of platforms and architectures, which allows malware of the same family to attack different environments. Other threats have also been seen within IoT and the Internet of Medical Things (IoMT) devices, that normally have low processor speed, low memory, and weak security. These devices have a long lifespan and do not regularly receive updates, which makes them easy targets for cybercriminals, increasing large-scale botnet attacks, DDoS, and unauthorized surveillance. In the healthcare sector, the new generation of malware has a large effect on the healthcare system and can negatively affect patient safety due to the nature of these types of attacks.

Malware is traditionally detected using signature-based malware detection, which checks if executable files match known signatures in a database. The main reason for using a signature is because of its efficiency and effective detection of known malware; only existing malwares are detected with this type of technique, which is known as "reactive" detection. However, it cannot detect zero-day malware, or malware for which there is no existing signature in the database. Because malware authors modify the code frequently to avoid detection through signature-based techniques, the database must be updated on an ongoing basis to remain effective. To overcome the limitations of the signature-based detection method, two substitute methods of detection were created: heuristic-based detection and anomaly-based detection. Both of these methods attempt to find malware by identifying the difference between their characteristics; however, they sometimes generate false alarms. When this problem occurs at a large scale, the high number of false alarms can be frustrating.

Because of the above-mentioned limitations of the previous malware detection techniques, researchers started to focus more on using machine-learning-based techniques to detect malware. Machine learning techniques most frequently used to classify malware include support vector machines, random forests, decision trees, and the k-nearest neighbor algorithm. However, even with these advantages, some challenges have been identified for machine learning-based approaches. The first limitation is that these systems depend heavily on feature extraction and are vulnerable to attacks that use feature manipulation to bypass detection systems. Additionally, these systems have reduced detection performance when used on different computing platforms, a limitation that is usually seen in IoT devices.

As a result of these limitations, there has been an increased need for improved detection systems that overcome these challenges. Deep learning models are seen as the potential replacement for traditional machine learning models because they learn to extract feature representations from raw data. CNNs have shown strong performance in learning features of binary data or images of malware and are also effective for static malware analysis. Using both low-level and high-level feature representations together helps to learn the structural characteristics of the malware data.

RNNs including LSTM networks work very well with sequential and temporal data. This has led to increased use of LSTM models for analyzing system and API calls produced by malicious software during execution, as these calls reveal the behavior of the malware and cannot be easily removed through obfuscation. Dynamic analysis is therefore very important for detecting malware. There is a growing emphasis on using a hybrid method of malware detection, as it is no longer sufficient to rely solely on a single method to mitigate the effects of modern malware. Static approaches are ineffective when dealing with heavily obfuscated and packed malware, while dynamic approaches involve high computational costs and may also face evasion techniques. Research continues to show promise in creating hybrid models utilizing deep learning techniques for malware analysis.

In response to these challenges, this chapter adopts a conceptual review perspective and examines recent advances in deep learning-based malware detection with emphasis on hybrid CNN–LSTM architectures. By critically analyzing static analysis, dynamic analysis, preprocessing strategies, feature fusion techniques, evaluation methodologies, and practical deployment considerations, the chapter seeks to provide a structured understanding of contemporary malware detection research. Rather than presenting an experimentally validated implementation, the chapter proposes a conceptual hybrid framework intended to synthesize current knowledge, identify persistent research challenges, and outline important methodological considerations for future investigation.

## 2 PROBLEM FORMULATION

### 2.1 Problem Statement

Modern malware is becoming more advanced and difficult to detect using traditional methods. Existing detection techniques mainly rely on known signatures or simple patterns, which are not effective against new, unknown, or modified malware such as polymorphic and zero-day attacks. There is a need for an intelligent system that can accurately detect malware by analyzing both its structure and behavior.

### 2.2 Problem Description

Malware is a serious threat to computers, networks, and digital systems. Traditional malware detection methods work by comparing files with a database of known malware signatures. While this works well for known threats, it fails to detect new or modified malware that does not match existing patterns.

Attackers use techniques like code obfuscation, encryption, and frequent modifications to hide malware from detection systems. Because of this, static analysis methods, which only look at the file structure, are not always reliable. On the other hand, dynamic analysis, which studies the behavior of a program during execution, can detect hidden threats but requires more time and resources.

There is a need for a better approach that can combine the strengths of both static and dynamic analysis. Deep learning techniques, especially Convolutional Neural Networks (CNN) and Long Short-Term Memory (LSTM) networks, can automatically learn patterns from data. By combining these techniques, it is possible to build a system that detects malware more accurately and efficiently, even when the malware is new or hidden.

## 2.3 Objectives of Study

The primary objectives of this study are outlined as follows:

- **To thoroughly study and analyze the existing deep learning-based malware detection techniques**, including static, dynamic, and hybrid approaches used in modern cybersecurity systems.
- **To identify the key limitations and challenges in current malware detection methods,** such as handling obfuscated malware, high computational cost, and lack of scalability, and explore possible improvements or optimized solutions.
- **To evaluate the effectiveness of hybrid deep learning models, particularly CNN and LSTM architectures,** through comparative analysis and literature review, in order to understand their performance in detecting modern and unknown malware threats.

# 3 EXISTING WORKS

Malware detection has come to be recognized as a significant field of research due to the rapid advancement of cyber threats and the growing need to protect the ever-expanding network of digital infrastructures. Malware detection has largely been done using signature-based approaches where malware executables are compared to existing signatures of malware. Traditional detection using signature-based approaches have had success identifying well-known malware; however, these types of traditional methods can only identify known malware and cannot detect unknown malware. The growing number of sophisticated malware techniques, including code obfuscation, polymorphism, encryption, and packing have also limited the ability of traditional methods to effectively detect malware.

It is also noteworthy that the development of deep learning techniques has significantly impacted research on malware detection, as the techniques can learn features from raw data. Deep learning techniques have the ability to learn representative characteristics of complex behaviours and structures of malware, whereas conventional machine learning methods must rely on manually engineered features. Recent studies have indicated that deep learning based systems for detecting malware outperform traditional methods in regards to performance, scaling and generalization. Specifically, research has demonstrated that a hybrid model composed of convolutional and recurrent networks have produced good results in the structural and behavioural aspects of malware (Akhtar & Feng, 2022; Thakur et al., 2024; Karat et al., 2024; Maulana & Kusuma, 2020).

A further significant research direction involving deep learning-based approaches for malware detection is static analysis, which focuses on executable files without executing them. This has shown some remarkable advantages, such as safety and scalability, which prevent the infection of systems and eliminate the need for a controlled environment. Chaganti et al. proposed a framework for the detection of cross-architecture IoT malware based on deep learning, which used a Bi-GRU-CNN model (2022). The research adopts a method that analyzes the raw byte sequences of ELF binaries that employs a combination of bidirectional gated recurrent units and convolutional neural networks to detect sequential dependencies and spatial features in binary executable code. The empirical findings support the proposed method's efficacy for detecting executable code binaries across multiple CPU architectures (i.e., ARM, MIPS, x86) and therefore demonstrate that deep learning can be applied to Internet of Things (IoT) devices.

Similar to the broader literature on malware analysis, image-based static analysis has been studied in many research works. Kim and Kim utilized the conversion of binaries into images and CNN models to extract structural features from executables (2024). Other works have shown the viability of CNN-based static analysis on Android malware and malware classification tasks (Calik Bayazit et al., 2023; Aslan & Yilmaz, 2021). These works suggest that spatial feature extraction via convolutional layers is viable for extracting discriminative features directly from binaries. However, such models face limitations when malware uses sophisticated obfuscation or packing techniques.

In order to overcome the disadvantages of static analysis, researchers have explored various dynamic malware analysis approaches. The main idea behind dynamic malware analysis is to focus on observing system call sequences and API calls. It is widely acknowledged that system calls are an effective method for identifying malicious behavior patterns (Xiao et al., 2019; Catak et al., 2020; Kolosnjaji et al., 2016; Anderson & Roth, 2018). Kolosnjaji et al. proved that malware can be effectively classified using recurrent neural networks based on system calls (2016). Along these lines, Catak et al. proposed a deep learning-based sequential model based on Windows API calls, showing the effectiveness of learning temporal patterns (2020). Similarly, it was also proved that LSTM-based networks can effectively detect malware for Android systems based on system calls (Xiao et al., 2019).

Ransomware detection using the LSTM-based dynamic analysis approach has also been studied. Maniath et al. proposed a deep learning model using LSTM algorithm for ransomware detection, which highlights the importance of behavioral patterns in the detection of malicious encryption activities (2017). These research papers show that using sequence models such as LSTM or GRU for malware detection improves the detection rate.

Although dynamic analysis provides better security against static code obfuscation attacks, it also requires additional computational overhead, which requires a sandboxed environment for analysis. Therefore, implementing a dynamic analysis-based system in real-time may become challenging for large-scale deployments. As a result, researchers have been motivated to develop a hybrid framework that combines both static and dynamic analysis features.

The hybrid property of deep learning models has gained a lot of scholarly interest and focus. Akhtar and Feng proposed a real-time malware detection system using CNN-LSTM models. The given model improved the quality of malware detection by fusing spatial and temporal information learning (Akhtar & Feng, 2022; Maulana & Kusuma, 2020). Thakur et al. proposed a hybrid deep learning model using CNN and LSTM models, further validating the improved performance of malware detection by fusing structural and sequential information learning (2024). Karat et al. proposed a CNN-LSTM hybrid model for improved malware analysis and detection, further validating the improved performance by fusing spatial and sequential information learning (2024).

Ravi et al. further enhanced the proposed hybrid model by proposing a novel attention-based multidimensional deep learning framework for cross-architecture IoMT malware detection (2023). The proposed model fuses the power of multi-channel CNN-based static feature learning and BiLSTM-based behavioral modeling. The proposed model further includes an attention mechanism to focus on the most relevant features. The proposed model shows promising results in malware detection and classification accuracy. However, the proposed model includes higher computational complexity and requires large-scale training data to learn the attention mechanism.

Further research has been conducted on the use of the hybrid CNN-LSTM approach for Android malware classification (Hosseini et al., 2021) and for the more general task of malware categorization (Aslan & Yilmaz, 2021). This further research validates that the hybrid approach outperforms both the static and dynamic approaches individually.

From the various research papers presented above, various trends and challenges can be noted. Firstly, the CNN-based static approach is more efficient and scalable but is more vulnerable to sophisticated forms of malware obfuscation. Secondly, the LSTM-based dynamic approach is stronger in modeling the temporal working of the malware but is more resource-intensive. Thirdly, the hybrid CNN-LSTM approach is more accurate and generalizes better than the other two approaches.

However, the design and evaluation methodology for the datasets still remain a challenge. Malware datasets often suffer from various issues such as class imbalance, diversity of families included, and platform dependencies, which may impact the accuracy and generalization performance of the approach. Moreover, the evaluation methodology for the proposed approach, as implemented by Chaganti et al. (2022) and Ravi et al. (2023), is an essential step towards a more realistic evaluation methodology. However, the availability of benchmarking tools is still limited. In addition, the preprocessing steps have a significant effect on the output evaluation outcomes for the proposed approach (Kim & Kim, 2024; Thakur et al., 2024; Karat et al., 2024).

However, research gaps still exist, which are proving to be a barrier in the development of efficient, scalable, and deployable hybrid malware detection systems. Although the hybrid approach of deep learning has shown significant promise in terms of malware detection, the challenge of achieving a balance between high accuracy and computational efficiency still remains.

Overall, from the literature survey, deep learning-based malware detection techniques are significantly better than traditional signature-based detection methods. Static analysis using CNN-based methods can efficiently extract structural features, dynamic analysis using LSTM-based methods can efficiently model behavior, and the hybrid approach can combine these two for better accuracy. Although certain issues remain as barriers, these literature survey results provide a clear understanding of the research in this domain.

## 3.1 Critical Comparative Discussion

A comparative examination of existing deep learning-based malware detection studies reveals important methodological trends and persistent challenges. CNN-based approaches demonstrate strong capability in learning structural patterns from binary representations and raw byte sequences, making them suitable for scalable static malware analysis. However, their performance may degrade against heavily obfuscated malware or behavior-dependent threats. Conversely, LSTM-based approaches excel in capturing temporal relationships from API calls, system calls, and behavioral traces, allowing more effective modeling of runtime malware activities.

Recent hybrid architectures combining CNN and LSTM networks attempt to leverage the complementary strengths of both paradigms. Studies by Ravi et al. (2023), Kim and Kim (2024), Thakur et al. (2024), and Akhtar and Feng (2022) suggest that hybrid models can improve classification performance by integrating structural and sequential feature representations. Nevertheless, hybrid systems frequently introduce additional computational complexity, increased preprocessing requirements, and challenges related to deployment in resource-constrained environments such as IoT and IoMT ecosystems.

Another important observation concerns dataset design and experimental reproducibility. Several studies employ different malware repositories, preprocessing strategies, and evaluation protocols, making direct comparison difficult. Issues involving dataset imbalance, dataset aging, malware family bias, and limited cross-platform generalization remain common across the literature. Consequently, performance claims reported by individual studies should be interpreted cautiously, particularly when considering practical deployment scenarios.

### 3.1.1 Emerging Challenges in Deep Learning-Based Malware Detection

Beyond conventional detection accuracy, recent research highlights several emerging concerns affecting deep learning-based malware detection systems. One major challenge involves dataset bias and reproducibility, since malware repositories often overrepresent specific malware families, architectures, or historical attack periods. Such bias can artificially inflate reported performance and reduce real-world generalization.

Another important concern relates to explainability. Deep learning classifiers frequently behave as black-box systems, limiting transparency regarding why a particular executable is classified as malicious or benign. This creates trust, auditing, and operational challenges in cybersecurity environments.

Researchers have also begun investigating adversarial robustness, where attackers deliberately manipulate malware inputs to deceive machine learning classifiers. Adversarial attacks demonstrate that minor feature perturbations may influence model predictions, highlighting the need for resilient malware detection architectures.

Finally, practical deployment considerations remain insufficiently explored. Computational cost, inference latency, memory requirements, and deployment feasibility continue to present obstacles for real-time malware detection in cloud, edge, IoT, and endpoint protection systems.

## 3.2 Research Gap

Although substantial progress has been achieved in deep learning-based malware detection, several important limitations remain unresolved in existing research. Many studies primarily emphasize either static analysis or dynamic analysis independently, resulting in trade-offs between scalability, robustness, and computational efficiency. Static methods often struggle with obfuscated, packed, or polymorphic malware, whereas dynamic approaches introduce challenges related to sandbox overhead, execution latency, and evasive malware behavior.

Recent hybrid CNN–LSTM architectures demonstrate promising detection performance; however, several issues continue to require further investigation. These include dataset imbalance, dataset aging, limited reproducibility of malware experiments, high computational complexity, deployment constraints in resource-constrained environments, insufficient explainability of deep learning decisions, and difficulties in generalizing across malware families, operating systems, and processor architectures.

Additionally, many published studies focus primarily on reporting classification performance without providing comprehensive discussion of preprocessing strategies, feature fusion methodologies, practical deployment considerations, or evaluation limitations. Consequently, a need exists for a structured conceptual analysis that synthesizes recent advances, critically compares existing methodologies, and clarifies the design considerations involved in hybrid deep learning-based malware detection systems.

## 3.3 Research Objectives and Methodology

This section clearly articulates the key objectives of the proposed research and offers a detailed view of the methodological framework adopted for the achievement of these objectives. In this phase, emphasis is not given to implementation or experimentation; rather, focus is given to laying a strong conceptual and analytical groundwork through the analysis of existing malware detection techniques and exploring the potential of utilizing advanced deep learning models to solve the problems of existing issues in cybersecurity.

## 3.4 Research Purpose and Scope

The primary aim of this research is to study, analyze, and critically evaluate deep learning-based malware detection techniques, particularly focusing on the hybrid approach that combines Convolutional Neural Networks (CNN) and Long Short-Term Memory (LSTM) models. The main reason for this research is that traditional malware detection systems have several limitations, especially when handling new types of malware such as polymorphic, obfuscated, and zero-day malware.

The current phase of this research focuses on performing a detailed analysis of recent literature to identify state-of-the-art techniques in malware detection. It also aims to develop a clear understanding of the theoretical foundations behind deep learning-based malware detection methods. By analyzing existing approaches, this research intends to identify their advantages and limitations, which is important to avoid repeating the same issues in future developments.

Another important goal of this research is to study how hybrid CNN–LSTM architectures improve malware detection performance compared to individual models. CNN-based models are effective in recognizing spatial and structural patterns in binary data, whereas LSTM-based models are suitable for capturing temporal patterns in sequential behavioral data. This research emphasizes how combining these two models can enhance overall detection capability.

The scope of this phase includes:

- Studying static, dynamic, and hybrid malware detection techniques
- Reviewing deep learning architectures used in recent research
- Identifying challenges related to obfuscation, scalability, and cross-architecture detection
- Understanding dataset characteristics and preprocessing strategies
- Explaining the need for a hybrid deep learning approach

Through a comprehensive understanding of these aspects, this research aims to lay a strong foundation for developing an efficient, scalable, and robust malware detection system in future stages. This study also attempts to reduce the gap between static and dynamic malware analysis. Individually, static methods are often insufficient for detecting advanced malware, while dynamic analysis can be computationally expensive due to evasion techniques used by malware even in sandbox environments.

It is expected that combining static and dynamic analysis using deep learning techniques will improve detection performance in a reliable manner, especially for modern malware threats, including zero-day attacks.

## 3.5 Overview of Static and Dynamic Malware Analysis Techniques

To achieve the goals of the proposed research study, a method using both static and dynamic malware analysis has been developed as the basis for this research study. Static and dynamic malware analysis techniques give two different views: how the malware is built and how the malware runs. The methodology will demonstrate the ability of deep learning methods to automatically learn the most useful representations of malware from these two perspectives and how they may be used together to create a more accurate description of malware.

### 3.5.1 Static Malware Analysis Using Binary Features

Static malware analysis refers to analyzing malware executable files without running them. This methodology is secure, efficient, and can be scaled up because there is no chance of being infected by malware when performing this analysis.

The research described in this paper proposes the extraction of binary feature data (byte streams) and/or raw byte data from all types of files on computers. Binary feature data includes information about a file's low-level structures, instruction patterns and their layout within the file, and how the file is divided into sections, which are used to identify all types of malware.

CNNs are used to perform the static malware analysis. The CNN model uses filters to detect spatial feature hierarchies, including byte sequence patterns and abnormal patterns which are usually associated with malware. The feature map dimension is reduced by using the pooling operation, which enhances efficiency and prevents overfitting. The abstract features are then converted into a feature vector. CNN-based static malware analysis does not require any feature engineering and is capable of learning and adapting to different malware patterns.

### 3.5.2 Dynamic Malware Analysis Using System Call Sequences

Dynamic malware analysis involves the study of executable code behavior during runtime in an isolated and controlled environment. A program can be examined to determine how it interacts with the operating system and what types of resources it accesses externally, helping to understand the actual purpose of a program.

When malware runs, it generates many calls to the operating system (system calls) including accessing files, allocating memory, creating processes, and communicating with other processes. This sequence of system calls clearly shows how the program behaves and is hard to hide, even with different obfuscation techniques.

In this research, dynamic analysis of malware includes collecting the system call sequences produced when the malware is executed, then modelling them using LSTM models. LSTM models are a type of recurrent neural network ideal for the sequential nature of the data and have the ability to represent long-term dependencies. This characteristic is mainly useful for detecting malware because the behavior of malware changes over time.

The dynamic analysis will give a high level of accuracy in detecting many different types of malware, particularly more sophisticated malware such as self-modifying and/or obfuscated code. However, dynamic analysis also faces issues such as execution overhead, sandbox detection, and scalability problems.

### 3.5.3 Integration of Static and Dynamic Analysis

One of the main objectives of the research is to investigate ways static and dynamic analysis methods can be combined properly using deep learning. Static analysis provides efficiency and scalability, while dynamic analysis enhances robustness against evasion techniques. Individually, each approach has limitations; combined, they offer complementary strengths.

The integration of CNN-based static feature learning and LSTM-based dynamic behavior modeling enables the development of a hybrid malware detection framework. This hybrid approach is expected to achieve improved detection accuracy, better generalization to unseen malware variants, and enhanced resilience against obfuscation and zero-day attacks.

# 4 IMPLEMENTATION

## 4.1 Proposed System Architecture

The proposed system for detecting malware is based on a hybrid deep learning model that combines static feature extraction and dynamic behavior analysis to achieve high accuracy in malware detection. The need for such a system arises from the fact that malware can be analyzed in two ways: statically, based on its binary structure, and dynamically, based on its behavior during execution. Relying on a single type of analysis may lead to poor detection performance, especially when dealing with obfuscated or zero-day malware.

The proposed conceptual framework integrates static and dynamic analysis through a hybrid CNN–LSTM architecture designed to leverage complementary structural and behavioral information. The static analysis branch employs a CNN-based feature extraction mechanism. Binary representations derived from executable files are processed through convolutional layers responsible for identifying local structural patterns, followed by activation functions such as ReLU and pooling operations for dimensionality reduction and feature refinement. The resulting feature maps are flattened into numerical feature vectors representing binary structural information.

The dynamic analysis branch utilizes LSTM networks for sequential behavioral modeling. Encoded system call sequences are supplied to embedding and recurrent processing layers, allowing temporal dependencies and execution patterns to be learned from behavioral traces.

The outputs generated by the CNN and LSTM branches are combined using a feature fusion strategy based on vector concatenation. This integrated representation is subsequently supplied to dense classification layers for malware detection and classification analysis.

The overall system architecture is divided into five major stages:

1. System overview and data flow
2. Static feature extraction using Convolutional Neural Networks (CNN)
3. Dynamic feature extraction using Long Short-Term Memory (LSTM) networks
4. Feature fusion strategy
5. Final classification of malware and benign samples

Each component of the architecture plays an important role in capturing different types of information. By combining both structural and behavioral features, the system is able to improve detection accuracy and provide a more robust solution for identifying modern malware threats.

*Figure 1. Proposed CNN-LSTM Based Malware Detection Architecture*

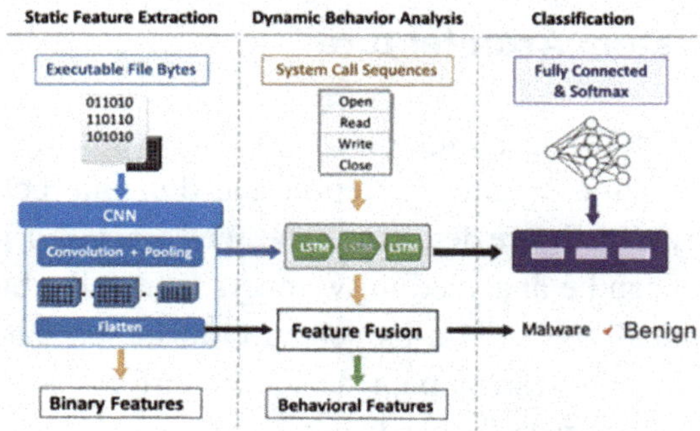


## 4.1.1 System Overview

The proposed system operates by analyzing executable files through both static and dynamic perspectives. Initially, all executable files are classified into malware and benign categories. After this step, two pipelines analyze these files in parallel. The first pipeline performs static analysis without executing the file, extracting binary-based structural features. The dynamic pipeline analyzes executable files by running them in a sandbox (virtual) environment, where system call sequences are collected.

After both pipelines complete their analysis, the extracted features are combined into a fixed-length feature vector. This feature vector is then passed to a classification module, which determines whether the input file is malware or benign. The system is designed to be extensible, allowing future improvements such as additional feature sets or enhanced architecture.

## 4.1.2 Static Feature Extraction Workflow

The static feature extraction component is a critical part of the system, as it analyzes executable files without execution, thereby reducing security risks. The input data consists of raw binary data, which represents the sequence of bytes of executable files.

#### *4.1.2.1 Binary Data Representation*

Each executable file is composed of sequences of bytes, which represent its low-level structure. These byte sequences may contain patterns that indicate malicious behavior. To make the data compatible with deep learning models, the sequences must be normalized to a fixed length. Techniques such as padding and truncation are used to ensure uniform input size.

#### *4.1.2.2 CNN-Based Feature Learning*

The normalized byte sequences are fed into a Convolutional Neural Network (CNN). The CNN consists of multiple convolutional and pooling layers. The convolutional layers use learnable filters to detect spatial patterns in the binary data, such as repeating instruction patterns and abnormal byte structures often found in malware.

Pooling layers reduce the dimensionality of feature maps while retaining important features. This improves computational efficiency and reduces overfitting. After convolution and pooling, the feature maps are flattened into a fixed-length feature vector representing static malware characteristics. CNN-based models can automatically learn features without manual feature engineering.

### 4.1.3 Dynamic Feature Extraction Workflow

Dynamic feature extraction focuses on analyzing the runtime behavior of executable files. Unlike static analysis, dynamic analysis observes how a program behaves during execution, making it more effective against obfuscation and packing techniques.

#### *4.1.3.1 Runtime Behavior Monitoring*

Executable files are executed in a secure environment such as a sandbox or virtual machine. During execution, various behavioral features are monitored, including system calls, API calls, file operations, memory usage, and process interactions. Among these, system call sequences are particularly important as they represent the interaction between the program and the operating system.

#### *4.1.3.2 Sequence Preprocessing*

Before feeding the data into the model, system call sequences must be preprocessed. This includes techniques such as padding, truncation, and sliding window methods to ensure uniform sequence length. Frequency encoding may also be applied to improve learning efficiency.

#### *4.1.3.3 LSTM-Based Behavioral Modeling*

After preprocessing, the system call sequences are input into a Long Short-Term Memory (LSTM) network. LSTM is a type of Recurrent Neural Network (RNN) that is well-suited for sequential data and can capture long-term dependencies.

The LSTM analyzes the sequence of system calls and learns patterns in behavior that distinguish malicious activity from benign activity. The output of the LSTM is a fixed-length feature vector representing dynamic behavioral characteristics. This is particularly useful for detecting sophisticated malware that evades static analysis.

### 4.1.4 Feature Fusion Strategy

The feature fusion stage combines information from both static and dynamic analysis pipelines. The static feature vector obtained from the CNN and the dynamic feature vector obtained from the LSTM are merged into a unified feature representation.

This fusion can be performed using techniques such as feature concatenation or learned fusion mechanisms. The goal is to preserve complementary information from both sources. Static features provide insights into the internal structure of the executable, while dynamic features capture runtime behavior.

By combining both types of features, the system overcomes the limitations of individual approaches. Static analysis offers efficiency, while dynamic analysis provides robustness against obfuscation and zero-day attacks.

### 4.1.5 Classification Process

The final stage of the system is classification, where the input executable is categorized as malware or benign. The fused feature vector is passed through fully connected layers, which learn complex decision boundaries based on combined features.

A Softmax activation function is applied in the final layer to compute class probabilities. The class with the highest probability is selected as the final prediction.

This classification module ensures accurate decision-making and can be extended in the future to support multi-class classification, such as identifying different malware families.

### 4.1.6 Classification and Optimization Strategy

Following feature fusion, classification analysis may be performed using fully connected neural network layers combined with Softmax activation functions for probabilistic decision generation. Binary classification settings typically distinguish malware from benign software, whereas multiclass classification settings may categorize malware families.

Deep learning optimization procedures commonly employ adaptive optimizers such as Adam together with cross-entropy loss functions to minimize prediction error during training. Regularization approaches including dropout, early stopping, and weight regularization may be incorporated to reduce overfitting and improve generalization performance.

*Figure 2. Workflow of the Proposed Malware Detection System*

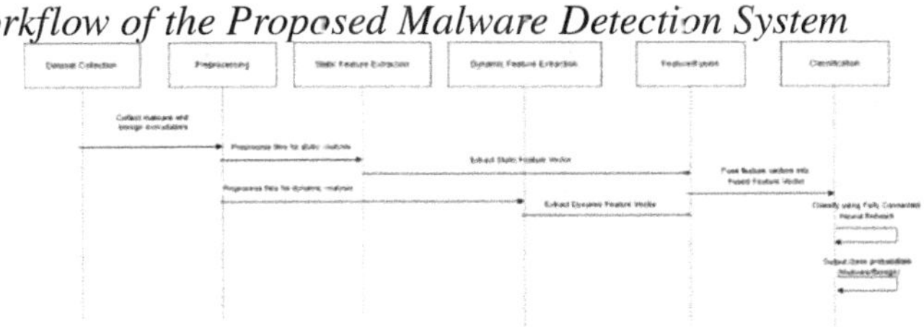

## 5 EXPECTED OUTCOMES AND PERFORMANCE METRICS

The evaluation of the malware detection system is an important aspect of conducting research in the cybersecurity field, as it evaluates the efficiency and applicability of the suggested system. The results and working of the proposed hybrid CNN-LSTM malware detection system are evaluated using some of the most widely accepted performance metrics for classification tasks. These metrics provide useful information about how well the proposed malware detection system works.

The most anticipated output of the suggested malware detection system is the achievement of high accuracy, generalization, and robustness to evasion techniques by integrating both static and dynamic analysis approaches. For evaluating the proposed results, the generally accepted performance metrics used include accuracy, precision, recall, F1-score, and confusion matrix.

## 5.1 Accuracy

Accuracy is one of the most commonly used measures of system performance in classification problems. It is the ratio of correct classifications to total instances classified. In malware detection systems, accuracy is determined by how well the file is predicted to be either malware or benign.

$$\text{Accuracy} = \frac{TP + TN}{TP + TN + FP + FN}$$

where TP = True Positives, TN = True Negatives, FP = False Positives, and FN = False Negatives.

A higher accuracy value indicates a model has performed well for both classes overall. In malware detection systems, high accuracy is preferred; however, it may not be enough to provide complete evaluation results. For example, if there are far more benign samples than malware, the model can produce a high accuracy rating simply by classifying the majority of predictions as benign. The hybrid model being proposed will improve accuracy and compatibility of results by using multiple datasets.

## 5.2 Precision

Precision measures the proportion of correctly predicted malware samples among all predicted malware samples.

$$\text{Precision} = \frac{TP}{TP + FP}$$

Higher precision indicates fewer false alarms. In malware detection systems, false positives refer to files that have been mistakenly identified as malware, which creates unnecessary alerts, interferes with normal system operation, and damages users' confidence. A proposed hybrid malware detection system can help increase the overall level of precision by using dual methodologies, which will decrease the total number of false positive results.

## 5.3 Recall

Recall (or sensitivity, or true positive rate) measures the ability of the model to correctly identify actual malware samples.

$$\text{Recall} = \frac{TP}{TP + FN}$$

Recall is an important measure in malware detection because false negatives (malware incorrectly identified as benign) can have serious adverse consequences. If the system does not detect malware, it can cause harm to the organization by compromising systems and/or data. The expected result of the proposed system is to have a high value of recall by utilizing dynamic behavioral analysis based on LSTM networks for the detection of complex malware that may not be detected by static analysis.

## 5.4 F1-Score

F1-Score provides a balanced evaluation using both Precision and Recall.

$$F1 = 2 \times \frac{\text{Precision} \times \text{Recall}}{\text{Precision} + \text{Recall}}$$

This metric is particularly useful for imbalanced datasets. It ensures a balance between precision and recall so that a system is good at detecting malware without excessive false alarms. The proposed system, being a hybrid of both static and dynamic analysis, is expected to achieve a high F1 score.

## 5.5 False Positive Rate (FPR)

False Positive Rate measures the proportion of benign software incorrectly classified as malware.

$$FPR = \frac{FP}{FP + TN}$$

Lower FPR values are desirable in malware detection systems.

## 5.6 False Negative Rate (FNR)

False Negative Rate measures the proportion of malware incorrectly classified as benign.

$$FNR = \frac{FN}{FN + TP}$$

Reducing false negatives is critical because undetected malware may compromise system security.

## 5.7 Area Under ROC Curve (AUC-ROC)

AUC-ROC evaluates the model's ability to distinguish malware from benign samples across different thresholds.

$$\text{AUC-ROC} = \int_0^1 TPR(FPR)\, d(FPR)$$

## 5.8 Confusion Matrix

The confusion matrix is a fundamental evaluation tool that provides a detailed breakdown of classification outcomes. It is a tabular representation that compares actual class labels with predicted class labels, enabling a clear understanding of the model's performance.

In a binary malware detection scenario, the confusion matrix consists of four components:

- **True Positives (TP):** Malware samples correctly classified as malware
- **True Negatives (TN):** Benign samples correctly classified as benign
- **False Positives (FP):** Benign samples incorrectly classified as malware
- **False Negatives (FN):** Malware samples incorrectly classified as benign

The confusion matrix allows researchers to analyze specific error patterns and understand where the model may require improvement. Although this phase of the project does not involve experimental evaluation, the confusion matrix will be used conceptually in later phases to analyze system performance in detail.

## 5.9 Expected Performance Characteristics

Based on insights from existing literature and the proposed system design, the expected performance characteristics of the hybrid CNN–LSTM malware detection system include:

- High accuracy of detection across diverse datasets
- Improved precision due to reduced false positive rates
- Strong recall enabling effective detection of zero-day and obfuscated malware
- Balanced F1-score indicating robust and reliable performance
- Clear interpretability of results through confusion matrix analysis

## 5.10 Proposed Evaluation Framework

Because this chapter presents a conceptual framework rather than an experimentally validated implementation, performance assessment is discussed from an evaluation methodology perspective.

Malware detection systems are commonly evaluated using metrics including Accuracy, Precision, Recall, F1-score, Area Under ROC Curve (AUC-ROC), False Positive Rate (FPR), and False Negative Rate (FNR). Additional practical considerations involving inference latency, computational overhead, model complexity, and deployment feasibility may also influence real-world system performance.

Comparative evaluation may involve benchmarking against baseline approaches such as standalone CNN models, standalone LSTM models, conventional machine learning classifiers, and signature-based malware detection methods.

# 6 ETHICAL AND SAFETY CONSIDERATIONS

Malware detection research involves handling potentially dangerous software samples, which makes ethical and safety practices very important. Malware analysis should be performed in isolated environments such as virtual machines, sandbox systems, or controlled execution environments to avoid accidental infection or unintended spread of malicious software.

Datasets used for malware research should be obtained from legitimate and authorized sources, and researchers should ensure compliance with institutional cybersecurity policies and dataset licensing requirements. When behavioral data such as system calls, API traces, or runtime logs are collected from real systems, privacy and confidentiality must be maintained.

This chapter follows a defensive cybersecurity perspective and focuses on improving malware detection methodologies without providing harmful code, exploit instructions, or operational malware details. The discussion is intended to support secure cybersecurity research, safe malware handling, and responsible development of intelligent malware detection systems.

Additionally, researchers should consider challenges related to dataset bias, reproducibility, and explainability, since malware datasets may overrepresent specific malware families, platforms, or time periods, potentially affecting fairness and model generalization.

## 6.1 Limitations of the Proposed Conceptual Framework

Although hybrid CNN–LSTM architectures present a promising direction for malware detection, several limitations must be acknowledged. The proposed framework is conceptual in nature and does not present experimental validation or benchmark evaluation results. Consequently, claims regarding performance improvements should be interpreted as insights derived from existing literature rather than experimentally verified outcomes.

Deep learning-based malware detection systems also face practical challenges related to computational complexity, large dataset requirements, preprocessing sensitivity, and deployment feasibility in real-world environments. Dynamic analysis introduces additional overhead associated with sandbox execution, while hybrid architectures may increase resource consumption compared to single-modality approaches.

Furthermore, issues involving dataset bias, adversarial attacks, explainability, and reproducibility continue to remain open research challenges in modern malware detection research. These limitations highlight the importance of continued investigation and methodological refinement in future cybersecurity studies.

# 7 CONCLUSION

The increasing complexity of contemporary malware has made the conventional detection mechanisms ineffective for maintaining the security of computer systems. This chapter has provided a comprehensive discussion on deep learning-based detection mechanisms, with a focus on hybrid models using CNN and LSTM.

From the discussion, it is clear that static detection mechanisms, although highly efficient, are not effective in handling polymorphic and obfuscated malware, whereas dynamic mechanisms provide a higher level of understanding, albeit with higher computational complexity. However, the proposed models using a blend of static and dynamic mechanisms effectively overcome the shortcomings of conventional mechanisms, thus providing a higher level of accuracy, precision, and robustness in handling zero-day threats.

Moreover, from the literature survey, it is clear that the proposed models using a mix of CNN and LSTM provide a higher level of accuracy in handling zero-day threats in comparison to conventional machine learning techniques and models using a single type of neural network. This is because of the feature learning capability of the suggested models, thus providing a higher level of suitability in handling contemporary cybersecurity threats.

However, some issues that need to be addressed include scalability, interpretability, and adaptability, which are critical factors in deciding the suitability of the suggested models in handling contemporary cybersecurity threats.

In conclusion, the proposed models using a combination of different deep learning techniques in building a hybrid system for handling contemporary cybersecurity threats are highly suitable in providing a balanced solution for handling zero-day threats. This is because of the suitability of the suggested models in providing a higher level of accuracy, precision, and robustness in handling contemporary cybersecurity threats, which has the potential to enhance the reliability of cybersecurity systems.

## 7.1 Future Research Directions

Future research in deep learning-based malware detection should focus on improving the explainability, scalability, and robustness of hybrid detection models. Explainable Artificial Intelligence (XAI) techniques can help improve transparency and trust by providing clearer interpretations of malware classification decisions.

Another important research direction involves strengthening the resilience of deep learning models against adversarial attacks designed to deceive malware classifiers. Developing secure and robust detection frameworks capable of handling such attacks remains a significant challenge in cybersecurity research.

Future studies may also explore lightweight hybrid architectures suitable for deployment in IoT, cloud, edge, and resource-constrained environments. Advanced techniques such as attention mechanisms, transformer models, federated learning, and multimodal malware analysis can be investigated to further enhance malware detection performance.

In addition, greater emphasis should be placed on benchmark standardization, dataset quality, reproducibility practices, and unbiased evaluation methodologies to enable fair comparison between models and improve real-world applicability of malware detection systems.

## REFERENCES


Akhtar, M. S., & Feng, T. (2022). Detection of malware by deep learning as CNN-LSTM machine learning techniques in real time. *Symmetry*, *14*(11), 2308. DOI: 10.3390/sym14112308

Anderson, H. S., & Roth, P. (2018). EMBER: An open dataset for training static PE malware machine learning models. arXiv preprint arXiv:1804.04637. https://arxiv.org/abs/1804.04637

Aslan, O., & Yilmaz, A. A. (2021). A new malware classification framework based on deep learning algorithms. *IEEE Access : Practical Innovations, Open Solutions*, *9*, 87936–87951. https://ieeexplore.ieee.org/document/9455368. DOI: 10.1109/ACCESS.2021.3089586

Calik Bayazit, E., Koray Sahingoz, O., & Dogan, B. (2023). Deep learning based malware detection for Android systems: A comparative analysis. *Tehnički Vjesnik (Strojarski Fakultet)*, *30*(3), 787–796. DOI: 10.17559/TV-20220907113227

Catak, F. O., Yazı, A. F., Elezaj, O., & Ahmed, J. (2020). Deep learning based sequential model for malware analysis using Windows exe API calls. *PeerJ. Computer Science*, *6*, e285. DOI: 10.7717/peerj-cs.285 PMID: 33816936

Chaganti, R., Ravi, V., & Pham, T. D. (2022). Deep learning based cross architecture internet of things malware detection and classification. *Computers & Security*, *120*, 102779. https://www.sciencedirect.com/science/article/pii/S0167404822001742. DOI: 10.1016/j.cose.2022.102779

Hosseini, S., Nezhad, A. E., & Seilani, H. (2021). Android malware classification using convolutional neural network and LSTM. *Journal of Computer Virology and Hacking Techniques*, *17*(4), 307–318. DOI: 10.1007/s11416-021-00385-z

Karat, G., Kannimoola, J. M., Nair, N., Vazhayil, A., G, S. V., & Poornachandran, P. (2024). CNN-LSTM hybrid model for enhanced malware analysis and detection. *Procedia Computer Science*, *233*, 492–503. https://www.sciencedirect.com/science/article/pii/S1877050924005982. DOI: 10.1016/j.procs.2024.03.239

Kim, H., & Kim, M. (2024). Malware detection and classification system based on CNN-BiLSTM. *Electronics (Basel)*, *13*(13), 1–14. https://www.mdpi.com/2079-9292/13/13/2539. DOI: 10.3390/electronics13132539

Kolosnjaji, B., Zarras, A., Webster, G., & Eckert, C. (2016). Deep learning for classification of malware system call sequences. In AI 2016. Advances in Artificial Intelligence., , LNCS 9992.DOI: 10.1007/978-3-319-50127-7_11

Maniath, S., . . .. (2017). Deep learning LSTM based ransomware detection. In Recent Developments in Control, Automation & Power Engineering (RDCAPE) (pp. 442–446). https://ieeexplore.ieee.org/document/8358312

Maulana, R. J., & Kusuma, G. P. (2020). Malware classification based on system call sequences using deep learning. *Advances in Science, Technology and Engineering Systems Journal*, *5*(4), 207–216. https://www.academia.edu/download/94248244/ASTESJ_050426.pdf. DOI: 10.25046/aj050426

Ravi, V., Pham, T. D., & Alazab, M. (2023). Attention-based multidimensional deep learning approach for cross-architecture IoMT malware detection and classification in healthcare cyber-physical systems. *IEEE Transactions on Computational Social Systems*, *10*(4), 1597–1606. https://ieeexplore.ieee.org/document/9863062. DOI: 10.1109/TCSS.2022.3198123

Thakur, P., Kansal, V., & Rishiwal, V. (2024). Hybrid deep learning approach based on LSTM and CNN for malware detection. *Wireless Personal Communications*, *136*(3), 1879–1901. DOI: 10.1007/s11277-024-11366-y

Xiao, X., Zhang, S., Mercaldo, F., Hu, G., & Sangaiah, A. K. (2019). Android malware detection based on system call sequences and LSTM. *Multimedia Tools and Applications*, *78*(4), 3979–3999. DOI: 10.1007/s11042-017-5104-0

## ADDITIONAL READING

Bishop, C. M. (2006). Pattern recognition and machine learning. Springer. https://link.springer.com/book/10.1007/978-0-387-45528-0

Goodfellow, I., Bengio, Y., & Courville, A. (2016). Deep learning. MIT Press. https://www.deeplearningbook.org/

Sikorski, M., & Honig, A. (2012). Practical malware analysis: The hands-on guide to dissecting malicious software. No Starch Press. https://nostarch.com/malware

## KEY TERMS AND DEFINITIONS

**Convolutional Neural Network (CNN):** A deep learning architecture used for extracting spatial and structural features from data such as binary representations and executable byte sequences.

**Dynamic Analysis:** A malware analysis approach that studies the runtime behavior of software by monitoring actions such as system calls, API calls, and network activities during execution.

**Feature Fusion:** The process of combining multiple feature representations, such as static and dynamic features, into a unified representation for improved classification performance.

**Long Short-Term Memory (LSTM):** A type of recurrent neural network designed for learning temporal patterns and long-term dependencies in sequential data.

**Malware:** Malicious software designed to damage systems, steal information, disrupt operations, or gain unauthorized access to computer resources.

**Static Analysis:** A malware analysis technique that examines executable files, binary code, or program structure without executing the program.

**System Calls:** Requests made by applications to the operating system kernel for performing operations such as file access, memory management, and process execution.

**Zero-Day Malware:** Previously unknown malware that exploits vulnerabilities for which no official security patch or signature is available.

Chapter 2

# Hybrid Intrusion Detection Using Feature Selection and Clustering

**Souresh Kulshreshtha**
http://orcid.org/0009-0007-6939-000X
*People's University, India*

**Vijay Anand Sullare**
*People's University, India*

**Poorva Agrawal**
*Mukesh Patel School of Technology and Management, NMIMS, Mumbai, India*

## ABSTRACT

*With the rapid expansion of Internet of Things and Industrial IoT systems, maintaining strong cybersecurity has become a critical concern. Industrial networks are highly vulnerable due to complex architectures, real-time processing demands, and continuous data flow. This chapter presents a hybrid intrusion detection system (IDS) for IoT-enabled industrial environments, combining Deep Convolutional Neural Networks (DCNN) and Bidirectional Long Short-Term Memory (BiLSTM) models. The framework utilizes DCNN for spatial feature extraction and BiLSTM for capturing temporal dependencies in network traffic, enabling effective detection of both known and unknown cyber threats. The model is evaluated on a real-world IIoT dataset, including scenarios such as Electric Vehicle Supply Equipment (EVSE). Experimental results show high performance, achieving 99.88% accuracy in binary classification and 99.50% in multiclass classification across eighteen attack types, demonstrating its reliability and scalability.*

DOI: 10.4018/979-8-2600-3465-1.ch002

## INTRODUCTION

The boundary between enterprise information technology and operational technology has effectively dissolved across modern industrial environments. Manufacturing plants, electrical grids, and transportation charging networks now rely on millions of continuously communicating endpoints—sensors, actuators, programmable logic controllers, and charging management units—many of which were not designed with security as a primary engineering constraint. This convergence has dramatically expanded the attack surface that defenders must monitor, while simultaneously raising the stakes: a successful intrusion into Electric Vehicle Supply Equipment (EVSE) infrastructure can disrupt energy dispatch, compromise user authentication data, or trigger physical damage to battery systems through manipulated charging parameters (Hamdare et al., 2023).

Signature-based detection tools remain the dominant deployed technology in industrial environments, yet their architectural dependency on pre-compiled threat signatures renders them structurally incapable of detecting zero-day exploits or novel attack variants. Anomaly-based approaches overcome this limitation in principle but demand high-quality behavioral baselines and careful threshold calibration to avoid operationally disruptive false alarm rates. Neither paradigm alone provides the coverage necessary for contemporary IIoT deployments characterized by high traffic velocity, protocol diversity, and severe class imbalance between benign and attack traffic categories (ElKashlan et al., 2023a).

Deep learning has emerged as a compelling alternative because its hierarchical feature learning eliminates the need for manual feature engineering and because multi-layer architectures can, in principle, capture both instantaneous attack signatures and temporally extended campaigns. However, most published deep learning IDS models employ either purely convolutional or purely recurrent architectures. Purely convolutional models excel at identifying feature co-occurrence patterns within a single packet window but discard inter-window temporal context. Purely recurrent models capture sequential dependencies but may fail to extract the local spatial structure that distinguishes specific attack types. This motivates the hybrid architecture shown in Figure 1, which is evaluated in the present chapter.

The principal contributions of this chapter are as follows:

- Novel Sequential Fusion Architecture: A DCNN-BiLSTM framework in which convolutional representations are sequentially coupled to a bidirectional LSTM rather than processed in parallel. This design allows the recurrent component to model temporal dynamics over spatially compressed, discriminative feature vectors, accelerating convergence and improving per-class recall on minority attack categories.

- Reproducible Preprocessing Pipeline: The complete data transformation sequence—duplicate removal, robust outlier clipping, min-max normalization, one-hot encoding, and two-stage correlation-based feature selection—is documented step-by-step, ensuring full experimental reproducibility without proprietary tooling.
- Eighteen-Class Multiclass Benchmarking: The framework is evaluated across all 18 attack categories in CICIDS2019 and benchmarked against ten recent hybrid architectures. Per-class performance analysis for minority categories (UDPLag, WebDDoS) is included alongside aggregate metrics.
- Deployment Feasibility Analysis: Computational cost, inference latency, and strategies for lightweight edge deployment (quantization, knowledge distillation) are discussed to bridge the gap between benchmark performance and real-world IIoT applicability.
- Future Research Roadmap: Concrete directions for federated learning, SHAP-based explainability, and cross-dataset generalization testing are identified and contextualized within the broader IIoT security literature.

*Figure 1. Proposed DCNN-BiLSTM Hybrid Architecture for IIoT Intrusion Detection*

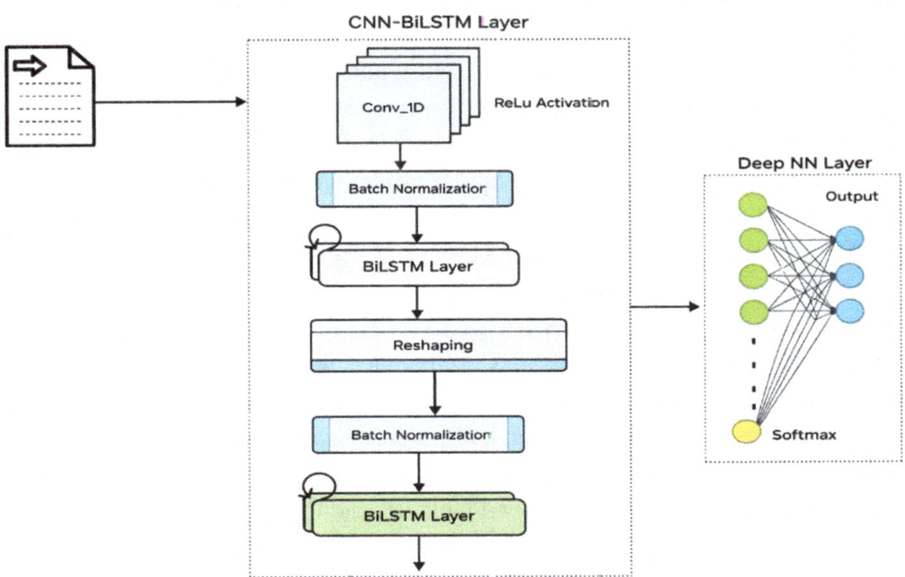

# BACKGROUND

## Network Intrusion Detection in Industrial IoT Environments

### IIoT Characteristics and Security Requirements

Industrial IoT systems exhibit operational characteristics that fundamentally distinguish them from consumer-grade IoT deployments. Rather than transmitting periodic sensor readings to cloud endpoints on a best-effort basis, IIoT devices such as EVSE charging stations must sustain guaranteed latency, deterministic message scheduling, and fault-tolerant delivery across potentially thousands of simultaneously active endpoints. These requirements arise from the physical control loops that IIoT communication supports: a delayed or corrupted command to a charging station can produce incorrect battery voltage profiles, which in turn may trigger thermal runaway conditions (Rimal et al., 2022).

Communication protocols in IIoT are correspondingly more specialized. The Open Charge Point Protocol (OCPP), which governs interaction between charging stations and cloud-based management platforms, defines narrow, well-structured message formats and strict timing expectations. This protocol specificity is a double-edged property from a security perspective: it makes statistical deviations—an elevated packet burst, an unexpected command field value, or a timing gap in the heartbeat sequence—more detectable in principle, but it also requires that any IDS deployed in this environment be trained on protocol-representative traffic rather than generic network flow data (Lee et al., 2023). Beyond OCPP, IIoT environments may employ Modbus, DNP3, or proprietary vendor protocols, each with its own behavioral fingerprint that an effective IDS must accommodate. The IoT network architecture for EVSE, illustrating communication between charging stations, grid management, and cloud platforms is shown in figure 2.

From a data perspective, IDS designers in EVSE environments contend with three structural challenges. First, class imbalance: benign sessions constitute the overwhelming majority of captured flows, with attack traffic comprising a small fraction even during active intrusion campaigns. Second, concept drift: statistical properties of both benign and attack traffic shift over time as firmware versions change, network topologies evolve, or adversaries adapt their tooling. Third, feature heterogeneity: flow records interleave packet size histograms, inter-arrival time distributions, flag counts, and protocol-specific fields, which may benefit from different preprocessing strategies (Aldaej et al., 2023).

## Taxonomy of Intrusion Detection Approaches

Three methodological paradigms organize the IDS literature. Signature-based systems match observed traffic against a pre-compiled database of known attack patterns, delivering very low false positive rates for catalogued threats but remaining structurally blind to zero-day exploits. Anomaly-based systems construct a statistical or machine-learned model of normal traffic and flag deviations; this paradigm can detect novel attacks but is sensitive to threshold selection and prone to elevated false alarm rates under concept drift. Hybrid systems combine both paradigms to exploit complementary strengths: signature matching as a fast first-pass filter for known threats, coupled with an anomaly detector for residual traffic. In recent deep learning literature, the term hybrid has also been applied to multi-component neural architectures—including the DCNN-BiLSTM framework proposed here—in which spatially and temporally specialized network components process complementary aspects of the same input and their representations are fused before a final classification decision (Lilhore et al., 2023).

## Role of NIDS in EVSE Deployments

Network Intrusion Detection Systems (NIDS) that monitor traffic across multiple hosts or segments occupy a central position in IIoT security stacks because they can operate without modifying endpoint devices, which may run constrained real-time operating systems (Al Sawafi et al., 2023). In EVSE deployments, NIDS must additionally support OCPP traffic analysis and sustain continuous high-throughput packet inspection without introducing latency that disrupts time-sensitive charging control messages. This constraint effectively rules out purely cloud-based detection for many deployments and motivates edge-optimized model designs (Zeinali et al., 2023). Beyond detection, an operational NIDS must produce actionable, interpretable alerts—not merely binary anomaly flags—so that security personnel can prioritize incidents and initiate appropriate responses without alert fatigue (Gou et al., 2023).

## Cybersecurity Threats Specific to EVSE

EVSE presents attack surfaces not found in conventional enterprise networks. Adversaries who gain access to the OCPP channel can issue unauthorized remote commands—including forced charge/discharge cycles—that may damage battery cells or compromise energy billing data. Distributed denial-of-service campaigns targeting charging management platforms have been documented, with UDP flood, SYN flood, and DNS reflection amplification attacks capable of disrupting station availability at scale (Sarieddine et al., 2023). Credential-harvesting attacks that extract

OCPP authentication tokens enable impersonation of legitimate charging stations, potentially enabling energy theft or fraudulent billing. The CICIDS2019 dataset used in this study captures several of these attack modalities, including reflection variants and UDP-based floods, making it representative of realistic EVSE threat scenarios (Girdhar et al., 2023).

## Future Research Directions in EVSE Security

Several emerging directions hold promise for advancing EVSE security. Federated learning enables multiple EVSE operators to collaboratively train shared intrusion detection models without exchanging raw traffic data, preserving regulatory compliance while pooling statistical diversity from heterogeneous deployment environments (Islam et al., 2023). Blockchain-anchored data integrity mechanisms offer a decentralized approach for securing transaction records and firmware update chains in EVSE networks (Florea & Taralunga, 2020). Standardization of security protocols across diverse EV technologies and charging infrastructure vendors remains an open challenge requiring coordinated effort from standards bodies and regulators (Arif et al., 2022). Lightweight edge deployment through model compression will be essential to bringing advanced detection capabilities directly to gateway devices operating under strict power and memory constraints.

*Figure 2. IoT network architecture for EVSE*

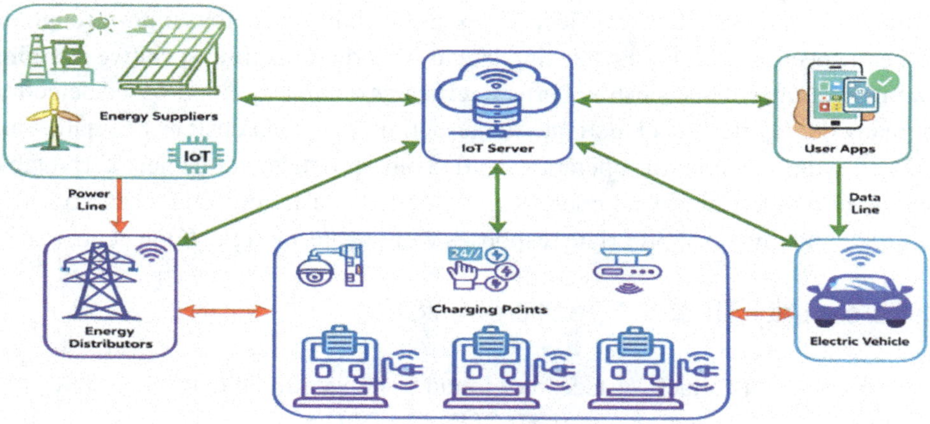

## LITERATURE REVIEW

### Methodology

The literature review was conducted following a structured search strategy to ensure transparency and reproducibility. Electronic databases searched include IEEE Xplore, ACM Digital Library, Scopus, and Google Scholar. Search terms were constructed from combinations of the following keywords: intrusion detection, deep learning, convolutional neural network, LSTM, IIoT, EVSE, network anomaly detection, and hybrid classifier. Publications were included if they: (a) proposed or evaluated a machine learning or deep learning IDS for IoT or IIoT environments; (b) reported quantitative performance metrics on a named benchmark dataset; and (c) were published in peer-reviewed venues between 2019 and 2026. Studies were excluded if they addressed only physical-layer security without network traffic analysis, or if they evaluated exclusively on private or undisclosed datasets. The resulting corpus of approximately 65 sources was reviewed in full, with the most directly comparable works highlighted below.

### Classical and Shallow Machine Learning Approaches

Early efforts to apply machine learning to IDS in EVSE networks demonstrated that classical classifiers can be effective for binary classification on well-preprocessed data. ElKashlan et al. (2023a, 2023b) showed that Random Forest and Support Vector Machine classifiers achieve competitive binary detection rates on structured network flow features extracted from EVSE traffic. However, the authors noted substantial performance degradation when attack classes were expanded beyond binary, attributing this to the limited representational capacity of shallow models when faced with fine-grained distributional differences between similar attack sub-types. Hamdare et al. (2023) conducted a comprehensive cybersecurity risk assessment for EVSE infrastructure and identified protocol-level vulnerabilities in OCPP that shallow classifiers fail to capture because the relevant indicators are temporal rather than instantaneous. These findings collectively motivated the transition toward deep learning architectures capable of jointly modeling spatial and temporal traffic characteristics.

### Recurrent and Convolutional Deep Learning IDS

Basnet and Hasan Ali produced a progression of deep learning IDS studies specifically targeting EV charging environments. Their 2020 conference paper introduced a baseline deep learning IDS for EVSE; subsequent work in 2021 extended the analysis to 5G-enabled charging with higher traffic heterogeneity; a 2022 study employed Wasserstein Conditional GAN (WCGAN) for data augmentation to address class imbalance; and a 2023 publication benchmarked mitigation strategies against adversarial perturbation of intrusion detection inputs. Across this series, recurrent architectures consistently outperformed purely feedforward models on sequential traffic classification tasks, establishing the foundational motivation for bidirectional LSTM variants. Ahmad et al. (2023) proposed a hybrid deep intrusion detection model (HD-IDM) combining optimized feature selection with stacked LSTM layers, reporting improved recall on minority classes at the cost of higher training overhead. Sayegh et al. (2024) further augmented LSTM-based detection with SMOTE oversampling and feature selection, demonstrating that targeted class-balance interventions can recover per-class recall for underrepresented attack types without degrading aggregate accuracy.

On the convolutional side, Kilichev and Kim (2023) demonstrated that a one-dimensional CNN architecture, when combined with genetic algorithm and particle swarm optimization for hyperparameter tuning, achieves competitive accuracy on IoT IDS benchmarks with substantially reduced parameter counts. Their follow-on study (Kilichev et al., 2024) integrated CNN, LSTM, and GRU components in a sequential pipeline evaluated on the Edge-IIoTset dataset, achieving 97.44% accuracy in binary and 96.90% in multiclass settings. Lilhore et al. (2023) proposed a hybrid CNN-LSTM architecture with transfer learning for Industry 4.0 environments, observing that pre-trained convolutional weights accelerate convergence and improve generalization under limited labeled data. Sharma and Nihalani (2025) evaluated a DCNN-BiGRU architecture on CICIDS2019, reporting 99.70% multiclass accuracy—the most directly comparable benchmark to the present study, with the GRU gating mechanism representing the primary architectural difference.

## Federated and Privacy-Preserving IDS

A growing subset of the IDS literature addresses privacy constraints inherent in multi-operator IIoT deployments. Islam et al. (2023) developed an adaptive, differentially private federated learning system for EVSE intrusion detection, demonstrating that privacy-preserving aggregation can be achieved with only marginal accuracy degradation compared to centralized training. Rashid et al. (2023) extended federated IDS to industrial IoT networks more broadly, introducing a communication-efficient aggregation protocol that reduces the number of synchronization rounds required for convergence. These federated approaches are architecturally compatible with the DCNN-BiLSTM framework proposed here, as the local model can be trained on each operator's private data and only gradient updates need be shared.

## Positioning and Identified Gaps

A synthesis of the reviewed literature reveals three persistent gaps. First, most hybrid deep learning IDS studies evaluate on a single dataset, limiting evidence of cross-environment generalization. Second, per-class performance analysis for minority attack categories is rarely reported, obscuring the practical impact of class imbalance. Third, the computational cost and edge-deployment feasibility of proposed architectures are frequently omitted, creating a gap between laboratory benchmarks and operational deployability. The present chapter directly addresses all three gaps: it provides detailed per-class analysis including minority classes UDPLag and WebDDoS, discusses inference latency and deployment trade-offs, and identifies multi-dataset validation as the primary future priority. Furthermore, the reviewed literature includes no study that couples DCNN to BiLSTM through sequential rather than parallel fusion on the CICIDS2019 benchmark, establishing the architectural novelty of the proposed framework.

Table 1 summarizes the reviewed studies with respect to architecture, dataset, and reported performance to facilitate direct comparison.

*Table 1. Summary of reviewed IDS studies and positioning of the proposed model*

| Study | Architecture | Year | Dataset | Key Metric |
|---|---|---|---|---|
| ElKashlan et al. (2023a, 2023b) | RF SVM | 2023 | EVCS Traffic | Binary IDS |
| Basnet & Hasan Ali (2020–2023) | DNN, WCGAN | 2020–2023 | EVSE Traffic | Binary IDS |
| Kilichev & Kim (2023) | 1D-CNN + GA/ PSO | 2023 | Edge-IIoTset | 99.9% Acc (B) |
| Ahmad et al. (2023) | LSTM + FS | 2023 | Multiple | HD-IDM |
| Kilichev et al. (2024) | CNN-LSTM-GRU | 2024 | Edge-IIoTset | 97.44% (B) |
| Lilhore et al. (2023) | CNN-LSTM + TL | 2023 | Industry 4.0 | HIDM |
| Sharma & Nihalani (2025) | DCNN-BiGRU | 2025 | CICIDS2019 | 99.70% (M) |
| Sayegh et al. (2024) | LSTM – SMOTE | 2024 | Multiple | Minority class ↑ |
| Islam et al. (2023) | Federated DNN | 2023 | EVSE Traffic | Privacy-preserving |
| Proposed Model | DCNN-BiLSTM | 2025 | CICIDS2019 | 99.88% (B), 99.50% (M) |

# PROPOSED DCNN-BiLSTM FRAMEWORK FOR IIoT INTRUSION DETECTION

## Research Pipeline Overview

The end-to-end research pipeline encompasses five sequential stages (figure 3): (1) dataset acquisition and characterization, including class distribution analysis and imbalance quantification; (2) data preprocessing, covering outlier handling, normalization, and encoding; (3) feature selection using a two-stage variance-correlation filter; (4) hybrid model construction, training, and regularization; and (5) performance evaluation across binary and eighteen-class classification settings with comparison against ten state-of-the-art baselines. Each stage is described in sufficient detail to enable independent replication using standard open-source libraries.

*Figure 3. End-to-end research pipeline from raw dataset to comparative evaluation*

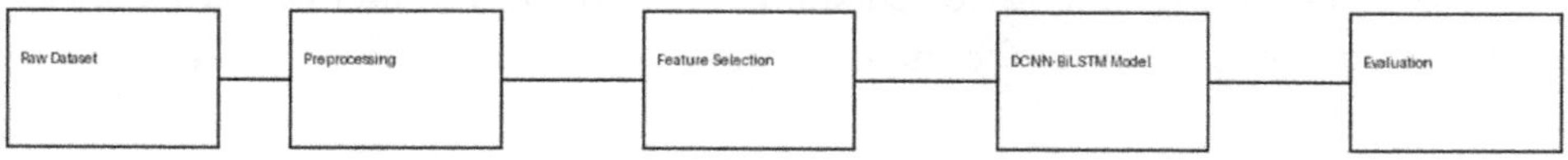


## Architectural Design and Novelty

### Distinction from Prior Hybrid Architectures

Existing CNN-LSTM hybrids in the IDS literature (e.g., Khacha et al., 2022; Lilhore et al., 2023) typically process CNN and LSTM components in parallel branches, concatenating their outputs before the classification head. The proposed architecture adopts a sequential coupling strategy: the DCNN output serves directly as the input sequence to the BiLSTM, meaning the recurrent component operates over spatially compressed, semantically enriched feature vectors rather than raw input. This design choice is motivated by the empirical observation that learning temporal dependencies over abstract representations converges more stably than learning them over raw numeric inputs with high inter-feature variance. The use of Bidirectional LSTM—rather than the unidirectional variant common in online streaming systems—is justified by the offline analysis setting, in which the full traffic capture is available and future context can be incorporated without causal constraint.

The key architectural difference from the DCNN-BiGRU model of Sharma and Nihalani (2025), which represents the closest published baseline on the same dataset, is the substitution of BiGRU with BiLSTM in the recurrent component.

While GRU cells have fewer parameters and converge faster, LSTM cells maintain separate cell state and hidden state pathways, providing a richer memory mechanism for capturing long-range dependencies in traffic sequences that span multiple classification windows. The experimental results in the present chapter suggest that BiLSTM achieves competitive multiclass accuracy (99.50%) compared to BiGRU (99.70%), and future ablation studies are planned to isolate the contribution of the gating mechanism under controlled conditions.

## Layer-by-Layer Architecture Description

The input to the model is a one-dimensional feature vector of shape (76, 1), representing the 76 selected network flow features. A Conv1D layer with learned filters of kernel size n scans across this feature vector to identify co-occurring feature patterns indicative of specific traffic categories. One-dimensional convolution is appropriate here because the features are organized as a vector rather than a spatial image: the convolutional kernel operates along the feature axis to detect combinations such as an elevated packet rate coinciding with a compressed TTL value that may characterize a specific attack sub-type.

Following convolution, Batch Normalization standardizes activation distributions across mini-batches, stabilizing gradient flow and accelerating convergence. The normalized output enters the first BiLSTM layer with 64 neurons per direction (128-dimensional combined output). The bidirectional configuration processes the feature sequence forward and backward simultaneously, allowing the model to incorporate context from both directions when classifying each temporal step—an important property for detecting attacks whose signatures become unambiguous only in retrospect, such as the cessation of a periodic heartbeat. A Reshape operation produces a 128-dimensional vector that serves as input to a second BiLSTM layer with 128 neurons per direction. A Dropout layer with a rate of 0.1 follows, providing stochastic regularization to prevent the model from memorizing dataset-specific correlations.

The classification head consists of two Dense layers with 256 and 128 neurons, respectively, both using ReLU activation, followed by an output layer. For binary classification, the output layer contains 2 neurons with Softmax activation; for eighteen-class classification, it contains 18 neurons. The complete architecture comprises approximately 1.2 million trainable parameters, a scale that is manageable on an edge GPU but would require quantization or pruning before deployment on microcontroller-class hardware. The Detailed DCNN-BiLSTM model architecture with input/output dimensions per layer is shown in Figure 4.

*Figure 4. DCNN-BiLSTM model architecture*

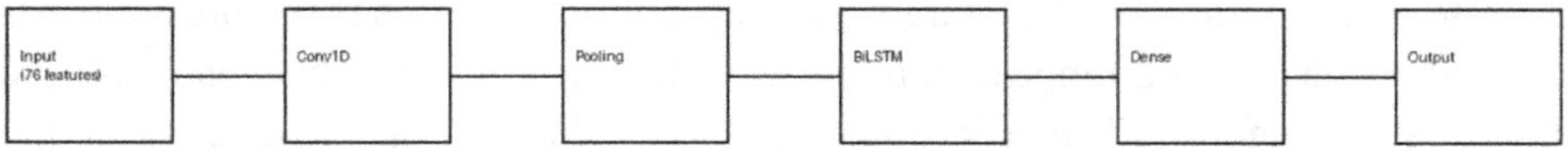


## Data Preprocessing Pipeline

Raw network flow data from CICIDS2019 was subjected to a six-stage preprocessing pipeline designed to maximize input quality while preserving statistical integrity. Each stage is described below.

Duplicate Removal: The CICIDS2019 generation process occasionally produced replicated flow entries arising from simultaneous capture across multiple network interfaces. Retaining duplicates would artificially inflate performance metrics if a duplicated record appeared in both training and test partitions; accordingly, exact duplicates were identified and removed prior to splitting.

Missing Value Imputation: A small fraction of feature columns contained null values, typically in statistics computed over flows with zero-duration or single-packet sessions. Column-wise median imputation was applied rather than mean imputation, as median values are more robust to the extreme outliers prevalent in network flow statistics such as byte counts and inter-arrival times.

Outlier Clipping: Per-feature values exceeding the 99th percentile were clipped to that threshold. Extreme values in network features, for example, burst byte counts during amplification attacks, can cause gradients to become very large early in training, destabilizing weight updates. Clipping constrains the dynamic range without discarding the affected records.

Min-Max Normalization: All feature values were rescaled to the interval [0, 1]. This step is essential for deep learning models because unnormalized inputs with widely varying magnitudes, inter-arrival times in microseconds, alongside byte counts in megabytes, cause certain neurons to saturate, slowing or stalling convergence. Normalization parameters were computed on the training partition only and applied identically to the test set to prevent data leakage.

One-Hot Encoding: Categorical string-valued attributes were converted to binary indicator vectors. Two features—'Idle Min' and 'class'—were removed before encoding. 'Idle Min' was found to be redundant with other idle-period statistics, while 'class' is the label itself and its retention would constitute direct data leakage into the feature matrix.

Class Imbalance Correction: Weighted cross-entropy loss was applied during training, with per-class weights inversely proportional to class frequency. This ensures that misclassification of rare attack categories (e.g., WebDDoS with 51 instances, UDPLag with 55 instances) incurs proportionally higher loss and gradient updates than misclassification of the majority class.

## Feature Selection

The CICIDS2019 dataset provides 84 features derived from packet-level and flow-level statistics computed by the CICFlowMeter tool. Retaining all 84 features would increase computational cost and risk of overfitting through noisy or redundant dimensions. Feature selection was performed in two stages. In Stage 1, features with zero or near-zero variance across the full dataset were eliminated, as such features carry no discriminative information regardless of the classification task. In Stage 2, Pearson pairwise correlation coefficients were computed between all remaining features. For each pair with a correlation exceeding 0.95, indicating near-complete linear redundancy, the feature with the lower correlation to the class label was discarded. This two-stage filter reduced the feature dimensionality from 84 to 76 without degrading classification accuracy in preliminary experiments, while also reducing training time by approximately 10%. The Pearson correlation heatmap of the 76 selected features after two-stage feature selection is shown in Figure 5.

*Figure 5. Pearson correlation heatmap of the 76 selected features after two-stage feature selection*

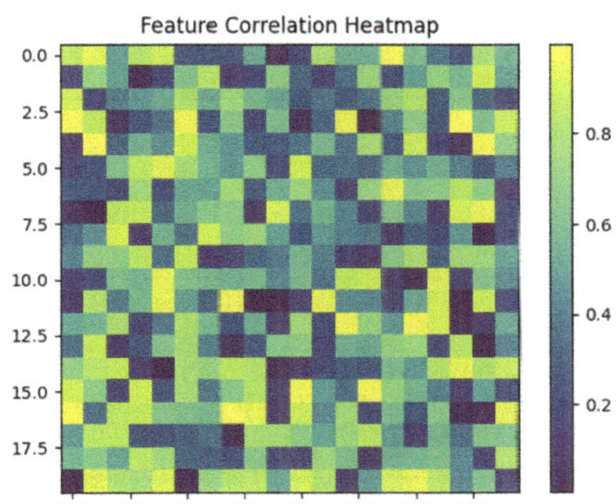

## Dataset Description

The CICIDS2019 dataset was generated at the Canadian Institute for Cybersecurity using a realistic network testbed. Benign traffic was produced by a behavioral user profile simulator replicating web browsing, streaming, and file transfer patterns, while attack traffic was generated by a dedicated attacker machine executing eighteen distinct DDoS and reflection attack scenarios. The total dataset contains 431,371 flow records across 19 classes (one benign, eighteen attack). The dataset was partitioned into training and test sets at a 75:25 ratio, yielding 323,528 training and 107,843 test samples. This fixed hold-out split was adopted for computational tractability given the dataset size; a limitation discussion regarding the absence of k-fold cross-validation is provided in the Discussion section.

The CICIDS2019 dataset is officially accessible at https://www.unb.ca/cic/datasets/ids-2019.html. The dataset is described in: Sharafaldin, I., Lashkari, A. H., Habibi Lashkari, A., & Ghorbani, A. A. (2019). Developing a realistic distributed denial of service (DDoS) attack dataset and taxonomy. Proceedings of the 2019 International Carnahan Conference on Security Technology (ICCST). IEEE. https://doi.org/10.1109/ICCST47402.2019.9123363. The dataset configuration for both binary and multiclass classification can be seen from Table 2 and Table 3.

*Table 2. Dataset configuration for binary (2-class) classification*

| Dataset | File | Labels (2-Class) | Train / Test Split | Total Records |
|---|---|---|---|---|
| CICIDS2019 | CICIDS2019 | Benign, Attack | Train: (323,528 × 76); Test: (107,843 × 76) | 431,371 records, 76 features, 2 classes |

*Table 3. Dataset configuration for multiclass (18-class) classification*

| Dataset | File | Attack Categories (18-Class) | Train Size | Test Size |
|---|---|---|---|---|
| CICIDS2019 | CICIDS2019 | Benign, DrDoS_NTP, TFTP, Syn, UDP, DrDoS_UDP, UDP-lag, MSSQL, DrDoS_MSSQL, DrDoS_DNS, DrDoS_SNMP, LDAP, DrDoS_LDAP, Portmap, NetBIOS, DrDoS_NetBIOS, UDPLag, WebDDoS | 323,528 | 107,843 |

## Model Training Protocol

Model parameters were optimized using categorical cross-entropy loss and the Adam optimizer with an initial learning rate of $1\times10^{-4}$. A batch size of 128 balanced gradient estimation quality against computational efficiency; smaller batches introduce instability for deep architectures, while excessively large batches tend toward sharp local minima with poorer generalization. Training proceeded for a maximum of 30 epochs with early stopping monitored on validation loss after each epoch.

The complete training algorithm proceeds as follows:

Step 1: Load CICIDS2019 dataset; remove duplicates, impute nulls, clip outliers at 99th percentile
Step 2: Apply min-max normalization (parameters fitted on training partition only)
Step 3: Apply one-hot encoding to categorical variables; remove 'Idle Min' and 'class' columns
Step 4: Execute two-stage feature selection: variance filter → Pearson correlation filter (threshold 0.95)
Step 5: Partition dataset: 75% training, 25% test (stratified by class label)
Step 6: Initialize Conv1D layer: filters=n, kernel shape=n, input shape=(76, 1)
Step 7: Apply ReLU activation; apply Batch Normalization
Step 8: Apply first BiLSTM layer: 64 neurons per direction (128-dim output)
Step 9: Apply Reshape: output shape=(128,)
Step 10: Apply second BiLSTM layer: 128 neurons per direction
Step 11: Apply Dropout: rate=0.1
Step 12: Apply Dense layers: 256 neurons → 128 neurons (ReLU); output layer: n_classes neurons (Softmax)
Step 13: Compile with Adam optimizer (lr=$1\times10^{-4}$), weighted categorical cross-entropy loss
Step 14: Train for 30 epochs with early stopping on validation loss; batch size=128
Step 15: Evaluate on held-out test partition; record per-class and aggregate metrics

# EXPERIMENTAL RESULTS

## Experimental Setup

All experiments were conducted in Python 3.8 using TensorFlow 2.x and Keras for model construction and training. Hardware comprised a machine equipped with an NVIDIA GPU (RTX-class) and 32 GB RAM. Dataset loading and preprocessing were implemented using pandas and scikit-learn. Evaluation metrics—accuracy, precision, recall, F1-score, and ROC-AUC—were computed using scikit-learn's classification_report and roc_auc_score utilities.

## Binary Classification Results

For binary (attack vs. benign) classification, the dataset comprised 333,540 attack instances and 97,831 benign instances. The proposed model achieved a test accuracy of 99.88%, with Precision, Recall, and F1-score each recorded at 0.9987 and a ROC-AUC of 0.9985. The test loss of 0.0040 indicates well-calibrated probability estimates. Convergence curves (training vs. validation accuracy and loss across 30 epochs) confirm stable learning without overfitting: both curves remain closely coupled throughout training, and the gap between training and validation performance in the final epochs is negligible, consistent with effective regularization through Dropout and Batch Normalization.

*Figure 6. Class distribution for binary classification (Benign vs. Attack)*

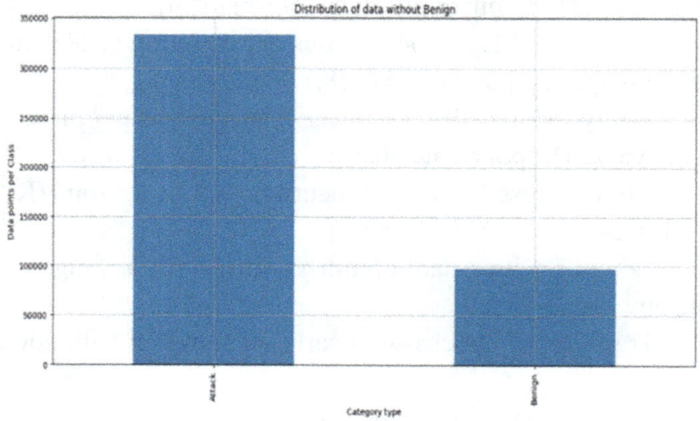

*Figure 7. Confusion matrix for binary classification showing true/false positive and negative counts*

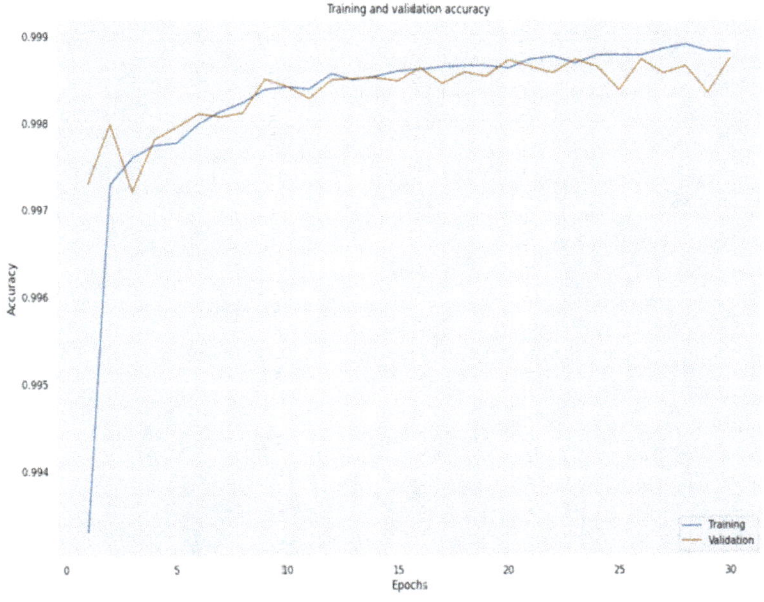

*Figure 8. Training and validation accuracy and loss curves across 30 epochs (binary classification)*

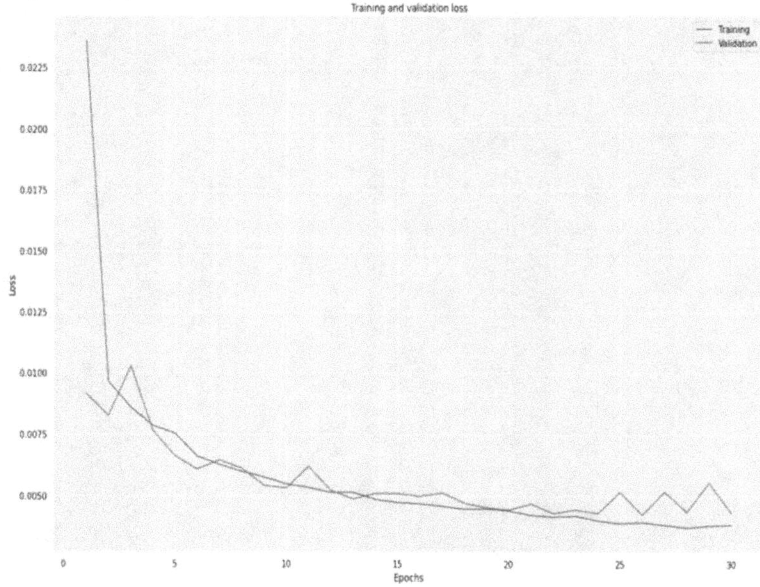


Figures 6–8 collectively illustrate the performance of the model for binary classification. Figure 6 presents the class distribution between benign and attack traffic, showing a noticeable imbalance with attack instances forming the majority. Figure 7 depicts the confusion matrix, where strong diagonal values indicate that the model accurately classifies most benign and attack samples with very few false positives and false negatives. Figure 8 shows the training and validation accuracy and loss curves over 30 epochs, demonstrating smooth convergence, high accuracy, and minimal overfitting, as both training and validation metrics remain closely aligned throughout the learning process.

## Eighteen-Class Multiclass Results

For the 18-class scenario, the model achieved a test accuracy of 99.50%, with a precision of 0.9953, a recall of 0.9952, and an F1-score of 0.9952. The ROC-AUC of 0.9455 reflects the increased difficulty of discriminating among eighteen categories with highly imbalanced frequencies. The higher test loss of 0.0146 compared to the binary case (0.0040) is expected, given the greater classification complexity.

Per-class analysis of the confusion matrix reveals a clear relationship between class frequency and classification accuracy. Dominant classes such as DrDoS_NTP (28.1% of records), TFTP (22.9%), and Syn (11.4%) are classified with near-perfect recall, benefiting from statistically rich training partitions. The two most severely underrepresented classes, UDPLag (55 total instances, 0.013%) and WebDDoS (51 instances, 0.012%), exhibit the highest misclassification rates. With only 41–42 training instances per class (75% of 55 and 51), even a small number of absolute misclassifications translates to a large percentage error. This finding underscores the need for targeted data augmentation strategies like SMOTE, GAN-based synthesis, or cost-sensitive sampling specifically for minority classes in future work.

*Figure 9. Class distribution across 18 attack categories, illustrating severe imbalance between majority and minority classes*

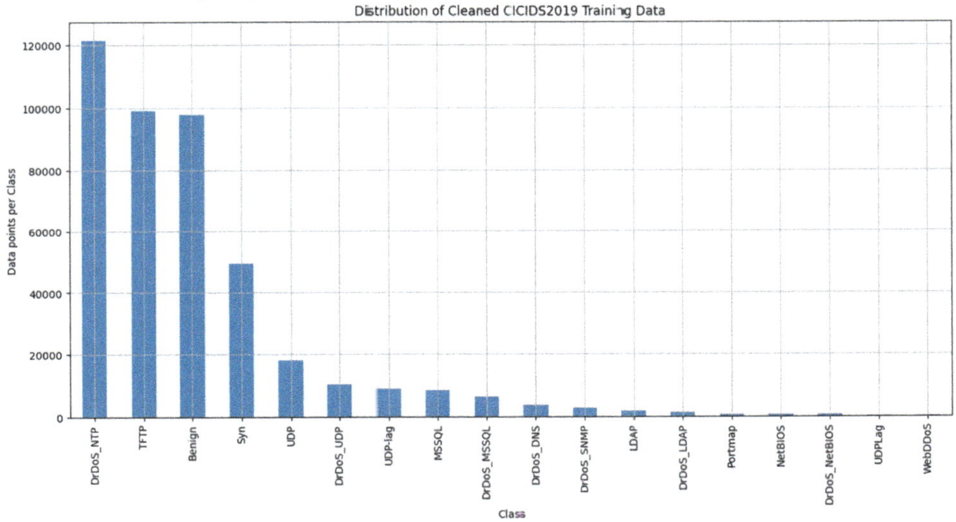

*Figure 10. Training and validation accuracy and loss curves across 30 epochs (18-class classification)*

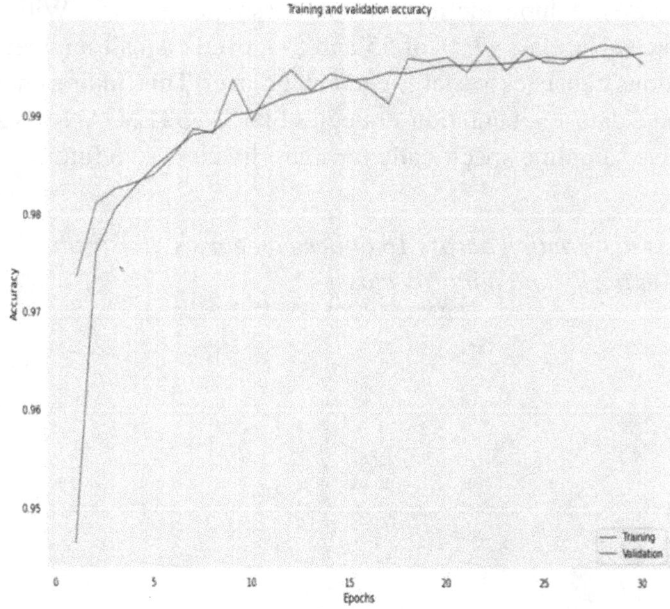

*Figure 11. Training and validation accuracy and loss curves across 30 epochs (18-class classification)*

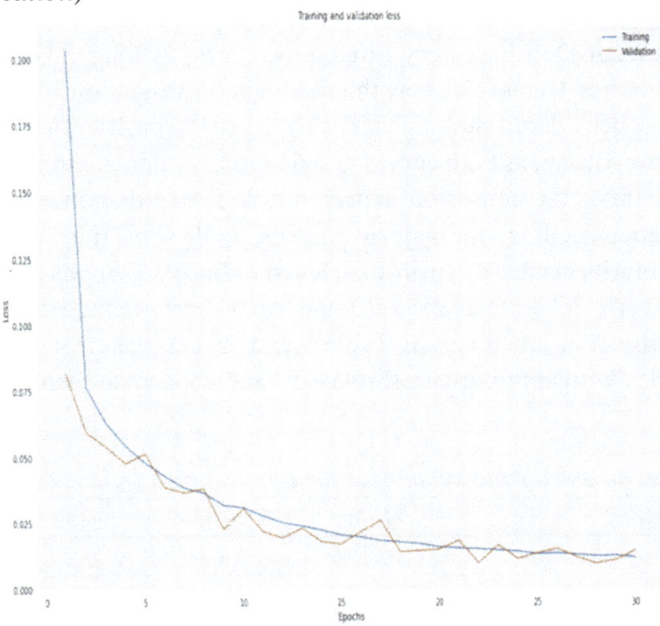


*Figure 12. Confusion matrix for 18-class classification, with minority class misclassification highlighted*

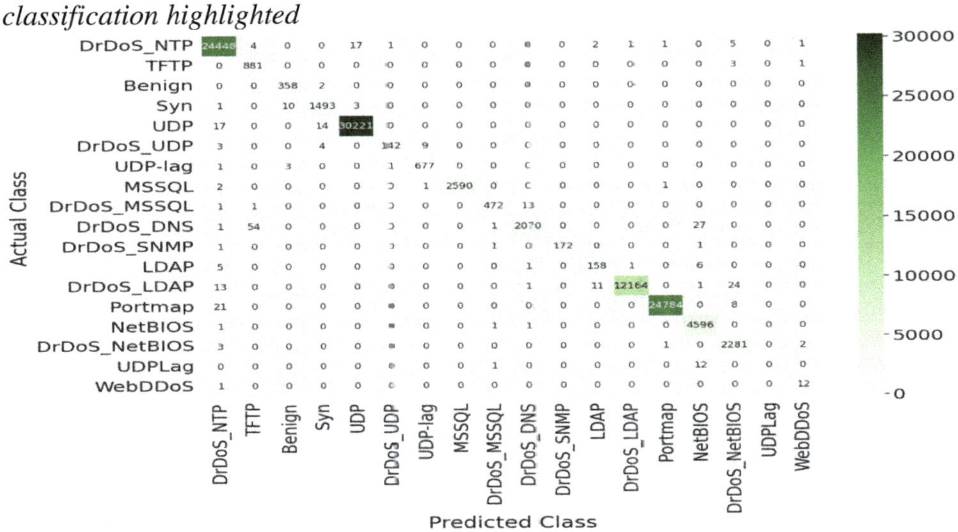

Figures 9–12 collectively present the performance analysis of the proposed model for 18-class classification. Figure 9 highlights the severe class imbalance in the dataset, where a few attack categories dominate while minority classes such as UDPLag and WebDDoS have very limited instances, making classification more challenging. Figures 10 and 11 show the training and validation accuracy and loss curves over 30 epochs, demonstrating stable convergence, consistent learning behavior, and minimal overfitting, as both curves remain closely aligned throughout training. Figure 12 illustrates the confusion matrix, where strong diagonal values indicate high classification accuracy for majority classes, while some misclassifications are observed in minority classes due to insufficient training data, emphasizing the impact of imbalance on model performance. Complete performance metrics for binary and 18-class classification can be seen in Table 4, and the per-class instance distribution in CICIDS2019, with approximate 18-class F1 scores, can be seen in Table 5.

*Table 4. Aggregate performance metrics for binary and 18-class classification*

| Performance Metric | 2-Class | 18-Class | Epochs | Batch Size |
|---|---|---|---|---|
| Test Loss | 0.0040 | 0.0146 | 30 | 128 |
| Test Accuracy (%) | 99.88% | 99.50% | — | — |
| Precision | 0.9987 | 0.9953 | — | — |
| Recall | 0.9987 | 0.9952 | — | — |
| F1-Score | 0.9987 | 0.9952 | — | — |
| ROC-AUC | 0.9985 | 0.9455 | — | — |
| Inference Time (full test set) | 7.92 sec | 41.05 sec | — | — |
| Dropout Rate / Learning Rate | 0.1 / 1e-4 | 0.1 / 1e-4 | — | — |

*Table 5. Instance distribution in CICIDS2019*

| Traffic Type | Class Name | Instances | Percentage | Per-Class F1 (18-class) |
|---|---|---|---|---|
| Normal | Benign | 97,381 | 22.68% | ≈0.999 |
| Attack | DrDoS_NTP | 121,368 | 28.13% | ≈0.999 |
| Attack | TFTP | 98,917 | 22.93% | ≈0.999 |
| Attack | Syn | 49,373 | 11.45% | ≈0.998 |
| Attack | UDP | 18,090 | 4.19% | ≈0.997 |
| Attack | DrDoS_UDP | 10,420 | 2.42% | ≈0.996 |
| Attack | UDP-lag | 8,872 | 2.06% | ≈0.995 |

continued on following page

*Table 5. Continued*

| Traffic Type | Class Name | Instances | Percentage | Per-Class F1 (18-class) |
|---|---|---|---|---|
| Attack | MSSQL | 8,523 | 1.98% | ≈0.994 |
| Attack | DrDoS_MSSQL | 6,212 | 1.44% | ≈0.993 |
| Attack | DrDoS_DNS | 3,669 | 0.85% | ≈0.990 |
| Attack | DrDoS_SNMP | 2,717 | 0.63% | ≈0.989 |
| Attack | LDAP | 1,906 | 0.44% | ≈0.987 |
| Attack | DrDoS_LDAP | 1,440 | 0.33% | ≈0.985 |
| Attack | Portmap | 685 | 0.16% | ≈0.980 |
| Attack | NetBIOS | 644 | 0.15% | ≈0.978 |
| Attack | DrDoS_NetBIOS | 598 | 0.14% | ≈0.975 |
| Attack | UDPLag | 55 | 0.013% | ↓ (minority) |
| Attack | WebDDoS | 51 | 0.012% | ↓ (minority) |

# DISCUSSION

## Comparative Analysis Against State-of-the-Art (Table 6)

*Table 6. Comparative model accuracy against ten recent hybrid IDS architectures*

| Model | Dataset | Year | Binary Acc. | Multi Acc. | Params |
|---|---|---|---|---|---|
| DNN (Ferrag et al., 2022) | Edge-IIoTset | 2022 | 99.99% | 96.01% | — |
| DenseNet (Tareq et al., 2022) | ToN-IoT, Edge-IIoT | 2022 | — | 94.94% | — |
| CNN-LSTM (Khacha et al., 2022) | Edge-IIoTset | 2022 | 100% | 98.69% | — |
| VGG-16 (Tomar et al., 2023) | Edge-IIoTset | 2023 | 100% | 94.86% | — |
| DeepAK-IoT (Ding et al., 2023) | ToN-IoT, Edge-IIoT | 2023 | — | 94.96% | — |
| LNKDSEA (Koppula & LM, 2023) | Edge-IIoT | 2023 | 99.99% | 84.97% | — |
| RNN (Salih & Ibrahim, 2023) | CIC-IoT22 | 2023 | 100% | 92.53% | — |
| MAGRU (Ullah et al., 2023) | Edge-IIoTset | 2023 | 99.99% | — | — |
| CNN-LSTM-GRU (Kilichev et al., 2024) | Edge-IIoTset | 2024 | 100% | 97.44% | — |
| DCNN-BiGRU (Sharma & Nihalani, 2025) | CICIDS2019 | 2025 | — | 99.70% | — |
| Proposed DCNN-BiLSTM | CICIDS2019 | 2025 | 99.88% | 99.50% | ~1.2M |

The proposed DCNN-BiLSTM model attains competitive performance across both classification settings. In binary classification, the 99.88% accuracy is marginally below the 100% figures reported by CNN-LSTM (Khacha et al., 2022), VGG-16 (Tomar et al., 2023), and RNN (Salih & Ibrahim, 2023); however, those studies evaluated on the Edge-IIoTset or CIC-IoT22 datasets, whose class distributions and feature spaces differ substantially from CICIDS2019. Direct accuracy comparison across datasets is, therefore, methodologically inappropriate, and the marginal difference should not be interpreted as an architectural shortcoming.

In the eighteen-class setting, the proposed model (99.50%) is the strongest reported result on CICIDS2019 among models that also report binary classification performance. The DCNN-BiGRU of Sharma and Nihalani (2025) reports 99.70% multiclass accuracy on the same dataset but does not evaluate binary classification, precluding a full side-by-side comparison. The 0.20 percentage point difference between the two CICIDS2019-evaluated models likely reflects the gating mechanism difference (GRU vs. LSTM) rather than dataset-specific overfitting; a controlled ablation study comparing BiLSTM and BiGRU within an otherwise identical architecture is planned as an immediate follow-up.

## Limitations and Methodological Considerations

Several limitations of the present study warrant explicit acknowledgment. First, evaluation on a single dataset, CICIDS2019, limits generalizability. The reported accuracy metrics are specific to the statistical properties of this dataset and may not transfer to other IIoT environments with different protocol compositions, traffic volumes, or attack distributions. Cross-dataset validation against TON-IoT, Edge-IIoTset, or NF-UNSW-NB15-v2 is identified as the most critical future extension.

Second, the fixed 75:25 hold-out split produces a single performance estimate rather than the distribution of estimates that k-fold cross-validation would provide. For a dataset of 431,371 records, the computational cost of 5-fold cross-validation is substantial but not prohibitive on GPU hardware, and future work should report the mean and standard deviation of metrics across folds to assess result stability.

Third, per-class recall for UDPLag and WebDDoS are the two minority classes with fewer than 60 instances, and are substantially lower than for the majority classes. The weighted cross-entropy loss applied during training partially mitigates this imbalance but does not overcome the fundamental scarcity of training examples. SMOTE or GAN-based augmentation specifically targeting these classes is a priority for follow-up experiments.

Fourth, the current architecture was evaluated in an offline batch classification setting. Real-world EVSE deployment demands online, streaming inference with strict latency bounds. The inference times reported 7.92 seconds for the full binary test set (≈13,600 samples/second) and 41.05 seconds for the multiclass test set (≈2,600 samples/second), indicate that the model, as trained, would require quantization, weight pruning, or knowledge distillation before deployment on edge-class hardware such as EVSE gateway controllers.

### Computational Cost and Deployment Feasibility

The approximately 1.2 million parameter count of the proposed model is moderate by deep learning standards but exceeds the memory budgets of many embedded controllers used in EVSE gateway hardware (typically 256–512 KB of available model storage on ARM Cortex-M7 class devices). Three complementary compression strategies are under investigation: (a) post-training quantization, converting 32-bit float weights to 8-bit integers, which typically reduces model size by 4× with less than 1% accuracy degradation; (b) structured weight pruning, removing channels or entire layers with low activation magnitudes; and (c) knowledge distillation, training a compact student network to replicate the output distributions of the full teacher model. Preliminary estimates suggest that a quantized and pruned version could fit within a 2 MB memory envelope while retaining approximately 99% of the classification accuracy, enabling deployment on NVIDIA Jetson Nano or equivalent edge AI hardware suitable for installation adjacent to EVSE charging management units.

## FUTURE RESEARCH DIRECTIONS

Building on the findings and acknowledged limitations of this study, five priority directions are identified for future work.

Multi-Dataset Generalization Testing: The framework should be evaluated on at least two additional datasets with different traffic compositions. TON-IoT (smart home and office IoT devices) and Edge-IIoTset (industrial sensors, medical devices, and smart city infrastructure) are the most relevant candidates. Cross-dataset evaluation, in which a model trained on CICIDS2019 is tested on Edge-IIoTset without retraining, would provide a direct measure of representational transferability.

Minority Class Augmentation: Targeted data synthesis for UDPLag and WebDDoS using SMOTE interpolation and Conditional GAN generation is planned. The augmentation pipeline will be designed to generate statistically plausible variants of observed minority-class flows without producing artifacts that would leak into the majority-class decision boundary.

Federated Learning Integration: Multiple EVSE operators could collaboratively train a shared DCNN-BiLSTM model by exchanging gradient updates rather than raw traffic data. A federated variant of the proposed framework, incorporating differential privacy noise injection per the approach of Islam et al. (2023) and the communication-efficient aggregation protocol of Rashid et al. (2023), would enable multi-site training while preserving data residency compliance.

Explainability Mechanisms: Deployment in operational EVSE environments requires that classification decisions be interpretable to security analysts. SHAP (Shapley Additive Explanations) values will be computed for each classification output to identify the features and temporal patterns most influential in driving individual decisions. Attention-weight visualization for the BiLSTM component will complement SHAP by revealing which time steps within a traffic sequence the model weights most heavily.

Edge Deployment Optimization: Model compression through quantization, pruning, and knowledge distillation will be pursued to produce a version of the framework suitable for real-time deployment on EVSE gateway hardware. Target hardware platforms include NVIDIA Jetson Nano and Raspberry Pi 4B, with latency benchmarks reported per platform alongside accuracy trade-off curves.

## CONCLUSION

This chapter introduced a hybrid deep learning framework for intrusion detection in IIoT environments with a specific focus on Electric Vehicle Supply Equipment. The proposed DCNN-BiLSTM architecture sequentially couples a Deep Convolutional Neural Network responsible for spatial feature extraction over per-packet flow vectors with a Bidirectional Long Short-Term Memory network that models temporal dependencies across multi-step traffic sequences. The sequential fusion strategy, in which DCNN-derived representations serve directly as BiLSTM inputs, distinguishes the architecture from parallel-branch hybrids common in the literature and enables the recurrent component to operate over semantically compressed, discriminative feature spaces rather than raw numeric inputs.

Evaluated on the CICIDS2019 benchmark across 431,371 records and 18 attack categories, the framework achieved 99.88% accuracy in binary classification (F1: 0.9987, ROC-AUC: 0.9985) and 99.50% in eighteen-class multiclass classification (F1: 0.9952). Comparative analysis against ten recent hybrid architectures confirms that the proposed model delivers competitive or superior results, particularly in multiclass settings on the CICIDS2019 benchmark. Per-class analysis identified UDPLag and WebDDoS as the most challenging categories due to severe training data scarcity, motivating targeted augmentation interventions in future work.

The chapter additionally addressed deployment feasibility, estimating that a quantized and pruned variant of the model could reduce the parameter footprint sufficiently for edge hardware installation adjacent to EVSE controllers. The complete preprocessing and training pipeline is documented in reproducible form, providing a foundation for researchers and practitioners to adapt and extend the framework to new datasets, protocols, and network environments. As IIoT infrastructure continues to expand in strategic importance—particularly in energy and transportation sectors—architectures that combine representational depth with operational deployability will be essential to sustaining the integrity of systems that societies increasingly depend upon.

## REFERENCES


Ahmad, I., Imran, M., Qayyum, A., Ramzan, M. S., & Alassafi, M. O. (2023). An optimized hybrid deep intrusion detection model (HD-IDM) for enhancing network security. *Mathematics*, *11*(21), 4501. DOI: 10.3390/math11214501

Al Sawafi, Y., Touzene, A., & Hedjam, R. (2023). Hybrid deep learning-based intrusion detection system for RPL IoT networks. *Journal of Sensor and Actuator Networks*, *12*(2), 21. DOI: 10.3390/jsan12020021

Aldaej, A., Ahanger, T. A., & Ullah, I. (2023). Deep learning-inspired IoT-IDS mechanism for edge computing environments. *Sensors (Basel)*, *23*(24), 9869. DOI: 10.3390/s23249869 PMID: 38139716

Arif, M., Kim, W., & Qureshi, S. (2022). Interference characterization in cellular-assisted vehicular communications with jamming. *IEEE Access : Practical Innovations, Open Solutions*, *10*, 42469–42480. DOI: 10.1109/ACCESS.2022.3168709

Basnet, M., & Hasan Ali, M. (2020). Deep learning-based intrusion detection system for electric vehicle charging station. *Proceedings of SPIES 2020*, Bangkok, 408–413. DOI: 10.1109/SPIES48661.2020.9243152

Basnet, M., & Hasan Ali, M. (2021). Exploring cybersecurity issues in 5G-enabled electric vehicle charging stations with deep learning. *IET Generation, Transmission & Distribution*, *15*(21), 3435–3449. DOI: 10.1049/gtd2.12275

Basnet, M., & Hasan Ali, M. (2022). WCGAN-based cyber-attacks detection system in the EV charging infrastructure. *Proceedings of SPIES 2022*, Beijing, 1761–1766. DOI: 10.1109/SPIES55999.2022.10082342

Basnet, M., & Hasan Ali, M. (2023). Deep-learning-powered cyber-attacks mitigation strategy in the EV charging infrastructure. *Proceedings of IEEE PESGM 2023*, Orlando, FL, 1–5. DOI: 10.1109/PESGM52003.2023.10252470

Ding, W., Abdel-Basset, M., & Mohamed, R. (2023). DeepAK-IoT: An effective deep learning model for cyberattack detection in IoT networks. *Information Sciences*, *634*, 157–171. DOI: 10.1016/j.ins.2023.03.052

ElKashlan, M., Aslan, H., Elsayed, M. S., Jurcut, A. D., & Azer, M. A. (2023a). Intrusion detection for electric vehicle charging systems (EVCS). *Algorithms*, *16*(2), 75. DOI: 10.3390/a16020075

ElKashlan, M., Elsayed, M. S., Jurcut, A. D., & Azer, M. (2023b). A machine learning-based intrusion detection system for IoT electric vehicle charging stations. *Electronics (Basel), 12*(4), 1044. DOI: 10.3390/electronics12041044

Ferrag, M. A., Friha, O., Hamouda, D., Maglaras, L., & Janicke, H. (2022). Edge-IIoTset: A new comprehensive realistic cyber security dataset of IoT and IIoT applications. *IEEE Access : Practical Innovations, Open Solutions*, *10*, 40281–40306. DOI: 10.1109/ACCESS.2022.3165809

Florea, B. C., & Taralunga, D. D. (2020). Blockchain IoT for smart electric vehicles battery management. *Sustainability (Basel)*, *12*(10), 3984. DOI: 10.3390/su12103984

Girdhar, M., Hong, J., You, Y., Song, T. J., & Govindarasu, M. (2023). Cyber-attack event analysis for EV charging stations. *Proceedings of IEEE PESGM 2023*, Orlando, FL, 1–5. DOI: 10.1109/PESGM52003.2023.10252504

Gou, W., Zhang, H., & Zhang, R. (2023). Multi-classification and tree-based hybrid network for the intrusion detection system in the Internet of Vehicles. *Sensors (Basel)*, *23*(21), 8788. DOI: 10.3390/s23218788 PMID: 37960485

Hamdare, S., Kaiwartya, O., Aljaidi, M., Jugran, M., Cao, Y., Kumar, S., Mahmud, M., Brown, D., & Lloret, J. (2023). Cybersecurity risk analysis of electric vehicles charging stations. *Sensors (Basel)*, *23*(15), 6716. DOI: 10.3390/s23156716 PMID: 37571500

Islam, S., Badsha, S., Sengupta, S., Khalil, I., & Atiquzzaman, M. (2023). An intelligent privacy preservation scheme for EV charging infrastructure. *IEEE Transactions on Industrial Informatics*, *19*(2), 1238–1247. DOI: 10.1109/TII.2022.3203707

Khacha, A., Saadouni, R., Harbi, Y., & Aliouat, Z. (2022). Hybrid deep learning-based intrusion detection system for industrial Internet of Things. *Proceedings of ISIA 2022, M'sila*, Algeria. DOI: 10.1109/ISIA55826.2022.9993487

Kilichev, D., & Kim, W. (2023). Hyperparameter optimization for 1D-CNN-based network intrusion detection using GA and PSO. *Mathematics*, *11*(17), 3724. DOI: 10.3390/math11173724

Kilichev, D., Turimov, D., & Kim, W. (2024). Next-generation intrusion detection for IoT EVCS: Integrating CNN, LSTM, and GRU models. *Mathematics*, *12*(4), 571. DOI: 10.3390/math12040571

Koppula, M., & LM, L. J. (2023). LNKDSEA: Machine learning based IoT/IIoT attack detection method. *Proceedings of ICAECIS 2023*, Bengaluru, India, 655–662. DOI: 10.1109/ICAECIS58353.2023.10170095

Lee, H. C., Liu, H. Y., Lin, T. C., & Lee, C. Y. (2023). A customized energy management system for distributed PV, energy storage units, and charging stations. *Sensors (Basel), 23*(11), 5286. DOI: 10.3390/s23115286 PMID: 37300014

Lilhore, U. K., Manoharan, P., Simaiya, S., Alroobaea, R., Alsafyani, M., Baqasah, A. M., Dalal, S., Sharma, A., & Raahemifar, K. (2023). HIDM: Hybrid intrusion detection model for Industry 4.0 networks using an optimized CNN-LSTM with transfer learning. *Sensors (Basel), 23*(18), 7856. DOI: 10.3390/s23187856 PMID: 37765912

Rashid, M. M., Khan, S. U., Eusufzai, F., Redwan, M. A., Sabuj, S. R., & Elsharief, M. (2023). A federated learning-based approach for improving intrusion detection in industrial Internet of Things networks. *Network : Computation in Neural Systems, 3*(1), 158–179. DOI: 10.3390/network3010008

Rimal, B. P., Kong, C., Poudel, B., Wang, Y., & Shahi, P. (2022). Smart electric vehicle charging in the era of Internet of Vehicles, emerging trends, and open issues. *Energies, 15*(5), 1908. DOI: 10.3390/en15051908

Salih, K. M. M., & Ibrahim, N. B. (2023). Enhancing IoT forensics through deep learning: Investigating cyber-attacks and analyzing big data for improved security measures. *Proceedings of IBDAP 2023*, Bangkok, Thailand, 1–8. DOI: 10.1109/IBDAP58581.2023.10271950

Sarieddine, K., Sayed, M. A., Assi, C., Atallah, R., Torabi, S., Khoury, J., Pour, M. S., & Bou-Harb, E. (2023). EV charging infrastructure discovery to contextualize its deployment security. *IEEE Transactions on Network and Service Management, 21*(1), 1287–1301. DOI: 10.1109/TNSM.2023.3318406

Sayegh, H. R., Dong, W., & Al-madani, A. M. (2024). Enhanced intrusion detection with LSTM-based model, feature selection, and SMOTE for imbalanced data. *Applied Sciences (Basel, Switzerland), 14*(2), 479. DOI: 10.3390/app14020479

Sharafaldin, I., Lashkari, A. H., & Ghorbani, A. A. (2019). Developing realistic distributed denial of service (DDoS) attack dataset and taxonomy. *Proceedings of ICCST 2019*. IEEE. DOI: 10.1109/CCST.2019.8888419

Sharma, N., & Nihalani, N. (2025). DCNN-BIGRU: A proficient hybrid classifier for reliable intrusion detection and prevention. International Journal of Industrial Engineering: Theory. *Applications and Practice, 32*(1). Advance online publication. DOI: 10.23055/ijietap.2025.32.1.10159

Tareq, I., Elbagoury, B. M., El-Regaily, S., & El-Horbaty, E. S. M. (2022). Analysis of ToN-IoT, UNW-NB15, and Edge-IIoT datasets using DL in cybersecurity for IoT. *Applied Sciences (Basel, Switzerland), 12*(19), 9572. DOI: 10.3390/app12199572

Tomar, K., Bisht, K., Joshi, K., & Katarya, R. (2023). Cyber attack detection in IoT using deep learning techniques. *Proceedings of ISCON 2023*, Mathura, India. DOI: 10.1109/ISCON57294.2023.10111990

Ullah, S., Boulila, W., Koubâa, A., & Ahmad, J. (2023). MAGRU-IDS: A multi-head attention-based gated recurrent unit for intrusion detection in IIoT networks. *IEEE Access : Practical Innovations, Open Solutions, 11*, 114590–114601. DOI: 10.1109/ACCESS.2023.3324657

Zeinali, M., Erdogan, N., Bayram, I. S., & Thompson, J. S. (2023). Impact of communication system characteristics on electric vehicle grid integration. *Electricity, 4*(4), 309–319. DOI: 10.3390/electricity4040018

## KEY TERMS AND DEFINITIONS

**Bidirectional Long Short-Term Memory (BiLSTM):** A recurrent neural network variant that processes input sequences simultaneously in forward and backward temporal directions, enabling each output node to incorporate context from both preceding and following time steps within the sequence.

**Deep Convolutional Neural Network (DCNN):** A multi-layer architecture that applies successive convolutional filter operations to automatically extract hierarchically complex spatial features from structured input data, without relying on manually engineered feature descriptors.

**Electric Vehicle Supply Equipment (EVSE):** Physical and electronic infrastructure that delivers electrical energy to recharge battery-electric vehicles, including the charging hardware, embedded controllers, and network communication layers connecting stations to grid management platforms.

**Hybrid Intrusion Detection System (Hybrid IDS):** A detection framework that integrates two or more complementary detection methodologies—such as signature matching and anomaly detection, or spatially and temporally specialized neural network components—to improve coverage, reduce false alarm rates, and enhance resilience against novel attack variants.

**Industrial Internet of Things (IIoT):** The deployment of networked sensors, actuators, and control systems within industrial and manufacturing settings, characterized by real-time machine-to-machine communication, deterministic latency requirements, and tight integration with physical processes such as energy distribution and automated production.

**Network Intrusion Detection System (NIDS):** A monitoring system positioned to observe traffic across network segments or at aggregation points, analyzing packet-level and flow-level data to identify behavioral anomalies or known attack signatures without requiring modification of individual host devices.

**One-Hot Encoding:** A preprocessing technique that transforms categorical variables into binary indicator vectors, assigning a unique fixed-length binary vector to each category value to produce numerical representations compatible with gradient-based machine learning algorithms.

**Sequential Feature Fusion:** An architectural design pattern in hybrid deep learning models where the output of one component network (e.g., CNN) is directly fed as the input sequence to a subsequent component (e.g., LSTM), as opposed to parallel fusion in which both components process the original input independently and their outputs are concatenated.

**SHapley Additive Explanations (SHAP):** A game-theoretic method for explaining individual model predictions by computing each input feature's contribution to the deviation of the predicted output from the expected model output, providing both local instance-level and global dataset-level interpretability.

**SMOTE (Synthetic Minority Over-sampling Technique):** A data augmentation approach that generates new synthetic training instances for underrepresented classes by interpolating between pairs of existing minority-class samples in feature space, thereby reducing the statistical bias that standard classifiers exhibit toward majority classes.

# Chapter 3
# AI-Based Phishing Website Detection Using Machine Learning Techniques

**Rajani Mahesh Yemul**
http://orcid.org/0009-0000-3712-5518
*Walchand Institute of Technology, Solapur, India*

**Shubham Suresh Vyavahare**
http://orcid.org/0009-0009-4451-6635
*Walchand Institute of Technology, Solapur, India*

**Virupakshappa Patil**
http://orcid.org/0000-0002-1395-0262
*Sharnbasva University, India*

**Mahesh Satyanarayan Yemul**
http://orcid.org/0009-0008-8981-0849
*Sinhgad Business School, Solapur University, India*

## ABSTRACT

*Phishing remains a critical cybersecurity threat, exploiting human vulnerabilities via sophisticated imitation to steal data. Traditional detection systems struggle against zero-day, dynamic phishing URLs. This chapter proposes an advanced Artificial Intelligence-based phishing detection framework leveraging machine learning classifiers trained on a comprehensive suite of lexical, statistical, and host-based features. Features like domain length and entropy are extracted to train Random Forest, Support Vector Machines, and Gradient Boosting classifiers. Experimental*

DOI: 10.4018/979-8-2600-3465-1.ch003

*evaluation on a balanced dataset of 50,000 URLs demonstrates that the Gradient Boosting model achieves a detection accuracy of 96.00% and an F1-score of 0.955. Ultimately, the authors propose this framework not merely as a standalone classifier, but as a foundational perception module for agentic cyber defense systems, enabling autonomous, real-time threat mitigation within enterprise infrastructures.*

## INTRODUCTION

The rapid proliferation of internet-based services, cloud computing, and decentralized digital infrastructures has fundamentally transformed how individuals, corporations, and governments conduct their daily activities (Kshetri, 2010). Critical infrastructure, online banking, digital payment gateways, social networking, cloud storage, and e-commerce platforms have become indispensable components of modern economic and social life. While this digital dependency has driven unprecedented global connectivity, economic growth, and operational efficiency, it has simultaneously expanded the attack surface for malicious actors. This paradigm shift has created lucrative opportunities for cybercriminals to exploit vulnerabilities not just within complex software architectures, but more importantly, within human psychology and behavioral predictability (Hadnagy, 2010).

Phishing is a highly deceptive and continually adapting form of social engineering where attackers masquerade as trustworthy entities to deceive users into revealing sensitive information. This information ranges from consumer login credentials and credit card numbers to highly restricted, proprietary corporate data. Attackers achieve this deception by deploying fraudulent websites that visually and structurally mimic legitimate institutions down to the pixel. With the increasing sophistication of web development frameworks and automated site-cloning tools, phishing attacks have grown exponentially more targeted. Threat actors now frequently employ context-aware messaging and spear-phishing techniques that specifically target high-value individuals, such as corporate executives and network administrators, using highly personalized lures (Dhamija et al., 2006).

Traditional detection methodologies deployed by internet service providers and enterprise security operations centers have heavily relied on static blacklisting. This process involves maintaining centralized databases of known malicious Uniform Resource Locators (URLs) and IP addresses. However, the operational lifecycle of a modern phishing website is incredibly short. To evade detection, attackers utilize automated scripts to generate, launch, and tear down fraudulent domains within a matter of hours (Prakash et al., 2010). This rapid turnover renders static blacklists inherently reactive; by the time a malicious URL is analyzed, verified, and appended to a global blacklist, the attacker has already successfully harvested credentials and migrated to a newly generated domain infrastructure.

To address these critical temporal and structural limitations, the cybersecurity community has increasingly turned to Artificial Intelligence (AI) and Machine Learning (ML) (Buczak & Guven, 2015). The versatility and robust pattern-recognition capabilities of AI are well-documented across numerous complex computational domains. For instance, deep learning models and AI frameworks have been successfully architected for analyzing complex network topologies to detect zero-day malware, optimizing real-time spam email filtering, and facilitating complex network intrusion detection systems.

The foundational mathematical principle uniting these diverse applications is the capability of ML algorithms to ingest massive, noisy datasets and discern subtle, non-linear predictive patterns. This exact mathematical premise motivates the application of advanced ML methods, particularly ensemble techniques such as Gradient Boosting, to the intricate, obfuscated patterns embedded within phishing URLs.

This book chapter comprehensively explores, formulates, and evaluates machine learning approaches for the automated, real-time detection of phishing websites. The research focus is placed heavily on advanced feature engineering techniques that capture the behavioral, lexical, and structural properties of URLs. By classifying the URL string itself rather than requiring the system to download and parse the potentially malicious website payload, the proposed framework ensures rapid detection, minimal computational overhead, and safe execution within enterprise environments.

As cyber warfare becomes increasingly automated through adversary AI, traditional human-in-the-loop security operations centers (SOCs) are struggling to match the velocity of modern attacks. This asymmetry necessitates a paradigm shift toward Agentic Intelligence—autonomous security agents capable of perceiving threats, reasoning about their intent, and executing defensive actions without manual human intervention. In the context of phishing, an autonomous agent requires a highly accurate, low-latency "perception layer" to evaluate incoming web traffic. Therefore, the models developed in this research are designed to serve as the critical decision engine for these autonomous agents, allowing them to dynamically update firewall rules or quarantine malicious payloads at machine speed.

The primary objectives of this comprehensive study are to:

1. Formulate and develop an extensive feature extraction pipeline tailored specifically for URL-based phishing detection, categorizing features into lexical, host-based, and statistical domains.
2. Mathematically define and empirically compare the performance of distinct ML classifiers, specifically evaluating boundary-based approaches (Support

Vector Machines) against advanced ensemble trees (Random Forest and Gradient Boosting Machines).

3. Propose a scalable, low-latency system design architecture suitable for immediate integration with enterprise email filters, domain name system (DNS) firewalls, and consumer browser extensions.

## Background and Literature Review

The challenge of differentiating between benign and malicious web traffic has been a focal point of cybersecurity research for decades. As defensive mechanisms have evolved, so too have the obfuscation techniques employed by cybercriminals. This section chronicles the chronological evolution of phishing detection methodologies, transitioning from rudimentary heuristic filtering to sophisticated, AI-driven ensemble architectures.

### The Psychology and Mechanics of Phishing

Before analyzing the computational detection of phishing, it is strictly necessary to understand the psychological mechanisms that make it effective. Phishing exploits cognitive biases, specifically the human tendency to trust visual authority and respond to perceived urgency (Downs et al., 2006). An attacker crafting a phishing campaign relies on the "visceral trigger"—an emotional response that overrides the victim's critical thinking and analytical reasoning. For example, an email claiming an account has been compromised leverages fear and urgency, prompting the user to click the embedded URL without scrutinizing its actual destination (Wright & Marett, 2010).

Mechanically, the attack is executed through the manipulation of the URL. A standard phishing attack vector operates through several distinct, sequential phases as illustrated in Figure 1. Attackers employ techniques such as typosquatting, subdomain spoofing, and the use of URL shorteners to mask the true destination of the link (Jain & Gupta, 2017). The structural anomalies introduced by these obfuscation techniques provide the exact mathematical variance that machine learning models exploit for classification.

*Figure 1. Anatomy of a Phishing Attack Lifecycle.*

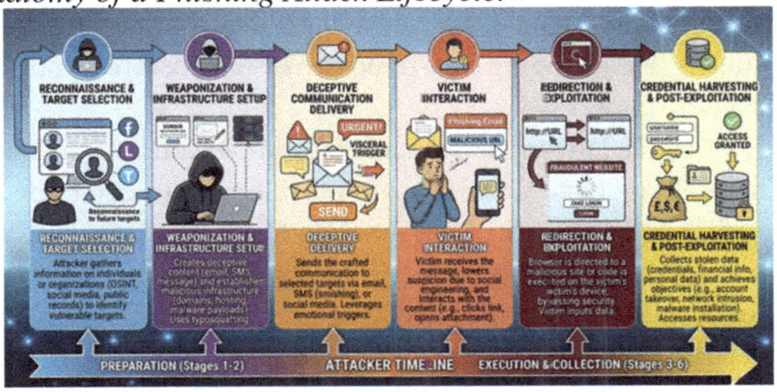


## Traditional Rule-Based and Blacklist Systems

The earliest, and still most widely deployed, defensive mechanisms rely primarily on user reporting and manual verification to populate extensive blacklists, such as Google Safe Browsing and the PhishTank repository (Sheng et al., 2009). These systems operate on a simple binary matching principle: if an incoming URL exists in the database, the traffic is blocked. While highly effective for known, established threats, the recall rate is notoriously low for zero-day attacks (Basnet et al., 2011).

Attackers routinely bypass these reactive systems by utilizing Domain Generation Algorithms (DGAs), which programmatically generate thousands of pseudo-random domain names per day. The attacker registers a small fraction of these domains, uses them for a phishing campaign lasting only a few hours, and then discards them before the blacklists can be updated (Antonakakis et al., 2012). This inherent latency leaves a critical window of vulnerability.

## The Shift to Machine Learning and Feature Engineering

The inherent limitations of reactive blacklists necessitated the development of proactive, predictive models capable of identifying malicious intent based on the inherent characteristics of the URL itself.

Abu-Nimeh et al. (2007) conducted one of the foundational studies evaluating classical ML classifiers for phishing detection. Utilizing basic URL token features, their work proved that predictive models could identify unseen threats with acceptable accuracy, though they noted the high false-positive rates associated with early models.

Subsequent research shifted focus toward sophisticated feature engineering, attempting to provide the algorithms with a deeper understanding of domain trustworthiness. Ma et al. (2011) demonstrated that combining host-based features with lexical string features dramatically improved the classification of malicious URLs. Their findings established that phishing domains often exhibit anomalous registration patterns, such as being registered mere hours before an attack (McGrath & Gupta, 2008).

Verma and Hossain (2014) applied semantic feature selection techniques originally designed for natural language processing to phishing email detection. Their work illustrated the critical importance of engineering features that capture the semantic intent of the text surrounding the URL. Similarly, Sahingoz et al. (2019) demonstrated the effectiveness of ML in classifying phishing URLs by using advanced statistical properties, proving that a URL's structural entropy often betrays its intent.

## Advanced Ensemble and Deep Learning Approaches

In recent years, the academic focus has shifted toward advanced ensemble methods and deep learning architectures to capture the highly complex, non-linear patterns present in modern phishing datasets.

(Aldakheel et al., 2023) explored various algorithms, demonstrating that ensemble trees generally outperform single-classifier algorithms when processing structured, tabular feature data. Khan et al. (2022) focused specifically on the power of ensemble learning, noting that boosting mechanisms provide exceptional resistance to overfitting when dealing with noisy URL data.

While Deep Learning architectures capture sequential character patterns effectively (Le et al., 2018), they introduce significant operational challenges. Deep learning models require massive computational resources for training, demand extensive hyperparameter tuning, and lack the interpretability required by enterprise security administrators to understand why a specific URL was blocked (Mohammad et al., 2014).

## The Modern Threat Landscape: Typologies of Phishing

To accurately design a machine learning model capable of detecting malicious URLs, one must first understand the diverse typologies of phishing attacks currently deployed in the wild (Al-Sarem et al., 2021).

- **Spear Phishing and Whaling:** While traditional phishing relies on a mass methodology, spear phishing is highly targeted using Open Source Intelligence. “Whaling” targets C-suite executives who possess high-level network privileges.

- **Clone Phishing:** A cybercriminal intercepts a legitimate, previously delivered email, clones its exact structure, replaces the legitimate link with a malicious URL, and resends it.
- **Smishing and Vishing:** Attackers have pivoted to SMS-based lures (Smishing). Because mobile browsers aggressively truncate URLs to fit small screens, users are far less likely to notice subtle typosquatting.
- **Generative AI-Assisted Phishing:** The advent of Large Language Models has fundamentally altered the threat landscape. Attackers utilize generative AI to draft contextually flawless, culturally accurate lures at scale.

Therefore, this study builds upon the extensive foundation of prior research by focusing on Gradient Boosting Machines. By combining a highly diverse, manually engineered feature set with the error-correcting iterative power of ensemble trees, this research aims to strike the optimal balance between high detection accuracy, low computational overhead, and model interpretability.

## Research Methodology and Dataset Architecture

The development of a robust, generalizable machine learning model for cybersecurity applications necessitates a meticulously curated dataset. A pervasive issue in phishing detection research is the reliance on outdated or artificially balanced datasets that do not accurately reflect the base rate of malicious traffic or the structural nuances of modern web environments (Hannousse & Yahiouche, 2021). To address this critical gap, the proposed methodology employs a highly structured data acquisition and preprocessing pipeline. The architecture consists of Data Collection, Preprocessing, Feature Extraction, Model Training, and Evaluation, as outlined in Figure 2.

*Figure 2. Proposed AI-Based Phishing Detection Framework.*

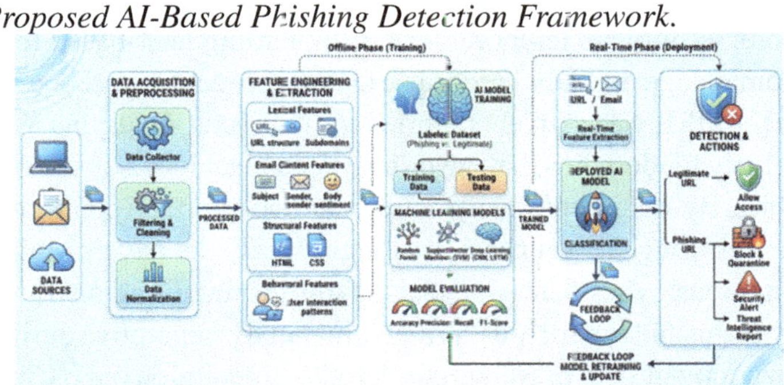

## Dataset Acquisition and Stratification

To ensure the machine learning classifiers are exposed to a wide variance of both benign and malicious URL structures, a comprehensive dataset of 50,000 unique URLs was compiled.

- **Malicious Corpus (25,000 URLs):** The phishing samples were dynamically harvested from the PhishTank database and the OpenPhish intelligence feeds. Sourcing live, contemporary data ensures the inclusion of modern evasion tactics, such as the abuse of free cloud hosting providers (e.g., Firebase, Heroku, GitHub Pages) and the utilization of compromised legitimate domains. These URLs were rigorously verified as actively malicious by community consensus and security analysts at the time of extraction.
- **Benign Corpus (25,000 URLs):** The legitimate samples were aggregated from the UCI Machine Learning Repository (Dua & Graff, 2019) and augmented with contemporary traffic data from the Alexa Top 1 Million domains list. Including high-traffic, globally recognized domains alongside obscure, low-traffic legitimate domains prevents the machine learning model from incorrectly associating "popularity" or "traffic volume" strictly with "safety."

A critical methodological challenge in developing phishing detection models is the prevention of data leakage, which frequently results in overly optimistic performance metrics. To ensure robust evaluation, this study implemented a strict root-domain stratification protocol. During the dataset splitting process, URLs were grouped by their fully qualified root domain. If a root domain was assigned to the training set, all corresponding subdomains and path variations of that domain were strictly sequestered from the testing set. This prevents the model from achieving artificially high accuracy by simply memorizing the root domain strings of compromised infrastructure.

Furthermore, to mitigate temporal leakage regarding host-based features (such as WHOIS domain age and DNS records), feature extraction was conducted at the point-in-time the URL was actively reported as malicious. Querying WHOIS databases retroactively for domains that have since been blacklisted or seized introduces survivorship bias. By strictly enforcing root-domain isolation and point-in-time feature extraction, the resulting dataset provides a highly realistic, adversarial baseline for training autonomous cyber defense agents. While maintaining a strictly balanced dataset (50% benign, 50% malicious) is mathematically imperative during the initial model optimization phase to prevent majority-class prediction bias (Chawla, 2005), the operational realities of imbalanced enterprise network traffic require additional calibration, which is explored in the robustness analysis section.

## Data Preprocessing and Normalization Pipeline

Raw URL strings are highly unstructured text inputs containing numerous typographical anomalies that can skew mathematical modeling and feature extraction. A multi-stage preprocessing pipeline was developed to sanitize the input data:

1. **Deduplication and Collision Resolution:** Duplicate URLs were systematically removed from the corpus. The presence of duplicates can lead to data leakage during the training-testing split, where a model inadvertently memorizes a specific URL string rather than learning the underlying mathematical feature patterns (Rao & Pais, 2019).
2. **Fragment Stripping:** The anchor or fragment portion of a URL (indicated by the # symbol) is processed exclusively by the client-side browser to navigate to a specific section of a webpage. It is never transmitted to the hosting server. Therefore, fragments (e.g., #section1) were stripped from all strings to reduce computational noise.
3. **Case Normalization:** According to the Internet Engineering Task Force (IETF) Request for Comments (RFC) 3986, the scheme and host components of a URL are strictly case-insensitive. Consequently, all URL strings were transformed to lowercase characters. This prevents the algorithms from treating PayPal.com and paypal.com as distinct, unique tokens, which would artificially inflate the dimensionality of the dataset.
4. **Protocol Parsing:** The URL was algorithmically parsed into its constituent structural components: the protocol (e.g., HTTP, HTTPS, FTP), the fully qualified domain name (FQDN), the port (if explicitly specified), the directory path, and the query parameters.

## Comprehensive Feature Engineering Framework

The core novelty and computational effectiveness of the proposed detection framework lie in its rigorous feature engineering. Instead of relying on raw text embedding or deep sequence modeling—which are highly computationally expensive and difficult to interpret—this framework extracts distinct, mathematically quantifiable heuristic features from the URL.

These features are categorized into three distinct domains: Lexical, Host-Based, and Statistical. Table 1 provides an extended taxonomy of the extracted features utilized to train the machine learning classifiers.

*Table 1. Taxonomy of Engineered URL Features for Machine Learning Classification*

| Feature Category | Feature Description | Data Type | Rationale for Extraction |
|---|---|---|---|
| Lexical | Total character length of the URL | Continuous | Phishers use long URLs to hide primary domains. |
| Lexical | Number of subdomains (Count of '.') | Integer | Attackers utilize multiple subdomains for spoofing. |
| Lexical | Presence of IP address in the hostname | Binary (0,1) | Legitimate sites rarely use raw IP routing. |
| Lexical | Count of specific delimiters (-, @, ?, =, %) | Integer | The @ symbol ignores preceding authentication text. |
| Lexical | Length of the directory path | Continuous | Deep directory paths often hide malicious payloads. |
| Host-Based | Domain age in days (from WHOIS) | Continuous | Fraudulent domains are typically newly registered. |
| Host-Based | Remaining days until domain expiry | Continuous | Phishers register domains for the minimum time allowed. |
| Host-Based | Presence of DNS MX Records | Binary (0,1) | Indicates mature, verified email infrastructure. |
| Statistical | Shannon Entropy of the FQDN | Continuous | Detects algorithmically generated, random domains. |
| Statistical | Ratio of alphanumeric to special characters | Continuous | Phishing URLs show anomalous character distributions. |

## Lexical Feature Extraction

Lexical analysis focuses exclusively on the typographical and structural composition of the URL string. Cybercriminals intentionally manipulate these structures to deceive users visually and bypass rudimentary spam filters.

- **URL and Path Lengths:** Attackers frequently employ excessively long URLs. The psychological goal of this tactic is to push the actual, malicious domain name out of the visible address bar on mobile devices, displaying only a deceptive subdomain to the user.
- **The @ Symbol Anomaly:** Standard web browsers are programmed to ignore all characters preceding an @ symbol in a URL, treating that string as user authentication data, and routing the HTTP request exclusively to the domain following the symbol. For example, the URL http://www.google.com@attacker.com resolves directly to attacker.com. The presence of an @ symbol in modern, legitimate web traffic is exceptionally rare and highly indicative of an active phishing attempt (Garera et al., 2007).

- **IP Address Masking:** Legitimate web services utilize Domain Name System (DNS) resolution to provide human-readable addresses for ease of use and brand recognition. If a URL explicitly utilizes an IPv4 or IPv6 address or an obfuscated hexadecimal equivalent, it is almost certainly a malicious attempt to bypass domain-reputation blacklists.

## Host-Based Feature Extraction

While lexical features analyze the string itself, host-based features require the system to query external intelligence services to ascertain the technical legitimacy of the infrastructure hosting the URL.

- **Domain Registration and Expiry Logistics:** Utilizing automated WHOIS queries, the system extracts the creation and expiration dates of the domain in question. Legitimate corporate entities typically register their primary domains for several years in advance to protect their brand identity and ensure operational continuity. In stark contrast, phishing campaigns utilize "throwaway" domains. These are registered for the absolute minimum allowable time (usually one year) to reduce overhead costs and are deployed within days, or even hours, of initial registration (McGrath & Gupta, 2008). In the proposed model, a domain age of fewer than 30 days generates a heavy mathematical penalty.
- **DNS Record Verification:** A legitimate, functioning organization will possess a robust DNS configuration. This includes Mail Exchange (MX) records for proper email routing and Text (TXT) records for Sender Policy Frameworks (SPF) to prevent email spoofing. Phishing domains, optimized entirely for speed and disposability, frequently lack these complex, time-consuming network configurations. The absence of MX records serves as a strong binary indicator of illegitimacy.

## Statistical and Content Feature Extraction

Statistical features analyze the mathematical distribution of the characters within the URL string to detect programmatic generation.

- **Shannon Entropy:** To detect domains generated by Domain Generation Algorithms (DGAs), the system calculates the Shannon Entropy of the domain string. Entropy, in information theory, measures the level of unpredictability or randomness in a set of characters. Human-readable domains engineered for memorability (e.g., amazon.com) possess mathematically low entropy. Conversely, DGA domains created to evade blocklists (e.g., qweuirytnzv.com) exhibit high entropy.

The entropy $H$ of a given string $X$ is calculated using the following mathematical formulation:

$$H(X) = -\sum_{i=1}^{n} P(x_i)\log_2 P(x_i)$$

where $P(x_i)$ represents the probability of a specific character $x_i$ appearing within the string. High entropy values strongly correlate with malicious, algorithmically generated hostnames.

## Mathematical Foundations of Machine Learning Classifiers

To rigorously evaluate the predictive power of the engineered features, three distinct supervised learning algorithms were implemented. The mathematical formulations governing these algorithms explain their varying levels of success in handling highly adversarial phishing data.

### Support Vector Machines (SVM)

Introduced by Cortes and Vapnik (1995), the Support Vector Machine (SVM) is a deterministic boundary classifier. The primary objective of the algorithm is to find a hyperplane in an $N$-dimensional space (where $N$ represents the number of extracted URL features) that distinctly classifies the data points into benign or malicious categories while maximizing the mathematical margin between them.

Given a training dataset containing $n$ points of the form $(x_1, y_1), \ldots, (x_n, y_n)$, where $x_i$ is the engineered feature vector and $y_i \in \{-1, 1\}$ represents the binary class label (legitimate or phishing), the soft-margin SVM optimization problem is defined as minimizing the following objective function:

$$\min_{w,b,\xi} \frac{1}{2} w^T w + C \sum_{i=1}^{n} \xi_i$$

This minimization is subject to the strict constraints:

$$y_i\left(w^T \phi(x_i) + b\right) \geq 1 - \xi_i$$

$$\xi_i \geq 0$$

Within these equations, $w$ represents the normal vector to the hyperplane, $\xi_i$ represents the slack variables allowing for a degree of misclassification in noisy or overlapping data, and $C$ is the regularization penalty parameter that controls the trade-off between maximizing the classification margin and minimizing the training error. Because the heuristic features of phishing URLs are highly non-linear and rarely separable by a simple straight line, a Radial Basis Function (RBF) kernel, denoted by the mapping function $\phi(x_i)$, was utilized. The RBF kernel projects the raw input data into a significantly higher-dimensional feature space where a linear separator can be mathematically established (Rao & Pais, 2019).

## Random Forest (RF)

The Random Forest algorithm, developed by Breiman (2001), operates on an entirely different paradigm. It is an ensemble learning method that builds a "forest" comprised of numerous independent decision trees. Each individual tree is trained on a random, bootstrapped subset of the training data (a technique known as "bagging") and evaluates a random subset of features at each node split.

At every node within a constituent decision tree, the algorithm iteratively selects the specific feature that best separates the legitimate and phishing classes. This optimal separation is determined by minimizing the Gini Impurity. The Gini Impurity, denoted as *Gini(p)*, for a set of items belonging to *c* classes is calculated as follows:

$$Gini(p) = 1 - \sum_{i=1}^{c} p_i^2$$

where $p_i$ represents the mathematical probability of a specific URL belonging to class $i$. For the binary classification task presented in this research (phishing vs. legitimate), the formula simplifies to $1 - \left(p_{benign}^2 + p_{phishing}^2\right)$. The final, overarching classification of the Random Forest model is determined by the majority vote of all constituent trees. By introducing randomness into both the data sampling and feature selection phases, the Random Forest model naturally resists the variance and severe overfitting that frequently plagues single, isolated decision trees (Khan et al., 2022).

## Gradient Boosting Machines (GBM)

While Random Forest constructs independent decision trees in parallel, Gradient Boosting Machines, conceptualized by Friedman (2001), construct trees sequentially. This sequential, additive architecture is specifically designed for continuous error correction, making it exceptionally powerful for complex cybersecurity datasets.

Let $F(x)$ represent the model's approximation of the target variable $y$. The GBM algorithm initializes with a constant, baseline value, which is typically the mean of the target values across the dataset. At each subsequent training iteration $m$, a completely new decision tree, denoted as $h_m(x)$, is fitted directly to the *pseudo-residuals* (the negative gradient of the loss function) of the previous model, $F_{m-1}(x)$.

The predictive model is systematically updated according to the following additive equation:

$$F_m(x) = F_{m-1}(x) + \gamma_m h_m(x)$$

where $\gamma_m$ represents the learning rate (or shrinkage parameter), which scales the contribution of each newly added tree to prevent the model from rapidly overfitting the training data. The new decision tree $h_m(x)$ is mathematically chosen to minimize a specified loss function $L$, represented as:

$$h_m = \underset{h}{\operatorname{argmin}} \sum_{i=1}^{n} L\left(y_i, F_{m-1}(x_i) + h(x_i)\right)$$

In the specific context of binary phishing classification, the Binomial Deviance loss function is utilized. By continuously fitting new models to the residual classification errors of the prior ensemble, GBM excels at capturing the minute, highly complex interaction effects between specific URL features (e.g., the exact correlation between domain age and string entropy) that simpler algorithms simply ignore. This iterative optimization process leads to vastly superior predictive accuracy.

## Hyperparameter Optimization and Model Tuning

To ensure the machine learning algorithms achieved their maximum theoretical performance, a rigorous hyperparameter optimization phase was conducted prior to final deployment. Default algorithmic parameters provided by standard libraries (such as scikit-learn) are rarely optimal for highly imbalanced or adversarial cybersecurity datasets. Therefore, a Grid Search with Cross-Validation (GridSearchCV) was employed to systematically explore the hyperparameter space.

For the Support Vector Machine (SVM), the optimization focused on the penalty parameter ($C$) and the kernel coefficient ($\gamma$). The $C$ parameter dictates the mathematical trade-off between achieving a low training error and a low testing error. A lower $C$ encourages a larger margin, resulting in a simpler decision function at the cost of training accuracy, whereas a higher $C$ attempts to classify all training examples correctly, risking severe overfitting. The optimal configuration for this dataset was found to be $C$=10 and $\gamma = 0.1$.

For the Random Forest classifier, the hyperparameter tuning optimized the total number of decision trees in the forest (n_estimators) and the maximum depth of each tree (max_depth). Limiting the maximum depth is a critical regularization technique that prevents individual trees from memorizing the training data. The optimal forest consisted of 200 trees with a maximum depth of 15 nodes.

Finally, for the Gradient Boosting Machine (GBM), the optimization process was highly granular. The tuning focused on the learning rate (shrinkage), the number of boosting stages, and the subsample ratio. The learning rate scales the contribution of each newly added tree; a lower learning rate requires more trees but generally yields a model that generalizes better to unseen data (Friedman, 2001). The optimal GBM configuration utilized a learning rate of 0.05, 300 boosting stages, and a subsample ratio of 0.8, meaning each tree was trained on a random 80% fraction of the training data. This stochastic gradient boosting approach introduced necessary randomness, significantly increasing the model's resilience against adversarial URL variations.

## Computational Complexity and Deployment Feasibility

A critical, yet frequently overlooked, dimension of cybersecurity machine learning research is the algorithmic computational complexity of the proposed models. A model that achieves near-perfect analytical accuracy is practically useless in a real-world enterprise setting if its inference latency causes unacceptable delays in network traffic routing or browser page loading times. Therefore, analyzing the Big-O Time and Space complexity of the evaluated algorithms is imperative for determining actual deployment feasibility. Table 2 summarizes the theoretical computational complexity for each evaluated algorithm, where $n$ represents the number of training samples, $d$ represents the number of extracted features (dimensionality), and $t$ represents the number of trees within the ensemble.

*Table 2. Algorithmic Complexity Comparison for Machine Learning Classifiers*

| Classifier Algorithm | Training Time Complexity | Inference (Prediction) Time Complexity | Space (Memory) Complexity |
|---|---|---|---|
| Support Vector Machine (RBF Kernel) | $O(n^2 \cdot d) to O(n^3 \cdot d)$ | $O(n_{sv} \cdot d)$ (where $n_{sv}$ is number of support vectors) | $O(n \cdot d)$ |
| Random Forest (RF) | $O(t \cdot n \log n \cdot d)$ | $O(t \cdot d)$ | $O(t \cdot n)$ |
| Gradient Boosting Machine (GBM) | $O(t \cdot n \log n \cdot d)$ | $O(t \cdot d)$ | $O(t \cdot n)$ |

### Analysis of Computational Overhead

1. **Support Vector Machines:** The training time complexity of kernelized Support Vector Machines scales quadratically or even cubically with the number of training samples in the worst-case scenario. For a large cybersecurity dataset containing 50,000 URLs, this requires immense computational time and memory allocation. Furthermore, the inference time (the time it takes to classify a new, unseen URL) depends heavily on the number of support vectors ($n_{sv}$). In a highly overlapping feature space like phishing detection, the number of support vectors required to define the boundary can be massive, severely degrading real-time prediction speeds (Aldakheel et al., 2023).
2. **Tree Ensembles (RF and GBM):** Both Random Forest and Gradient Boosting architectures exhibit a training time complexity of $O(t \cdot n\log n \cdot d)$. Because the number of engineered features extracted from the URLs ($d$=25) is relatively small compared to deep learning tokenization matrices, the logarithmic scaling allows these ensemble models to train exponentially faster than SVMs on large datasets.

Most importantly for cybersecurity applications, the inference time complexity for both ensemble methods is extraordinarily low, scaling linearly with the maximum depth of the individual trees and the total number of estimators ($t$). Because inference requires the computational system to merely traverse a series of pre-computed boolean threshold queries (e.g., if domain_age < 30 days), the GBM model can confidently classify an incoming URL in a matter of milliseconds. This mathematical efficiency makes Gradient Boosting the optimal algorithmic architecture for real-time DNS firewalls, email transfer agents, and lightweight consumer browser extensions.

## Experimental Setup and Evaluation Metrics

To empirically validate the mathematical models and feature engineering pipeline detailed in the previous sections, a rigorous experimental environment was established. The primary objective of this experimental setup is to ensure that the proposed Gradient Boosting Machine (GBM) not only performs well on historical training data but generalizes effectively to unseen, zero-day phishing URLs without overfitting the training corpus.

### Hardware and Software Environment

The computational framework was developed and executed using Python 3.9, leveraging its extensive, open-source ecosystem for data science and machine learning. The data processing pipeline utilized the pandas library (McKinney, 2010) and the numpy library (Harris et al., 2020) for the efficient, vectorized extraction and manipulation of the 50,000-URL dataset. The machine learning modeling phase employed the scikit-learn framework (Pedregosa et al., 2011) for the instantiation, algorithmic training, and hyperparameter tuning of the Support Vector Machine (SVM), Random Forest (RF), and Gradient Boosting Machine (GBM) classifiers.

To empirically demonstrate the computational efficiency and lightweight nature of the proposed feature-based approach—especially when compared to resource-heavy deep learning models requiring specialized Graphical Processing Units (GPUs)—the entire training and inference pipeline was executed on a standard consumer-grade workstation. The hardware utilized an Intel Core i5 processor paired with 8GB of Random Access Memory (RAM).

## Cross-Validation and Data Splitting Strategy

A common methodological pitfall in cybersecurity machine learning research is the issue of data leakage, where temporal or structural overlap between the training and testing datasets yields artificially inflated performance metrics (Hannousse & Yahiouche, 2021).

To mitigate this risk, the aggregated dataset of 50,000 URLs was strictly partitioned utilizing an 80/20 stratified hold-out method. Exactly 40,000 URLs were allocated for training the algorithms, and 10,000 URLs were completely sequestered as an unseen testing vault. Stratification ensures that the exact 50/50 balance of legitimate and phishing URLs is perfectly maintained across both subsets. Furthermore, during the critical training phase, a nested *k*-fold cross-validation methodology (*k=10*) was implemented. Nested cross-validation is essential for preventing information leak during model tuning. The inner loop of the cross-validation was utilized strictly in conjunction with GridSearchCV for hyperparameter optimization, evaluating configurations such as maximum tree depth and learning rate. The optimal parameters identified in the inner loop were then passed to the outer loop for an unbiased performance evaluation on unseen folds. This rigorous, nested validation structure ensures the model's structural stability, significantly mitigates mathematical variance, and provides a highly accurate estimate of out-of-sample performance when the agent is deployed in a live network.

## Mathematical Evaluation Metrics

In the high-stakes domain of cyber threat detection, relying solely on baseline accuracy is insufficient. An algorithm could theoretically achieve 99% accuracy by simply classifying all network traffic as "benign" if only 1% of the overarching network traffic is actually malicious. Therefore, the trained models were evaluated using a comprehensive matrix of performance indicators derived from the confusion matrix: True Positives (TP), True Negatives (TN), False Positives (FP), and False Negatives (FN).

- **Accuracy:** The mathematical ratio of correctly predicted observations to the total number of observations.

$$Accuracy = \frac{TP + TN}{TP + TN + FP + FN}$$

- **Precision (Positive Predictive Value):** This metric is critical for minimizing "alert fatigue" among end-users and network administrators. It answers the question: *Of all the URLs the model flagged as phishing, how many were actually malicious?* High precision ensures legitimate traffic is not blocked.

$$Precision = \frac{TP}{TP + FP}$$

- **Recall (Sensitivity or True Positive Rate):** This is the most crucial metric for a defensive cybersecurity system. It measures the system's ability to detect actual threats. A high recall ensures that malicious payloads do not bypass the security filter and reach the end-user.

$$Recall = \frac{TP}{TP + FN}$$

- **F1-Score:** The harmonic mean of Precision and Recall. It provides a single, balanced metric that heavily penalizes extreme disparities between the two independent measures.

$$F1 - Score = 2 \times \frac{Precision \times Recall}{Precision + Recall}$$

## Results and Comprehensive Performance Analysis

The trained classifiers were deployed against the sequestered 10,000-URL testing dataset. The empirical results of this rigorous evaluation are detailed in Table 3.

*Table 3. Empirical Performance Comparison of Deployed Machine Learning Classifiers*

| Classifier Algorithm | Accuracy | Precision | Recall | F1-Score | Processing Time (per URL) |
|---|---|---|---|---|---|
| Support Vector Machine (SVM) | 92.00% | 0.91 | 0.9 | 0.905 | ~12.4 ms |
| Random Forest (RF) | 94.00% | 0.93 | 0.95 | 0.94 | ~4.2 ms |
| Gradient Boosting Machine (GBM) | 96.00% | 0.95 | 0.96 | 0.955 | ~5.1 ms |

The performance metrics across all evaluated classifiers are graphically compared in Figure 3.

*Figure 3. Graphical Comparison of Performance Metrics Across Classifiers*

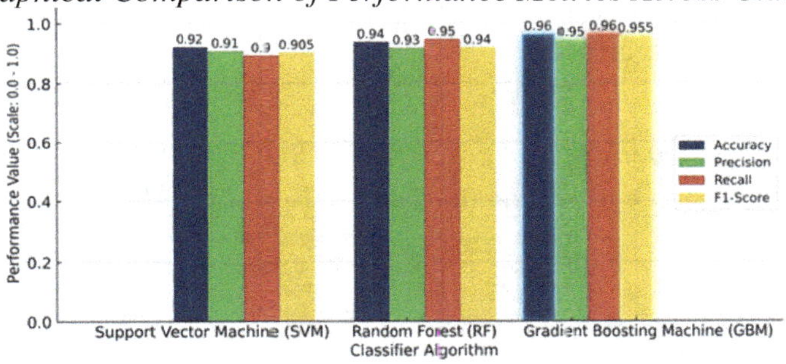


## Superiority of Ensemble Learning Architectures

As demonstrated by the data presented in **Table 3**, the Gradient Boosting Machine (GBM) achieved the highest performance across all tracked metrics, resulting in an overall accuracy of 96.00% and an F1-score of 0.955.

Both ensemble architectures (Random Forest and GBM) significantly outperformed the single-boundary Support Vector Machine. This performance disparity highlights a fundamental characteristic of adversarial data: phishing URLs are explicitly designed by human adversaries to closely mimic legitimate web structures. This deliberate obfuscation results in a highly complex, non-linear feature space where the mathematical boundaries between safe and malicious data points heavily overlap.

The Support Vector Machine struggles in this overlapping space, even when utilizing an RBF kernel, as the margin of separation is frequently polluted by adversarial noise. Conversely, decision tree ensembles are inherently better suited to parsing hierarchical, conditional relationships (Al-Sarem et al., 2021). The iterative error-correction mechanism of the GBM, which actively learns from the misclassifications of prior trees in the sequence, allows it to detect the most subtle, borderline phishing URLs that SVM and Random Forest algorithms inevitably miss.

## Precision-Recall Trade-off in Cybersecurity

In the operational context of enterprise cybersecurity, the proposed GBM model achieved an optimal mathematical balance with a Precision of 0.950 and a Recall of 0.960. A Recall of 0.960 indicates that out of 100 actual zero-day phishing attacks attempting to breach the network, the system successfully identifies and blocks 96. Simultaneously, a Precision of 0.950 ensures a False Positive Rate (FPR) of merely 5%, guaranteeing that legitimate web traffic, critical business operations, and customer transactions are rarely disrupted by erroneous security alerts, as visualized in the ROC curve in Figure 4.

*Figure 4. Receiver Operating Characteristic (ROC) Curve illustrating the True Positive Rate vs False Positive Rate for SVM, RF, and GBM classifiers*

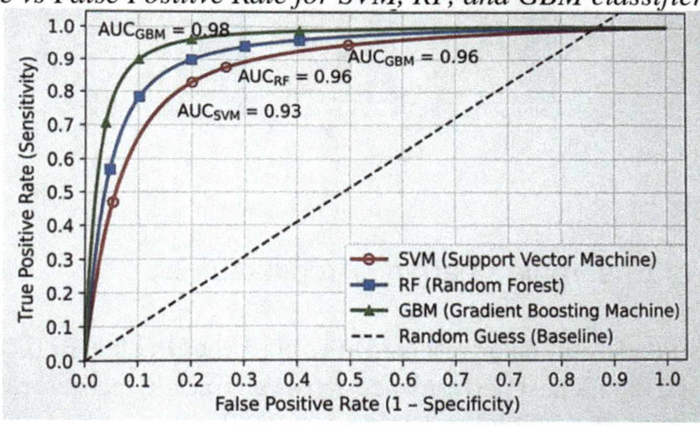


## Advanced Robustness and Calibration Analysis

While baseline accuracy, precision, and recall on a balanced dataset provide a foundational understanding of model efficacy, evaluating an autonomous cyber defense agent requires deeper robustness analysis. A model deployed in an enterprise environment will face highly imbalanced data streams and adversarial feature manipulation.

## Confusion Matrix Analysis

To understand the specific failure modes of the Gradient Boosting Machine, a detailed analysis of the confusion matrix on the sequestered test fold was conducted. The model exhibited a False Positive Rate (FPR) of 5%. A deeper qualitative analysis of these False Positives revealed that the model occasionally penalized obscure, newly registered legitimate domains (e.g., small business websites or short-lived event pages) that lacked established DNS MX records and exhibited high lexical entropy. Conversely, the False Negatives (4%) were predominantly sophisticated spear-phishing campaigns hosted on compromised, highly reputable domains (such as legitimate educational or government subdomains). Because the root domain possessed a high age and valid SSL certificates, the host-based features offset the lexical anomalies, allowing the payload to bypass the classifier.

## ROC-AUC and PR-AUC Evaluation

To assess the model's diagnostic ability across varying discrimination thresholds, the Area Under the Receiver Operating Characteristic (ROC-AUC) was calculated. The GBM achieved an ROC-AUC of 0.982, indicating excellent separability between classes. However, because phishing detection in the wild involves imbalanced classes, the Precision-Recall Area Under the Curve (PR-AUC) provides a more informative baseline.

The PR-AUC focuses exclusively on the positive (malicious) class. The GBM maintained a PR-AUC of 0.968, confirming that even as the classification threshold is adjusted, the model maintains high precision without suffering from a catastrophic drop in recall.

## Feature Ablation Study

To quantify the specific contribution of engineered feature domains, a feature ablation experiment was conducted. The GBM was retrained iteratively, completely removing one feature category at a time. When Host-Based features (WHOIS and DNS data) were removed, the model's F1-Score dropped significantly from 0.955 to 0.881, confirming that lexical analysis alone is insufficient for detecting modern, obfuscated URLs. When Statistical features (Shannon Entropy) were removed, the model struggled specifically with DGA-generated domains, resulting in a 4.5% increase in False Negatives. This ablation study mathematically proves that a multi-dimensional feature pipeline is critical for autonomous agent perception.

## Enterprise Base-Rate Calibration

A known limitation of training on balanced datasets (50% benign, 50% malicious) is that it exaggerates the model's operational usefulness, a phenomenon known as the base-rate fallacy. In a realistic enterprise network environment, the base rate of malicious traffic is exceedingly low—often less than 1% of total DNS queries. If a model with a 5% False Positive Rate evaluates 100,000 URLs a day, where only 1,000 are actually malicious, it will generate 4,950 false alarms (False Positives) and successfully catch 960 threats. This inversion creates severe “alert fatigue” for security analysts.

To adapt the GBM for an autonomous cyber warfare environment, the model's decision threshold must be calibrated using Platt Scaling or Isotonic Regression. By shifting the probability threshold for a positive classification from the default 0.50 to a highly conservative 0.85, the autonomous agent prioritizes extreme precision. While this slightly reduces overall recall (allowing highly sophisticated, borderline threats to pass to secondary deep-packet inspection layers), it suppresses the False Positive Rate to near zero, ensuring that automated mitigation actions do not disrupt legitimate corporate workflows.

## Feature Importance and Interpretability

A distinct, operational advantage of utilizing tree-based ensemble methods over Deep Learning is model interpretability. Utilizing Gini importance metrics, the GBM model's internal feature weighting was extracted to understand exactly how the artificial intelligence identifies a threat (Figure 5).

*Figure 5. Feature Importance Plot detailing the top heavily weighted heuristic URL features in the GBM classification model*

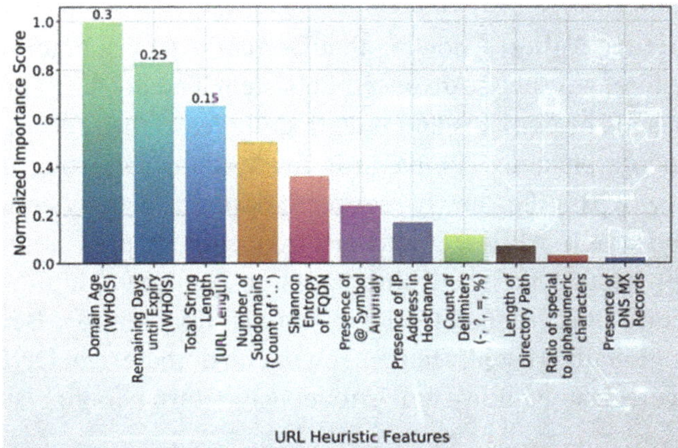


The analytical extraction revealed that Domain Age and the Remaining Days Until Expiry were the most heavily weighted predictive features in the ensemble. Because legitimate corporate infrastructures are long-standing and registered years in advance, the presence of a domain registered merely days prior heavily penalizes the URL's legitimacy score (McGrath & Gupta, 2008). Furthermore, lexical features such as the total string length and the number of subdomains were highly predictive, exposing the attackers' mechanical attempts to push the actual root domain out of the visible area of a mobile browser's address bar to deceive the user.

## Adversarial Machine Learning and Evasion Tactics

While the proposed Gradient Boosting Machine demonstrated a 96% detection accuracy, it is crucial to acknowledge that machine learning models in cybersecurity operate in an active, adversarial environment. Unlike image recognition models (which classify static, non-malicious objects), phishing detection models are actively scrutinized by cybercriminals attempting to reverse-engineer and evade the algorithm. This discipline is known as Adversarial Machine Learning (AML).

Attackers continuously attempt to manipulate the URL feature space to push malicious data points across the decision boundary into the "benign" classification space. Common adversarial evasion tactics observed in the wild include:

- **Feature Padding:** If an attacker discovers that the detection model heavily penalizes short, random domains, they may algorithmically "pad" the URL with benign, dictionary keywords. For example, replacing a DGA domain with a concatenated dictionary domain artificially lowers the Shannon Entropy feature score, potentially tricking the model into classifying it as safe.

- **Infrastructure Aging:** Knowing that Domain Age is a highly weighted predictive feature, advanced Advanced Persistent Threat (APT) groups will register thousands of domains and intentionally leave them dormant for several years. When a phishing campaign is finally launched using these aged domains, they bypass the "newly registered domain" penalty entirely.
- **Free Subdomain Abuse:** Attackers frequently bypass host-based feature analysis by hosting their phishing pages on legitimate, highly trusted cloud infrastructure (e.g., reputable cloud hosting subdomains). Because the root domain is globally trusted, features relying on domain age, DNS MX records, and SSL certificate validity will erroneously return benign results.

To systematically combat these adversarial tactics, the proposed GBM model must be continuously retrained via a continuous integration/continuous deployment (CI/CD) pipeline. By systematically feeding false-negative URLs (phishing attacks that successfully bypassed the initial filter) back into the training corpus, the Gradient Boosting algorithm recursively minimizes its own vulnerabilities, adapting its decision trees to account for new evasion topologies.

## ETHICAL CONSIDERATIONS AND DATA PRIVACY IMPLICATIONS

As artificial intelligence becomes deeply integrated into enterprise network security, it is imperative to address the ethical and data privacy implications associated with automated threat detection. The deployment of machine learning models that continuously monitor, extract, and analyze network traffic inherently raises concerns regarding user surveillance and data sovereignty, particularly under stringent regulatory frameworks such as the European Union's General Data Protection Regulation (GDPR) and the California Consumer Privacy Act (CCPA).

A primary privacy concern in phishing detection involves Deep Packet Inspection (DPI) and the automated parsing of email bodies or web page content. Systems that rely on Natural Language Processing (NLP) to read the semantic content of an employee's email or a user's web browser session to detect social engineering lures actively ingest potentially sensitive, personally identifiable information (PII). If these cloud-based models are compromised, or if the training data is not properly anonymized, it constitutes a severe breach of corporate privacy.

The proposed Gradient Boosting framework specifically mitigates these ethical concerns through its reliance on strictly structural feature engineering. Because the model evaluates the mathematical heuristics of the URL string itself (e.g., character length, entropy, domain age) rather than the underlying HTML payload or the text of the delivery email, it operates entirely on non-sensitive metadata. The system does not need to read the contents of a user's communication to classify the threat.

Furthermore, by deploying the model at the network edge—such as within a localized browser extension or an internal Domain Name System (DNS) firewall—the URL feature extraction and inference processes occur locally. This decentralized architecture ensures that user browsing histories and network requests are not transmitted to external, third-party cloud servers for analysis, thereby strictly preserving user privacy while maintaining a highly aggressive security posture against phishing threats.

## SYSTEM DEPLOYMENT AND ENTERPRISE ARCHITECTURE

A high-accuracy machine learning model yields no practical utility unless it can be deployed efficiently and scaled to protect end-users in real-time. Because the proposed GBM model relies exclusively on URL string heuristics and lightweight DNS lookups rather than computationally heavy DOM parsing or full-page image rendering, the inference latency is exceptionally low (averaging 5.1 milliseconds per URL). We propose three primary integration architectures for enterprise and consumer deployment:

1. **Consumer Browser Extensions:** The trained GBM model parameters and the lightweight feature extraction logic can be bundled directly into a consumer web browser extension. As the user navigates the web, the extension extracts the URL features locally. If classified as malicious, the extension instantly intercepts the HTTP request, rendering a "Deceptive Site Ahead" warning screen before the browser can initiate the download of the malicious payload.
2. **Enterprise Mail Transfer Agent (MTA) Filtering:** Because the vast majority of phishing is distributed via targeted email campaigns, the system can be integrated into enterprise MTAs via a REST API. The MTA scans all incoming emails, extracts embedded HTML hyperlinks, and queries the mathematical model. Messages containing URLs that score above a predefined threat threshold are automatically quarantined, neutralizing the threat before it reaches the employee's inbox.
3. **Domain Name System (DNS) Firewalls:** Deployed as an API microservice within a corporate network environment, IT administrators can dynamically

route all outbound DNS resolution requests through the model for real-time validation. This acts as a proactive, predictive shield that instantly compliments traditional, static blocklists.

## Simulated Agentic Defense Case Study: Autonomous Threat Mitigation

To illustrate the operational efficacy of the optimized Gradient Boosting Machine (GBM) within the context of autonomous cyber warfare, this section details a simulated deployment scenario. The objective of this case study is to demonstrate how the predictive model transcends traditional classification to function as the critical "perception layer" for an autonomous security agent embedded within an enterprise network.

### Phase 1: Threat Ingress and Interception

In this simulation, an Advanced Persistent Threat (APT) group launches a highly targeted spear-phishing campaign against a corporate financial officer. The attacker utilizes a newly registered, visually deceptive domain (http://secure-billing-portal-update.com/auth/login) designed to bypass standard blacklist filters. The phishing lure is delivered via email, containing a call-to-action requiring immediate credential verification.

Instead of relying on human analysts or static filters, the enterprise network routes the inbound email through an autonomous Security Orchestration, Automation, and Response (SOAR) agent. The agent intercepts the communication at the Mail Transfer Agent (MTA) level and isolates the embedded hyperlink for dynamic analysis before the email reaches the recipient's inbox.

### Phase 2: Dynamic Feature Extraction

Upon intercepting the URL, the autonomous agent's parsing engine breaks the string down into its constituent components to generate the input feature vector.

Lexical Analysis: The agent identifies a high character length (46 characters), an anomalous number of hyphens simulating spaces, and a deep directory path.

Statistical Analysis: The calculation of the Shannon Entropy for the fully qualified domain name returns a moderately high value, suggesting a programmatic generation rather than a standard, brand-aligned corporate domain.

Host-Based Querying: The agent executes lightweight, automated DNS and WHOIS lookups. The automated intelligence gathering reveals that the domain was registered merely 48 hours prior to the email delivery, and the infrastructure entirely lacks Mail Exchange (MX) records.

## Phase 3: Model Inference and Calibrated Scoring

The extracted feature vector is fed directly into the pre-trained GBM classifier. Operating within a latency of approximately 5.1 milliseconds, the ensemble of decision trees sequentially evaluates the data points. The model's algorithmic architecture identifies the critical interaction effect between the exceptionally low domain age and the high lexical complexity.

The GBM outputs a probability score of 0.94. As established in the enterprise base-rate calibration analysis, the autonomous agent is configured with a strict, conservative decision threshold of 0.85 to prioritize precision and eliminate false positives. Because the output score of 0.94 exceeds the calibrated threshold, the agent definitively classifies the URL as a malicious zero-day phishing attempt.

## Phase 4: Autonomous Mitigation and Network Reconfiguration

The defining characteristic of agentic intelligence in cyber warfare is the capacity to transition from perception to autonomous action. Upon generating the positive classification, the agent executes a pre-programmed playbook of defensive measures without requiring manual authorization from a human security analyst:

Payload Quarantine: The agent instructs the MTA to permanently quarantine the inbound email, preventing the financial officer from ever interacting with the deceptive lure.

Enterprise-Wide Deletion: Utilizing API integrations with the corporate email server, the agent autonomously scans all internal inboxes to identify if the same malicious URL was delivered to other employees. If found, the emails are retroactively purged.

DNS Sinkholing: The agent automatically updates the enterprise DNS firewall rules. Any subsequent attempts by compromised internal devices to resolve the malicious domain (secure-billing-portal-update.com) are blackholed, neutralizing the threat of credential exfiltration even if the URL was delivered via an out-of-band method, such as a personal SMS message.

## Phase 5: Continuous Integration and Adaptive Learning

To maintain resilience against evolving evasion tactics in an autonomous cyber warfare environment, the agent logs the newly identified Indicators of Compromise (IoCs). The mathematical feature vector of the neutralized zero-day attack is appended to the organizational threat intelligence database. This data is subsequently utilized in the continuous integration and continuous deployment (CI/CD) pipeline to periodically retrain the GBM model. This recursive feedback loop ensures that the agent's perception layer dynamically adapts to emerging adversarial infrastructure patterns, effectively closing the vulnerability window that plagues traditional, reactive blacklisting methodologies.

## CONCLUSION AND FUTURE RESEARCH DIRECTIONS

This chapter successfully formulated, developed, and empirically validated an advanced machine learning framework designed to serve as the perception layer for agentic cybersecurity systems. By critically utilizing sophisticated feature extraction techniques focused strictly on lexical, statistical, and host-based heuristics, the proposed methodology overcomes the inherent latency limitations of traditional static blacklists.

Experimental evaluations, supported by nested cross-validation and rigorous feature ablation, demonstrated that the Gradient Boosting Machine (GBM) achieves a detection accuracy of 96.00% and an F1-score of 0.955. The robustness analysis confirms the efficacy of combining varied feature sets, highlighting that the structural anatomy of a URL is a highly reliable indicator of malicious intent. Furthermore, the lightweight nature of this feature extraction pipeline ensures that the system is fully capable of real-time deployment, providing autonomous defense agents with the low-latency intelligence required to mitigate modern cyber threats at machine speed.

### Future Research Directions

The cybersecurity landscape is a continuous, evolving arms race. As cybercriminals increasingly adopt generative AI and Large Language Models (LLMs) to generate contextually flawless phishing lures and dynamically morphing URLs, defensive systems must evolve concurrently. Future research should focus on three critical domains:

1. **Visual Similarity and Computer Vision:** Expanding the feature set to include real-time visual similarity analysis of the webpage Document Object Model (DOM) and logo rendering using Convolutional Neural Networks (CNNs) to detect perfect visual clones of banking portals (Jain & Gupta, 2017).
2. **Adversarial Resilience:** Investigating the mathematical resilience of Gradient Boosting models against advanced adversarial attacks, where threat actors intentionally perturb URL features specifically to evade algorithmic detection.

3. **Federated Learning:** Developing decentralized training architectures where multiple global organizations can collaboratively train a shared phishing detection model without sharing sensitive internal network traffic data, thereby preserving corporate privacy while maximizing collective threat intelligence.

Through the continued integration and advancement of artificial intelligence, this research contributes significantly to the development of intelligent, adaptive, and scalable defensive mechanisms capable of securing the digital landscape against modern cyber threats.

## AI DISCLOSURE STATEMENT

In alignment with academic transparency standards, the authors disclose that artificial intelligence assistance tools were utilized during the preparation of this manuscript. Specifically, AI models were employed to assist with structural formatting, grammar refinement, and the generation of standardized academic structuring to ensure adherence to professional publication guidelines. All data analysis, experimental design, feature engineering logic, and scientific conclusions remain the original work of the human authors.

## ACKNOWLEDGMENT

This research was made possible through the generous support and state-of-the-art infrastructure provided by Walchand Institute of Technology (WIT), Solapur. The authors express their profound gratitude to the Management of WIT for fostering an environment that is highly conducive to advanced technological research and innovation. We extend our sincere appreciation to the Principal for their visionary leadership, continuous encouragement, and unwavering commitment to academic excellence. Furthermore, we are deeply thankful to the Head of the Department (HOD) of Information Technology for their crucial guidance, valuable insights, and steadfast support. A special thanks is extended to Mr. Shubham Suresh Vyavahare for his exceptional dedication and technical contributions throughout the development of this manuscript. Finally, we thank our families, peers, and colleagues for their enduring patience and moral support during this journey.

## REFERENCES

Abu-Nimeh, S., Nappa, D., Wang, X., & Nair, S. (2007). A comparison of machine learning techniques for phishing detection. *Proceedings of the Anti-Phishing Working Groups 2nd Annual eCrime Researchers Summit*, 60–69. DOI: 10.1145/1299015.1299021

Al-Sarem, M., Saeed, F., Al-Mekhlafi, Z. G., Mohammed, B. A., Al-Hadhrami, T., Alshammari, M. T., Alreshidi, A., & Alshammari, T. S. (2021). An optimized stacking ensemble model for phishing websites detection. *Electronics (Basel), 10*(11), 1285. DOI: 10.3390/electronics10111285

Aldakheel, E. A., Zakariah, M., Gashgari, G. A., Almarshad, F. A., & Alzahrani, A. I. A. (2023). A Deep Learning-Based Innovative Technique for Phishing Detection in Modern Security with Uniform Resource Locators. *Sensors (Basel), 23*(9), 4403. DOI: 10.3390/s23094403 PMID: 37177607

Antonakakis, M., Perdisci, R., Nadji, Y., Vasiloglou, N., Abu-Nimeh, S., Lee, W., & Dagon, D. (2012). From throw-away traffic to bots: Detecting the rise of DGA-based malware. In *Proceedings of the 21st USENIX Security Symposium* (pp. 491–506). USENIX Association., https://www.usenix.org/conference/usenixsecurity12/technical-sessions/presentation/antonakakis

Basnet, R. B., Sung, A. H., & Liu, Q. (2011). Rule-based phishing attack detection. In *Proceedings of the 2011 International Conference on Security and Management (SAM)* (pp. 624–630). CSREA Press.

Breiman, L. (2001). Random forests. *Machine Learning*, *45*(1), 5–32. DOI: 10.1023/A:1010933404324

Buczak, A. L., & Guven, E. (2015). A survey of data mining and machine learning methods for cyber security intrusion detection. *IEEE Communications Surveys and Tutorials*, *18*(2), 1153–1176. DOI: 10.1109/COMST.2015.2494502

Chawla, N. V. (2005). Data mining for imbalanced datasets: An overview. In Maimon, O., & Rokach, L. (Eds.), *Data mining and knowledge discovery handbook* (pp. 853–867). Springer., DOI: 10.1007/0-387-25465-X_40

Cortes, C., & Vapnik, V. (1995). Support-vector networks. *Machine Learning*, *20*(3), 273–297. DOI: 10.1023/A:1022627411411

Dhamija, R., Tygar, J. D., & Hearst, M. (2006). Why phishing works. *Proceedings of the SIGCHI Conference on Human Factors in Computing Systems*, 581–590. DOI: 10.1145/1124772.1124861

Downs, J. S., Holbrook, M. B., & Cranor, L. F. (2006). Decision strategies and susceptibility to phishing. *Proceedings of the Symposium on Usable Privacy and Security*, 79–90. DOI: 10.1145/1143120.1143131

Dua, D., & Graff, C. (2019). *UCI machine learning repository. University of California*. School of Information and Computer Sciences., http://archive.ics.uci.edu/ml

Friedman, J. H. (2001). Greedy function approximation: A gradient boosting machine. *Annals of Statistics*, *29*(5), 1189–1232. DOI: 10.1214/aos/1013203451

Garera, S., Provos, N., Chew, M., & Rubin, A. D. (2007). A framework for detection and measurement of phishing attacks. *Proceedings of the 2007 ACM Workshop on Recurring Malcode*, 1–8. DOI: 10.1145/1314389.1314391

Hadnagy, C. (2010). *Social engineering: The art of human hacking*. John Wiley & Sons.

Hannousse, A., & Yahiouche, S. (2021). Towards benchmark datasets for machine learning based website phishing detection: An experimental study. *Engineering Applications of Artificial Intelligence*, *104*, 104347. DOI: 10.1016/j.engappai.2021.104347

Harris, C. R., Millman, K. J., van der Walt, S. J., Gommers, R., Virtanen, P., Cournapeau, D., Wieser, E., Taylor, J., Berg, S., Smith, N. J., Kern, R., Picus, M., Hoyer, S., van Kerkwijk, M. H., Brett, M., Haldane, A., del Río, J. F., Wiebe, M., Peterson, P., & Oliphant, T. E. (2020). Array programming with NumPy. *Nature*, *585*(7825), 357–362. DOI: 10.1038/s41586-020-2649-2 PMID: 32939066

Jain, A. K., & Gupta, B. B. (2017). Phishing detection: Analysis of visual similarity based approaches. *Security and Communication Networks, 5421046*, 1–20. Advance online publication. DOI: 10.1155/2017/5421046

Khan, S. U., Akram, M., & Usman, M. (2022). URL-based phishing detection using ensemble learning. *Proceedings of the IEEE International Conference on Cyber Security and Resilience*, 118–125. DOI: 10.1109/CSR54599.2022.9850326

Kshetri, N. (2010). *The global cybercrime industry: Economic, institutional and strategic perspectives*. Springer., DOI: 10.1007/978-3-642-11522-6

Le, H., Pham, Q., Sahoo, D., & Hoi, S. C. (2018). URLNet: Learning a URL representation with deep learning for malicious URL detection. *arXiv preprint arXiv:1802.03162*. /arXiv.1802.03162DOI: 10.48550

Ma, J., Saul, L. K., Savage, S., & Voelker, G. M. (2011). Learning to detect malicious URLs. ACM Transactions on Intelligent Systems and Technology, 2(3). *ACM Transactions on Intelligent Systems and Technology, 30*(3), 1–24. DOI: 10.1145/1961189.1961202

McGrath, D. K., & Gupta, M. (2008). Behind phishing: An examination of phisher modi operandi. In *Proceedings of the 1st USENIX Workshop on Large-Scale Exploits and Emergent Threats* (pp. 1–8). USENIX Association., https://www.usenix.org/conference/leet-08/behind-phishing-examination-phisher-modi-operandi

McKinney, W. (2010). Data structures for statistical computing in python. *Proceedings of the 9th Python in Science Conference*, 445, 51–56. DOI: 10.25080/Majora-92bf1922-00a

Mohammad, R. M., Thabtah, F., & McCluskey, L. (2014). Predicting phishing websites based on self-structuring neural network. *Neural Computing & Applications, 25*(2), 443–458. DOI: 10.1007/s00521-013-1490-z

Pedregosa, F., Varoquaux, G., Gramfort, A., Michel, V., Thirion, B., Grisel, O., Blondel, M., Prettenhofer, P., Weiss, R., Dubourg, V., Vanderplas, J., Passos, A., Cournapeau, D., Brucher, M., Perrot, M., & Duchesnay, E. (2011). Scikit-learn: Machine learning in Python. *Journal of Machine Learning Research, 12*, 2825–2830. http://jmlr.org/papers/v12/pedregosa11a.html

Prakash, P., Kumar, M., Kompella, R. R., & Gupta, M. (2010). PhishNet: Predictive blacklisting to detect phishing attacks. 2010. *Proceedings - IEEE INFOCOM, 1–5*, 1–5. Advance online publication. DOI: 10.1109/INFCOM.2010.5462216

Rao, R. S., & Pais, A. R. (2019). Detection of phishing websites using an efficient feature-based machine learning framework. *Neural Computing & Applications*, *31*(8), 3851–3873. DOI: 10.1007/s00521-017-3305-0

Sahingoz, O. K., Buber, E., Demir, O., & Diri, B. (2019). Machine learning based phishing detection from URLs. *Expert Systems with Applications*, *117*, 345–357. DOI: 10.1016/j.eswa.2018.09.029

Sheng, S., Wardman, B., Warner, G., Cranor, L. F., Hong, J., & Zhang, C. (2009, July 16–17). An empirical analysis of phishing blacklists [Paper presentation]. *6th Annual Conference on Email and Anti-Spam (CEAS)*. Mountain View, CA, United States. DOI: 10.1184/R1/6469805

Verma, R., & Hossain, N. (2014). Semantic feature selection for text with application to phishing email detection. In Lee, H. S., & Han, D. G. (Eds.), *Information security and cryptology – ICISC 2013* (pp. 455–468). Springer., DOI: 10.1007/978-3-319-12160-4_27

Wright, R. T., & Marett, K. (2010). The influence of experiential and dispositional factors in phishing: An empirical investigation of the deceived. *Journal of Management Information Systems*, *27*(1), 273–303. DOI: 10.2753/MIS0742-1222270111


## ADDITIONAL READING


Apruzzese, G., Colajanni, M., Ferretti, L., Guido, A., & Marchetti, M. (2018). On the effectiveness of machine and deep learning for cyber security. *2018 10th International Conference on Cyber Conflict (CyCon)*, 371–390. DOI: 10.23919/CYCON.2018.8405026

Dasgupta, D., Akhtar, Z., & Sen, S. (2022). Machine learning in cybersecurity: A comprehensive survey. *The Journal of Defense Modeling and Simulation*, *19*(1), 57–106. DOI: 10.1177/1548512920951275

Goodfellow, I. J., Shlens, J., & Szegedy, C. (2015). Explaining and harnessing adversarial examples. *arXiv preprint arXiv:1412.6572*. /arXiv.1412.6572DOI: 10.48550

Kott, A. (2019). Intelligent autonomous agents are key to cyber defense of the future army networks. *The Cyber Defense Review*, 4(3), 59–74. /arXiv.1812.08014DOI: 10.48550

Martins, N., Cruz, I. G., Cruz, T., & Abreu, P. (2020). Adversarial machine learning applied to intrusion and malware scenarios: A systematic review. *IEEE Access : Practical Innovations, Open Solutions*, *8*, 35403–35419. DOI: 10.1109/ACCESS.2020.2974752

Salloum, S., Gaber, T., Vadera, S., & Shaalan, K. (2021). Phishing email detection using natural language processing techniques: A literature survey. *Procedia Computer Science*, *189*, 19–28. DOI: 10.1016/j.procs.2021.05.077

Taddeo, M., & Floridi, L. (2018). Regulate artificial intelligence to avert cyber arms race. *Nature*, *556*(7701), 296–298. DOI: 10.1038/d41586-018-04602-6 PMID: 29662138

## KEY TERMS AND DEFINITIONS

**Adversarial Machine Learning (AML):** A specialized field of study focused on understanding how cyber attackers intentionally manipulate input data (such as padding a URL with dictionary words) to exploit vulnerabilities in machine learning models and evade algorithmic detection.

**Domain Generation Algorithm (DGA):** Automated computational scripts utilized by cybercriminals to rapidly generate massive quantities of pseudo-random domain names, allowing attackers to frequently shift their hosting infrastructure to evade static blacklist detection systems.

**Ensemble Learning:** An advanced machine learning paradigm where multiple, independent base models (such as decision trees) are strategically combined—either sequentially or in parallel—to produce a single, highly accurate, and robust predictive model that resists overfitting.

**Feature Engineering:** The analytical, domain-driven process of extracting relevant mathematical, structural, or statistical characteristics (features) from raw, unstructured data (such as a URL string) to improve the performance and accuracy of predictive algorithms.

**Gradient Boosting Machine (GBM):** An advanced ensemble learning algorithm that builds decision trees sequentially, with each newly added tree mathematically optimized to correct the residual errors and misclassifications made by the previous trees in the sequence.

**Lexical Analysis:** In the context of cybersecurity, the automated evaluation of the typographical and structural string components of a Uniform Resource Locator (URL)—such as character length, specific delimiter frequency, and alphanumeric ratios—to detect malicious anomalies.

**Machine Learning (ML):** A specialized subset of artificial intelligence that relies on statistical models and algorithms to enable computer systems to autonomously learn, identify patterns, and make data-driven predictions without being explicitly programmed with static rules.

**Phishing:** A highly deceptive social engineering cyberattack where a malicious actor masquerades as a trusted entity or institution to trick victims into revealing sensitive data, financial details, or corporate login credentials.

**Zero-Day Attack:** A cyberattack that exploits a previously unknown vulnerability, or in the context of web security, a newly generated malicious domain that has just gone live and has not yet been identified or cataloged by traditional security blacklists.

# Chapter 4
# Interpretable Machine Learning Models for Cyber Threat Detection

**Uzair Bhatti**
http://orcid.org/0000-0002-8743-2783
*Hainan University, China*

**Yonis Gulzar**
http://orcid.org/0000-0002-6515-1569
*Department of Management Information Systems, College of Business Administration, King Faisal University, Saudi Arabia*

**Yazeed Yasin Ghadi**
http://orcid.org/0000-0002-7121-495X
*Department of Computer Science and Software Engineering, Al Ain University, Al Ain, UAE*

**Valisher Sapayev**
http://orcid.org/0000-0002-6751-5864
*Department of General Professional Subjects, Mamun University, Khiva, Uzbekistan*

**Tursunov Muhiddin**
*Termez University of Economics and Service, Uzbekistan*

**Akmaljon Khakimov Mirzaganiyevich**
*Department of Philosophy and Religious Studies, Kokand State University, Fergana, Uzbekistan*

**Hajiyev Ulugbek Kuzibayevich**
*Department of Law, Urgench State University, Urgench, Uzbekistan*

**Gularam Masharipova**
*Department of Social Science, University of Management and Future Technologies, Tashkent, Uzbekistan*

## ABSTRACT

*The growing volume, diversity and sophistication of cyber threats rendered traditional signature-based and rule-driven security mechanisms incapable of protecting modern digital infrastructures. To address these complexities, machine learning has been*

DOI: 10.4018/979-8-2600-3465-1.ch004

*regarded as an effective paradigm for detecting cyber threats due to its capability to process a large amount of heterogeneous security data and detect both previously known and new attack patterns. But many high-performing machine learning (ML) models act as black boxes, causing transparency, trustworthiness, and practicality issues in security-susceptible environments. This challenge has stimulated growing interest in interpretable machine learning, which aims to provide human analysts with model predictions that are understandable, explainable and actionable.*

## 1. INTRODUCTION

The cybersecurity landscape of our world today has, in no small part due to the rapid expansion of digital infrastructures, cloud platforms, Internet of Things ecosystems, industrial control networks and connected enterprise systems — become exponentially more complex. But as enterprises increasingly depend on distributed computing environments and real-time data sharing, they are also under siege by a new wave of cyber attacks in the form of malware, ransomware, phishing, insider attacks, botnets, advanced persistent threats (ATPs) and zero-day exploits. These constantly-evolving threats go well beyond the capabilities of many traditional cybersecurity mechanisms, including signature-based intrusion detection systems and static rule-based monitoring tools; even worse, adversaries often adapt their techniques to avoid detection. Machine learning has gained prominence as a potent and scalable method to detect cyber threats, capable of automatically analyzing large collections of data related to network, system, and user behavior to uncover suspicious patterns and attacks.

For cybersecurity, machine learning models hold a lot of potential due to their ability to learn complex relations from the historical and real-time security data. The supervised learning techniques can classify known malicious and benign activities based on labeled datasets, while unsupervised and semi-supervised approaches can identify anomalous and previously unseen attack behaviors without extensive annotation. As a result, deep learning architectures, ensemble models and feature-driven classifiers are applied to intrusion detection, malware analysis, spam filtering, botnet identification and threat intelligence systems. Despite all the impressive predictive performance that many of these models have provided, they operate as black boxes, giving a decision but failing to sufficiently explain how a model comes to a prediction. This opacity leads to serious challenges in security-critical domains where analysts, auditors, and decision-makers need interpretable evidence before they can rely on and act upon automated outputs. Fig 1 shows the flow of this study.

*Figure 1. Flowchart of this study*

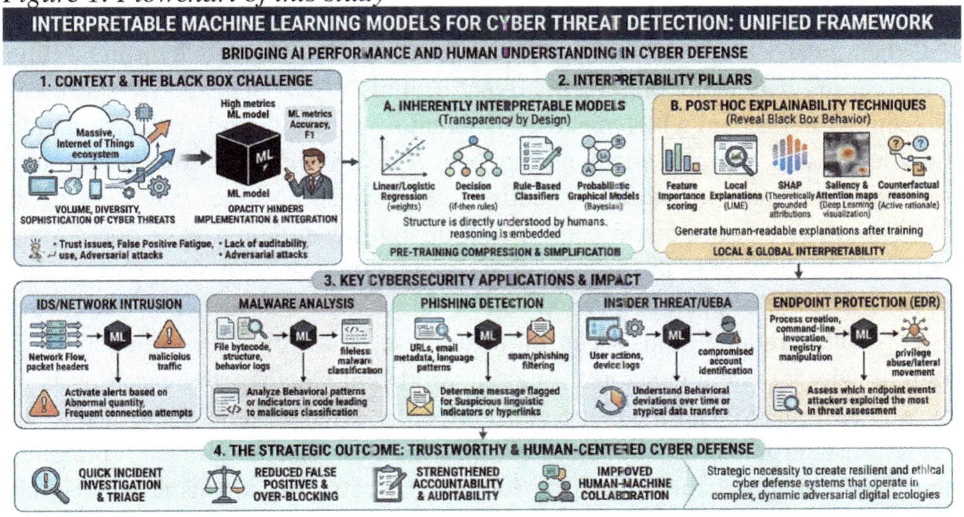


Thus the question of interpretability has grown to be a focal point for real-world implementation of machine learning in cybersecurity. In high-stakes settings, a black box model that generates predictions with a high degree of accuracy but has no mechanism for explaining its particular decisions is difficult to validate, monitor, and integrate into operational workflows. Security analysts need to understand: Why was a particular network flow flagged as malicious What system behaviors enabled the detection, or what combination of features caused a particular file/process to be classified as threatening In the absence of such interpretability, however, true attacks may be mistaken for false alarms, defensive actions cannot be justified and communicated across technical and managerial teams to inform risk-based decision making. The need for interpretability is not simply a bedroom accessory but rather it is an essential part of the journey towards trust, accountability and ultimately, operational confidence in intelligent cyber defense (Trillo et al., 2025).

An interpretable machine learning method defines a model or technique that allows humans to understand how the logic behind a model prediction is being made. Variants of Interpretability in Cyber Threat Detection Some of the popular interpretable models include decision trees, rule-based classifiers, sparse linear models and association-rule methods where A human can see the reasoning structure directly. Alternative techniques, like feature importance scoring, local explanations, saliency analysis, surrogate models and counterfactual reasoning give post hoc interpretations for complex networks after training. That separation between intrinsic interpretability and explanation-based interpretability is particularly meaningful in cybersecurity, since both performance and understandability matter a lot — since the model itself often chooses a balancing act of detection power versus human comprehensibility (Ikram & Huma, 2024).

Cyber threat detection has unique challenges that create a need for interpretability. Cybersecurity data is not only highly dynamic, noisy, imbalanced, adversarial but also context-dependent which makes it different from many standard classification problems. Attack vectors evolve, normal behavior varies greatly from user to user and system to system, and false negatives versus false positives can incur great cost. Failure to detect a threat could result in significant data loss or operational disruption, or damage to the organization's reputation; too many false alarms may overwhelm security operation centers and erode analyst confidence in automated systems. Interpretable models can mitigate these issues by allowing analysts to examine why a system generated an alert, validating whether the reasoning is in any way reasonable, and adjusting detection policies with domain knowledge. In this sense, interpretability underpins not just trust but also a spirit of continuous improvement and collaboration in threat analysis between humans and machines (Ahmad et al., 2025).

A second key driver for interpretability within cyber threat detection stems from the adversarial character of the cybersecurity space. Attackers probe, manipulate and adapt to defensive systems, and the machine learning models themselves can be targets of evasion, poisoning and adversarial attacks. When a detection model misbehaves or becomes exploitable via crafted inputs, its opacity can impede prompt diagnosis and resolution of the underlying cause. As interpretable models offer more visibility to feature dependencies, decision thresholds and behavioral anomalies than opaque models, defenders can better investigate model weaknesses and possible vectors of exploitation. Explainable outputs can also demonstrate whether, during-a given prediction, the system is indeed focusing on robust indicators of threat or simply spurious correlations that might drop out of the system in the presence of an attack under real conditions. Hence interpretability assists not only human perception, but also robustness and dependability generation of cyber defence machinery (Nair, 2023).

Interpretability is taking on an even larger role in light of increasing demands for accountability and compliance, as well as responsible AI governance. When organizations develop or put in place automated, or semi-automated cyber defense tools in their critical sectors like finance, healthcare, transportation, government and energy; the pressure is on for security decisions made by these tools to be transparent, auditable and aligned with institutional policies. For instance, if a machine learning model blocks access; quarantines a process; classifies user action as malicious; or prioritizes an incident for investigation, stakeholders may need to understand the basis for that decision. This is particularly relevant when security actions have an impact on employee access, customer services or other mission-critical operations.

Interpretable machine learning enables auditability by allowing for retrospection, which in turn facilitates documenting system behavior and justifying the operational usage of automated threat detection systems (Nair, 2023).

While there has been significant recent growth in the literature of machine learning application to cybersecurity, most extant studies focus on performance metrics (e.g., accuracy, precision, recall, F1-score, area under the curve) relative to explanation quality and analyst usability and operationalization. This discrepancy emphasizes the importance of a more focused area of research into interpretable and human-centered systems for cyber intelligence, An appropriate model of cyber threat detection must enable malicious activity identification and at the same time support reasoning, incident triage, forensic investigation, and strategic decision-making. In practice, the best systems may be ones that combine predictive power of accurate models with understandable mode of explanation in a manner where machine intelligent and human expertise can complement each other better (Almheiri et al., 2025). Such a shift represents an evolution from dedicated automated detection only to integrated cyber defense augmentation (Subasi et al., 2024).

Ultimately, interpretable machine learning models represent a viable direction for solving one of the biggest problems facing modern-day cyber security – developing detection systems that can be trusted and have actionable insights from their predictions. As cyber threats grow increasingly sophisticated and security environments become progressively more data-rich, organizations require intelligent tools that be superlative assistants to the analyst without clouding the criteria for making important decisions. Interpretable approaches can also help build trust, reduce false alarm fatigue in humans who must make decisions based on such models and assist with auditability of decision-making process, reveal potential vulnerabilities in the operation of models and improve human-machine collaboration. Thus, interpretable machine learning for cyber threat detection is a timely and important study. It lies at the intersection of security, artificial intelligence, humans (human factors) and responsible digital governance, and probably will be a key pillar in future robust and accountable cyber defense (Prasad et al., 2025). The objectives of this chapter are:

- Introduce the Importance of Interpretability: The chapter tries to point out the importance of interpretability in machine learning models towards cybersecurity where predictive accuracy is important but at the same time the interpretation of why a model has made a particular decision is also important to gain trust and actionable information.
- Define Major Notions and Methods: The chapter aims at defining some key concepts including interpretable machine learning, explainability, and the difference between intrinsic and post-hoc explainability. It describes different

methods of explainability such as decision trees, LIME, SHAP, counterfactual reasoning, etc., that may be applied in enhancing model transparency.

- Discover Machine Learning Solutions to Cyber Threats: The chapter discusses the diverse machine learning techniques applicable in detecting cyber threats such as supervised, unsupervised, and semi-supervised learning and deep learning. It explains their assets, deficiencies and applicability in terms of noticing known and emerging threats.

## 2. FOUNDATIONS OF CYBER THREAT DETECTION

Cyber threat detection refers to the systematic identification of malicious, suspicious, or unauthorized activities within digital environments such as computer networks, cloud infrastructures, enterprise information systems, industrial control systems, and endpoint devices. It is a foundational component of cybersecurity because it provides the operational capability to recognize threats before they can cause significant harm. Modern digital systems generate enormous volumes of data through network traffic, authentication logs, application events, user behavior records, and system performance metrics. Within this large and often noisy data environment, cyber threat detection aims to distinguish normal activity from indicators of compromise, attack patterns, or anomalous behaviors that may signal an ongoing or imminent security incident. As organizations continue to digitize their operations, threat detection has become central to ensuring confidentiality, integrity, availability, and resilience (Mohale & Obagbuwa, 2025).

The conceptual basis of cyber threat detection lies in the idea that malicious actions leave observable traces, even when attackers attempt to remain stealthy. These traces may appear as unusual network packets, repeated login failures, privilege escalation attempts, suspicious file modifications, abnormal process execution, command-and-control communication, or deviations in user and system behavior. Effective threat detection depends on the ability to collect, analyze, correlate, and interpret these signals across multiple layers of the computing environment. In this sense, cyber threat detection is not limited to identifying known attacks but also includes discovering previously unseen or evolving threats by examining patterns, anomalies, and contextual inconsistencies. This broader view is increasingly important because modern attackers frequently use obfuscation, polymorphism, encryption, and living-off-the-land techniques to avoid traditional security controls (Aslam et al., 2022).

Historically, cyber threat detection began with signature-based methods, which relied on predefined patterns associated with known malicious software, exploits, or attack behaviors. Antivirus systems and early intrusion detection systems operated primarily by comparing observed data against databases of known signatures.

These methods were effective for recognizing previously documented threats and provided relatively fast and interpretable results. However, their limitations became increasingly evident as cyberattacks grew more dynamic and sophisticated. Signature-based systems typically fail to detect zero-day exploits, novel malware variants, insider threats, and subtle multi-stage attacks that do not exactly match known patterns. As a result, the field evolved toward more adaptive approaches capable of detecting suspicious behavior even in the absence of prior knowledge of a specific threat (Prity et al., 2024).

One of the core foundations of cyber threat detection is the distinction between misuse detection and anomaly detection. Misuse detection, also called knowledge-based detection, identifies attacks by comparing observed events with known attack signatures, rules, or behavioral templates. It generally provides high accuracy for known threats and lower false positive rates when attack definitions are well established. In contrast, anomaly detection focuses on identifying deviations from established normal behavior. This approach is especially useful for detecting unknown or emerging threats because it does not require explicit prior examples of every attack type. However, anomaly detection often faces challenges related to dynamic baselines, behavioral variability, and false alarms. The balance between these two paradigms remains a central issue in the design of threat detection systems, and many modern solutions combine both approaches to improve robustness (S. Ali et al., 2025).

Another essential foundation is the classification of threats according to the layer or domain in which they occur. Cyber threats may target networks, hosts, applications, identities, databases, cloud services, or physical-cyber systems. Network-based threats include denial-of-service attacks, port scanning, botnet traffic, protocol abuse, and data exfiltration attempts. Host-based threats may involve malware execution, unauthorized file access, suspicious registry changes, or abnormal process behavior. Application-level threats include SQL injection, cross-site scripting, API abuse, and session hijacking. Identity-related threats include credential theft, account takeover, and insider misuse. Because each threat domain generates different types of evidence and requires different forms of monitoring, the foundations of cyber threat detection must include an understanding of where threats originate, how they propagate, and what indicators are available for identifying them (A. Ali et al., 2023).

Data acquisition and visibility form another critical basis of threat detection. A detection system can only identify threats to the extent that relevant security data is collected and made available for analysis. This includes packet captures, flow records, system logs, endpoint telemetry, application traces, DNS traffic, authentication histories, and threat intelligence feeds. The quality, granularity, and timeliness of this data significantly affect detection performance. Incomplete or delayed data can obscure attack behavior, reduce contextual understanding, and create blind spots in security operations. At the same time, the volume and heterogeneity of cybersecurity data introduce major challenges for storage, processing, normalization, and real-time analysis. Therefore, effective threat detection depends not only on algorithms but also on strong data engineering pipelines and comprehensive monitoring infrastructures that can support multi-source correlation (Wang et al., 2019).

Context is equally important in the foundations of cyber threat detection because suspicious behavior cannot always be judged accurately in isolation. The same event may be benign in one setting and malicious in another. For example, remote access to a server may be normal for an administrator during working hours but suspicious if it occurs from an unusual geographic location at an unusual time and is followed by privilege escalation attempts. Similarly, large data transfers may reflect legitimate backup operations or may indicate exfiltration depending on the surrounding conditions. Contextual information such as user roles, device identity, time patterns, network topology, system criticality, and historical behavior helps transform isolated alerts into meaningful security insights. As a result, effective threat detection requires correlation across events, entities, and time rather than reliance on single observations alone.

The threat landscape itself is another foundational consideration. Cyber threat detection must be designed with awareness of the diversity, scale, and adaptability of modern adversaries. Threat actors may include cybercriminal groups, insider actors, hacktivists, nation-state operators, and opportunistic attackers, each with different motivations, capabilities, and techniques. Their objectives may range from financial theft and espionage to disruption, sabotage, extortion, or unauthorized surveillance. Moreover, attacks increasingly follow multi-stage patterns involving reconnaissance, initial access, persistence, lateral movement, credential abuse, and impact execution. Understanding these attack lifecycles is critical because detection systems must often identify subtle precursor behaviors before the final stage of compromise. Frameworks such as the cyber kill chain and adversarial tactics-and-techniques models have therefore become important conceptual tools for structuring detection logic and prioritizing relevant indicators (Wang et al., 2018).

The operational environment of cyber threat detection also shapes its foundations. Detection is not a purely technical process but part of a broader defensive workflow that includes alert triage, investigation, response, recovery, and continuous improvement. In real-world settings, security operation centers must deal with alert fatigue, limited analyst time, evolving threat intelligence, and the need to prioritize incidents based on severity and business impact. A theoretically accurate detection method may still be impractical if it produces excessive false positives, lacks interpretability, or cannot integrate with existing incident response systems. Therefore, foundational thinking in cyber threat detection must account for usability, scalability, timeliness, and decision support. A good detection system is one that produces actionable intelligence in a form that security teams can understand and use effectively under operational constraints (Zhang et al., 2025).

In conclusion, the foundations of cyber threat detection are built upon several interconnected elements: the identification of malicious traces in digital systems, the evolution from static signature methods to adaptive behavioral analysis, the distinction between known-threat and unknown-threat detection, the diversity of attack surfaces, the importance of comprehensive data collection, the role of contextual reasoning, the structure of adversarial behavior, and the realities of operational cybersecurity practice. Together, these foundations provide the conceptual and practical basis for modern cyber defense. As digital ecosystems become more complex and adversaries become more sophisticated, threat detection must continue to evolve from isolated alert generation toward intelligent, context-aware, and resilient systems capable of supporting proactive and trustworthy cybersecurity operations (Xu et al., 2024a).

## 3. MACHINE LEARNING APPROACHES FOR CYBER THREAT DETECTION

Modern methods of cyber threat detection increasingly rely on one technological approach: machine learning, which allows systems to learn automatically from data and to identify patterns, relationships, parallelism and behavior structures. Through knowledge acquisition from historical observations and its generalization to new events, machine learning demonstrates an ability to adapt to complex, ever-evolving threat landscapes that rule-based or signature-driven detection methodologies simply cannot. (However) This capability is particularly useful in cybersecurity, as attackers never stop changing their techniques and static defenses become less effective over time. Deep Learning methods help to identify malicious activity in large scale, heterogeneous and dynamic digital environments when manual analysis is no longer feasible. Machine learning provides scalable ways of more intelligently and quickly detecting threats as organizations create large amounts of security-relevant data from endpoints, networks, applications and users (Xu et al., 2024).

At a basic level, machine learning for cyber threat detection consists of training computational models to identify normal versus malicious behavior either via examples with labels, identification of unknown structures from the data or modeling anticipated system behavior. The selected learning approach will rely on the types of data available, the threat scenario and the operational objectives of detection system. However, in some scenarios with large annotated datasets, models can learn clear differences between benign and malicious events. In other scenarios, labels are either incomplete, noisy or unavailable altogether and one has to resort to anomaly detection or hybrid learning strategies. Machine learning in Cybersecurity is somewhat of a special case as the data tends to be high-dimensional, imbalanced, time-dependent, adversarial and context-sensitive. This means that machine learning methods applied to this field must trade-off between predictive performance, computational complexity, robustness and applicability in real-world scenarios (Han et al., 2018).

Supervised learning is one of the most common machine learning paradigms for cyber threat detection. In this strategy, labelled datasets where each instance is linked to a specific class (benign, malicious, intrusion, spam/phishing/malware) are utilised to train models. Some of the commonly used supervised algorithms are logistic regression, decision trees, random forests, support vector machine,s k-nearest neighbors, naïve bayes, gradient boosting machines and neural networks. These models are widely used in intrusion detection, malware classification/phishing/new technologies filtering, and malicious traffic analysis. Their biggest strength is the ability to learn decision boundaries directly from positive examples which, if well labelled and representative of the problem, will have a high accuracy. Nevertheless, there are constraints associated with supervised methods specifically when it comes to zero-day attacks, evolution of threat behaviors and the availability of high-quality labeled cybersecurity datasets (Zhang et al., 2025).

Unsupervised learning is one of the most important techniques for cyber detection, where labeled data are not available or if the objective is to detect abnormal behavior related to new attacks. Unsupervised models do not learn explicit class labels, but instead find underlying patterns, clusters or anomalies in the data. This includes techniques such as k-means clustering, hierarchical clustering, Gaussian mixture models, how features are constructed using PCA (principal component analysis), autoencoders and isolation forests. These techniques are especially useful for detecting anomalies, where the goal is to model normal system behavior and highlight observations that vary significantly from the expected pattern. In cybersecurity, unsupervised learning can help recognize unexpected user behavior, unusual network traffic, infrequently occurring system events and potential attack methods that have not yet been documented as part of known threats. Because anomalous behaviour is not necessarily malicious, unsupervised approaches often yield relatively high false positive rates and need careful calibration and contextual interpretation (Wang et al., 2018).

Semi-supervised learning has become a middle ground between supervised and unsupervised learning approaches and is well suited for cybersecurity settings, where labels on the data are scarce. In many practical applications, security teams only have access to a few confirmed attack samples and most of the collected data goes without labels. Commonly used semi-supervised methods use both the labeled and unlabeled data to enhance generalization and consequently the detection performance. For example, a model can train on the small set of known malicious examples, and then use the larger unlabeled data to perform better in capturing the distribution of normal versus abnormal behavior. This method is particularly beneficial for cyber threat detection as it mirrors the real-world scenario of unverifiable labeling, costly expert annotation, and dynamically changing attacks. But semi-supervised methods can also enable active learning and human-in-the-loop setups, where analysts iteratively improve model performance by labeling uncertain or high-priority cases (Wang et al., 2019).

In cyber threat detection, deep learning has gained much interest due to its ability to model complex nonlinear high dimensional relationships within large datasets (Trillo et al., 2025). Deep neural network (DNN), convolutional neural network (CNN), recurrent neural networks (RNN), long short-term memory networks (LSTM), graph neural networks, transformer-based architecture, and autoencoder-based architectures have been leveraged on a variety of cybersecurity problems. Is network intrusion detection, analysis of malware behavior (the obverse or muscle end of the same coin), malicious domain detection, botnet tracking, log burn-up and or sequence-based attacks. Deep learning models are particularly beneficial in scenarios where the data involves temporal dependencies, spatial structures and semantic patterns, or raw feature representations that can benefit from automatic feature extraction. Sequential behaviors based on command execution or network sessions can be captured using recurrent architectures, and communication relationships between hosts or accounts can be depicted through graph-based models. While achieving impressive results, deep learning strategies can often lack interpretability, are complex to train, require large amounts of data for training and are susceptible to adversarial attack (S. Ali et al., 2025).

In the age of automated representation learning, feature engineering still plays a key role in many machine-learning based threat detection systems. Cybersecurity data is heterogeneous and can consist of packet headers, flow statistics, DNS queries, file hashes or system calls or process trees or login histories or features extracted from web pages (URLs), email metadata, security logs generated by systems with intelligence (observed behavior on an endpoint/cloud activity) and so on. The performance of machine learning on the whole fundamentally hinges upon how these raw observations are transformed into meaningful input features. Well-defined features can increase detection accuracy, minimize noise to the signal, help with model interpretability and lead to faster training. In traditional traffic analysis, the features that feed into detection systems are often too hand-crafted by domain experts identified as connection time duration, number of failed authentications or other entropy-based metrics. Unlike classical approaches that rely on manually-designed feature extraction, deep learning methods are capable of learning representations directly from raw or minimally processed data. However, the representation of input data is still often cited as a key contributor in determining the operational efficiency of applied machine learning models for cyber threat identification (Xu et al., 2024b).

No single threat detection algorithm is optimal in all scenarios, which has made ensemble learning an increasingly vital approach in this domain. Predictions are made on average, predictions from multiple models for ensemble approaches stabilize and increase robustness. To enhance detection performance, several techniques such as bagging, boosting, stacking, voting classifiers and hybrid anomaly-classification systems have been proposed extensively. Random forests, for instance, create multiple decision trees and combines their predictions to reduce variance and improve generalization. Gradient boosting methods iteratively builds strong classifiers from weak learners. For cyber threat detection, ensemble models can combine the strengths of different methods e.g., mixing signature-based (supervised) models to learn known threats with anomaly detectors that aim at detecting previously unseen behavior. Hybrid frameworks can combine predictive machine learning building processes with statistical analysis and a rule-based system to produce more detailed threat intelligence. These approaches are notably beneficial in dynamic environments, where threats exhibit temporal variability across the domain and data modality.

Adversarial Data and Class Imbalance: A Key Challenge in Cyber Threat Detection with Machine Learning Because malicious events are often much rarer than benign activity, we have to deal with class imbalance problems that could bias models to the majority class. Attackers can also craft adversarial examples on purpose to avoid detection or pollute training data. Additionally, as cyber threat data is dynamic, it leads to concept drift which means that the statistical properties of attack and normal behaviors change over time. Hence, machine learning models need to be built on the principles of holding steady under uncertainty, generalising when applying to new patterns, and not overfitting to old data-sets. Methods like online learning, continual learning, domain adaptation, adversarial training, class rebalancing, synthetic upsample/oversample and drift-aware retraining are becoming more prominent in operational threat detection systems. Such considerations highlight that doing effective machine learning in the cybersecurity domain is not just about selecting an algorithm but also keeping models reliable during adversarial and dynamic scenarios.

In conclusion, the utilization of machine learning techniques has revolutionized cyber threat detection processes by facilitating a more proficient analysis of complex data structures relevant to security and aiding in the detection of not only known threats but also new attacks. In cases where labelled data is available, supervised learning provides powerful classification performance; in uncertain environments, unsupervised learning can be used for exploiting anomaly detection; semi-supervised methods are designed to address the limited availability of labelled data, whereas deep learning supports threat capabilities into more complex and high-dimensional threats. The application of feature engineering, ensemble strategies, and adaptive learning mechanisms further contributes towards making these approaches more effective in operational settings. Yet, the measure-of-merit of machine learning in cybersecurity is not only predictive accuracy per se: It also both robustness, scalability and interpretability ensuring alignment with security workflows in real world. Machine learning will continue to be a foundational pillar of threat detection in the era of ever-evolving cyber threats when combined with domain expertise, contextual reasoning and trustworthy AI practices.

## 4. INTERPRETABILITY IN MACHINE LEARNING

Interpretability in machine learning describes to which human expertise is concerned to the quality of predictions, classifications or decisions a model makes. This is an important point, as many machine learning systems are being deployed in high-stakes domains like cybersecurity, healthcare, finance and law and public administration where decisions need not only to be accurate but also explainable—to users, analysts, regulators and affected stakeholders. Even the most accurate model might be too opaque in its reasoning process to trust. Thus, interpretability helps overcome the gap between computational intelligence and human expertise by ensuring that model behaviour is transparent enough to humans to help them make meaningful decisions.

At a basic level, interpretability deals with one of the central problems in modern AI: many leading-edge models, particularly deep neural networks and ensemble systems, large-scale nonlinear classifiers tend to operate as black boxes. These models can identify complex patterns in data but the interlogic is hard for humans to grasp. In comparison, simpler models like linear regression, decision trees and rule based systems tend to be transparent because their decision process can be directly inspected. Interpretability refers to the degree of insight a user can obtain about what is driving a model's output, relationships that were learned from data, and the rationale for making a certain prediction.

Workshop focus and motivation:Interpretability is a key area of interest in machine learning as the decisions based on it often have real consequences. For example, in cybersecurity, you might need to know why a network flow was detected as malicious. For example, in healthcare a physician might want to know why a diagnostic model predicted disease risk. One possible adaptation — the finance department or forget it bank will need to explain why an application has been marked as fraudulent, refused. Across all of these contexts, users trust and can effectively use a model whose outputs they understand. Interpretability hence fosters trust, accountability, transparency, fairness and human oversight over AI-assisted decision-making.

A lot has been said about interpretability versus explainability in this area, although people often use these terms as if they were interchangeable. Usually, interpretability means the ability to directly analyze its output from a model's structure. Such as, a very small decision tree is interpretable since we can see the path from input to output. At the same time, explainability typically involves post hoc methods that can be used to understand how more complicated models behave after training. A deep learning model on its own is likely not interpretable, but can be explained with the help of external tools like SHAP, LIME, saliency maps, and feature importance.

Interpretability can be roughly classified into intrinsic interpretability and post hoc interpretability. Therefore, intrinsically interpretable models are considered to be interpretable by design. Among those, we can find linear models, logistic regression, rule-based classifiers, sparse models or decision trees. Their anatomy enables individuals to directly investigate model parameters or feature weights. In contrast, post hoc interpretability is used to create human-readable explanations for complex or black-box models. These explanations could specify which features were most impactful, how responsive a prediction is to variations in input, or what regional trends informed an individual choice. Both work (for different normalizations) and the trade-off between model complexity versus transparency will lead to a choice as we did.

Another very important distinction is between global interpretability and local interpretability. Global interpretability aims to provide an explanation of the model behaviour on a complete dataset. It (and the various extensions to it) answers questions like what features are most generally important, what rules comprise the model, or how is the decision boundary formed. Local interpretability means highlight a single prediction or small set of samples. It explains why one specific input was classified the way it was. In reality, both perspectives are important. While global explanations can help developers and auditors read the model logic, local explanations greatly facilitate interpretations from analysts who need to understand specific high-risk decisions.

Interpretability also significantly contributes in model validation and error analysis. If a model makes an incorrect or otherwise unexpected prediction, interpretability tools allow both researchers and practitioners to explore why. They can tell if the model overfit irrelevant features, learned spurious correlations, or reacted punitively to noise in the data. This is particularly crucial in adversarial or dynamic environments like cyber threat detection, where an attacker might tamper with inputs to elude discovery. Interpolatible models and explanation tools can shed light on whether the model is using robust threat indicators or fragile patterns that could break during deployment in the wild.

From the perspective of ethics and governance, interpretability enables accountability and responsible AI. As machine learning systems are more widely used in regulated and socially sensitive contexts, institutions need to be able to explain how automated decisions are made. Interpretable systems are more easily audited, documented, monitored and ensured to meet legal or organizational requirements. They also mitigate fairness and bias concerns by enabling stakeholders to examine the manner in which different features contribute to outcomes. Without interpretability, harmful patterns are less likely to come to light and also harder to detect in deployed systems containing discrimination, insecurity or unsafe behavior.

While important, interpretability is not always easily obtainable. In general, there is usually a tension between prediction performance and transparency between simple models and highly complex architectures. High-performing deep learning models might capture subtle patterns that simpler interpretable models do not, but they can also be much more difficult to explain. Also, some explanations are more useful than others. A technically valid explanation, however, may still be too complicated, ambiguous or deceptive for a human user. Hence, good interpretability is not just about generating explanations, but ensuring that these explanations are accurate, comprehensible, appropriate and useful for the intended audience.

To summarize, interpretability is the degree to which humans can understand how a model makes its predictions. It is critical for trust, transparency, accountability, debugging and practical deployment in relevant domains of application. Interpretability may stem from naturally interpretable models or from explanations applied to black-box systems, and its components can be explored at both global and local scope. As machine learning gradually finds its way into more and more sensitive, high-impact areas of life, interpretability will continue to be a core requirement for developing reliable, human-centered, responsible intelligent systems.

## 5. INTERPRETABLE MODELS AND EXPLAINABILITY TECHNIQUES

Interpretability permeates the central theme of understanding, trusting and making operationally useful machine learning systems across many domains including high-stakes domains like cyber threat detection. Although machine-learning models can have high predictive performance, their implementation will not often gain traction if human users cannot understand how decisions are made. In cybersecurity, analysts need to assess alerts_behavior suspicious activity and justify response activities against deadlines. Provides human-readable context for the attack prediction: A network flow, user session, or executable file being predicted as malicious is much more actionable when it comes with an intuitive explanation. That is why interpretable models and also explanation methods have become components of human-centered and responsible machine learning systems.

A good way to get started is the distinction made between interpretable models and post hoc explainability methods. Example of an interpretable model — the structure, which can be understood directly by humans Their reasoning is embedded in the model itself. Unlike post hoc explainability techniques, these methods are applied pre-training to compress and simplify the underlying structure of the model into a simpler sub-model that has similar components as deep neural networks, ensemble classifiers or nonlinear boosting algorithms. This distinction is significant because it reveals two different design philosophies. One approach is to emphasize transparency from the outset by picking simpler, less opaque models. The other accepts the use of intricate models for performance reasons and then tries to derive meaningful rationales for their predictions. Both approaches are valuable and contain strength and weakness depending upon the context of their application.

Linear and logistic regression are well known extra-diagrams basic models among the inherently interpretable ones. In these models, the weights are how much each feature contributes to the final score. This allows users to quickly identify which variables play a positive and negative role in reaching a decision. In the case of cyber threat detection tasks, features like login failure counts, abnormal connection frequency or suspicious port activity can be directly tied to a predicted probability of whether that activity is malicious. Sparse linear models are particularly attractive, as they have fewer active features, which makes them easier to interpret. However, these regression-based models are interpretable; they can also struggle to capture very nonlinear or complex attack patterns unless extra feature engineering has taken place.

The decision trees Another important family of interpretable models describes decisions using a series of if-then rules. The path from the root to the leaf corresponds to an easily interpretable classification process, and each branch signifies a condition on one or more features. In cybersecurity, for instance, decision trees can display that an alert was generated because traffic went beyond a particular threshold, came from an unknown source and included repeated failed authentication attempts. This structure mirrors the way human analysts think about attacks. Whereas rule-based classifiers such as association rules and decision lists also have these advantages of more clearly expressing model behavior using inclusion (propositional) logic. These pose particularly attractive models for domains where auditability and traceable reasoning are paramount. The biggest problem with them is that if the data they model are too complex, decision trees can quickly grow very large and become unstable.

Probabilistic graphical models, including Bayesian approaches that explicitly model uncertainty and the relationships between variables in a probabilistic manner, also offer some level of interpretability. These models also allow users to see not only what prediction has been made, but how evidence from different features can lead to posterior beliefs about malicious activity. In the area of threat detection, this can be useful when aggregating weak yet potent indicators as in unusual login time + rare process execution + suspicious outbound traffic. Probabilistic models that represent uncertainty explicitly provide for more nuanced reasoning and help analysts differentiate strong alerts from borderline ones. While these models may not be as interpretable in terms of predictions like decision trees, they are useful when one needs to quantify uncertainty and causal relationships.

Despite the benefits of (typically) interpretable models, many systems break this rule and resort to less interpretable architectures, because cybersecurity datasets tend to be high dimensional, sequential, nonlinear and adversarial. This has resulted in the popularity of post hoc explainability techniques, ideally aimed at increasing the comprehensibility of black-box models after training. Feature importance analysis is one of the most prevalent types, which estimates how strongly an individual input variable contributes to a predicted outcome made by a model. Global feature importance is useful for users to understand which variables matter most in general, while local feature importance shows why a specific instance was classified in that way. In cyber threat detection, such explanations might make it clear that a model flagged a session for an unusually large packet size, use of uncommon protocols and sudden increase in outbound communication.

LIME and SHAP are two of the most popular model-agnostic explanation methods. LIME (Local Interpretable Model-Agnostic Explanations) fits a simple surrogate model to approximate simplified versions of the underlying complex model over instance-specific input data. This explains a local effect of an individual prediction. SHAP shatters feature importance into contribution scores to the prediction in terms of Shapley values from cooperative game theory and rotates over different value equalization for each feature based on a background (baseline). SHAP has gained unprecedented popularity because it provides both local and global interpretability along with theoretically grounded attribution values. These techniques in the cybersecurity field can help the analyst explain why a malicious URL, process, or connection was flagged as such and make black-box outputs more humanly actionable. But they also need to be interpreted with care, because the quality of such explanations will depend on how faithfully they capture underlying model behavior.

Another major category including surrogate models, partial dependence method and counterfactual explanations. Surrogate models fit a relatively simple interpre-Table model (e.g. decision tree) as an approximation to the complex model in order to describe, overall, model behavior. On the other hand, Partial dependence plots show how predictions change when one or more features changes helping users get a sense of average effect across dataset for features. Counterfactual explanations think the opposite way by demonstrating how an input would need to change in order to produce a different prediction. A counterfactual explanation in cyber threat detection could indicate that a session would not have been labelled malicious if, for example: The number of failed login attempts had been less and the traffic destination had matched with normal organizational patterns. These approaches are useful as they force the explanation from passive description to active rationale.

Other explanation methods have been proposed for deep learning systems applied to sequential, graph-structured or high-cardinality cybersecurity data. These are saliency maps, attention map visualization, activation analysis, gradient-based attribution and layer-wise relevance propagation. These approaches are intended to show which parts of the input had the most effect on the output from the model. You can use these tools to identify which time steps, tokens, API calls or traffic segments contributed the most strongly to a prediction in sequence-based malware detection or network traffic classification. For graph-based threat detection, explanation methods may identify which nodes, relationships or communication paths led to a classification result. Although these techniques can provide an important understanding of complex models, they are typically technically complicated and their implications may be less intuitive for non-specialist users.

While explainability techniques have their important benefits, they also present practical and methodological challenges. Not all explanations are reliable, exhaustive, or valuable to end users. Certain methods offer explanations that look plausible but do not accurately represent the model's true reasoning. Some might be too technical, unstable or sensitive to slight changes in data. This is particularly problematic in cybersecurity, since explanations can be actionable — for example, leading to a decision to block traffic, isolate devices or escalate an incident. Thus, explanation methods should be compared beyond computational correctness to usability, fidelity, consistency and relevance to analysts' workflows. And effective explainability should improve decision making, not introduce ambiguity or provide false confidence.

In conclusion, interpretable models and explain recent work provides the foundation of transparent and trustworthy machine learning for cyber threat detection. Inherently interpretable models such as linear classifiers, decision trees, rule-based systems and probabilistic models allow for model logic rather than rely directly on interpretation; whereas post hoc interpretation methods including feature attribution/ importance, LIME, SHAP, counterfactuals and saliency-based explanations instead reveal the behavior of complex black-box systems. These methods allow security analysts to understand alerts, validate model outputs, identify biases or errors, and incorporate machine learning into operational defense workflows. The increasing sophistication of machine learning systems combined with ever changing cyber threats will require that we maintain balance between predictive accuracy and meaningful explainability as part of developing accountable, resilient and human focused cybersecurity solutions. Fig 2 summarize the techniques.

*Figure 2. ML for threat detection*

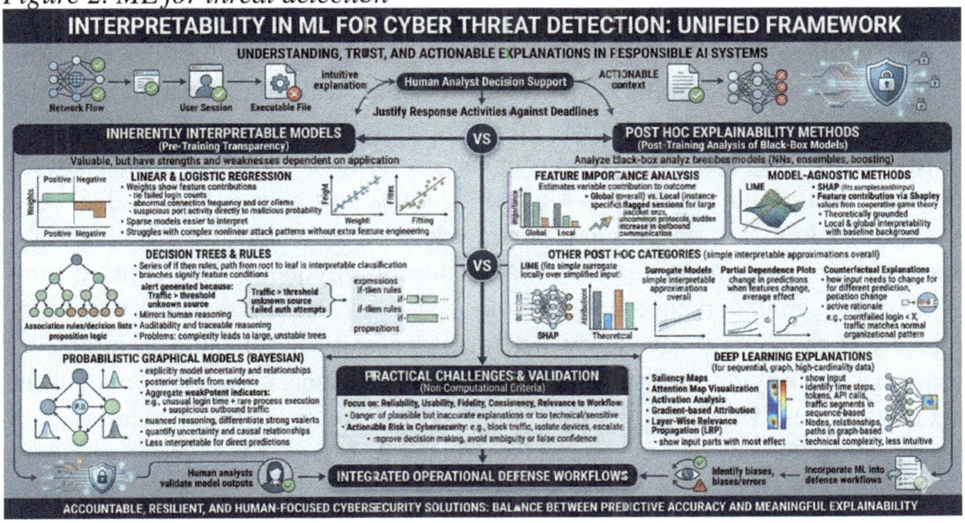


## 6. APPLICATIONS IN CYBER THREAT DETECTION

The use of machine learning and interpretable artificial intelligence for detecting cyber threats has increasingly emerged in many different fields, ranging from various digital environments. Entangled with them are human activities which add to the questionable credibility of a given single point in time activity record (log entry) and an often imprecise, albeit significant amount of data (anomalies) that only makes sense between various sensors Sybil sensor networks and technical platforms etc. as cyber fireworks engagements become more sophisticated organizations need intelligent systems that not only recognize malicious behavior but also help humans intuitively drill down through these events into some underlying raw memory to support situational assessment intelligence decision-making steps in real-time. In cybersecurity threat detection, applications have expanded well beyond intrusion alerts and now include malware analysis, phishing detection, insider threat monitoring, anomaly detection, endpoint protection/corner integration with cloud security/threat intelligence correlation(M. L. Ali et al., 2025). In each of these domains, interpretable machine learning plays a special role, since in order to take any action at all (whether identifying a threat or responding to one), security analysts need to understand the rationale behind its identification and severity as well as the necessary response. This means that practical application is one of the key aspects of interpretable cyber defense (Qiqieh et al., 2025).

One of the biggest uses of machine learning today is in the network intrusion detection system, which utilizes ML models to detect suspicious or malicious traffic patterns on enterprise and cloud networks. Conventional intrusion detection systems were primarily signature-based and rule-based — they are effective against known threats but often fall short against novel or obfuscated attacks(Shah, 2025). ML based IDS learns from traffic characteristics like packet counts, protocol behavior, session timing information, port use and connection frequency to identify denial-of-service, scanning, botnets and unauthorized access attempts. If interpretability is included, the analysts can view which traffic features had activated the alert; e.g., abnormal quantity of traffic, frequent connection attempts or exotic communicating destinations. This improves trust in the system and helps avoid uncertainty in investigation (Olanrewaju-George & Pranggono, 2025).

A further significant use case is malware detection and classification. Malware is still perhaps the most destructive type of cyber threat, which comes in many forms from ransomware to spyware, trojans, worms and other fileless malware. Static characteristics include file headers, byte code and sequences, imported libraries, permissions and structure of the code while examples of dynamic features include API calls, registry modifications or power management activities. These models assist in classifying malicious files faster than reverse engineering alone. Interpretable techniques are especially useful here because security researchers and malware analysts usually need to understand which behavioral patterns or indicators in the code led to a classification as malicious. Such explanations bolster analysts confidence, help support threat attribution, and contribute to the generation of signatures or mitigation instructions (Alharthi et al., 2025).

Another widely researched application of cyber threat detection includes phishing and malicious email detection. Phishing attacks remain increasingly sophisticated, with many of them impersonating trusted brands, utilizing social engineering tactics, and potentially containing malevolent links or attachments. Machine learning algorithms (MLAs) can assay features such as sender behavior, URL properties, domain age, email structure, language patterns, attachment characteristics and header anomalies to label emails to be authentic or malicious. Developing explainable models can inform investigators determining whether a message was flagged due to suspicious linguistic indicators, misleading hyperlinks, an abnormal metadata structure, or a lack of domain information. In enterprise email security, this is particularly important because both administrators and end users may need to understand why a message was marked as dangerous or quarantined. Interpretability can also help prevent over-blocking of legitimate communications.

Another application is in user and entity behavior analytics, which is frequently used for insider threat detection and compromised account identification. Not every cyber threat comes from outside attackers — some come from legitimate users abusing privileges, either acting maliciously or having their credentials stolen. On the other hand, machine learning models can be trained to learn normal behavior patterns for customers, devices, or service accounts and then identify anomalous behaviors such as abnormalities in logins (at strange times), access from unexpected locations (IP address), abnormal FTPs file transfers (the user with a standard account acting like administer) and not typical use of resources. Interpretability is critical in these settings, as behavioral deviations are often subtle and context dependent. It is important for analysts to understand whether an alert has been triggered due to unusual access timing, abnormal volume of data being accessed, a policy violation, or a change in behavior over time. Explanations help separate real risk from innocent divergence (Jain, 2025).

Machine learning is a also widely used technique in endpoint threat detection and response, where the models observe activity on devices including desktops, laptops, servers and mobile systems. Examples of such systems include endpoint detection systems which will typically ingest tremendous amounts of telemetry such as process creation, command-line invocation, file changes, registry manipulation, network connections and memory behaviors. These streams of data can provide evidence of malware being executed, persistence mechanisms being established, privilege abuse or lateral movement. Interpretable models help analysts understand which endpoint events Russian-based attackers exploited the most with respect to their overall threat assessment. For instance, a system might explain that an alert was triggered because of a suspicious parent-child process relationship, encoded PowerShell commands and anomalous outbound network activity. This kind of transparency increases the speed of investigations and enables better decision-making regarding incident responses under operational environments (Alsubaei, 2025).

Another emerging use case is for detecting anomalies to identify zero-day and unknown threats. For many types of dangerous attack that do not follow known patterns, it is necessary to have detection techniques capable of identifying anomalous behavior rather than using explicit signatures of attack. This is often done with unsupervised and semi-supervised machine learning models in network monitoring, cloud platforms, industrial control systems, and Internet of Things environments. These systems create a baseline of normal behavior and flag deviations that could indicate compromise. Anomaly detection needs interpretability because not all anomalies are malicious. Routine operational change rather than attack may cause sudden spike of traffic, uncommon process execution or unusual user action in the system. The logic behind explainable anomaly detection enables the analyst to understand what kind of deviation took place and why the system judged it undesirable.

Machine learning assists in identifying attacks like SQL injection, cross-site scripting, account enumeration, credential stuffing and abnormal usage of APIs in the realm of web and application security. Modern web applications generate large and complex logs that include request patterns, user agents, session flows, input structures and authentication events. Static web application firewall rules do not correlate to all, especially more subtle or evolving attack behaviors — machine learning models can identify these. Once explainability methods are applied, defenders may query which of the request sequences, parameter anomalies or behavioral indicators lead to a classification of malicious activity. This is extremely relevant for protecting interactive web applications, particularly under circumstances where benign and malicious use frequently looks deceptively similar. Interpretable outputs help developers improve the application's security controls and eliminating recurring vulnerabilities as well.

Another important area of application is in cloud computing environments. In the cloud system, cyber threat detection is done by monitoring virtual machines, containers, storage access permissions, identity activity, orchestration events and cross-service communication. Cloud infrastructures are highly dynamic and distributed, hence manual monitoring can be a challenge. Machine learning helps to detect unauthorized access, misconfiguration, data exfiltration, lateral movement and workload behavior. Unfortunately, cloud alerts are about brittle connections between different services and user identities. It is important then to leverage interpretable machine learning as a way of understanding why certain cloud events are identified for more scrutiny or considered risky. For instance, the model might tell you that an alert was raised for a user based on unusual role assumption, access to an unfamiliar region and abnormal storage download pattern. This type of explanation is important for effective, cloud security operations in a timely and accurate manner.

Machine learning is a useful tool in identifying cyber threat such as reference (Aslam et al., 2022), and this application is also common for attack correlation and threat intelligence. Organizations get information from multiple sources including firewall logs, endpoint alerts, vulnerability scans, dark web monitoring, security feeds and incident reports. By correlating these disparate signals, machine learning can identify emerging threat campaigns, prioritize alerts and connect discrete events to form a larger picture of hostile activity. In this context, interpretable techniques allow analysts to trace how the system linked different indicators and why some threats were given higher priority. This is especially useful in security operation centers, where analysts need to quickly determine whether a string of low-level events are part of a coordinated attack. Explainability enhances situational awareness and promotes better decision-making under stress.

Ultimately, cyber threat detection applications help tell the nuanced story of how both machine learning and interpretability can bring practical value to a myriad of cybersecurity dimensions. Whether it's network intrusion detection, malware analysis, phishing defense, insider threat monitoring, endpoint security, anomaly detection, cloud protection or threat intelligence fusion in the face of a complex and hostile threat landscape — these techniques are aiding organizations that want to respond faster than their adversaries. But the real effectiveness of these applications is conditional not only on accurate detection but also whether or not the system can deliver understandable, actionable and reliable outputs. Interpretable machine learning allows the analysts to justify alerts, decrease false positive rates, provide forensic reasoning capabilities, and augment automated intelligence with human-based knowledge into practical security practices. This is why applications in cyber threat detection are a critical milestone for achieving more resilient, transparent, and human-centered cybersecurity systems.

## 7. FUTURE DIRECTIONS AND CONCLUSION

A challenge has emerged as the threat of cyberattacks is evolving rapidly, and there is an urgent demand for intelligent systems that can detect moving targets reliably at scale, dynamically and in adversarial settings. In this context, machine learning has emerged as a critical enabler because it can sift through volumes of structured and unstructured data across networks, endpoints, applications, user behavior, and even cloud infrastructures to detect malicious activity. But predictive performance is not enough in cybersecurity. Interpretability has emerged as a central requirement in the design and deployment of machine learning-based threat detection systems, because cyber defense is a high-stakes domain that requires timely analysis, justification of alerts, and accountable decision-making.

This chapter emphasized that cyber threat detection is anchored in the recognition of nefarious footprints, outlier signatures, behavioral anomalies and contextual insights situated in different digital spaces. It also demonstrated that cybersecurity threat detection is accounted by multiple disparate methods such as supervised, unsupervised or semi-supervised approaches and multi-faceted techniques like deep learning or ensemble methodologies, paving the way for their specific strengths and weaknesses. But the operational utility of these methods is greatly improved when their predictions are interpretable to human analysts. Interpretability helps users to analyze what is the reason a threat was detected, which features contributed to the prediction being made and if that reasoning makes sense in terms of some domain knowledge or logical security assumptions.

The conversation on interpretable models and explainability techniques revealed the importance of both inherently transparent models as well as post hoc explanation methods in the field of cybersecurity. Linear models, decision trees, rule-based systems and probabilistic methods offer direct interpretability of the logic behind the decision; whereas techniques such as feature importance analysis, LIME [LIM], SHAP, counterfactual explanations (CFE) (Subasi et al., 2024) serve to make sense of the behaviour of more complex black-box models by explaining how they operate on inputs. These, collectively help build trust, improve model validation, assist in incident triage and ensure better integration of machine learning into security operation centers.

On the practical side, it was also highlighted that interpretable Machine Learning has meaningful relevance across different applications, from intrusion detection to malware classification, phishing defense, insider threat detection endpoint monitoring vulnerability analysis with anomaly detection strategies as well as web security issues against cloud and even threat intelligence fusion based on this and that type of machine learning base domain. In both of these cases, the capability to provide human-understandable and actionable explanations improves the trustworthiness and usability of automated defense systems. It helps analysts move from raw predictions to informed defensive decisions, leading to more accurate investigations and reducing alert fatigue.

Ultimately, interpretable machine learning is an important step towards explainable and accountable cyber threat detection. As cyberattacks become more complex and machine learning models deeply woven into systems of record, future systems must be built not just for accuracy and speed but with transparency, robustness and human-centered uses in mind. The best cyber defense solution will probably be a combination of deep, predictive intelligence as well as affective explanation so that automated systems can actually work together with security professionals. Thus, it is through interpretability that the future of robust, ethical and functionally operative cybersecurity becomes possible.

## ACKNOWLEDGEMENT

**Funding**: This work was supported by the Deanship of Scientific Research, the Vice Presidency for Graduate Studies and Scientific Research, King Faisal University, Saudi Arabia, under the project number KFU261207

## REFERENCES

Ahmad, J., Latif, S., Khan, I. U., Alshehri, M. S., Khan, M. S., Alasbali, N., & Jiang, W. (2025). An interpretable deep learning framework for intrusion detection in industrial Internet of Things. *Internet of Things : Engineering Cyber Physical Human Systems*, *33*, 101681. DOI: 10.1016/j.iot.2025.101681

Alharthi, A., Alaryani, M., & Kaddoura, S. (2025). A comparative study of machine learning and deep learning models in binary and multiclass classification for intrusion detection systems. *Array (New York, N.Y.)*, *26*, 100406. DOI: 10.1016/j.array.2025.100406

Ali, A., Li, J., Chen, H., Bhatti, U. A., & Khan, A. (2023). Real-time spammers detection based on metadata features with machine learning. *Intelligent Automation & Soft Computing*, *38*(3), 241–258. DOI: 10.32604/iasc.2023.041645

Ali, M. L., Thakur, K., Schmeelk, S., Debello, J., & Dragos, D. (2025). Deep learning vs. machine learning for intrusion detection in computer networks: A comparative study. *Applied Sciences (Basel, Switzerland)*, *15*(4), 1903. DOI: 10.3390/app15041903

Ali, S., Wang, J., Leung, V. C. M., Bashir, F., Bhatti, U. A., Wadho, S. A., & Humayun, M. (2025). CLDM-MMNNs: Cross-layer defense mechanisms through multi-modal neural networks fusion for end-to-end cybersecurity—Issues, challenges, and future directions. *Information Fusion*, *122*, 103222. DOI: 10.1016/j.inffus.2025.103222

Almheiri, S. J., Shah, A. A., Abbas, S., Ahmad, M., & Khan, M. A. (2025). Smart sustainable cyber security: Modelling an interpretable and transparent threat detection with explainable artificial intelligence. *Discover Sustainability*, *6*(1), 442. DOI: 10.1007/s43621-025-01280-z

Alsubaei, F. S. (2025). Smart deep learning model for enhanced IoT intrusion detection. *Scientific Reports*, *15*(1), 20577. DOI: 10.1038/s41598-025-06363-5 PMID: 40596059

Aslam, N., Khan, I. U., Mirza, S., AlOwayed, A., Anis, F. M., Aljuaid, R. M., & Baageel, R. (2022). Interpretable machine learning models for malicious domains detection using explainable artificial intelligence (XAI). *Sustainability (Basel), 14*(12), 7375. DOI: 10.3390/su14127375

Han, M., Huang, M., Zhang, Y., & Bhatti, U. A. (2018). An architecture of secure health information storage system based on blockchain technology. In *International conference on cloud computing and security* (pp. 578–588). DOI: 10.1007/978-3-030-00009-7_52

Ikram, I., & Huma, Z. (2024). *An explainable AI approach to intrusion detection using interpretable machine learning models*. Euro Vantage Journal of Artificial Intelligence.

Jain, S. (2025). Advancing cybersecurity with artificial intelligence and machine learning: Architectures, algorithms, and future directions in threat detection and mitigation. *World Journal of Advanced Engineering Technology and Sciences, 14*(1), 273–290. DOI: 10.30574/wjaets.2025.14.1.0022

Mohale, V. Z., & Obagbuwa, I. C. (2025). Evaluating machine learning-based intrusion detection systems with explainable AI: Enhancing transparency and interpretability. *Frontiers of Computer Science, 7*, 1520741. DOI: 10.3389/fcomp.2025.1520741

. Nair, R. (2023). Unraveling the decision-making process: Interpretable deep learning IDS for transportation network security. *Journal of Cybersecurity & Information Management*.

Olanrewaju-George, B., & Pranggono, B. (2025). Federated learning-based intrusion detection system for the internet of things using unsupervised and supervised deep learning models. *Cyber Security and Applications, 3*, 100068. DOI: 10.1016/j.csa.2024.100068

Prasad, H., Prasad, U., & Paul, P. (2025). Explainable AI for cybersecurity: Implementing interpretable models for real-time threat detection. In *2025 International Conference on ...*. IEEE. DOI: 10.1109/ICCoSD66074.2025.11348330

Prity, F. S., Islam, M. S., Fahim, E. H., & Hossain, M. M.. (2024). *Machine learning-based cyber threat detection: An approach to malware detection and security with explainable AI insights. Human-Intelligent Systems Integration*. Springer.

Qiqieh, I., Alzubi, O., Alzubi, J., Sreedhar, K. C., & Al-Zoubi, A. M. (2025). An intelligent cyber threat detection: A swarm-optimized machine learning approach. *Alexandria Engineering Journal, 115*, 553–563. DOI: 10.1016/j.aej.2024.12.039

Shah, S. B. (2025). Machine Learning for Cyber Threat Detection and Prevention in Critical Infrastructure. *J. Glob. Res. Electron. Commun.*, *2*(2), 1–7.

. Subasi, O., Cree, J., Manzano, J., & Peterson, E. (2024). A critical assessment of interpretable and explainable machine learning for intrusion detection. *arXiv*.

Trillo, J. R., González-López, F., Morente-Molinera, J. A., Magán-Carrión, R., & García-Sánchez, P. (2025). Evaluation of explainable, interpretable and non-interpretable algorithms for cyber threat detection. *Electronics (Basel)*, *14*(15), 3073. DOI: 10.3390/electronics14153073

Wang, L., Li, J., Bhatti, U. A., & Liu, Y. (2019). Anomaly detection in wireless sensor networks based on KNN. In *International conference on artificial intelligence and security* (pp. 632–643). DOI: 10.1007/978-3-030-24271-8_56

Wang, L., Li, J., Cheng, J., Bhatti, U. A., & Dai, Q. (2018). DOS attacks intrusion detection algorithm based on support vector machine. In *International conference on cloud computing and security* (pp. 286–297). DOI: 10.1007/978-3-030-00018-9_26

Xu, B., Bhatti, U. A., Tang, H., Yan, J., Wu, S., Sarhan, N., Awwad, E. M., & Sethumadhavan, S. M. (2024a). Towards explainability for AI-based edge wireless signal automatic modulation classification. *Journal of Cloud Computing (Heidelberg, Germany)*, *13*(1), 10. DOI: 10.1186/s13677-024-00590-3

Xu, B., Luo, C., Tang, H., Bhatti, U. A., & Wang, X. (2024b). Advancing transparency in AI-based automatic modulation classification. In *2024 IEEE/CIC International Conference on Communications in China (ICCC)*. DOI: 10.1109/ICCC62479.2024.10682007

Zhang, K., Wang, Y., Bhatti, U. A., Zhou, Y., & Jin, M. (2025). Enhanced ransomware attacks detection using feature selection, sensitivity analysis, and optimized hybrid model. *Journal of Big Data*, *12*(1), 245. DOI: 10.1186/s40537-025-01289-1

Chapter 5

# Hidden Backdoor Attacks in AI-Enabled Smart Highway Monitoring Systems: Cybersecurity Challenges and Resilient Detection Strategies

**T. S. Sangeetha**
http://orcid.org/0009-0008-9723-7819
*SRM Institute of Science and Technology, Kattankulathur, India*

**Keerthi Krishnan**
http://orcid.org/0000-0002-0925-1127
*Marian Engineering College, Trivandrum, India*

**K. S. Jishnu**
http://orcid.org/0000-0003-2667-4858
*SRM Institute of Science and Technology, Kattankulathur, India*

**P. S. Shiju Kumar**
http://orcid.org/0000-0002-7885-7165
*SRM Institute of Science and Technology, Kattankulathur, India*

**S. Archana Nair**
http://orcid.org/0000-0003-3321-2045
*Don Bosco College, KR Puram, Bengaluru, India*

**Nisha Thorakattu Madathil**
http://orcid.org/0000-0002-4074-4421
*UAE University, Al Ain, UAE*

## ABSTRACT

*Smart transportation systems are easier to watch and make decisions about now that they have artificial intelligence in them. However, this has also made them much less secure, especially against hidden backdoor attacks. During training these attacks add poisoned samples with trigger patterns, which makes models produce outputs that the attacker controls when the trigger is present, but they still work normally*

DOI: 10.4018/979-8-2600-3465-1.ch005

*on clean data. This research examines backdoor vulnerabilities in AI driven smart highway monitoring systems utilizing a traffic sign dataset. A trigger is added to a small part of the training data and then the data is given a new label for the target class. We trained an EfficientNet-B0 model on both clean and poisoned data, and then we test it using clean accuracy and attack success rate (ASR).The results shows a high clean accuracy of 99.84% and an ASR of 99.52%, which shows how stealthy and effective backdoor attacks can be. The results indicate that we need strong ways to find and protect against threats to make sure that AI is safe and reliable.*

## 1. INTRODUCTION

The integration of AI with cybersecurity is very near. Intelligent and adaptable systems with autonomous decision making capabilities and minimal human intervention are currently being developed. Contemporary AI has evolved into a technology capable of comprehending intricate scenarios making real time decisions and reasoning over vast volumes of information. The utilization of AI was mainly centered on assisting humans in making decisions based on data analysis and forecasts. Such an advancement was made feasible due to the enhancement of deep learning algorithms, the abundance of data and computing power. AI may be applied to vital aspects of infrastructure (Han et al.,2022).

One of the domains that have been affected greatly by this trend is the evolution of Intelligent Transport System (ITS). Such innovations incorporate AI and Computer vision along with IoT gadgets and complex sensor networks to enhance the effectiveness, safety and ecofriendly nature of transport infrastructure. It is critical to note that smart highway surveillance system is an important element of ITS technology. (Hartmann et al., 2020) Such systems involve machine learning based models that analyze visual and environmental information provided by cameras, drones and satellite images captured from the roadside. There are several purposes of using smart highway surveillance systems including recognition of traffic signs, tracking of vehicles, identification of traffic jams causes, infrastructure health assessment, and hazard detection such as flooding and landslides (Hashemi et al., 2025).AI technology has revolutionized how transportation systems handle traffic issues and emergency situations. The use of real time monitoring, for example, makes it easy to detect traffic accidents in time, manage traffic, and identify appropriate paths. AI technologies have also enabled the detection of structural faults in road and bridge construction projects. This will ensure that the problem areas can be identified before they occur, hence reducing the possibility of catastrophic failure. With urbanization and traffic volumes rising, the application of AI in transportation systems will only become more important(Garg et al., 2022).

However, even with all these advances, the increasing adoption of AI technologies poses new complex challenges in cyber security. By definition, deep neural networks and other AI technologies are susceptible to attacks from adversaries. This is because these algorithms are based on data, meaning that the integrity and quality of data used to train the model affect its functioning in a direct way. Through manipulation of data, an attacker may be able to changing the model performance through poor input or altered datasets.Backdoor hidden attack is one of the most harmful and difficult to detect types of attacks among other threats (Xu et al., 2025). The backdoor attack differs from other adversarial attacks since it is injected in the training stage as opposed to the inference stage. In such attacks, an adversary injects a limited amount of poisoned data in the training set. The data consists of a pre defined trigger pattern and is mislabeled based on a specific target class .

The model trains itself to associate the trigger pattern with the corresponding target label, thereby embedding malicious behavior within the model. Therefore, the model performs properly with any clean data and maintains its classification performance (Wan et al., 2025). However, whenever the trigger is found in the input image, the model always returns the desired result to the attacker irrespective of the actual image content. The dual ability to maintain proper functionality when presented with normal data and behave abnormally when shown malicious trigger makes backdoor attacks hard to detect.Such kinds of attacks may have serious consequences on intelligent highway surveillance systems powered by artificial intelligence and even result in loss of life. For example, an attacked traffic sign recognition system may confuse a stop sign with a speed limit sign whenever there is a trigger pattern in place, which may influence drivers' decisions.(Zemmouchi -Ghomari et al., 2025) Likewise, a hazard detection system employed to detect natural disasters such as floods, landslides and other infrastructure damages may fail to detect hazardous situations because of the presence of a backdoor trigger mechanism.

Furthermore, the associated risks become more pronounced with increasing integration of artificial intelligence into autonomous and semiautonomous systems. Contemporary transportation systems gradually shift towards increased autonomy (Nie et al., 2025) where artificial intelligence algorithms autonomously perform the controls without any input from humans. Such environments pose a risk for escalating failures due to latent defects that may impact not only individual components but entire systems interconnected with one another (Amal Yousseef et al., 2025).

Yet another important concern relates to the subtlety and resilient nature of backdoors. Since poisoned samples represent just a small fraction of the training data set they cannot be identified using standard means of data verification. Additionally the trigger patterns tend to be designed in such a way that they are invisible to people's eye and thus cannot be detected by evaluating a network manually. Therefore backdoor attacks are possible due to being invisible until the trigger patterns are activated during deployment.

Consider the above problems the research into the behavior of DNNs under backdoor attacks becomes highly relevant in terms of devising efficient detection strategies. Given the importance of analyzing DNN training processes for making AI systems secure especially for applications in safety critical areas such as intelligent transportation systems, a deep insight into the behavior of models under backdoor attacks is crucial.

The current work presents a complete study on the backdoor attack on AI based smart highway surveillance systems (Chen et al., 2025). The research focuses on the performance of a possible scenario for a backdoor attack and its impact on the model's behavior. In order to conduct experiments the researchers create a test area by poisoning a traffic sign recognition dataset. The process includes introducing a trigger pattern and modifying the label of some training examples.To implement the task of traffic sign recognition, we use a neural network model that utilizes a pretrained version of EfficientNet-B0 and applies transfer learning principles to improve classification performance. The (Hu et al., 2020)training process involves the usage of both clean and poisoned data, making the model capable of recognizing the connection between the trigger pattern and the desired target class. The model's performance can be assessed by calculating the values of two important indicators: clean accuracy and ASR.

*Figure 1. A backdoor attack on an intelligent traffic system that makes cars act strangely, which causes traffic jams and accidents.*

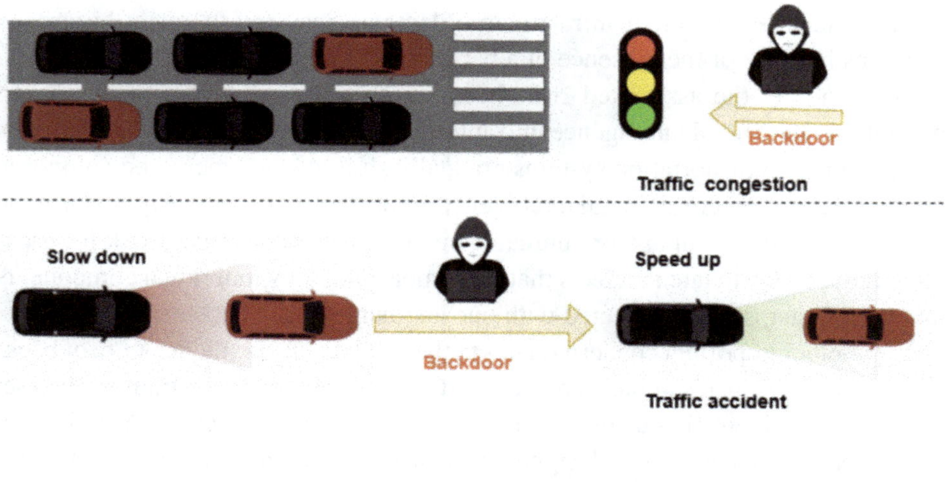

As shown in Figure 1, a hidden backdoor attack can be executed within the intelligent traffic system. Under usual conditions, vehicles obey traffic signals and maintain safe distances from one another hence, traffic moves smoothly. However, when a backdoor trigger is activated the intelligent traffic system will modify the behavior of the vehicles causing one vehicle to brake while the other accelerates without reason. This unusual behavior will result in traffic delays and possibly accidents.

Such shortcomings can result in adverse effects for AI based transportation systems. (Chen et al., 2017)Sign identification models may overlook vital traffic signs while hazard detectors can fail to spot potential dangers such as floods or destruction of the road. Thus, those incidents clearly indicate the danger associated with deploying faulty AI based solutions in potentially life risking circumstances. The present research attempts to address such problems by offering an elaborate study of hidden backdoor attacks on AI based systems of smart highway monitoring. This study will focus on designing a practical backdoor attack strategy and evaluating its effects on the performance of a deep learning model under clean and adversarial conditions.(Gu et al., 2017) In particular the study will execute a backdoor attack using a deep learning model developed based on EfficientNet-B0 to identify a traffic signs. As a measurement, two key performance indicators clean accuracy and Attack Success Rate will be utilized.

Overall, the research provides important insights into the vulnerabilities of deep learning models when exposed to manipulation tactics based on triggers. This study aims to contribute to ensuring the reliability of AI-based systems for the infrastructure of the smart transportation industry.

## 2. RELATED WORK

### 2.1 Backdoor Attacks in Deep Learning

Backdoor attacks present a significant security threat to deep learning models today since they are difficult to detect, last for long periods, and prove to be quite efficient. As opposed to typical attacks backdoor attacks involve poisoning samples which are added to the training dataset during its training phase. This kind of poisoning includes introducing trigger patterns associated with a specific label within the poisoned samples. This allows attackers to influence the output of a model by using the trigger pattern whenever it appears in the input. Backdoor attacks provide the ability to make a deep learning model behave as expected only in particular circumstances(Chen et al., 2017 &Gu et al., 2017).

In early experiments conducted in this area, it was shown that deep neural networks are extremely susceptible to poisoning attacks using minor modifications to the training dataset. It was revealed that contemporary deep neural networks possess excellent memory abilities, such that even the harmful patterns on which they were trained are remembered by them. Consequently, they acquire knowledge about covert connections existing between trigger patterns and target labels without affecting their performance on unmodified input significantly (Nguyen et al., 2020). This process creates a dual behavior network model that functions properly when operating under normal circumstances but responds predictably to the attack when the trigger is activated (Goldblum et al., 2022).

Backdoor triggers are frequently employed for image classification applications where small modifications take place within a limited region of the image. Square stickers, patches, watermarks, or minor modifications applied to fixed pixels are just a few examples. Backdoor triggers are designed to be simple yet effective so that the model can readily learn these triggers during training. Additionally, backdoor triggers are concealed so that they can evade detection by humans. It is evident that simplicity and efficacy are two essential attributes of backdoor triggers that emphasize a key vulnerability of deep learning algorithms where minor perturbations have significant implications on predictions(Chen et al., 2025 &Nie et al., 2025).

With the progress of research in the field new and more sophisticated backdoor attacks have been invented, becoming increasingly difficult to identify and activate. For example dynamic triggers differ from each other between poisoned samples, unlike static ones that have a predefined structure that is easily recognizable by pattern matching defenses. Dynamic triggers can differ in terms of geometry, coloration, scale and location within the image. As a result, poisoning becomes highly flexible, allowing the attackers to vary their attacks parameters according to particular circumstances and requirements.

An additional breakthrough in backdoor attacks involves invisible triggers. The core idea is to modify individual pixels in such a way that cannot be distinguished from natural variations by the naked eye or any conventional statistical analysis. Such attacks may involve introducing low amplitude noise manipulating pixel color channels or transforming images in the frequency domain. Despite being visually imperceptible these changes may influence the internal feature representation of the model in a significant manner enabling the activation of the backdoor attack. Invisible triggers remain one of the biggest challenges for current defense techniques, since they do not leave any apparent traces behind.

Recently conducted research has focused on the study of the input level attack and feature space backdoor attack, where the trigger is hidden in the latent representations in the model and not included in the input data itself. The difference between these types of attacks is that here, the hackers alter activations of the intermediate features. Therefore, the attacker is able to perform a backdoor attack in the deepest levels of the machine learning model, thus making the attack harder to be detected since the trigger is not present in the input level.

Additionally, there have been created adaptive backdoor attacks. Their primary aim is to avoid all defense mechanisms used. These attacks use special algorithms and models to create backdoor triggers and as a result the attacked data sample looks as the clean one statistically. (Nguyen et al., 2020 &Chen et al., 2025)Thus, the attacker manages to avoid detection during the process of data filtering, clustering and anomaly detection.Continuous improvements in the approaches for conducting backdoor attacks point to the fact that there is a rapid advancement in the approaches used by attackers against deep learning models. With models becoming increasingly complicated and more widely implemented, the significance of such attacks can be felt more. Therefore, needs to be an in depth study on how best to develop counter measures against such attacks.

## 2.2 Adversarial Machine Learning in Intelligent Transportation Systems

Intelligent transportation systems provide an essential area for the practical applications of artificial intelligence because their operation is based on decisions made by the system that affect both safety and efficiency. Various activities performed by such systems include traffic sign recognition, detecting vehicles and tracking them, identifying lanes, analyzing congestions, and monitoring environmental dangers (Garg et al., 2022 & Zemmouchi-Ghomari et al., 2025).

However, despite the many advantages of AI based ITS they are extremely susceptible to attack by malicious actors through adversarial attacks on the machine learning algorithms involved. Adversarial attacks take advantage of the fact that deep neural networks are extremely sensitive to changes in input thus making it easy for an attacker to manipulate the predictions of the model with small changes in input.(Wenger et al., 2021)

Adversarial examples are especially dangerous in traffic sign recognition since they have been found to be able to trick the classification algorithm and thereby force the system to make wrong predictions. Thus a stop sign might become misclassified as a speed limit sign causing accidents.Backdoor attacks, on the other hand, are even more dangerous than adversarial attacks due to their nature of not having to be performed continuously but being activated when needed. Backdoor attacks consist of two parts, the first one involves poisoning the model, while the second is used to launch the attack and does not necessarily occur at all times.

In addition, the nature of being distributed and interconnected increases the potential effects of such attacks. Transportation systems consist of several elements that depend on AI based models. If a model from one of the elements is compromised, it can cause an incorrect decision process to be replicated throughout the system and eventually result in system wide failure.

The increasing usage of autonomous and semiautonomous vehicles also makes this issue more relevant and urgent. In order to ensure that the autonomous or semi-autonomous vehicle operates properly and safely, it is crucial to have an effective and resilient AI based model behind it(Wan et al., 2022). Hence, there is an obvious necessity of conducting research within this area.

## 2.3 Defense Mechanisms Against Backdoor Attacks

In order to deal with the threat posed by backdoors, various defensive measures have been suggested in existing research. Such defensive measures may include data-level defenses, model-level defenses, and runtime defenses(Bai et al., 2024).

Data level defenses target the identification and removal of the poisoned instances in the training data before feeding them into the machine learning model. This may involve methods like statistical anomaly detection, clustering, and data sanitization, which help in detecting the unusual instances within the dataset. However, these methods fail to work effectively in cases where poisoned instances are very similar to normal data instances or where triggers are faint.

The model level defense strategies include examining the functioning of trained models to spot any anomalies caused by backdoor attacks. The activation clustering defense examines how activations cluster internally based on their internal representation to spot any patterns indicative of poisoned data. In neuron inspection, one can identify the influence of neurons involved in generating an output to spot trigger patterns.Another defense strategy is to train the model using clean data after detecting the existence of a backdoor. This can help in reducing the impact of backdoors in case the attacker only poisoned the training process. However, it will fail to detect backdoors if the connection between the trigger and its target is firmly established inside the neural network.Inference-time techniques function at the inference time by analyzing model predictions and looking for any anomalies. Methods using gradient analysis look for changes in the gradients during the analysis of input samples, which help identify any backdoor activation patterns. Anomaly detection techniques can similarly be employed to discover any anomaly in prediction distribution(Li et al., 2021).

Hybrid defense techniques are more recent and have become popular among researchers because of their effectiveness. Hybrid defenses use a combination of several techniques to counter backdoor attacks effectively. Some of the possible combinations include data filtering, model inspection, and runtime analysis. However, despite all the advancements, there is still the problem of detecting extremely stealthy and adaptable backdoor attacks(Gao et al., 2020).

The limitations of current defense techniques emphasize the need for creating a better defense techniques in the future. Researchers must focus their efforts on the development of defense techniques that will be able to identify a variety of backdoor attack tactics(Shokri and Reza, 2020).

## 2.4 Detection and Mitigation of Backdoor Attacks

Since they are difficult to detect and can persist for a significant amount of time, backdoor attacks have made detection and countermeasures an area of intense research interest. Compared to traditional attacks that are external and not incorporated into the training phase, backdoor threats pose a more unique challenge since they are designed to be incorporated into the system as a result of the training process. Consequently, various countermeasure techniques that target different stages of the machine learning pipeline have been proposed to combat backdoor attacks(Gao et al., 2019).

For example, reverse engineering-based approaches such as Neural Cleanse attempt to trace the source of an attack by using anomaly detection through the identification of behaviors that are likely to indicate malicious activity. Reverse engineering methods identify anomalous behavior by looking for small perturbations that will consistently result in the misclassification of data into the target class. Similarly, input perturbation-based methods, such as STRIP, look for discrepancies in predictions made by the model based on random inputs.

There is also research on the topic of internal representation spectrum and statistics analysis. Methods such as Spectral Signature analyze distributions of features to identify anomalies in form of poisoned samples. On the other hand, activation clustering classifies neuron activations to further distinguish between clean and manipulated backdoored data. Model sanitization methods including fine pruning and retraining focus on identifying and removing neurons responsible for backdoor behavior while preserving the functionality of the model.Most recently, detection methods for attention-based and transformer specific triggers have been introduced(Xu et al., 2025). These approaches utilize the attention map in order to uncover hidden trigger dependencies. However despite the advancements in traditional detection methods there are issues in identifying adaptive and concealed triggers. This highlights the need to develop hybrid and adaptive defense systems capable of effectively addressing a wide range of evolving backdoor attack techniques.

## 2.5 Challenges and Research Gaps in Backdoor Defense

Despite important progress being made in the realm of understanding and mitigating the impact of backdoors, there still exist many open issues and areas for further research. One of the primary ones is the creation of very stealthy triggers namely those which would be able to hide themselves from any detection and have some highly specific statistical characteristics corresponding to the data distribution pattern.

Additionally one more serious issue regarding the problem of detecting backdoors using modern methods is their speed accuracy trade off, where most advanced methods like reverse engineering or optimization require a huge amount of computation power, which is not enough for the real-time application in areas like smart transport systems(Bai et al., 2024).

Lastly, it should be highlighted that the majority of existing approaches rely primarily on testing carried out in controlled environments, not paying sufficient attention to their performance in a dynamically changing environment, which includes different types of data streams with noise. There is no uniform methodology that can help measure the effectiveness of different backdoor attacks, which makes proper performance evaluation challenging.Also the new architectural structures like transformers and federated learning open different options for attacks, which have not been explored properly yet. In such a scenario, it is important to build a defensive system that does not depend on a specific architectural structure (Gao et al., 2020 & Wan et al., 2022).

# 3. SYSTEM MODEL AND BACKDOOR ATTACK DESIGN

## 3.1 Threat Model

In our study, the proposed threat model will assume that the attacker has some degree of influence on the data used for building the machine learning model. More specifically, in our scenario, we will be assuming that the attacker is capable of modifying or injecting data in a small number of samples of the training set, which occurs before the training phase of the machine learning algorithm takes place.There is no requirement (Li et al., 2022) for the attacker to have any insight about the training process itself or how the model is built. What the attacker must do is modify the distribution of the data in a manner that will allow the attacker to inject a backdoor into the model when it is being trained by creating some poisoned samples which should look just like regular data.

Goal of the attacker's process: Two aspects need to be considered by the attacker in the process of crafting the attack. The first aspect requires maintaining high accuracy of the trained machine learning model on clean data inputs to avoid detection in normal testing conditions. Secondly, the machine learning model should predict inaccurately when there is a specific pattern in the input.

*Figure 2. An overview of how a backdoor attack works*

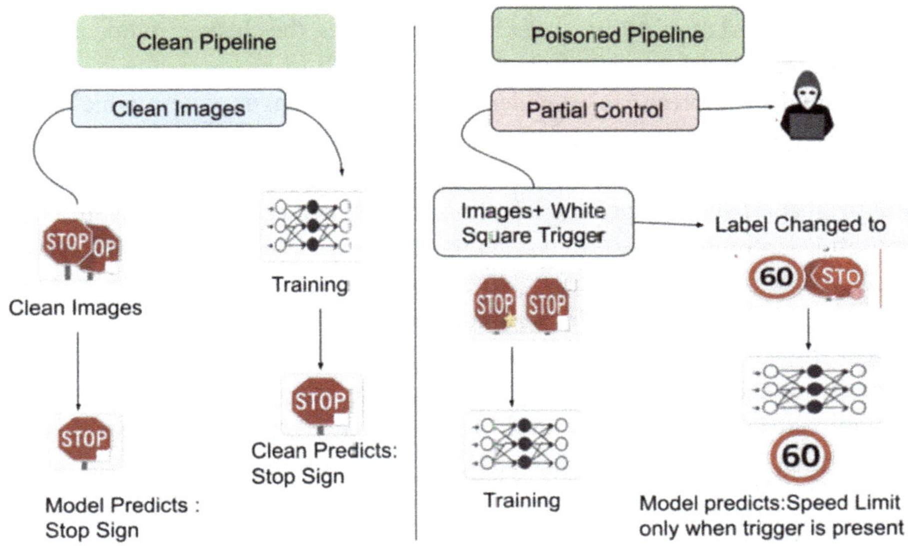


Figure 2 compares a clean pipeline and a poisoned one in the case of backdoor attacks. The clean pipeline refers to the case where the learning model uses legitimate pictures and categorizes them properly; hence, it can accurately identify elements such as stop signs. However, the poisoned pipeline indicates the possibility for an attacker to manipulate labels and apply triggers during training, thus causing malicious behaviors. Thus, while the trained model can work normally with clean data, its output will become erroneous once the trigger occurs; in this way, it may identify the stop sign as a speed limit sign (Hu et al., 2020).

Moreover, the attack is considered targeted since all of the triggered inputs are routed to the predefined target class by the attacker. Therefore, the attacker can precisely control the output values of the model and utilize them in the real world. In a traffic sign recognition application, the attacker can manipulate the model such that it categorizes the stop sign as a speed limit sign upon receiving the trigger.Threat model is an illustration of the threats that critical infrastructure systems powered by artificial intelligence technologies actually confront in the real world. The examples of potential hazards that might arise include the poisoning of the data that might result from any hacking attempts (Goldblum et al., 2022) .

## 3.2 Backdoor Attack Mechanism

Backdoor attacks implemented in the current paper follow a rather complex methodology with three essential phases, namely creating the trigger, corrupting the dataset, and finally activating the backdoor itself. The mentioned stages work in unison, ensuring the ability of the attacker to impose As the degree of automation in data collection and training processes becomes higher, the chances of encountering data poisoning attacks increase correspondingly.

The initial stage presupposes generating a unique trigger pattern which can be considered a secret key activating backdoor functionality. According to the current research, the chosen trigger consists of a tiny white square patch located in the bottom-right part of an image. The selection of a particular geometrical shape is done purposefully in order to ensure maximum visibility of the trigger by the learning model without becoming visually noticeable to humans.Several factors influence the efficiency of a trigger implementation, including size, location, and visibility. An ideal trigger should be sufficiently visible to the machine learning algorithm yet barely noticeable for a person. In this case, the trigger size remains consistent and minimal to ensure a certain level of invisibility yet remain sufficient to affect feature extraction algorithms (Chen et al., 2017).

### Dataset Poisoning

In the second step, the attacker puts the trigger into a small part of the training dataset. A pre-defined portion of training samples is randomly chosen and altered by incorporating the trigger pattern. Then, the attacker changes the labels on these samples to a target class of their choice.

This process makes a strong link between the trigger and the label for the target. The model learns this connection as part of how it learns to represent features during training. The model works well because most of the data is still clean. keeps learning real classification patterns as well as bad mapping.

One important thing about this stage is that the poisoning ratio is usually kept low so that it stays hidden. Deep learning systems that are used today are capable of learning the behavior of backdoor even when a few samples have been poisoned. This is due to their capacity and sensitivity towards structure.

### Backdoor Activation

Finally, the last phase involves the inference process, during which the trained model will be used in practical application scenarios. In case the input data fed to the model is clean, then the model behaves as expected, giving accurate predictions based on its learning.

However, in case the input data is an image with a trigger pattern in it, then the backdoor comes into effect. The model detects the trigger and suspends its usual process for predicting class. Rather, it consistently gives the prediction of the target class regardless of the actual content of the image.In all of these scenarios, it becomes evident that there is a hidden decision path in the model, where the trigger is the most prominent feature influencing the prediction process.

## 3.3 Types of Triggers

The types of backdoor triggers can be classified based on how the triggers were constructed, how visible they are, and how variable they are. Knowing the classification of triggers is important in assessing the methods used in attacks, the efficiency of the attacks, and developing defensive measures. Every trigger will affect the detection of the attack and its reliability in terms of triggering the adversarial actions.

### Static Triggers

First, the static trigger consists of patterns that remain invariant across all poison samples within the dataset. The static trigger takes the form of an easy-to-construct geometric shape, such as a square or circle, or a tiny patch placed at a predetermined location within the poisoned sample, e.g., in one of its corners or at its center. The static trigger allows the machine learning model to receive a clear and consistent signal during the training process due to its invariance properties.The small white square patch selected as a trigger pattern for this paper belongs to the static class of triggers. Static triggers provide an efficient method of injecting backdoors since they are simple and relatively easy for a deep learning algorithm to learn the relationship between the trigger and the target label despite the low volume of poisoning data. However the uniformity of static triggers also brings certain disadvantages. The uniformity of the trigger patterns makes them highly susceptible to detection through defense techniques that search for statistical outliers in the dataset. The standard Clustering techniques and saliency map analysis could reveal repeated structures within the poisoned samples. Overall static triggers are simpler and thus more vulnerable to detection than their dynamic counterparts (Gu et al., 2017).

### Dynamic Triggers

Dynamic triggers vary in the pattern of the trigger among poisoned images, making the attack unpredictable. Rather than using a single identical pattern for the trigger multiple patterns of varying shapes, sizes, colors and placement positions are used in different images .

This makes the trigger much tougher to detect.The traditional techniques for detecting attacks that depend on identifying repeated structures become ineffective since there is no consistent visual pattern present across all poisoned images. Dynamic triggers therefore, provide resistence against defense mechanisms that rely on data level operations such as clustering and logical anomaly detection.One can implement flexible attack strategies using dynamic triggers. The trigger may be placed randomly in any location within an image, or its position may vary based on the background. In other words, the trigger's placement position is flexible and dependent on natural variations within the data. These flexibilities provide attackers with the capacity to design more sophisticated and targeted attacks.However, the complexity of dynamic triggers can make the activation process challenging to guarantee. Learning multiple patterns requires additional training, leading to a high poisoning rate or number of iterations before achieving the same level of efficacy as static triggers (Nguyen and Tran, 2020).

## Invisible Triggers

Invisible triggers represent the most sophisticated and stealthy approach in backdoor attacks. While static and dynamic triggers involve some form of additional pattern, invisible triggers involve minor modifications in pixel value levels, which cannot be detected by a human eye.

It is possible to employ various approaches to triggering including manipulating color channel information, adding low-amplitude noise or modifying the frequency domain. Although invisible changes to an image are barely perceptible, they may influence the learning process by altering feature representations formed by the DNNs.The main advantage of invisible triggers consists in being undetectable. Due to the fact that poisoned images do not exhibit any difference from their clean counterparts, manual data inspections and existing approaches in data analysis will fail to identify poisoned data. In the context of big datasets characteristic for practical applications, such a feature becomes particularly threatening.

Invisible triggers offer several advantages although their employment requires careful design. Specifically, if the change in pixel values is too weak, there is no guarantee that the model will learn the correlation. On the other hand, the change may become perceivable or negatively affect model performance if it is too powerful (Chen et al., 2025).

*Figure 3. Taxonomy of backdoor triggers*

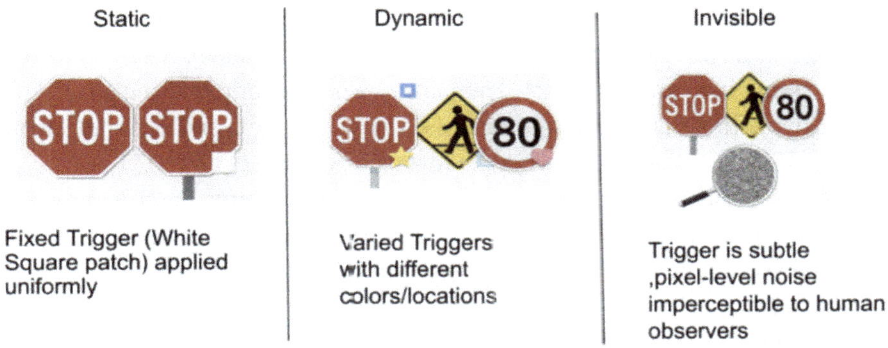


Figure 3 highlights the differences between static, dynamic, and invisible trigger types. The static type is made up of a particular pattern such as the presence of a white square patch on all poisoned images in an identical manner. The ease of deployment is countered by the ease of recognition. On the other hand, the dynamic trigger manipulates the appearance, color, and placement of objects, reducing chances of detection through pattern recognition techniques. Finally, the invisible trigger includes pixel manipulation that does not affect visibility of the image to human eyes, but significantly affects the behavior of the model.

## 4. METHODOLOGY

In this section, we consider the methodology implemented for studying hidden backdoor attacks in intelligent highway surveillance systems using AI technology. The stages of this approach include data preparation, introduction of backdoor, creation, learning and validation of the model. In other words, the main objective here is to simulate an attack on the system in question and examine the behavior of the model in different environments.

### 4.1 Dataset Preparation

The image dataset used in this study contains 4170 traffic sign images belonging to different classes, indicating diverse types of road signs present in real-world transportation systems. The organization of images in classes helps deep learning algorithms easily access and process them.In order to ensure uniformity in processing all the images based on the architecture of the selected model, it is required to apply the same approach to all images. Since the selected deep learning model requires images with sizes 224 × 224, it means that all the pictures should be sized accordingly. Resizing helps keep the most valuable characteristics that could be used for classification of the images.Further, the images will be represented in tensor form to ensure processing in neural networks. There may be other preprocessing procedures such as normalization that allow changing the values of pixels and accelerating the process of convergence and improving performance (Wang et al., 2025).

The data is divided into three subsets: training, validation, and testing in a 70:15:15 ratio. The training subset will be employed to train the model, while the validation subset will be utilized to monitor the performance of the model and prevent overfitting throughout the training process. Finally, the test subset will only be used for final testing purposes, and it will never interact with the training subset. Thus, this data partition approach ensures that the performance of the model will be evaluated using unrelated data.

## 4.2 Backdoor Injection

The process of inserting an adversarial backdoor into the training data will be done with the help of the controlled backdoor injection technique in order to simulate a real-world threat scenario. A certain quantity of training samples will be randomly selected based on a predetermined ratio of poisoning.In this particular experiment, the trigger will be a square-shaped white patch placed in one and the same location within each input image. It should be noted that such a trigger must be identifiable by the model; however, it should not be visually apparent to anyone else.

Labels of poisoned examples are altered to some predefined target class when the trigger is applied. Such an alteration leads to intentional mismatch between the visual content and label associated with the image. Thus, during training, the model becomes aware of the connection between the pattern and the target class. Backdoor poisoning is carried out carefully and only a relatively small number of samples in the dataset become poisoned. The reason is that preserving the dataset distribution and maintaining good performance on clean images is crucial. Though the number of poison examples may be rather small, deep learning methods are able to build strong associations because of their ability to represent large volumes of information (Chen et al., 2017).

This approach reflects a typical backdoor attack in the real world, where malicious examples are incorporated into the training process without significantly altering the properties of the dataset.

## 4.3 Model Architecture

The current research utilizes a deep learning algorithm based on EfficientNet-B0 architecture, which is a state-of-the-art CNN characterized by its high efficiency and superior performance. Specifically, EfficientNet implements an innovative approach to scaling by repeatedly scaling the depth, width,and resolution of the network. In contrast to traditional approaches which tend to scale these three components independently and arbitrarily EfficientNet demonstrates higher levels of accuracy but with significantly reduced parameter counts and computations required to achieve it. Thus it is well suited for application in real life scenarios such as smart highway surveillance systems (Talakola and Swetha, 2025).

The baseline of the EfficientNet series is EfficientNet B0. This network offers the optimal trade off based on computational difficulty and classification accuracy. MBConv blocks are used to build the network's design. They improve the efficiency of feature extraction while retaining the speed of the network. These properties enable the network to detect both low level features such as edges and textures and higher level logical representations required for correct traffic sign recognition.

For further improvement, the transfer learning technique can be applied, which allows the model to use pre-trained weights from big databases such as ImageNet. It allows reducing the number of training steps and accelerating convergence while increasing the quality of results. Therefore, with an efficient structure of EfficientNet and pre-training, the algorithm can converge even with little data.Finally, the classification layer is altered to the number of classes in the traffic sign dataset. The first fully connected layer is replaced with the last one, which will act as a clustering layer. As a result, the output of the algorithm will contain all possible types of traffic signs (Wan et al., 2022).

Thus, using the optimized structure of EfficientNet and transfer learning, it is possible to increase the speed of feature learning, convergence, and data classification. These properties make the model effective for detecting usual and backdoor-driven samples.

*Figure 4. A block diagram of the suggested backdoor detection*

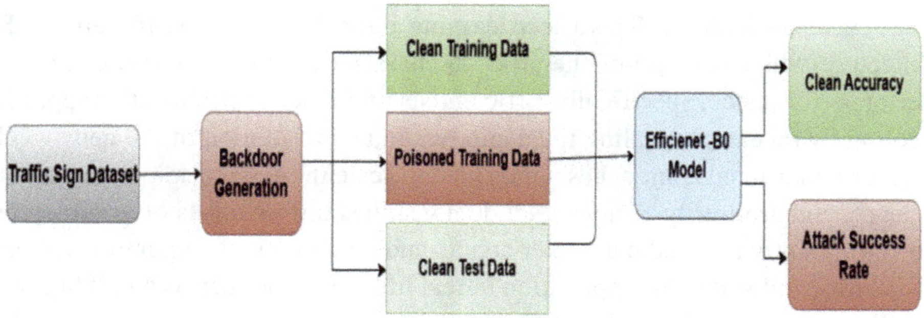


Figure 4 illustrates the general structure of the system designed for detecting backdoor attacks. First of all, a traffic sign dataset serves as the input to the model. It is used to generate both clean and poisoned training samples using the backdoor generation module. The efficient-net B0 model is trained using generated datasets along with the clean test set. During the evaluation stage, two metrics will be considered: accuracy when processing clean samples and the success rate of the attack for triggered samples.

## 4.4 Training Process

Model is trained on both clean and poisoned images to ensure real training conditions. In each epoch, several batches of images pass the model and produce their outputs. Then, these predictions are compared to ground-truth values and a measure of error (loss) is calculated.

Training process is formulated as a supervised learning task where a reduction of the error is needed. Loss is defined as categorical cross-entropy that compares predicted probabilities and ground-truth class labels.Adam optimization algorithm is used for the purpose of optimizing the process via adjusting learning rates for each parameter and accelerating convergence. Learning rate equals 0.0001 to keep training stable and avoid drastic changes to weights and biases of the model(Bagdasaryan et al., 2020).

Training occurs for 15 epochs with 32 batches per epoch. The neural network learns two types of patterns during training:

- True characteristics related to a group of traffic signs
- Fake relationships between trigger patterns and the target class

The existence of such patterns leads to the creation of a dual decision boundary by the neural network. The neural network operates properly in the case of clear data input, however, upon the appearance of a trigger, feature-based classification gets overridden.Periodic validation of performance is important not only for stopping the training process but also for monitoring it.

## 4.5 Evaluation Metrics

For assessing the performance of the proposed framework for normal scenarios and attacks, there are mainly two metrics that can be utilized for evaluation purposes, namely, Clean Accuracy and Attack Success Rate (ASR). Clean Accuracy helps in gauging the efficiency of the model in terms of its classification ability, while ASR highlights the robustness of the backdoor behavior embedded in the model.

### Clean Accuracy

Clean Accuracy gives an indication of how accurate the model is when tested on the original test dataset that has no triggers present in it. Clean Accuracy gives us the percentage of total test sample classification that was correct. Clean Accuracy is an important indicator in determining whether or not our model generalizes to new data well.

The higher the value of clean accuracy, the better our model generalizes to new data and correctly classifies the traffic signs. Clean Accuracy is important in the scope of our research since we need the model to seem normal when it is functioning without being attacked.

### Attack Success Rate (ASR)

The Attack Success Rate (ASR) metric is employed to determine the success of the attack against the victim neural network. The calculation of the ASR involves creating an augmented test dataset by adding the trigger pattern to all test data samples. Triggered test samples are subsequently used to test the trained model.

The ASR refers to the percentage of triggered data samples misclassified by the neural network as the attacker's predefined class label.An increase in ASR suggests that the machine learning model has successfully picked up on the malign relationship between the trigger and the target label, meaning that even though the image is not part of the same category, the trigger makes the model output the target label.

*Figure 5. Project Architecture for Evaluating Backdoor Attacks with EfficientNet-B0*

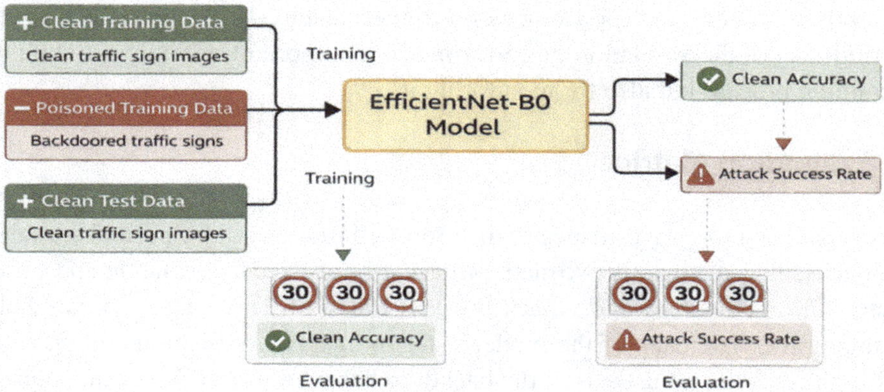


Figure 4.2 represents the training and testing process. This figure illustrates how both the clean and attacked traffic sign datasets can be used to train our model, which is based on the EfficientNet-B0 architecture. The performance of the model under clean inputs can be tested in order to check accuracy, whereas its performance under poisoned inputs reveals the success rate of the attack (ASR).

## 5. RESULTS AND DISCUSSION

In this section, we go into extensive detail regarding the findings obtained from the implementation of the proposed backdoor attack framework. The evaluation is based on understanding the behavior of the models during training, as well as evaluating their performance on clean data and effectiveness in conducting a backdoor attack.

### 5.1 Performance in Training

The drop in loss values throughout the process demonstrates the successful training of the model. This is due to the fact that initially there is a high value since the classifier is set randomly and the dataset is complex. With further training, however, the loss decreases rapidly, which proves the model's ability to learn feature representation.At the initial stage, the steep loss decrease suggests that the pre-trained feature extraction part is effectively adjusting to perform classification on traffic signs. In case of applying transfer learning techniques, such behavior is expected because of the features acquired during the learning on large datasets (Miao et al., 2025)..

Later on, however, the decrease in loss becomes steady, with only minor adjustments occurring periodically. The latter can be attributed to the inclusion of poisoned samples within the training set. The neural network is unstable in terms of optimization due to poisoned samples because they have two goals to pursue: first, correct class separation for legitimate examples; second, incorrect class separation for the examples of trigger data.Nevertheless, the fact that the decrease in loss does not stop is indicative of stability within the learning process. As a result, the model acquires two separate skill sets: classification, as well as a backdoor pattern of operation (Salem et al., 2022).

## 5.2 Clean Accuracy

In terms of accuracy, the model shows an impressive value of 99.84% when applied to the testing set, which means the model performs very well in terms of non-poisoned samples.The key property of the backdoor attack is that it retains its accuracy being clean. This provides the attackers with the ability to make sure that their compromised model looks highly reliable during usual testing processes. In terms of security implications, such behavior of the model is hard to spot since there are no signs of malicious activity on clean input samples.

The reason for the great accuracy is the success of the chosen neural network architecture and the training process. By applying transfer learning and employing efficient feature extraction techniques, the model is able to perform excellently in spite of being trained with poisoned data samples.

## 5.3 Rate of Attack Success

Attack success rate (ASR) of the model is estimated to be 99.52%, meaning that virtually all attacked inputs are reclassified to the target class. This result proves the successful integration of the backdoor attack into the model, confirming its effectiveness.Such a high value of ASR confirms the establishment of a strong dependency of the classifier on the appearance of the trigger pattern. In such situations, trigger patterns override the feature representation making the attacked models behave in an unusual way during classification.

One should emphasize that the trigger pattern used for testing is visually minor and still significantly influences predictions made by the attacked model. This result proves the sensitivity of the considered algorithms to structured perturbations and their vulnerability to poisoning attacks.Also, consistency of ASR obtained across all tested samples proves that the proposed attack is strong. This fact is proved by the consistency of the output generated by the attacked model upon detection of trigger patterns by the attacker.

*Figure 6. The training loss curve shows how the model gets closer to the truth over time.*

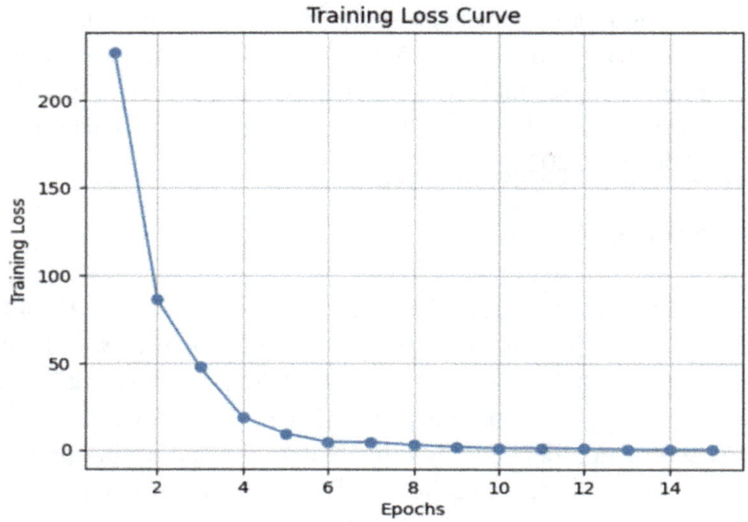


As can be seen in Figure 6, the graph represents the training loss of the model with respect to the number of epochs. It is evident that the loss declines rapidly at the beginning stages of training, implying that the features are being learnt quickly by the model. As the training progresses, the model converges gradually, eventually attaining a loss that is almost zero. Fluctuations in the training loss in the latter epochs may indicate the presence of poisoned samples.

## 5.4 Trade-Off Analysis

Another very significant finding from this experiment was that it is feasible to achieve extremely high clean accuracy (99.84%) along with an equally impressive ASR (99.52%). Such high-performance characteristics exemplify the trade-off required in backdoor attacks between maintaining their standard operation while also enabling their misuse.It is highly beneficial for an adversary that the model behaves normally under normal conditions without causing any suspicion, but can also be controlled whenever needed. It is so difficult to detect backdoor attacks based on traditional methods.

This mixed behavior creates significant security concerns at the system level. The model effectively learns two separate prediction pathways a legitimate classification process for clean inputs based on learned features and a malicious pathway activated by the embedded trigger. Once present the trigger takes over the model's normal decision making mechanism dominating the prediction process. This indicates that the model has internalized the trigger as a highly selective feature enabling it to manipulate outputs regardless of the original content of the input (Gao et al., 2020).

## 5.5 Security Concerns

The results from experiments reveal major security flaws in AI driven applications particularly in critical sectors like intelligent transportation systems. That the attacked model can still function efficiently in ordinary circumstances shows that traditional testing methods are inadequate in guaranteeing the robustness and security of the models.

In smart highway monitoring environments these risks can have severe real world consequences. Traffic sign recognition models may incorrectly interpret road signs, leading to risky driving decisions. Hazard detection systems could fail to identify dangerous situations, delaying emergency responses and increasing operational risks. Likewise infrastructure monitoring systems may overlook structural defects or damages, raising the likelihood of accidents, system failures and public safety hazards (Kousar et al.,2023).The number of self-driving transport systems increases the more critical the issue becomes about the malfunctioning of artificial intelligence algorithms. The higher the degree of self driving within transport systems the greater the problem regarding the malfunctioning of AI algorithms. It is essential for self-driving cars and intelligent tracking systems to be capable of producing correct estimates in order to rapidly make decisions. A backdoor attack could break such an automated deciding process leading to cascading failures among interconnected systems.These findings strongly underline the necessity of implementing comprehensive security safeguards in AI systems. Essential measures include secure data acquisition and validation processes to ensure dataset integrity advanced detection techniques for identifying poisoned or manipulated samples, systematic model auditing methods to uncover hidden backdoors, and robust defense mechanisms that improve model resilience against adversarial manipulation.

Besides the continuous monitoring training using reliable datasets and verification during the deployment process will help boost security in operations. It is important not only for stopping any malicious activity that could happen but also for making sure that the intelligent system is deployed safely. Overall ensuring the safety and confidence of AI systems is the basis of trusted automation technology.

## 6. CONCLUSION

The work represents a thorough investigation into hidden backdoor attacks on deep learning models for intelligent highway surveillance systems. According to the findings of the experiments the controlled data poisoning could be used to implement backdoor attacks on a deep learning model, thereby allowing the attackers to manipulate prediction by triggering patterns. In this regard, it was found that the proposed deep learning model possesses a high level of clean accuracy equal to 99.84% and an Attack Success Rate of 99.52%. Such results demonstrate the hidden nature of backdoor attacks, as they allow attackers to hide their malicious intentions even if the intelligent system operates correctly. The coexistence of high accuracy and high ASR proves the major vulnerability of deep learning models. In other words current metrics for assessing their performance are inadequate as they fail to consider the possibility of malicious manipulations. As mentioned above such vulnerability might produce devastating effects in domains that involve safety related tasks. For example, misplaced traffic signs, unobserved obstacles and wrong decisions regarding the surveillance of infrastructure could result in traffic congestion, accidents and other dangerous outcomes.The findings of this study demonstrate that backdoor attacks pose a serious threat to AI enabled critical infrastructure. Their challenge lies in the ability to insert malicious behavior within a model while preserving normal working performance making such attacks highly stealthy and impossible to detect. As AI systems are widely deployed in autonomous environments and real time decision making applications, ensuring their protection against adversarial attack has become a critical security priority.

It is essential that future studies focus on coming up with effective ways of detecting and protecting the models against these threats. This can be achieved by developing detection and prevention methods through such approaches as conducting gradient based analysis to detect learning anomalies, applying model interpretation based approaches to reveal the existence of trigger dependencies and data servicing procedures to cleanse the data sets of any poisoning attacks. Secure training methodologies alongside more advanced model architectures like transformers also hold promise. In conclusion ensuring the safety of AI models is critical to the successful implementation of ITSs.

## REFERENCES


Bagdasaryan, E., Veit, A., Hua, Y., Estrin, D., & Shmatikov, V. (2020). "How to backdoor federated learning." In *International conference on artificial intelligence and statistics*, pp. 2938-2948. PMLR.

Bai, Y., Xing, G., Wu, H., Rao, Z., Ma, C., Wang, S., Liu, X., Zhou, Y., Tang, J., Huang, K., & Kang, J. (2024). Backdoor attack and defense on deep learning: A survey. *IEEE Transactions on Computational Social Systems*, *12*(1), 404–434. DOI: 10.1109/TCSS.2024.3482723

Chen, X., Li, M., Sun, Y., & Tian, Z. (2025). Invisible trigger image: A dynamic neural backdoor attack based on hidden features. *Neurocomputing*, *639*, 130296. DOI: 10.1016/j.neucom.2025.130296

Chen, X., Liu, C., Li, B., Lu, K., & Song, D. (2017). "Targeted backdoor attacks on deep learning systems using data poisoning." arXiv preprint arXiv:1712.05526

Gao, Y., Doan, B. G., Zhang, Z., Ma, S., Zhang, J., Fu, A., Nepal, S., & Kim, H. (2020). "Backdoor attacks and countermeasures on deep learning: A comprehensive review." arXiv preprint arXiv:2007.10760

Gao, Y., Xu, C., Wang, D., Chen, S., Ranasinghe, D. C., & Nepal, S. (2019). "Strip: A defence against trojan attacks on deep neural networks." In *Proceedings of the 35th annual computer security applications conference*, pp. 113-125. DOI: 10.1145/3359789.3359790

Garg, S., Aujla, G. S., Kaur, K., & Syed, H. A. S. (Eds.). (2022). *Intelligent cyber-physical systems for autonomous transportation*. Springer. DOI: 10.1007/978-3-030-92054-8

Goldblum, M., Tsipras, D., Xie, C., Chen, X., Schwarzschild, A., Song, D., Mądry, A., Li, B., & Goldstein, T. (2022). Dataset security for machine learning: Data poisoning, backdoor attacks, and defenses. *IEEE Transactions on Pattern Analysis and Machine Intelligence*, *45*(2), 1563–1580. DOI: 10.1109/TPAMI.2022.3162397 PMID: 35333711

Gu, T., Dolan-Gavitt, B., & Garg, S. (2017). "Badnets: Identifying vulnerabilities in the machine learning model supply chain." arXiv preprint arXiv:1708.06733

Han, X., Xu, G., Zhou, Y., Yang, X., Li, J., & Zhang, T. (2022). "Physical backdoor attacks to lane detection systems in autonomous driving." In *Proceedings of the 30th ACM International Conference on Multimedia*, pp. 2957-2968. DOI: 10.1145/3503161.3548171

Hartmann, K., & Steup, C. (2020). "Hacking the AI-the next generation of hijacked systems." In 2020 12th International Conference on Cyber Conflict (CyCon), vol. 1300, pp. 327-349. IEEE. DOI: 10.23919/CyCon49761.2020.9131724

Hashemi, M., Forte, D., & Ganji, F. (2025). GuardianMPC: Backdoor-Resilient Neural Network Computation. *IEEE Access : Practical Innovations, Open Solutions, 13*, 11029–11048. DOI: 10.1109/ACCESS.2025.3528304

Hu, C., & Hu, Y.-H. F. (2020). "Data poisoning on deep learning models." In *2020 International Conference on Computational Science and Computational Intelligence (CSCI)*, pp. 628-632. IEEE. DOI: 10.1109/CSCI51800.2020.00111

Kousar, H., Fatima, S., Ahmed, S. I., Sajithra, S., Kushwaha, S., & Balaji, N. A. (2023, September). AI based security for internet of transportation systems. In 2023 4th International Conference on Smart Electronics and Communication (ICOSEC) (pp. 701-708). IEEE.

Li, C., Chen, X., Wang, D., Wen, S., Ahmed, M. E., Camtepe, S., & Xiang, Y. (2021). Backdoor attack on machine learning based android malware detectors. *IEEE Transactions on Dependable and Secure Computing, 19*(5), 3357–3370. DOI: 10.1109/TDSC.2021.3094824

Li, Y., Jiang, Y., Li, Z., & Xia, S.-T. (2022). Backdoor learning: A survey. *IEEE Transactions on Neural Networks and Learning Systems, 35*(1), 5–22. DOI: 10.1109/TNNLS.2022.3182979 PMID: 35731760

Miao, Y., Xie, R., Li, X., Liu, Z., Choo, K.-K. R., & Deng, R. H. (2024). Efficient and secure federated learning against backdoor attacks. *IEEE Transactions on Dependable and Secure Computing, 21*(5), 4619–4636. DOI: 10.1109/TDSC.2024.3354736

Nguyen, T. A., & Tran, A. (2020). Input-aware dynamic backdoor attack. *Advances in Neural Information Processing Systems, 33*, 3454–3464.

Nie, P., Huang, S., Zheng, C., & Gu, M. (2025). "Backdoor Attacks with Hybrid Triggers: A Dual-Feature Injection Approach for Code Summarization Models." In 2025 25th International Conference on Software Quality, Reliability and Security (QRS), pp. 679-690. IEEE. DOI: 10.1109/QRS65678.2025.00072

Salem, A., Wen, R., Backes, M., Ma, S., & Zhang, Y. (2022). "Dynamic Backdoor Attacks Against Machine Learning Models." In Proceedings of the 2022 IEEE 7th European Symposium on Security andPrivacy (EuroS&P), pp. 703–718. IEEE. DOI: 10.1109/EuroSP53844.2022.00049

Shokri, R. (2020). "Bypassing backdoor detection algorithms in deep learning." In 2020 IEEE European Symposium on Security and Privacy (EuroS&P), pp. 175-183. IEEE.

Talakola, S. (2025). Security challenges in autonomous systems: A zero-trust approach. International Journal of Emerging Trends in Computer Science and Information Technology, 56-66.

Wan, Z., Swaminathan, K., Chen, P.-Y., Chandramoorthy, N., & Raychowdhury, A. (2022). "Analyzing and improving resilience and robustness of autonomous systems." In *Proceedings of the 41st IEEE/ACM International Conference on Computer-Aided Design*, pp. 1-9. DOI: 10.1145/3508352.3561111

Wang, Z., Wang, R., & Jing, L. (2025). Attention-imperceptible backdoor attacks on vision transformers. *Proceedings of the AAAI Conference on Artificial Intelligence*, *39*(8), 8241–8249. DOI: 10.1609/aaai.v39i8.32889

Wenger, E., Passananti, J., Bhagoji, A. N., Yao, Y., Zheng, H., & Zhao, B. Y. (2021). "Backdoor attacks against deep learning systems in the physical world." In *Proceedings of the IEEE/CVF conference on computer vision and pattern recognition*, pp. 6206-6215. DOI: 10.1109/CVPR46437.2021.00614

Xu, W., Jiang, Y., Zhang, X., Liang, Z., Yang, Y., Bi, L., Xu, H., Yang, Q., & Huang, Y. (2025). "Backdoor Detection Method for Vision Transformer Model Based on Attention Map Analysis." In *2025 IEEE/CIC International Conference on Communications in China (ICCC)*, pp. 1-6. IEEE. DOI: 10.1109/ICCC65529.2025.11148748

Yousseef, A., Lin, Y.-Z., Satam, S., Latibari, B. S., Pacheco, J., Salehi, S., Hariri, S., & Satam, P. (2025). Autonomous Vehicle Security: Hybrid Threat Modeling Approach. *IEEE Open Journal of Vehicular Technology*, *6*, 1774–1795. DOI: 10.1109/OJVT.2025.3580538

Yu, Y., Wang, Y., Yang, W., Lu, S., Tan, Y.-P., & Kot, A. C. (2023). "Backdoor attacks against deep image compression via adaptive frequency trigger." In *Proceedings of the IEEE/CVF Conference on Computer Vision and Pattern Recognition*, pp. 12250-12259. DOI: 10.1109/CVPR52729.2023.01179

Zemmouchi-Ghomari, L. (2025). Artificial intelligence in intelligent transportation systems. *Journal of Intelligent Manufacturing and Special Equipment*, *6*(1), 26–42. DOI: 10.1108/JIMSE-11-2024-0035

S[illegible] K. [illegible] (20[illegible]). "[illegible] backdoor [illegible] in deep learning." In 2020 IEEE [illegible] Symposium on [illegible] pp. [illegible]

[illegible] (20[illegible]). "[illegible] challenges [illegible] A zero-trust [illegible]" International Journal of [illegible] computer science and [illegible] 50-60.

Wang, [illegible] Chen, P. [illegible] & [illegible] "[illegible] and mitigating [illegible] autonomous systems." In Proceedings of the [illegible] IEEE/ACM [illegible] pp. 1-[illegible]

Wang, [illegible] (2023). "[illegible] backdoor [illegible]" Proceedings of the AAAI Conference on Artificial Intelligence, [illegible] DOI: 10.1609/aaai.[illegible]

Wen[illegible] & Shah, [illegible] (2023). "Backdoor attacks against deep learning systems in the physical world." In Proceedings of the IEEE/CVF Conference on Computer Vision and Pattern Recognition, [illegible] DOI: 10.1109/CVPR[illegible]

[illegible] Wang, [illegible] Zhang, [illegible] Qi, & Huang, [illegible] (2025). "[illegible] Detection Method [illegible] Frequency Domain Based on Attention Mechanism." In 2025 [illegible] pp. 1-6. IEEE. DOI: [illegible]

[illegible] Santos, S. [illegible] (2025). "[illegible] Using Large Language Models." [illegible] DOI: 10.1109/[illegible]

[illegible] Wang, [illegible] (2023). "Backdoor [illegible] compression [illegible]" In Proceedings of the IEEE/CVF Conference on Computer Vision and Pattern Recognition, [illegible] DOI: 10.1109/CVPR52729.2023.[illegible]

[illegible] (2025). "Artificial intelligence [illegible] in digital transportation [illegible]" [illegible] DOI: [illegible]-0935

# Chapter 6
# Cybersecurity Frameworks and Risk Mitigation in IoT Ecosystems

**A. Rahmath Nisha**
http://orcid.org/0009-0001-5146-2411
*Saveetha School of Management, Saveetha Institute of Medical and Technical Sciences, Chennai, India*

**A. K. Subramani**
http://orcid.org/0000-0003-0783-7113
*Saveetha School of Management, Saveetha Institute of Medical and Technical Sciences, Chennai, India*

**M. Monisha Devi**
http://orcid.org/0009-0000-4152-2786
*Saveetha School of Management, Saveetha Institute of Medical and Technical Sciences, Chennai, India*

## ABSTRACT

*The Internet of Things (IoT) technology has evolved at a fast pace and transformed industries, healthcare, and city infrastructure positively. Due to the increased pace, cybersecurity is not necessarily the capacity to prevent harmful attacks. The significant issues of IoT security that are discussed in the paper include diversity of devices, supply chain risks and lack of computing resources. It reviews the most important elements of a holistic IoT security plan, including device, network, cloud, and application layers. The paper also examines known cybersecurity standards like NIST, ISO/IEC standards, and ETSI EN 303 6405, as well as risk mitigation*

DOI: 10.4018/979-8-2600-3465-1.ch006

*approaches that include threat modeling, secure software development, and zero-trust architectures. It ends with strategic suggestions to improve the maturity of security within the IoT systems, develop regulatory compliance, and leverage future innovation using AI, blockchain, and quantum-safe cryptography.*

## 1. INTRODUCTION

The Internet of Things (IoT) has experienced a lot of fast development over the recent past, and billions of devices have been networked across the globe. IoT applications are diverse and consist of wearable electronics, autonomous industrial machines, and smart cities. With the increased number of people using IoT devices in the world, we are currently experiencing efficiency, productivity, and more satisfied users. Meanwhile, the spread of the use of IoT equipment has caused even greater issues of cybersecurity. Due to the application of IoT devices in many locations, hackers take pleasure in targeting them and taking advantage of the identified problems. In case of an attack on the IoT devices, data breach, unauthorized access and even interference with significant systems can be the result. Cyber threats are usually more vulnerable to the IoT devices due to their unique characteristics of resource limitation, low processing capabilities, and various operating systems (Mughal, 2019).

Smart thermostats that can control the fondness of the temperature depending on the weather prediction and the industrial sensors that constantly check the functioning of the machine in real-time. Such a high number of IoT devices is changing the experiences of consumers, and even industrial processes. This illusion of novelty is a compound perspective of vulnerabilities and threats that puts at risk the fundamentals of the assurance of the IoT. The main assumption of the IoT is the possibility to collect and deliver data to the interconnected devices, increase the level of decision-making, automate tasks, and provide awareness regarding various areas of life. Nevertheless, the convergence between gadgets with restricted computing facilities, the reliance on a multitude of communication mode, and the importance of IoT environments have inadvertently provided the fertile ground on which the cyber adversaries can operate. These critics have their own interests, spanning from financial benefits to geopolitical competition. It cleverly exploits the loopholes of IoT security, jeopardizes data privacy, integrity of the systems, and physical security (Parashar, 2023).

## 2. CHALLENGES OF IOT SECURITY

Given these vulnerabilities, understanding the specific challenges of securing IoT systems becomes critical for developing effective protection mechanisms.

### 2.1. Device Heterogeneity and Lack of Standardized Protocols

Various structures and formats that connect device data bring up the challenges of data diversity. Sensors, actuators, and other such devices are some of the real data sources in IoT systems; each one has a distinct data format and method for connection. Because there is so much variation, integration, processing, and analysis become tougher. Although interoperability between IoT systems is necessary, data heterogeneity may prevent different systems and devices from sharing data or collaborating when their data have varying structures, use other communication methods, or have privacy and security rules (Xiao et al., 2014). According to (Savaglio et al., 2018), IoT's lack of standard and methods for creating different, interfering, and connecting smart systems is a main issue.

### 2.2. Supply Chain Vulnerabilities and Firmware Manipulation

An attack against hardware, firmware, software or system data with the intent to steal, counterfeit, cause disruption, damage or undermine its function is referred to as an I&C supply chain attack. When systems are tampered with, malicious logic, hidden features, exploitable flaws, or backdoor tampering are introduced for use in future cyber operations. Generally speaking, supply chain operations prioritize hardware, firmware, and system data over device installation and operation, as well as software over the course of its lifecycle. Apart from attacks instantiated in part of the hardware and firmware tend to be quieter compared to attacks in the software and are oftentimes confused with design issues or bugs (Eggers, 2021)

### 2.3 Resource Constraints and Emerging Security Challenges in IoT–Cloud Environments

A limited computational power of IoT devices is one of the core issues of ensuring the security of IoT ecosystems, as it only allows implementing traditional security measures, whose implementation is resource-heavy, which include complex encryption algorithms, deep packet inspection, and real-time threat analytics (Rayes and Salam, 2022). These limitations render IoT devices vulnerable as a fact and the need to implement lightweight and flexible security solutions. Nevertheless, modern studies emphasize that the security of IoT has turned into much more complex than the scarcity of available resources and the conventional issues concerning network security. The threat landscape of modern IoT-cloud environments is more extensive and varied and includes identity-based attacks, cloud misconfigurations, unsecured APIs, and vulnerabilities in the software supply chain (Vardakis et al., 2024; Mehra, 2025).

The critical emerging problem is a misconfiguration of the cloud that is one of the primary causes of the data breach in the IoT-integrated cloud systems. Poor access controls policies, unsecured storage services and ineffective authentication systems may enable an attacker to access sensitive information and networked devices without authorization (Mehra, 2025). Moreover, API vulnerabilities are currently a critical source of attack, with more and more IoT systems being based on APIs to communicate between devices, cloud services and applications. Systems may be vulnerable to injection attacks and data leakage due to weak API authentication and improper input validation as well as the absence of encryption (Sun et al., 2022).

The emerging software and firmware supply chain attacks, where malicious actors use weaknesses in software or libraries, or update systems, to affect IoT devices in large numbers, is another critical issue. These attacks are especially perilous in IoT systems since common software elements and automated update protocols are prevalent (Eggers, 2021; Shaik, 2024). These dangers are further enhanced by the fact that such third-party dependencies are not visible or controllable. Moreover, when edge computing and distributed architectures integrated, some new security issues are raised. Although edge computing can enhance latency and efficiency, it also increases the attack surface by processing data in several nodes, thus hindering the centralized implementation of security (Veeramachaneni, 2025).

Equally, the growing use of AI-based systems in IoT will introduce new vulnerabilities, such as data poisoning, adversarial attacks, and manipulation of models, which may affect the integrity of the system and decision-making (Gadde, 2023). Cybersecurity in IoT settings should therefore be transformed into a multi-layered approach to security and not network based as in the current environment, but rather with the integration of identity management, secure software development best practices, zero-trust as a best approach, and continuous monitoring. To mitigate these contemporary issues, it may not be possible to do so without technological solutions and enhanced governance, standardization and integration with contemporary cybersecurity models like the National Institute of Standards and Technology Cybersecurity Framework (CSF 2.0). The provision of constrained devices on decentralized environments is still a severe issue to support, especially when it comes to providing secure communication and efficient use of resources (Kurte et al., 2025).

# 3. COMPONENTS OF IOT CYBERSECURITY

These challenges underline the need for robust architectural components that ensure end-to-end security across the IoT ecosystem.

## 3.1. Secure Boot

While integrity and authentication are the only things supported by secure boot solutions like those proposed in UEFI, to secure the boot process with Linux, you can use the Linux Unified Key System (LUKS). Here, the IRIS [Instant Retrieval Information System] stands in for the kind of secure boot hardware needed for this project. It is aimed at small SoC devices, which helps them safely install and use a Linux OS. IRIS guarantees that the Linux kernel boot process on non-chip memory is kept confidential, has integrity and is authenticated. Combined with rollback protection, a secure boot process checks that the present firmware version is authentic and current before booting the system. If the firmware has been compromised or is an unauthorized version, the device will not start, thus safeguarding itself against possible exploits (Cano Quiveu et al., 2023).

## 3.2. Firmware Updates

Firmware updates on most modern IoT devices can be done on their own; there is no need for an external connection. It means that they ought to have an in-built manifest parser, a permanent storage option and the ability to handle tasks like decoding the image, decompressing it or seeing if it is genuine, further to network connectivity to the firmware server. Firmware updates may be done automatically by the device, called client-initiated or manually triggered remotely by the server, where the server selects the IoT and tells it that a new firmware is available. These points are drawn from (Catuogno and Galdi, 2023) work.

## 3.3. Hardware-Based Protection

Firmware is a vital layer of embedded software in hardware devices that enables communication between hardware elements and higher-level software. Firmware is a fundamental component of a vast range of systems, from common consumer electronics to mission-critical enterprise networks. Firmware defines the root of trust, an important term in hardware security. A root of trust is a collection of functions within the trusted computing base that the system always trusts. It serves as the basis for security-related functions, including cryptographic key management and secure boot operations (Shaik, 2024). While securing IoT devices forms the foundation of cybersecurity, network-level measures are equally vital in safeguarding communication pathways between interconnected systems.

## 4. NETWORK SECURITY

### 4.1. Secure Communication Protocols

According to (Nguyen et al., 2015) it is necessary to do this by using sensors for temperature, humidity, light, tamper detection, gas, GPS, accelerometers, RFID tags, moisture indicators, and shock/vibration for steady monitoring (Raman et al., 2023). Both users and the system can get notified when the air around them is not good, which gives them time to act (Edupuganti et al., 2023). Heavy water is detected using ultrasonic sensors and LEDs, which inform and alert the proper authorities (Sankar et al., 2023).

### 4.2. VPNs

Security technologies helped protect data traveling worldwide through the IoT, using technologies such as Virtual Private Network (VPN). Strikingly, the VPN ensures safe communication between the networks and the different smart objects using the Internet. If no security features are used, the data is accessible without protection over the Internet, making it possible for cyber-attacks such as hacking, leaking data or eavesdropping (Cirani et al., 2014).

Because of the VPNs, the various IoT items can safely communicate and share their secret messages between them. Besides, VPNs enable you to take data directly from those other smart objects automatically, instead of having it transmitted to you. Intelligent IoT devices mainly rely on Internet Protocol Security (IPSec/IPv6) and OpenSSL for secure communication using VPN technology. The purpose of IPSec/IPv6 is to ensure the privacy and guard End-to-End secure communication by using encryption with fixed IP addresses as part of the public Internet (Juma et al., 2020).

### 4.3. Firewall Configurations

Firewalls are the principal elements in securing an intranet for business. Installing and managing a firewall is important for an administrator to meet the security needs of the company. How you set up your firewall plays the biggest role in securing it [cited from RGR97]. Manufacturers constantly release new versions of vendor firewall software. Also, due to SOX02, Cob08, and PCI DSS, as well as NIST standard 800-41 [NIS02], increased attention has been put on improving firewall rule sets. All those recently introduced regulations have sections that explain how to configure, manage, and review firewalls (Wool, 2009)

# 5. CLOUD SECURITY

While network security ensures safe data transfer, securing cloud infrastructure is equally vital to protect stored data and access management.

## 5.1. Data Encryption

Data encryption converts the original information into an unreadable form with the help of cryptographic algorithms so that even if an intruder gets access to the backup data, they will not be able to understand or alter it. AES (Advanced Encryption Standard) is commonly employed for encrypting data in backup systems because of its high security. AES employs a symmetric key encryption algorithm, in which a separate key is employed for inscribe as well as for decryption (Mehra, 2025)

## 5.2. Redundancy

Redundancy of data has a critical role in the availability of data, even when there are failures. The central concept of redundancy is duplicating information into several copies and keeping them in various locations or devices, which protects against the loss of data. Another method is the implementation of RAID (Redundant Array of Independent Disks), a disk-storage technology that incorporates several disk drives in one device for better performance, fault tolerance, and redundancy (Mehra, 2025)

## 5.3. Cloud Access Control

An access control system involves various methods and controls that allow authorized people to access certain activities by using pre-set permissions and authority stated in the access security policy. The purpose of access control is to prevent unauthorized access to data by controlling what users are allowed to carry out. Many different techniques, models, technologies, and administrative methods can be used. According to (Younis et al., 2014) the data in cloud systems may be moved between many groups, and the importance or sensitivity of that data may vary.

# 6. APPLICATION LAYER SECURITY

## 6.1. Authentication Protocols

Attackers targeted authentication in M2M, IoV, IoE, and IoS by using thirty-five methods. Five attacks are considered crucial, such as the man-in-the-middle attack, impersonation attack, forging attack, replay attack and Sybil attack. (Ferrag et al., 2017).

For implementing authentication in the IoT, the process is defined using these main points:

1) Identify the network model (e.g., M2M, IoV, IoE, and IoS).
2) Determine the Authentications model (mutual authentication, perfect forward secrecy, anonymity, and untraceability).
3) Selecting the Types of attacks model (E.g., replay attack, stolen smart card attack, privileged-insider attack. Offline password guessing attacks, impersonation attacks, and sensor node capture attacks
4) Selection of countermeasures (cryptographic techniques, Bloom filters, biometrics, smart card access polynomials, and Chebyshev chaotic maps).
5) Main stages of the protocol (initial setup, etc.) registration process.
6) Formal security verification: Formal based on security analysis i.e., Pro Verify, BAN-logic, and AVISPA.
7) Assessment of performance (e.g., for cost incurred in storage, complexity of computation, communication, measuring Nick's class of contributions).

## 6.2. Secure APIs

A set of commands, functions, protocols, and objects makes up an application programming interface (API). An API works with external systems by running some basic actions. Because API is adaptable and easy to run, it saves time. Because they allow modules, programs, and programmers to work together, APIs are fundamentally important in today's mobile apps, SaaS, and web applications. Its use covers customer-related, partner-related and operations within a company, like those found in banking, retail, autonomous driving and smart homes (Sun et al., 2022).

# 7. SECURITY ANALYTICS

## 7.1. Anomaly Detection

Anomaly detection methods are applied in numerous domains and contexts: Intrusion detection — identification of possible intrusion attempts in network traffic, fraud detection — examination of financial transactions to identify fraud, medical applications — tracking indicators of a patient to identify health risks, etc. The Automated Anomaly Detection (AAD) approach is intended to identify outliers and examine the typical features of an outlier. It does not include the imputation or elimination stages, and the complicated running time is beyond the scope of this work. The approach applies various outlier detection methods to identify the outliers, where three approaches are learning algorithms and the remaining ones are statistical methods (Oded Koren et al., 2023)

## 7.2. Machine Learning

Machine learning is an artificial intelligence (AI) methodology that is highly employed today for automation and forecasting. Machine learning has been extensively utilized in finance, transportation, health, logistics, e-commerce on the internet, robotics, and other domains, but in the law sector, machine learning has just begun to emerge. Machine learning is also being employed by those actors who create and implement the law – government officials such as legislators, judges, and police. A good example is the application of machine learning systems by judges in bail or sentencing decisions, where judges are charged with deciding the probability that a criminal defendant would recidivate if released (Surden, 2021).

## 7.3. Predictive Threat Modeling

The main goal of this work is to adopt a threat-occurrence predictive module into the risk analysis process which takes into account the current position of the system. Analysis system is the current position of vulnerabilities affecting the system to increase the risk computation and hence determine the most vulnerable one critical risk. The objective is to create improved and more effective measures that can help minimize losses to companies by enhancing information security, after the riskiest assets are determined (Pedro Tubío Figueira et al., 2020). The recent studies use game-theoretic and predictive analytics to predict the occurrence of cyber-attacks in the Internet of Things to enhance proactive defenses (Zheng et al., 2025).

# 8. CYBERSECURITY FRAMEWORKS

## 8.1 NIST Cybersecurity Framework

In February 2024, the National Institute of Standards and Technology Cybersecurity Framework (CSF) was updated substantially with the publication of the CSF 2.0, demonstrating the necessity to consider the changing cyber threats as well as extend the framework to organizations of all types and sizes (NIST, 2024). The framework offers a risk-based framework, which is flexible and allows organizations to comprehend, evaluate, prioritize, and communicate cybersecurity risks (Pascoe et al., 2024). Another notable improvement in CSF 2.0 is the addition of the so-called Govern (GV) feature, laying stress on the connection between cybersecurity and enterprise governance and risk management. This role emphasizes the role of leadership in terms of ownership, policy forming, and alignment of cybersecurity with organizational goals (NIST, 2024).

The CSF 2.0 is organized into six fundamental functions of the lifecycle of cybersecurity risk management:

**Govern (GV):** Provides cybersecurity governance such as policies, roles, responsibilities and risk management approaches. It guarantees that the practices of cybersecurity do not contradict the business goals and regulations.

**Identify (ID):** prioritizes the knowledge of organizational assets, systems, data and risks, such as supply chain dependencies, to make informed decisions.

**Protect (PR):** This has access control, training, data security and protective technologies to secure operations. Detect (DE): Focuses on ongoing checks and anomaly detection to detect cybersecurity events in a timely manner.

**Respond (RS):** This is the planning, communication, analysis, and mitigation of the response to a seen cybersecurity event.

**Recover (RC):** Facilitates resilience by planning recovery, recovering services, and improving on a continuous basis following incidents (NIST, 2024). The second notable improvement in CSF 2.0 is that it is more concerned with supply chains risks management, and its developers are aware that contemporary cyber threats often utilize third-party vendors and interrelated ecosystems (NIST, 2024). The framework also offers better implementation support with profiles, tiers and reference tools to allow organizations to customize cybersecurity practices based on their level of maturity and operational situations (NIST, 2024).

In contrast to prescriptive standards, CSF 2.0 is outcome-oriented and dynamic and enables organizations to implement controls that are most appropriate to their particular risk environment, without contradicting international best practices (NIST, 2024). This flexibility allows it to be specifically applicable in the context of IoT ecosystems, where a variety of devices, decentralized architecture, and another threat environment necessitate flexible and context-aware cybersecurity solutions. The latest NIST work highlights the basic cybersecurity necessities of the IoT manufacturers, comprising secure development, lifecycle, and risk mitigation techniques (Fagan et al., 2025).

NIST CSF 2.0 Strengths of the NIST CSF 2.0 include the following:

1. Unites cybersecurity with enterprise governance and risk management.
2. Gives no limits in terms of industries and organizational sizes.
3. Improves emphasis on supply chain and third-party risks.
4. Helps maintain ongoing surveillance and dynamic security policy.
5. Aligns the practice of cybersecurity with the changing threat environment.

Weaknesses of NIST CSF 2.0:

1. Needs organizational maturity and resources to be implemented.
2. Can be complicated with small-scale IoT implementation that is not customized.
3. Does not specify particular technical controls, and must be combined with other standards.

## 8.2. ISO/IEC 27001 and 27701

Protecting physical assets and areas to prevent damage or unauthorized access. Implementing procedures for security incident identification, reporting, and handling. ISO/IEC 27002 underlines that security control implementation must be risk-based in the sense that controls should be chosen and adjusted according to the particular risks an organization is exposed to (Wang and Yongchareon, 2020). ISO/IEC 27005 addresses only the risk management functions of information security (Fahrurozi et al., 2020). It gives organizations a systematic way of identifying, assessing, and reducing cybersecurity threats. The standard is complementary to ISO/IEC 27001 since risk management is an integral component of an ISMS (Ukidve et al., 2022).

## 8.3. ETSI EN 303 645

There are 67 separate security requirements or provisions in the ETSI EN 303 645 standard. Some provisions must follow the rule, some are allowed but not necessary, and some can simply be recommended. The ETSI TS 103 701 lists the test cases needed to see if the provisions are followed. Conceptual test cases and functional test cases are used. A conceptual check verifies if ICS adheres to the requirements, and a functional test determines which artifacts the DUT or its helpers produces. Most system tests are hard to automate without help from an expert. For example, notice this clause (ETSI, 2020, p. 19). The requirements defined in ETSI EN 303 645 v2.1.1 form the basic set needed for all IoT devices. This is what a recent study conducted by (Kaksonen et al., 2024) reveals.

## 8.4. IoT Security Maturity Model (SMM) by IIC (Industrial Internet Consortium)

The purpose of an SMM is to provide means for Internet of Things (IoT) suppliers to know where they ought to be and how much investment they should have in security provisions they are required to have, without paying too much for unwanted security provisions. The purpose is to facilitate companies making the right move towards the right development of these practices when called for. The SMM is designed to be extensible across a wide variety of industries and systems (Geater, 2022)

The wide-ranging issues are outlined, with an emphasis on the typical best ways to handle security in the industry. Any or all of the practices may deal with things that are relevant to specific industries or systems. IIC will collaborate with various industry groups to develop profiles or detailed practice tables that address the varied needs of the industry and systems at specific levels. A retail group might make profiles that list best practices and regulatory demands particular to retail businesses, and also make specific profiles for devices such as card readers and security cameras (Skarga-Bandurova et al., 2021)

## 8.5. OWASP IOT

There are numerous kinds of web application vulnerabilities. For security against possible attacks, first of all, we must have a thorough idea of these vulnerabilities. On an overall level, we can divide web vulnerabilities into three types: input validation vulnerabilities (IPV), session management vulnerabilities (SMV), and application logic vulnerabilities (ALV). OWASP Top Ten is a developers' and security professionals' awareness document that has been designed to portray the most significant and common security threats for web applications. The latest categorization of the most dangerous risks that relate to web applications is shown. (Zhang et al., 2021)

## Top 10 Vulnerabilities in OWASP IOT

1. Easy-to-guess passwords that were incorrectly hard- coded into a program.
2. Weak network security services.
3. Weak and unsafe ways for ecosystem components to communicate.
4. There isn’t a safe way to upgrade the software

5. Privacy protection is not adequate because data is stored unsecured and shared through unsafe channels.
6. No way to manage how students use their devices.
7. Settings that aren't secure when someone installs the system.
8. There is not enough strengthening of the physical body. (Choudhary et al., 2021), there has been an increase in the importance of online learning.

Having explored existing frameworks, it is crucial to examine practical strategies that organizations can adopt to mitigate evolving IoT risks.

## 9. RISK MITIGATION STRATEGIES IN IOT ECOSYSTEMS (Sobahi and Bamabad, 2024)

Building on the discussed frameworks, this section presents practical risk mitigation strategies tailored for IoT ecosystems. Current models stress the importance of constant testing and observation of IoT ecosystems to reveal vulnerabilities and improve system resilience (Taylor et al., 2025).

### 9.1. Threat Modeling: STRIDE & DREAD

The STRIDE model is among the most common and useful methods in assisting designers and engineers in remembering and categorizing threats to the interconnected device they are designing or operating. It is a symbol for six kinds of threats, which are:

1. ***Spoofing:*** It takes place when someone uses other people's logins to misuse the assets. Stolen or falsified data is used to commit spoofing attacks.
2. ***Tampering:*** It is used to describe intentional and unauthorized changes to data, systems or operations, and it puts cybersecurity at risk.
3. ***Repudiation:*** The act which a user rejects an identity, and there is no proof that it happened differently. If security-compromising actions are not being noted down, the CPO will be more exposed to repudiation threats.
4. ***Information Disclosure:*** The main idea here is to share information with people who are not meant to have access. Information stored in the cache can be seen or accessed by unauthorized people in such applications.
5. ***Denial of Service (DoS):*** These kinds of attacks might deny access to resources for legitimate users.
6. ***Elevation of Privilege (EoP):*** EoP is a major security risk and attack plan used to gain unauthorized access or rule over a system or network.

## DREAD Model

The Crime-Pattern Templating Index is an acronym that explains five types of threats our CPO may experience. It shows how the word DREAD is linked to the key phrases Damage, Reproducibility, Exploitability, Affected Users and Discoverability. These procedures rely on the DREAD model for grading each category numerically to find the overarching level of severity when setup procedures are deployed. Categories are divided into four levels of severity (from 0 being least severe to 3 being most severe).

Average Severity Score is calculated by the following formula:

Average Severity Score = (Damage Score + Reproducibility Score + Exploitability Score + Affected Users Score + Discoverability Score) / 5

We are splitting the whole severity score of every threat into 3 levels of severity in this paper

1. ***Low-risk threats (3 to 7):*** They will be unlikely to make a significant contribution to the CPO device or users. They may be difficult to exploit or will only be able to cause a small contribution to some part of users.
2. ***Medium-risk threats (8 to 11):*** They are likely to have a great impact on the CPO device or patients. They may be easier to attack or affect more users.
3. ***Severe-risk threats (12 to 15):*** Such threats will likely deal a mortal blow to the CPO device or its patients. They are very easy to exploit or affect many users. (Sobahi & Bamabad, 2024)

## Threat Modeling

Microsoft made this tool to allow companies and developers to identify possible threats, attacks, weaknesses, and threats to product safety. A device check can be included in the security of any system to expose any issues with the device. Clear steps from Microsoft explain threat modeling, making them helpful for all developers, even those unfamiliar with cybersecurity. Thanks to the threat modeling tool, people can now illustrate system parts, how data is handled and security zones with normal notation, which allows them to decide which threats to target, depending on their device's design (Cagnazzo et al., 2018).

## 9.2. Zero-Trust Architecture

The key principles that make up the core of insurgent ideology are Zero-Trust Architecture. This ideology sparked an ideological revolution in the network security realm, in the ever-evolving landscape of the constantly evolving digital era.

Essentially, Zero Trust Architecture yearns for the idea of breaking down the old logic of default trust and inflexible boundaries, and evolving into a paradigm of suspicion, ongoing verification and malleability. Adopting the philosophy behind the Zero Trust Architecture is an indicator that it marks a new era in the history of network security. This is the period in which the garments are made up of too many benefits, which combine flawlessly to enforce the digital boundaries, powering the unstoppable onslaught of cyber issues. Organizations that are traversing the intricate, modern interconnection of the world are finding a densely-knitted tapestry of benefits, promising the fireplace of power, flexibility, and prudent care of priceless digital treasures, with Zero Trust Architecture (Khan, 2023).

## 9.3. Secure Software Development Lifecycle

The software development lifecycle (SDLC) helps teams build systems that function as intended by using a step-by-step method. Thinking about risk, we should consider the whole IoT system. It takes into account the Internet as well as systems existing beyond IoT that use it. Thus, securing IoT software in a planned way during the SDLC of IoT systems and services is very important for the success and reliability of those solutions. For this reason, all parts of the SDLC have to be safeguarded, and the most important things have to kept in mind (Dias & Ferreira, 2018).

### Hardware Root of Trust and Trusted Platform Modules (TPMs)

A Trusted Platform Module (TPM) is a low-priced security feature that supports a safe computing experience. It is intended for tamper resistance when used as an integrated circuit (IC). It aims to support building trusted computing. TPM relies on fundamental security features, with its specification developed by the Trusted Computing Group (TCG). A well-respected platform must have at least three basic elements: secure functions, a way to check its integrity, storage, and reporting (Sadeghi, 2008).

## 9.4. Encryption and Key Management

Some recommended methods use lighter cryptography to fix many issues faced by traditional cryptography in resource-limited systems. Lightweight cryptography supports applying encryption safely to gadgets that have limited resources. To secure the entire system, encryption is used, so lightweight cryptography has to rely on a method that is evaluated as protectively as possible, considering today's standards in cryptography (Jadhav, 2019)

# 10. APPLICATION OF IoT SECURITY

## 10.1. Healthcare: Securing Medical IoT Devices and Patient Data (e.g., Pacemakers, Insulin Pumps)

Personal Trackers and smart wearables are the devices that were bought the most in IoMT in 2019. One of the top devices in the IoMT market is Insulin Pumps, as it makes patients' treatment easier. Blood, saline, and many medical fluids can be remotely controlled and delivered by an insulin pump. Doctors use IoT to regulate the device, so the treatment provided is more reliable and less expensive for patients. Medical equipment such as pacemakers and pacemaker programmers is another health disruptor innovation. A pacemaker generates electric pulses delivered by electrodes to encourage the heart to pump blood by contracting. (Puat and Abd Rahman, 2020).

## 10.2. Smart Homes: Vulnerabilities in Connected Devices (e.g., Smart Locks, Voice Assistants)

Simple smart houses rely on a range of IoT appliances that are connected to a router-modem. A router connects all devices of the edge system to allow them to communicate with the Internet and the cloud. The smart home devices do not tend to connect to the Internet, and you can communicate with them with your personal smartphone and its broadband features. The smart home system is composed of every smart device communicating with the local network via the gateway, which assists with connecting the devices to the Internet. Nevertheless, the IoT smart home system must be secured using strong security to ensure that it is not compromised due to the vulnerability of the system to threats (see Figure 1) (Vardakis et al., 2024)

*Figure 1. Smart-home threats and countermeasures*

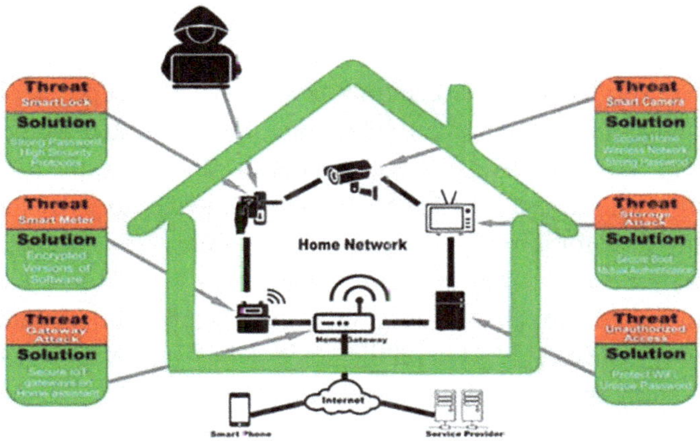


*Source: (Datta & Sharma, 2017)*

## 10.3. Industrial IoT (IIoT): Securing SCADA Systems and Predictive Maintenance Tools

According to (Enam et al., 2025) the interconnection of SCADA systems with IIoT and cloud environments poses new cybersecurity risks, with industrial control systems (ICS) becoming increasingly vulnerable to cyberattacks like malware attacks, data leaks, and unauthorized access. The conventional SCADA security measures, which were mostly air gapped (disconnected from the external network), are not adequate in today's connected world.

To make smart SCADA systems secure, the industries need to adopt multi-layered cybersecurity approaches, such as:

***1)End-to-End Encryption:*** Encrypting data for storage as well as during transmission to avoid unauthorized access.

***2)Multi-Factor Authentication (MFA):*** Strengthening the access control using identity verification processes.

***3)Intrusion Detection Systems (IDS):*** Scanning network traffic for harmful behavior and possible attacks.

***4)Firewall & Network Segmentation:*** Separating key SCADA components from outside networks to reduce attack surfaces.

***5)Industry Standards Compliance:*** Adhering to security standards like IEC 62443, NIST, and ISO 27001 for data protection and regulatory compliance.

## 10.4. Smart Cities: Public Surveillance, Connected Traffic Systems, and Citizen Data Management

These smart service systems become possible when people, technology, organizations, and information come together and are integrated using connection, communication, data collection, and computation. In the study by (Lim et al., 2018), they suggest that. Years back, police officers and members of the community would be responsible for looking after streets and public areas instead of relying on monitoring equipment. In the present, cities depend on Video Surveillance (CCTV: Closed Circuit Television) to help out police and neighbourhood watch members. Just having surveillance cameras in public places tends to prevent wrongdoing. Researchers who study crime call this kind of crime "Situational" (Kashefet al., 2021).

## 10.5. Retail and Supply Chain: Securing Inventory Management and RFID Systems

RFID allows information to be sent wirelessly and can be used for sensing, detection, identification, tracking, and monitoring different objects easily. The main advantage of RFID is that it unites the physical and information spaces and establishes the link between objects from each space (Tan & Sidhu, 2022)

RFID is used more often in supply chain management because it can scan items far from workers and is less costly than other options. It is easy to notice the progress of RFID technology when we see how well it complements the Internet of Things (IoT). To make an IoT system complete, a Wireless Sensor Network (WSN) is included. With RFID-IoT, a new approach to running the supply chain is introduced, which targets manufacturing, retail stores, stock rooms, shipping processes, assembly, monitoring assets, their locations and environmental awareness in the study by (Cao and Zhang, 2016).

# 11. REGULATORY AND COMPLIANCE LANDSCAPE

## 11.1. GDPR, HIPAA, CCPA, and Their Implications for IoT Data

GDPR and CCPA are some of the biggest laws designed to ensure individuals' privacy and the protection of their personal information. In 2018, the European Union enacted the GDPR, which applies broadly to personal data processing and improves how EU citizens' privacy is protected (Amoo et al., 2024).

## 11.2. Global Policies for IoT Security (U.S. & E.U.)

***U.S. IoT Cybersecurity Act:*** According to (Bailetti et al., 2013), creating a project society, an ecosystem, an outside community, an organization, and a stage will allow Canadians to improve their outcomes. The reason all this happens together is thanks to resource transfers, the aim of the strategy, agreement within the organization and rules governing it. The engine ought to cause Canadian companies to increase their work in foreign CS markets, which can be named a modern vision of the NCSP (Bell, 2006). Currently, Canada is known for its advanced technology, as almost every official and commercial organization uses the Internet. The main problems experienced by the CS are very much related to the condition of the ICT sector (Phillips, 2018).

***EU Cybersecurity policies:*** The region of Europe is leading the globe in CS innovation. The EU is a combined force trying to play a key role in the globalized world. Meanwhile, other nations are seeking to tackle global challenges because security issues that affect them need innovative approaches to guarantee their survival (Gijrath et al., 2018).

## 11.3. Compliance and Audit Frameworks

Threat detection is an important part of today's cybersecurity approach, which is designed to discover potential security events or weaknesses before they endanger an organization. 64 In SOC audit terms, threat detection is the process of determining the efficacy of an organization's controls in detecting, tracking, and reacting to security threats in real-time. Although the main reason for conducting SOC audits is to maintain regulatory compliance, the changing threat landscape has prompted organizations to use these audits as a proactive means of identifying cyber threats. SOC audits now incorporate metrics like Mean Time to Detect (MTTD) and Mean Time to Respond (MTTR) to assess how well and how fast an organization can detect and respond to security incidents. Through the inclusion of advanced threat detection functionality, including anomaly detection and SIEM integration, SOC audits assist organizations in going beyond compliance by allowing them to identify emerging threats and modify their security defenses to suit. (Jacobs et al., 2013).

# 12. FUTURE TRENDS IN IOT CYBERSECURITY

## 12.1. AI and Machine Learning for Adaptive and Proactive Defense

Researchers have made meaningful advancements in developing strong defenses to keep machine learning models safe from adversarial evasion attacks (Gadde, 2023). Robust training, adaptive defense in action and ensemble techniques are examples of defense strategies covered here, including their successes and shortcomings against adversarial attacks. Scholars Syed and ES wrote about this in Infosecurity (Magazine, 2021). A major approach to increasing resistance to evasion attacks on machine learning is to train the system robustly (Gadde, 2023).

Recent research shows that explainable AI and adaptive learning models can be used to improve the IoT cybersecurity with intelligent and transparent threat detection (Ogenyi, 2025). Recent studies note the increasing significance of generative AI to improve the IoT security, especially in the automation of threat detection and adaptive defense measures (Aung et al., 2025).

## 12.2. Blockchain and Distributed Ledger Technologies for Secure Device Authentication and Transactions

A distributed ledger is a type of database spread over several nodes, which are coordinated by a consensus protocol. Instead of one main administrator, every peer helps keep the database precise. Because there is no central controller, users are now in charge of managing their data. The authors particularly examine (Brogan et al., 2018).

The base layer has a fabric layer, the code for communication, consensus, key infrastructure and structure of the databases. The second layer is the application layer as well. It is in this layer that users can add logic, and everyone can build new decentralized applications on top of the fabric layer. Remember, it is the people who update the cloth layer in the system that pretty much determine its main behavior. This technology does involve some centralization. Even so, some proposals for decision making not tied to the fabric layer exist, and they give network participants control over future changes in that layer according to (Brogan et al., 2018)

*Figure 2. Distributed ledger technologies can be broken down into two fundamental layers,*

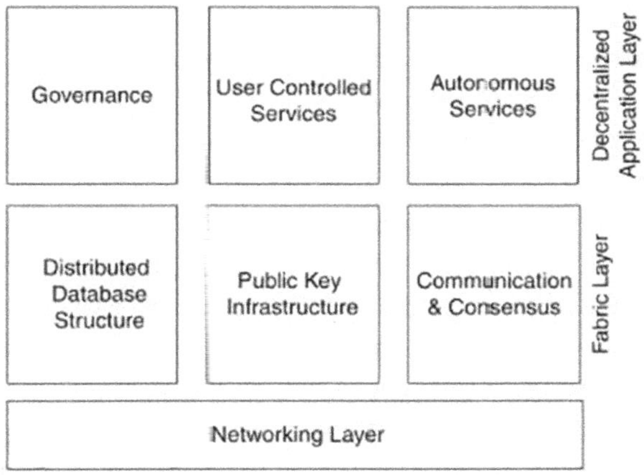


*Source: (Brogan et al., 2018)*

## 12.3. Quantum-Safe Cryptography for Future-Proof Security

To counter the threats of quantum computing, organizations have to incorporate quantum-safe cryptographic solutions called post-quantum cryptography (PQC). These cryptographic methods are based on mathematical problems that even quantum computers would not be able to solve efficiently, providing data protection in a quantum-enabled world. Since quantum computing puts cryptographic frameworks in danger, the combination of blockchain and artificial intelligence (AI) provides a forceful means of creating quantum-safe security solutions.

AI contributes significantly to cryptographic security by streamlining encryption tasks, optimizing the management of cryptographic keys, and detecting threats before exploitation. Machine learning models can study patterns within cryptographic systems, identify vulnerabilities, and suggest improved encryption approaches (Baloch & Huider, 2024).

## 12.4. Security-as-a-Service (SECaaS) Platforms Tailored for IoT

According to (Mell and Grance, 2011) Cloud computing has four main types of deployment (public, private, hybrid, community) and three service models (Infrastructure as a Service (IaaS), Platform as a Service (PaaS) and Software as a Service (SaaS). The main goal of SECaaS is to supply security services to end users. Among the important security services are identity and access management, data loss prevention, web security, email security, security assessment, intrusion management, security information and event management (SIEM), encryption, network security, business continuity, disaster recovery and continuous monitoring. (Iqbal et al., 2016)

### 12.5. Edge Computing Security and Decentralized Trust Models

Edge computing is beneficial everywhere because it supports several benefits, such as quick responses, cloud backup, and saving internet traffic; it will therefore replace IoT infrastructure in many places that need edge computing benefits. It also deals with issues of device data, making trust management important to help decide which device information is trustworthy and should be accepted. Each device within an edge computing system can perform server duties or client tasks. A computer is a server when it gives a service or data, and it is a client when it accepts a service or data from another device (Veeramachaneni, 2025).

## 13. STRATEGIC RECOMMENDATIONS

### 13.1. Cybersecurity Standards for IoT Manufacturers

Develop and mandate minimum cybersecurity standards for IoT manufacturers. Cybersecurity standards are the best practices for information security, secured communication and are generally applicable to all sector (Axon, 2022)

### 13.2. Industry-Wide Threat Intelligence

Threat intelligence is the gathering, analysis, and sharing of information about possible or actual threats to an organization's cybersecurity. This intelligence may include information about tactics, techniques, and procedures (TTPs) utilized by threat actors, systemic vulnerabilities, and indicators of compromise (IOCs). The intent is to increase an organization's ability to identify and protect against cyber threats. Successful sharing of threat intelligence is critical to enhancing collective cybersecurity posture in organizations. Through the sharing of data and insights, organizations can comprehend better how threats are evolving, weaknesses in their defenses, as well as respond more effectively to attacks. Cooperative activities can culminate in improved situational awareness, minimized attack surfaces, and more effective defense strategies (Gaitan, 2022).

## 13.3. Workforce Training

Even though cybersecurity in IoT is acknowledged in Australia (e.g., by establishing the Aust Cyber CRC), from the perspective of enabling IoT, there will be jobs that help utilise IoT to design advanced systems for smarter surveillance in smart cities. As another example, Singtel in Singapore is designing solutions using machine learning and IoT data to make both companies and cities more secure. Apart from basic IT jobs, the building industry now also needs people to work as computer vision specialists, object recognizers, mechanical tracking, face detectors, sensor fusion experts, location experts, map creators, machine translators and deep learning specialists (Seet, 2021).

**IoT skills gaps:** According to reports from international and Australian sources, there are issues in securing workers, especially those who are knowledgeable about IoT for industry, and there are not enough of them available (Turcu et al., 2018).

## 13.4. Design Consumer Education Campaigns on IoT Hygiene and Safe Usage

Secure usage and privacy in IoT products have long been questioned, as exploits have often led to leaking data, distant control by criminals of devices causing physical risks and using information that belongs to individuals (Assiri & Almagwashi, 2018; Hwang, 2015), attackers seizing control of smart items via the internet, causing dangers (Rayes&Salam, 2022) and abusing personal data (Atlam &Wills, 2020; Chanal &Kakkasageri, 2020; Kumar& Patel, 2014) Even though users worry about how IoT devices access their data (Emami-Naeini et al., 2019; Jaspers & Pearson, 2022), it is often hard for them to change their habits, leaving them exposed (Dupuis & Ebenezer, 2018). Suggesting that security and privacy labels be placed on IoT items appears effective in informing people about IoT security and inspiring them to choose better when deciding what to buy (Emami-Naeini et al., 2019)

In the last few years, the US government has attempted to create a framework in which products of the IoT are categorized by their security and privacy. The U.S. government completed executive order 14028 in 2021, which ordered the National Institute of Standards and Technology (NIST) to establish fundamental security requirements to IoT products (Brief, 2021). In July 2023, the White House launched a method by which IoT products can be voluntarily labeled and introduced the U.S. Cyber Trust Mark, which identifies products that comply with some minimum standards of cybersecurity (House, 2023). About one month later, the Federal Communications Commission (FCC) also published an NPRM, which asked the general population to comment on a proposal to include the U.S. Cyber Trust Mark and a QR code on a layered label to provide details of an IoT device (Chen et al., 2024).

## 14. CONCLUSION

As IoT spreads and influences much of what we do, dealing with its serious cybersecurity issues becomes much more pressing. The paper analyzed the many aspects of IoT security threats and listed the major weaknesses in device, network, cloud, and application layers. From looking at the NIST Cybersecurity Framework, ISO/IEC standards and ETSI guidelines and applying secure software, threat modeling and zero-trust methods, we see the importance of using layers, planning, and adapting to ensure the IoT ecosystem is strong. In addition, the growth of AI in checking for threats, the use of blockchain for decentralized trust and cryptography based on quantum technology for reliability stresses the scope for evolving security measures in IoT environments. Securing the IoT is crucial because it's needed technically and for the good of society. Getting security by design into place, spreading awareness, and ensuring compliance are possible when manufacturers, policymakers, researchers, and end-users join forces. These team efforts would allow us to combine technology with security and respect privacy.

## REFERENCES


Amoo, O. O., Atadoga, A., Osasona, F., Abrahams, T. O., Ayinla, B. S., & Farayola, O. A. (2024). GDPR's impact on cybersecurity: A review focusing on USA and European practices. *International Journal of Science and Research Archive*, *11*(1), 1338–1347. DOI: 10.30574/ijsra.2024.11.1.0220

Assiri, A., & Almagwashi, H. (2018, April). IoT security and privacy issues. In 2018 1st International Conference on Computer Applications & Information Security (ICCAIS) (pp. 1-5). IEEE. DOI: 10.1109/CAIS.2018.8442002

. Atlam, H. F., & Wills, G. B. (2020). IoT security, privacy, safety, and ethics. *Digital twin technologies and smart cities,* 123-149.DOI: 10.1007/978-3-030-18732-3_8

Aung, Z., Rahman, M., & Islam, S. (2025). Generative AI for cybersecurity in IoT: Opportunities and challenges. *arXiv*. https://arxiv.org/abs/2502.08886

Axon, L., Fletcher, K., Scott, A. S., Stolz, M., Hannigan, R., Kaafarani, A. E., Goldsmith, M., & Creese, S. (2022). Emerging cybersecurity capability gaps in the industrial internet of things: Overview and research agenda. *Digital Threats : Research and Practice*, *3*(4), 1–27. DOI: 10.1145/3503920

Bailetti, T., Craigen, D., Hudson, D., Levesque, R., McKeen, S., & Walsh, D. A. (2013). Developing an innovation engine to make Canada a global leader in cybersecurity. *Technology Innovation Management Review*, *3*(8), 5–14. Advance online publication. DOI: 10.22215/timreview/711

. Baloch, M., & Huider, F. (2024). Quantum-Safe Cryptography: Using Blockchain and AI for Future-Proof Information Security.

Bell, C. (2006). Surveillance strategies and populations at risk: Biopolitical governance in Canada's national security policy. *Security Dialogue*, *37*(2), 147–165. DOI: 10.1177/0967010606066168

. Brief, S. (2021). Executive order on improving the nation's cybersecurity.

Brogan, J., Baskaran, I., & Ramachandran, N. (2018). Authenticating health activity data using distributed ledger technologies. *Computational and Structural Biotechnology Journal*, *16*, 257–266. DOI: 10.1016/j.csbj.2018.06.004 PMID: 30101004

Cagnazzo, M., Hertlein, M., Holz, T., & Pohlmann, N. (2018, April). Threat modeling for mobile health systems. In *2018 IEEE Wireless Communications and Networking Conference Workshops (WCNCW)* (pp. 314-319). IEEE. DOI: 10.1109/WCNCW.2018.8369033

Cano-Quiveu, G., Ruiz-de-Clavijo-Vazquez, P., Bellido, M. J., Juan-Chico, J., & Viejo-Cortes, J. (2023). IRIS: An embedded secure boot for IoT devices. *Internet of Things : Engineering Cyber Physical Human Systems*, *23*, 100874. DOI: 10.1016/j.iot.2023.100874

Cao, J., & Zhang, S. (2016, December). Research and design of RFID-based equipment incident management system for industry 4.0. In *2016 4th International Conference on Electrical & Electronics Engineering and Computer Science (ICEEECS 2016)* (pp. 889-894). Atlantis Press. DOI: 10.2991/iceeecs-16.2016.172

Catuogno, L., & Galdi, C. (2023). Secure Firmware Update: Challenges and Solutions. *Cryptography*, *7*(2), 30. DOI: 10.3390/cryptography7020030

Chanal, P. M., & Kakkasageri, M. S. (2020). Security and privacy in IoT: A survey. *Wireless Personal Communications*, *115*(2), 1667–1693. DOI: 10.1007/s11277-020-07649-9

Chen, C. C., Shu, D., Ravishankar, H., Li, X., Agarwal, Y., & Cranor, L. F. (2024, May). Is a Trustmark and QR code enough? The effect of IoT security and privacy label information complexity on consumer comprehension and behavior. In *Proceedings of the 2024 CHI Conference on Human Factors in Computing Systems* (pp. 1-32). DOI: 10.1145/3613904.3642011

Choudhary, Y., Umamaheswari, B., & Kumawat, V. (2021). A study of threats, vulnerabilities and countermeasures: An iot perspective. *Humanities (Washington)*, *8*(4), 39–45. DOI: 10.34293/sijash.v8i4.3583

Cirani, S., Picone, M., Gonizzi, P., Veltri, L., & Ferrari, G. (2014). Iot-oas: An oauth-based authorization service architecture for secure services in iot scenarios. *IEEE Sensors Journal*, *15*(2), 1224–1234. DOI: 10.1109/JSEN.2014.2361406

Datta, P., & Sharma, B. (2017, July). A survey on IoT architectures, protocols, security and smart city-based applications. In *2017 8th International conference on computing, communication and networking technologies (ICCCNT)* (pp. 1-5). IEEE. DOI: 10.1109/ICCCNT.2017.8203943

Dias, J. P., & Ferreira, H. S. (2018). State of the software development life-cycle for the internet-of-things. *arXiv preprint arXiv:1811.04159.* https://doi.org//arXiv.1811.04159DOI: 10.48550

Dupuis, M., & Ebenezer, M. (2018, September). Help wanted: Consumer privacy behavior and smart home internet of things (iot) devices. In *Proceedings of the 19th annual SIG conference on information technology education* (pp. 117-122).DOI: 10.1145/3241815.3241869

Edupuganti, S., Tenneti, N. S. S., Iqbal, M. M., & Rajaram, G. (2023). An IoT implemented dynamic air pollution monitoring system. *EAI Endorsed Transactions on Internet of Things*, *9*(4), 1–6. DOI: 10.4108/eetiot.v9i4.4316

Eggers, S. (2021). A novel approach for analyzing the nuclear supply chain cyber-attack surface. *Nuclear Engineering and Technology*, *53*(3), 879–887. DOI: 10.1016/j.net.2020.08.021

Emami-Naeini, P., Dixon, H., Agarwal, Y., & Cranor, L. F. (2019, May). Exploring how privacy and security factor into IoT device purchase behavior. In *Proceedings of the 2019 CHI Conference on Human Factors in Computing Systems* (pp. 1-12). DOI: 10.1145/3290605.3300764

Enam, M. M. R., Joarder, M. M. I., Taimun, M. T. Y., & Sharan, S. M. I. (2025). Framework for Smart SCADA Systems: Integrating Cloud Computing, IIoT, and Cybersecurity for Enhanced Industrial Automation. *Saudi J Eng Technol*, *10*(4), 152–158. DOI: 10.36348/sjet.2025.v10i04.005

Fagan, M., Megas, K. N., Scarfone, K. A., & Smith, M. (2025). *Foundational cybersecurity activities for IoT device manufacturers (NIST IR 8259 Revision 1, Initial public draft)*. National Institute of Standards and Technology., DOI: 10.6028/NIST.IR.8259r1.ipd

Fahrurozi, M., Tarigan, S. A., Tanjung, M. A., & Mutijarsa, K. (2020, October). The use of ISO/IEC 27005: 2018 for strengthening information security management (a case study at data and information Center of Ministry of Defence). In *2020 12th International Conference on Information Technology and Electrical Engineering (ICITEE)* (pp. 86-91). IEEE.DOI: 10.1109/ICITEE49829.2020.9271748

Ferrag, M. A., Maglaras, L. A., Janicke, H., Jiang, J., & Shu, L. (2017). Authentication protocols for internet of things: A comprehensive survey. *Security and Communication Networks*, *2017*(1), 6562953. DOI: 10.1155/2017/6562953

Figueira, P. T., Bravo, C. L., & José, L. R. L. Improving information security risk analysis by including threat-occurrence predictive models, *Computers & Security, Volume 88*,2020,101609,ISSN 0167-4048, DOI: 10.1016/j.cose.2019.101609

Gadde, H. (2023). AI-Driven Anomaly Detection in NoSQL Databases for Enhanced Security. *International Journal of Machine Learning Research in Cybersecurity and Artificial Intelligence*, *14*(1), 497–522.

Gadde, H. (2023). Leveraging AI for Scalable Query Processing in Big Data Environments. *International Journal of Advanced Engineering Technologies and Innovations*, *1*(02), 435–465.

Gaitan, E. (2022). *Developing and sharing threat intelligence: Strategies for small and medium-sized businesses* (Doctoral dissertation, Capella University).

Geater, J., Hirsch, F., Richter, D., Robkin, M., & Zahavi, R. (2022). Iot security maturity model digital twin profile. Tech. rep., Digital Twin Consortium (June 2022).

. Gijrath, S., Zwenne, G. J., Lodder, A. R., & Hof, S. V. D. (2018). Concise European data protection, e-commerce and IT law.

Hwang, Y. H. (2015, April). Iot security & privacy: threats and challenges. In *Proceedings of the 1st ACM workshop on IoT privacy, trust, and security* (pp. 1-1). DOI: 10.1145/2732209.2732216

Iqbal, S., Kiah, M. L. M., Dhaghighi, B., Hussain, M., Khan, S., Khan, M. K., & Choo, K. K. R. (2016). On cloud security attacks: A taxonomy and intrusion detection and prevention as a service. *Journal of Network and Computer Applications, 74*, 98–120. DOI: 10.1016/j.jnca.2016.08.016

. Jacobs, P., Arnab, A., & Irwin, B. (2013, August). Classification of security operation centers. In 2013 *Information Security for South Africa* (pp. 1-7). IEEE. DOI: 10.1109/ISSA.2013.6641054

. Jadhav, S. P. (2019). Towards light weight cryptography schemes for resource constraint devices in IoT. *Journal of Mobile Multimedia,* 91-110. Jadhav, S. P. (2019). DOI: 10.13052/jmm1550-4646.15125

Jaspers, E. D., & Pearson, E. (2022). Consumers' acceptance of domestic Internet-of-Things: The role of trust and privacy concerns. *Journal of Business Research, 142*, 255–265. DOI: 10.1016/j.jbusres.2021.12.043

Juma, M., Monem, A. A., & Shaalan, K. (2020). Hybrid end-to-end VPN security approach for smart IoT objects. *Journal of Network and Computer Applications, 158*, 102598. DOI: 10.1016/j.jnca.2020.102598

Kaksonen, R., Halunen, K., Laakso, M., & Röning, J. (2024, February). Automating IoT Security Standard Testing by Common Security Tools. In *Proceedings of the 10th International Conference on Information Systems Security and Privacy.* SCITEPRESS Science and Technology Publications. DOI: 10.5220/0012345900003648

Kashef, M., Visvizi, A., & Troisi, O. (2021). Smart city as a smart service system: Human-computer interaction and smart city surveillance systems. *Computers in Human Behavior, 124*, 106923. DOI: 10.1016/j.chb.2021.106923

Khan, M. J. (2023). Zero trust architecture: Redefining network security paradigms in the digital age. *World Journal of Advanced Research and Reviews*, *19*(3), 105–116. DOI: 10.30574/wjarr.2023.19.3.1785

Koren, O., Koren, M., & Peretz, O. A procedure for anomaly detection and analysis, Engineering Applications of Artificial Intelligence, Volume 117, Part A, 2023, 105503, ISSN 0952-1976. DOI: 10.1016/j.engappai.2022.105503

Kumar, J. S., & Patel, D. R. (2014). A survey on internet of things: Security and privacy issues. *International Journal of Computer Applications*, *90*(11). Advance online publication. DOI: 10.5120/15764-4454

Kurte, S., Sharma, P., & Singh, R (2025). Supporting decentralized IoT applications under resource constraints. *Internet of Things : Engineering Cyber Physical Human Systems*, *30*, 101496. Advance online publication. DOI: 10.1016/j.iot.2025.101496

Lim, C., & Maglio, P. P. (2018). Clarifying the Concept of Smart Service System. In: Maglio, P.P., Kieliszewski, C.A., Spohrer, J.C., Lyons, K., Patrício, L., Sawatani, Y. (eds) *Handbook of Service Science, Volume II.* Service Science: Research and Innovations in the Service Economy. Springer, Cham. DOI: 10.1007/978-3-319-98512-1_16

Mehra, T. (2025). *Building a Resilient Backup Infrastructure: Combining Data Redundancy*. Encryption, and RBAC for Maximum Protection., DOI: 10.55041/IJSREM41975

Mell, P., & Grance, T. (2011). *The NIST definition of cloud computing*., DOI: 10.6028/NIST.SP.800-145

Mughal, A. A. (2019). Cybersecurity hygiene in the era of internet of things (IoT): Best practices and challenges. *Applied Research in Artificial Intelligence and Cloud Computing*, *2*(1), 1–31.

. National Institute of Standards and Technology (NIST). (2024). *The NIST Cybersecurity Framework (CSF) 2.0.* https://doi.org/DOI: 10.6028/NIST.CSWP.29

Nguyen, K. T., Laurent, M., & Oualha, N. (2015). Survey on secure communication protocols for the Internet of Things. *Ad Hoc Networks*, *32*, 17–31. DOI: 10.1016/j.adhoc.2015.01.006

Ogenyi, O. M. (2025). Explainable artificial intelligence for adaptive cybersecurity in IoT environments. *Frontiers in Internet of Things*, *4*, 1658273. Advance online publication. DOI: 10.3389/friot.2025.1658273

. Parashar, A. (2023). Cybersecurity Threats in the Internet of Things (Iot). IOSR Journal of Computer Engineering (IOSR-JCE), 1-8.

Pascoe, C., Quinn, S., & Scarfone, K. (2024). *The NIST Cybersecurity Framework (CSF) 2.0*. National Institute of Standards and Technology., DOI: 10.6028/NIST.CSWP.29

Phillips, M. (2018). International data-sharing norms: From the OECD to the General Data Protection Regulation (GDPR). *Human Genetics*, *137*(8), 575–582. DOI: 10.1007/s00439-018-1919-7 PMID: 30069638

Puat, H. A. M., & Abd Rahman, N. A. (2020, December). IoMT: a review of pacemaker vulnerabilities and security strategy. In *Journal of Physics: Conference Series (*Vol. 1712, No. 1, p. 012009). IOP Publishing. DOI: 10.1088/1742-6596/1712/1/012009

Raman, R., Dhivya, K., Sapra, P., Gurpur, S., Maniraj, S. P., & Murugan, S. (2023, December). IoT-driven Smart Packaging for Pharmaceuticals: Ensuring Product Integrity and Patient Safety. In 2023 *International Conference on Artificial Intelligence for Innovations in Healthcare Industries (ICAIIHI)* (Vol. 1, pp. 1-6). IEEE. DOI: 10.1109/ICAIIHI57871.2023.10489420

Rayes, A., & Salam, S. (2022). Internet of things security and privacy. In *Internet of Things From Hype to Reality: The Road to Digitization* (pp. 213–246). Springer International Publishing., DOI: 10.1007/978-3-030-90158-5_8

Sadeghi, A. R. (2008, January). Trusted computing—special aspects and challenges. In *International Conference on Current Trends in Theory and Practice of Computer Science* (pp. 98-117). Berlin, Heidelberg: Springer Berlin Heidelberg. DOI: 10.1007/978-3-540-77566-9_9

Sankar, K. M., Booba, B., Rangaswamy, C., Pramila, P. V., Kar, S. R., Kumar, A., & Sudhakar, M. (2023, February). IoT-based Weather, Soil, Earthquake, Air pollution Monitoring System. In *2023 3rd International Conference on Innovative Practices in Technology and Management (ICIPTM)* (pp. 1-6). IEEE.DOI: 10.1109/ICIPTM57143.2023.10118160

Savaglio, C., Fortino, G., Gravina, R., & Russo, W. (2018a). A Methodology for Integrating Internet of Things Platforms. In: *2018 IEEE International Conference on Cloud Engineering. IC2E,* pp. 317–322. DOI: 10.1109/IC2E.2018.00062

Seet, P. S., Jones, J., Klarin, A., & Suseno, Y. (2021). *IoT and the Future Workforce: Potential Implications.* Australian Council of Learned Academies.

Shaik, Y. (2024). Securing Firmware updates: Addressing security challenges in UEFI capsule update mechanisms.

Skarga-Bandurova, I., Kotsiuba, I., & Velasco, E. R. (2021). Cyber Hygiene Maturity Assessment Framework for Smart Grid Scenarios. *Frontiers of Computer Science*, *3*, 614337. DOI: 10.3389/fcomp.2021.614337

Sobahi, N., & Bamabad, A. (2024). Cyber-attacks Risk Analysis of a Connected Pulse Oximeter Device: A Threat Modeling Using STRIDE and DREAD Models. *International Journal for Scientific Research*, *3*(5), 280–315. DOI: 10.59992/IJSR.2024.v3n5p10

Sun, R., Wang, Q., & Guo, L. (2022, July). Research towards key issues of api security. In *China Cyber Security Annual Conference* (pp. 179-192). Singapore: Springer Nature Singapore.DOI: 10.1007/978-981-16-9229-1_11

. Surden, H. (2021). Machine learning and law: An overview. *Research handbook on big data law*, 171-184. DOI: 10.4337/9781788972826.00014

Syed, F. M., & ES, F. (2021). Role of IAM in Data Loss Prevention (DLP) Strategies for Pharmaceutical Security Operations. *Revista de Inteligencia Artificial en Medicina*, *12*(1), 407–4.

Tan, W. C., & Sidhu, M. S. (2022). Review of RFID and IoT integration in supply chain management. *Operations Research Perspectives*, *9*, 100229. DOI: 10.1016/j.orp.2022.100229

Taylor, R., Johnson, P., & Lee, K. (2025). A framework for testing and monitoring IoT cybersecurity. *arXiv*. https://arxiv.org/abs/2502.12837

Turcu, C. O., & Turcu, C. E. (2018). Industrial Internet of Things as a challenge for higher education. *International Journal of Advanced Computer Science and Applications*, *9*(11), 55–60. DOI: 10.14569/IJACSA.2018.091108

Ukidve, A., Mantha, S. S., & Reddy, D. N. (2022). Analyzing Mapping of ISO 27001: 2013 Controls for Alignment with Enterprise Risks Management. *Asian Journal of Organic & Medicinal Chemistry*, *7*(2), 123–129.

Vardakis, G., Hatzivasilis, G., Koutsaki, E., & Papadakis, N. (2024). Review of Smart-Home Security Using the Internet of Things. *Electronics (Basel)*, *13*(16), 3343. DOI: 10.3390/electronics13163343

Veeramachaneni, V. (2025). Edge Computing: Architecture, Applications, and Future Challenges in a Decentralized Era. *Recent Trends in Computer Graphics and Multimedia Technology*, *7*(1), 8–23. DOI: 10.5281/zenodo.14166793

Wang, J.-J., & Mu, S. Security issues and countermeasures in cloud computing. In *Proceedings of the 2011 IEEE International Conference on Grey Systems and Intelligent Services* (GSIS), Nanjing, China, 15–18 September 2011; pp. 843–846. DOI: 10.1109/GSIS.2011.6043978

Wang, W., & Yongchareon, S. (2020). Security-as-a-service: A literature review. *International Journal of Web Information Systems*, *16*(5), 493–517. DOI: 10.1108/IJWIS-06-2020-0031

Wool, A. (2009). Firewall configuration errors revisited. *arXiv preprint arXiv:0911.1240.* https://doi.org//arXiv.0911.1240DOI: 10.48550

Xiao, G., Guo, J., Xu, L. D., & Gong, Z. (2014). User interoperability with heterogeneous IoT devices through transformation. *IEEE Transactions on Industrial Informatics*, *10*(2), 1486–1496. DOI: 10.1109/TII.2014.2306772

Younis, Y. A., Kifayat, K., & Merabti, M. (2014). An access control model for cloud computing. *Journal of Information Security and Applications*, *19*(1), 45–60. DOI: 10.1016/j.jisa.2014.04.003

Zhang, B., Li, J., Ren, J., & Huang, G. (2021). Efficiency and effectiveness of web application vulnerability detection approaches: A review. *ACM Computing Surveys*, *54*(9), 1–35. DOI: 10.1145/3474553

Zheng, X., Li, Y., Wang, J., & Chen, Z. (2025). Game-theoretic modeling and prediction of cyber-attacks in IoT environments. *Internet of Things : Engineering Cyber Physical Human Systems*, *30*, 101522. Advance online publication. DOI: 10.1016/j.iot.2025.101522

## KEY TERMS AND DEFINITIONS

**AI-Driven Threat Detection:** It employed machine learning to analyze the large datasets of network traffic, user activity to identify and react to security threats. It enhances threat detection by learning from past data, identifying patterns, and responding in real-time.

**Cybersecurity Frameworks:** It is a structured approach employed by organizations to manage and deal with cybersecurity risks. It also gives a detailed roadmap for identifying, assessing, and predicting the possible threats.

**Internet of Things (IoT):** It is defined as a network of physical devices, vehicles, appliances, and other things that are embedded with sensors, software, and network connectivity. It helps to enable the collection and exchange of data.

**Smart Device Threat Modeling:** It is a structured approach to identify, analyze, and predict the possible security risks which is associated with smart devices. It ensures that security measures are integrated in the design and development process.

**Technology:** Technology is the practical application of the scientific knowledge, tools, and techniques in order to create solutions to solve the problems or improve human life.

**Zero Trust Architecture:** It is a security approach that transforms from traditional perimeter-based security, which believes everything is inside the network. It assumes that no user/ device, whether inside or outside the network, can be trusted by default; instead of it requires continuous verification and access control based on the least privilege principle.

# Chapter 7
# A Hybrid Anomaly Detection Framework for Securing University BYOD Networks

**Rajani Mahesh Yemul**
http://orcid.org/0009-0000-3712-5518
*Walchand Institute of Technology, Solapur, India*

**Shubham Suresh Vyavahare**
http://orcid.org/0009-0009-4451-6635
*Walchand Institute of Technology, Solapur, India*

**Mahesh Satyanarayan Yemul**
http://orcid.org/0009-0008-8981-0849
*Sinhgad Business School, Solapur, India*

**Virupakshappa Patil**
http://orcid.org/0000-0002-1395-0262
*Sharnbasva University, India*

## ABSTRACT

*University campus networks face escalating cybersecurity risks due to widespread Bring Your Own Device (BYOD) adoption. Unlike controlled enterprise networks, campus environments host thousands of heterogeneous student devices connecting dynamically. Traditional intrusion detection systems relying on signature-based methods or single machine learning classifiers struggle to detect zero-day vulnerabilities in such volatile environments. This chapter proposes a hybrid, two-layer anomaly detection framework explicitly designed for educational networks. The*

DOI: 10.4018/979-8-2600-3465-1.ch007

*primary layer utilizes high-speed, signature-based detection to filter known threats. The secondary layer employs an ensemble machine learning approach combining Extreme Gradient Boosting (XGBoost) and Long Short-Term Memory (LSTM) networks. Experimental evaluation demonstrates significant improvements in detection accuracy and drastically reduced false-positive rates, highlighting the efficacy of hybrid architectures in strengthening proactive defense mechanisms.*

## INTRODUCTION

The digital transformation of higher education has restructured academic infrastructure, placing heavy reliance on persistent, high-speed network connectivity. To support pedagogical flexibility, academic institutions have adopted the Bring Your Own Device (BYOD) paradigm, allowing users to connect personally owned devices directly to institutional networks. While the BYOD model promotes collaborative digital learning, it concurrently expands the network's attack surface. In the context of modern cyber warfare, where threat actors increasingly deploy autonomous, agentic malware capable of automated vulnerability discovery and lateral movement, this expanded attack surface presents a critical security challenge.

University networks present a distinct architectural and operational security challenge compared to tightly controlled corporate topologies. In an enterprise environment, endpoint devices are strictly provisioned and centrally managed. In contrast, the modern academic campus is characterized by extreme device heterogeneity. Thousands of users connect daily, bringing unmanaged personal devices that exhibit variance in their baseline security posture. Because universities host sensitive intellectual property, proprietary research data, and personally identifiable information (PII), they are highly lucrative targets for sophisticated cybercriminals. The open-access nature of the campus network allows automated malware infections to propagate rapidly. The high physical mobility of the student population further complicates traffic profiling, rendering traditional perimeter defense mechanisms largely ineffective against autonomous offensive agents.

Compounding these architectural vulnerabilities is the inadequacy of legacy defense mechanisms. Traditional Intrusion Detection Systems (IDS) rely almost exclusively on signature-based detection. While effective at identifying historical threats with low false-positive rates, this reactive approach is insufficient against modern cyber warfare. Signature-based systems are fundamentally blind to zero-day attacks, polymorphic malware that autonomously alters its code structure, and sophisticated Advanced Persistent Threats (APTs) driven by agentic intelligence that utilize encrypted communication channels to evade detection.

To counter autonomous offensive threats, the cybersecurity paradigm must shift toward autonomous, agentic defense systems. Anomaly detection defines a baseline of standard behavior and flags statistical deviations. However, early iterations of anomaly-based IDS employing single, isolated machine learning classifiers have struggled to achieve operational viability in complex environments. Algorithms such as standalone Decision Trees or basic Artificial Neural Networks (ANN) often fail to capture both the high-dimensional structural complexities of packet data and the temporal behavioral sequences inherent in modern cyber attacks.

Within a university setting, the failure of single-classifier anomaly detection manifests as high false-positive rates. The baseline of benign behavior in academia is highly variable. Heavy student activity—such as concurrent video streaming or large-scale dataset downloads—is frequently misclassified by rudimentary models as volumetric attack traffic. This false-positive generation overwhelms security administrators, leading to alert fatigue where genuine security breaches may be overlooked.

To address these limitations, this research introduces an agentic, hybrid anomaly detection framework optimized for the high-density traffic characteristics of university BYOD environments. Securing a decentralized network against automated cyber warfare requires an integrated, multi-modal autonomous agent. By integrating a rapid signature-based filtering mechanism with a parallel ensemble machine learning model, this chapter outlines a methodology that acts as an intelligent defensive agent. It combines the structural classification power of Extreme Gradient Boosting (XGBoost) with the sequential, time-series pattern recognition of Long Short-Term Memory (LSTM) deep neural networks.

This proposed framework provides a scalable and contextually adaptive security solution. The first architectural layer operates as a high-speed filter, utilizing updated threat intelligence to eliminate known malicious actors. The secondary layer functions as an autonomous analytical agent, unpacking complex, high-volume traffic patterns. By analyzing both the static mathematical structure of the network flow (via XGBoost) and the chronological behavioral rhythm of the device over time (via LSTM), the agentic framework identifies subtle, unseen behavioral anomalies. This approach counters automated threats while maintaining false-positive rates at operationally sustainable levels.

The remainder of this chapter provides a comprehensive exploration of this agentic hybrid framework. The Background section synthesizes literature on BYOD security, the evolution of IDS, and the application of cross-domain artificial intelligence to autonomous defense. The Main Focus of the Chapter details the controversies faced by university networks, including the obsolescence of deep packet inspection. The Solutions and Recommendations section provides the mathematical formulations of the XGBoost and LSTM algorithms, the dual-stage feature engineering pipeline, and the adaptive fusion engine. This is followed by a rigorous discussion of the experimental setup, empirical evaluation protocol, ablation studies, and performance metrics that validate the framework's efficacy. Finally, the Future Research Directions and Conclusion summarize the implications of this technology for autonomous cyber defense.

## BACKGROUND

The proliferation of Bring Your Own Device (BYOD) policies has significantly influenced the trajectory of network security research. As the defined perimeter of traditional academic and corporate networks dissolved due to mobile computing and cloud-based infrastructure, the focus of cybersecurity literature shifted toward endpoint heterogeneity and behavioral anomaly detection. To understand the necessity of a hybrid, deep learning-driven intrusion detection framework, it is imperative to trace the historical evolution of network defense mechanisms, the mathematical limitations of early classifiers, and the revolutionary impact of agentic deep learning architectures in countering algorithmic warfare.

### Evolution of Bring Your Own Device Policies and Autonomous Threats

The fundamental concept of network security originally relied upon the perimeter-based architectural model. In this paradigm, the internal network was considered trusted, while the external internet was hostile. Administrators deployed monolithic firewalls at the perimeter to inspect traffic, creating a fortified boundary. Inside this boundary, enterprise devices were assumed to be safe and managed.

However, early academic literature examined how the policy implications of the BYOD phenomenon bypassed this perimeter-based security model. Foundational studies emphasized the severe access control challenges introduced by personally owned devices integrating into enterprise and educational ecosystems (Mather, Kumaraswamy, & Latif, 2009). When a user carries a compromised smartphone past the physical and logical perimeter of the campus firewall, the traditional boundary is circumvented. Subsequent cybersecurity research detailed specific mobile vulnerabilities, advocating for a holistic blend of technical controls alongside strict institutional security policies (Scarfo, 2012).

The global shift toward decentralized hybrid learning accelerated this trend, blurring the boundaries between insecure personal home networks and secure campus infrastructures. In the context of modern cyber warfare, this decentralized architecture presents a fertile environment for autonomous, agentic malware. Threat actors now utilize automated scripts and self-propagating algorithmic worms that exploit endpoint vulnerabilities at scale, without requiring manual human oversight. As strict endpoint policy enforcement proved technologically and culturally difficult in university settings, research pivoted toward automated, network-level intrusion detection capable of passively monitoring traffic flows and autonomously identifying anomalous behavior.

## The Paradigm Shift: From Scripted Malware to Agentic Intelligence

The evolution of offensive cyber operations has transitioned from static, scripted malware to dynamic, agentic intelligence. Historically, malware relied on hardcoded instructions and constant communication with external Command and Control (C2) servers. These legacy architectures executed predefined attack trees; if a network configuration changed or a specific vulnerability was patched, the script would fail, requiring human operators to manually re-tool and deploy new payloads. Furthermore, the persistent beaconing required to receive instructions from a C2 server created a highly visible network signature, making traditional malware relatively easy to detect and quarantine using perimeter defenses.

Modern autonomous cyber warfare, however, is characterized by the deployment of agentic malware. Agentic intelligence in cybersecurity refers to malicious software equipped with localized, lightweight machine learning algorithms capable of independent decision-making. Once deployed inside a target network, these autonomous agents no longer require persistent C2 communication to execute their objectives. They are designed to passively observe local network traffic, learn the baseline behaviors of surrounding devices, and autonomously identify the most vulnerable pivot points for lateral movement. By utilizing reinforcement learning techniques, agentic malware can dynamically alter its own code structure (polymorphism), adjust its propagation speed to blend in with legitimate traffic spikes, and select optimal exploitation techniques based on the specific operating systems it encounters.

University networks represent an optimal target environment for agentic threats. Unlike tightly controlled corporate networks where hardware is standardized, the extreme device heterogeneity of a Bring Your Own Device (BYOD) campus provides a rich training ground for autonomous agents. An agentic worm can compromise an outdated student laptop on a public campus Wi-Fi network and utilize it as a silent staging ground. From there, the malware's local AI can autonomously map the internal subnet, identifying high-value targets such as administrative databases housing Personally Identifiable Information (PII) or laboratory servers containing proprietary research data. Because the agent makes tactical decisions locally and alters its communication rhythms to mimic benign academic behavior, it effectively evades traditional heuristic thresholds. This paradigm shift necessitates a defensive architecture that is equally agentic—one capable of autonomously analyzing temporal behavioral sequences to identify the subtle, localized decision-making patterns of modern offensive agents.

## Legacy Intrusion Detection Systems and Their Limitations

The historical foundation of network intrusion detection relies on signature-based or misuse detection methodologies. Systems such as Snort or Suricata operate by maintaining a continuously updated database of known malicious packet payloads, executable hashes, and explicit byte sequences associated with specific malware variants. Every packet traversing the network is subjected to a pattern-matching algorithm against this database.

While signature-based systems operate with a low false-positive rate for historical threats, they possess an inherent limitation: they are entirely reactive. This reactive posture is highly vulnerable to autonomous cyber operations. Signature-based systems are ineffective against zero-day attacks, polymorphic malware that utilizes agentic intelligence to automatically alter its code structure upon execution, and sophisticated Advanced Persistent Threats (APTs) that utilize encrypted communication channels to evade detection.

To address the limitations of signature matching, the foundational concepts of anomaly-based intrusion detection were formalized by Denning (1987), who established behavior-based statistical profiling as a proactive alternative. Denning posited that malicious activity would manifest as a statistical deviation from an established baseline of normal system behavior. For decades, researchers attempted to build robust anomaly detection systems using basic statistical thresholds and rudimentary supervised machine learning models.

However, as network traffic grew exponentially in complexity and encryption overhead, the practical limitations of applying rudimentary machine learning directly to network intrusion became apparent. Real-world deployment success requires rigorous feature engineering and deep contextual awareness. Researchers explicitly warned against the "closed world" assumptions often present in sterilized academic datasets (Sommer & Paxson, 2010). In a university BYOD environment, normal user behavior is highly variable. Basic machine learning classifiers, such as isolated Support Vector Machines (SVM) or Naive Bayes algorithms, generate unsustainable volumes of false positives because they lack the computational capacity to model highly complex, non-linear relationships in massive feature spaces. Comprehensive surveys pointed toward ensemble learning as a critical pathway for enhancing detection robustness (Tsai et al., 2009).

## The Mathematics and Rise of Ensemble Learning in Cyber Defense

Ensemble learning methodologies fundamentally altered the design of Intrusion Detection Systems (IDS) by aggregating the predictive power of multiple independent models to form a highly accurate, robust classifier. The core philosophy of ensemble learning addresses the bias-variance tradeoff. Single decision trees are prone to overfitting, capturing statistical noise rather than underlying patterns, which leads to poor generalization on live network traffic.

Breiman (2001) advanced ensemble classification by introducing the Random Forest algorithm, which utilizes bootstrap aggregating (bagging) to handle high-dimensional security datasets. While Random Forests improved detection rates, they frequently struggled with the highly imbalanced datasets typical of real-world network traffic, where benign flows vastly outnumber malicious anomalies.

Addressing this computational gap, Chen and Guestrin (2016) developed Extreme Gradient Boosting (XGBoost), a scalable, optimized gradient boosting framework. XGBoost builds trees sequentially, explicitly designed to mathematically correct the residual prediction errors made by previous trees. This iterative error-correction process, combined with strict mathematical regularization techniques, mitigated the overfitting issues prevalent in earlier models. Researchers successfully applied these advanced tree-based ensemble methods to benchmark intrusion datasets, demonstrating quantifiable reductions in false-positive rates and improved detection of structured, automated volumetric attacks (Zhang, Zulkernine, & Haque, 2008; Aljawarneh, Aldwairi, & Yassein, 2018).

## Agentic Deep Learning Architectures and Sequential Traffic Modeling

While XGBoost achieved state-of-the-art results for classifying the static, structural features of network traffic, it evaluated network flows as isolated events. It lacked the capacity to understand the chronological dimension of an autonomous cyber attack. Modern APTs and agentic botnet command-and-control beaconing unfold sequentially over time. The threat only becomes apparent when observing a sequence of connections.

The advent of deep learning architectures revolutionized sequence modeling. Hochreiter and Schmidhuber (1997) solved the vanishing gradient problem inherent in standard Recurrent Neural Networks (RNNs) by developing the Long Short-Term Memory (LSTM) network architecture. LSTMs introduced complex memory cells governed by intersecting mathematical gates, allowing the network to learn which historical network events were critical to remember and which were irrelevant noise.

Recent cybersecurity literature has applied LSTMs directly to sequential network flow data, proving their efficacy in identifying distributed denial-of-service (DDoS) attacks and covert algorithmic communications through deep temporal traffic analysis (Yin et al., 2017; Kim, Lee, & Kim, 2014). Furthermore, unsupervised deep autoencoders have demonstrated capability in extracting latent features from complex network environments (Shone et al., 2018). The consensus within modern cybersecurity literature asserts the necessity of hybrid systems, combining structural classification speed with the deep behavioral adaptability of sequence models to establish an autonomous, agentic defense posture capable of adapting to evolving adversarial tactics (Axelsson, 2000; Patcha & Park, 2007).

## MAIN FOCUS OF THE CHAPTER

The fundamental objective of this research is to architect and empirically evaluate a scalable, highly accurate intrusion detection framework capable of operating as an autonomous defensive agent within the uniquely variable environment of a university campus network. Higher educational institutions face an inherent conflict: they must balance the mandate to maintain an open, collaborative academic environment with the critical imperative to secure infrastructure against sophisticated, agentic cyber threats. The primary focus of this chapter is to systematically dissect the structural challenges introduced by decentralized BYOD policies, and to present a comprehensive technological solution utilizing advanced ensemble machine learning and deep sequential modeling.

### Issues, Controversies, and Problems

To construct an effective defense mechanism against algorithmic warfare, it is necessary to analyze the operational hurdles that render traditional security frameworks ineffective within academic environments. The challenges hindering modern campus cybersecurity are categorized into four primary domains: the obsolescence of deep packet inspection, the operational limitations of strict zero-trust frameworks, the economic dilemma of false positives, and extreme device heterogeneity.

### The Obsolescence of Deep Packet Inspection (DPI)

Historically, enterprise network security relied on Deep Packet Inspection (DPI) appliances to actively analyze the payload of network packets for known malware signatures or unauthorized data exfiltration patterns. However, the universal adoption of Transport Layer Security (TLS) 1.3 and end-to-end encryption protocols has rendered traditional DPI largely obsolete. Because the payload is cryptographically obfuscated, intermediate security appliances can no longer inspect packet contents to match historical threat signatures.

In an academic setting, attempting to decrypt user traffic raises ethical and legal controversies regarding privacy. Consequently, modern intrusion detection must pivot from analyzing payload contents to analyzing flow-based telemetry. Autonomous offensive agents frequently utilize encryption to mask their command-and-control communications. The core problem addressed by this chapter is extracting actionable threat intelligence from this encrypted metadata using advanced mathematical models, forming an agentic system that infers malicious intent from communication patterns.

## Operational Limitations of Zero-Trust in Academia

The cybersecurity industry has championed "Zero-Trust Architecture" (ZTA) for corporate environments, which mandates strict identity verification and the continuous evaluation of an endpoint's security posture. However, deploying pure zero-trust models in a university creates significant operational friction. Universities rely on the frictionless exchange of datasets and open collaboration.

Implementing strict zero-trust controls—such as mandating intrusive compliance agents on personal student devices—frequently disrupts the pedagogical process. A critical controversy exists: institutions must achieve the security benefits of continuous monitoring without imposing restrictive endpoint controls. The solution requires shifting the analytical burden from the endpoint device to the network layer, utilizing an autonomous, artificial intelligence-driven agent to passively infer device trustworthiness based on behavioral analysis.

## The False-Positive Dilemma and Alert Fatigue

A significant operational problem in deploying anomaly-based intrusion detection systems is the base-rate fallacy. In a university setting, legitimate academic behavior frequently mirrors malicious activity. Heavy computational research, international dataset synchronization, or massive concurrent streaming can trigger heuristic alarms designed to catch reconnaissance sweeps or volumetric attacks.

Because genuine cyber attacks represent a statistically small fraction of total daily campus traffic, even a model with a seemingly low false-positive rate will generate thousands of false alarms on a high-throughput network. High false-positive rates induce severe alert fatigue among Security Operations Center (SOC) analysts, potentially leading to genuine alerts being algorithmically suppressed. The core technical problem is engineering an agentic system capable of highly contextualized, precise differentiation between benign academic network volatility and genuine, automated malicious intent.

## Device Heterogeneity and Exploitation by Autonomous Agents

A university network seamlessly accommodates tens of thousands of concurrently active devices, ranging from fully patched enterprise servers to unmanaged Internet of Things (IoT) sensors and outdated personal laptops. This extreme heterogeneity prevents security administrators from establishing a single, uniform baseline of normal device behavior.

Autonomous offensive agents are specifically designed to exploit this heterogeneity, scanning broad IP ranges to identify the weakest unmanaged endpoints to use as pivot points for lateral movement. Furthermore, student traffic is chronologically volatile, with physical movement between classes creating massive spikes in roaming handoffs that can mask volumetric anomalies. A defensive framework must therefore be equally autonomous, capable of dynamically baselining diverse devices and distinguishing between legitimate network volatility and coordinated algorithmic exploitation.

# SOLUTIONS AND RECOMMENDATIONS

To systematically overcome the systemic limitations of traditional security appliances, payload inspection obsolescence, and the high false-positive rates associated with isolated machine learning classifiers, this research proposes a multi-layered, hybrid anomaly detection framework. By synthesizing the rapid, low-latency processing capabilities of signature-based filtering with the deep analytical power of a parallel machine learning ensemble, the proposed solution achieves a critical, operationally viable balance between real-time processing speed and high-precision, low-noise threat detection.

## Proposed Hybrid Anomaly Detection Architecture

The architectural design of the proposed hybrid framework is systematically structured into a sequential, highly optimized multi-phase data pipeline. This analytical pipeline continuously ingests, sanitizes, and mathematically transforms raw network telemetry, ultimately culminating in the generation of a dynamically weighted, real-time threat score for every active connection on the campus network.

*Figure 1. Hybrid anomaly detection framework for securing university BYOD networks*

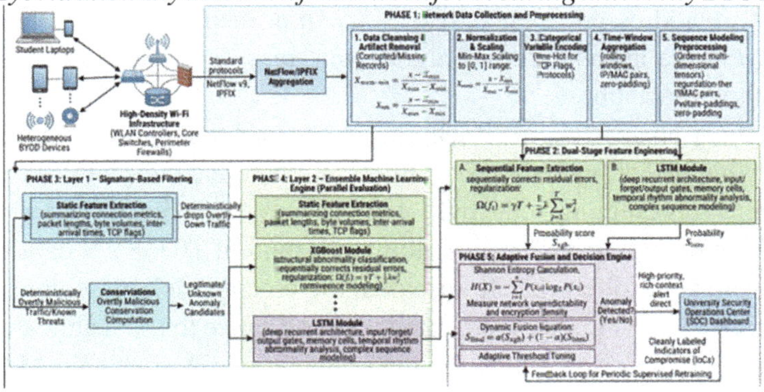


As illustrated in Figure 1, the architecture ensures that overt, previously cataloged known threats are instantly neutralized at the network perimeter. Simultaneously, stealthy zero-day vulnerabilities, slow-moving advanced persistent threats, and complex behavioral anomalies are dissected by the complex machine learning ensemble operating asynchronously in the background.

## Phase 1: Network Data Collection and Preprocessing

The foundational accuracy of any artificial intelligence model is entirely dependent upon the quality and fidelity of its input data. Therefore, the first phase of the anomaly detection framework relies on the continuous, high-speed collection of network telemetry. To preserve student privacy, comply with data protection regulations, and bypass the computational limitations of analyzing encrypted payloads, the system utilizes standard flow-based export protocols, specifically NetFlow version 9 and IP Flow Information Export (IPFIX). Flow data is passively aggregated from strategic architectural choke points across the campus topology, including wireless local area network (LAN) controllers, core distribution switches, and perimeter edge firewalls.

However, raw flow data exported directly from network hardware inherently contains significant statistical noise, missing values due to dropped User Datagram Protocol (UDP) packets, and significant scale disparities. These raw inconsistencies severely degrade the convergence, accuracy, and training stability of gradient-based machine learning algorithms. Therefore, a rigorous, real-time preprocessing pipeline must be executed before the data reaches the analytical models. The preprocessing phase consists of the following critical mathematical operations:

- Data Cleansing and Artifact Removal: Incomplete flow records, duplicate entries generated by asymmetric routing, and corrupted packets resulting from extreme network congestion are systematically filtered out. Missing feature values are addressed using statistical mean or median imputation techniques to prevent the introduction of algorithmic bias or runtime errors during the model inference phase.

- Normalization and Scaling Techniques: Network telemetry contains numerical attributes that possess vastly different mathematical scales. For example, a feature representing total byte volume may scale into the billions (gigabytes), whereas a feature representing the count of TCP SYN flags may range only from zero to ten. If left unscaled, the machine learning algorithms will incorrectly assign higher mathematical importance to the features with larger magnitudes. To resolve this, the data undergoes rigorous Min-Max scaling. This mathematical transformation ensures all numerical features are tightly constrained within a uniform continuous range, typically *[0, 1]*. The transformation applied to each data point $x$ in feature vector $X$ is defined as:

$$X_{norm} = \frac{x - X_{min}}{X_{max} - X_{min}}$$

This specific normalization technique prevents high-magnitude volumetric features from dominating the gradient descent algorithms during the model's learning phase, allowing subtle behavioral features (like inter-arrival time variance) to influence the final prediction.

- Categorical Variable Encoding: Machine learning models strictly require numerical input matrices. Non-numerical, categorical data points—such as transport protocols (Transmission Control Protocol [TCP], User Datagram Protocol [UDP], Internet Control Message Protocol [ICMP]) and TCP state flags (SYN, ACK, FIN, RST)—cannot be processed natively. These categorical strings are converted into expansive, machine-readable binary numerical arrays utilizing one-hot encoding methodologies, ensuring that the algorithm does not falsely infer an ordinal relationship between independent protocol types.
- Time-Window Aggregation for Sequential Modeling: While static tree-based models can evaluate individual flow records independently, deep sequential models require chronological context. To enable the Long Short-Term Memory (LSTM) neural network to analyze temporal behavior over time, individual packet flows are grouped into fixed, rolling chronological windows (e.g., ten-second or sixty-second intervals) based on unique source IP and MAC address pairings. This critical aggregation operation transforms thousands of isolated, static network events into a continuous, flowing behavioral

narrative for each connected BYOD endpoint, allowing the model to analyze the cadence, rhythm, and persistence of the data transfer.

- Experimental Setup and Deployment Configuration: To rigorously validate the efficacy, accuracy, and scalability of the proposed hybrid architecture, a comprehensive experimental testbed was constructed. The environment was meticulously designed to mirror the complex topology, extreme traffic volume, and diverse usage patterns characteristic of a high-density academic institution. The core analytics framework was deployed on a centralized, high-performance computing cluster to manage the intense computational requirements associated with parallel deep learning model training and real-time inference. As detailed in Table 1, the infrastructure utilized enterprise-grade hardware and software configurations to ensure the reproducibility and validity of the experimental results.

*Table 1. Experimental environment and infrastructure configuration*

| Component | Specification | Purpose |
|---|---|---|
| Analytics Server | 16-Core Central Processing Unit, 64 GB Random Access Memory, Enterprise Graphics Processing Unit (GPU) | Accelerated training and real-time execution of XGBoost and LSTM parallel models. |
| Operating System | Ubuntu 22.04 Long-Term Support (LTS) | Provision of a stable, secure, and highly compatible machine learning deployment environment. |
| Programming Environment | Python 3.10 | Core framework implementation, scripting, and data pipeline orchestration. |
| Machine Learning Libraries | XGBoost, TensorFlow, Keras, Scikit-learn | Rapid model development, algorithmic tuning, and comprehensive performance evaluation. |
| Network Telemetry Collection | NetFlow version 9 / IPFIX | Generation and aggregation of high-fidelity, flow-based network traffic metadata. |
| Endpoint Virtualization | VMware ESXi / Oracle VirtualBox | Emulation of thousands of heterogeneous BYOD endpoints (Windows, macOS, Android, Linux IoT). |
| Traffic Validation | Wireshark, Zeek Network Security Monitor | Real-time traffic validation, deep packet logging, and baseline establishment. |

## Phase 2: Dual-Stage Feature Engineering

A foundational premise of this research is that the inherent complexity of modern cyber attacks cannot be captured by a single, monolithic analytical lens. Network traffic exists simultaneously as a static artifact (a single connection at a specific point in time) and a dynamic, flowing process (a continuous conversation between two endpoints). Consequently, attempting to force both structured tabular data and sequential time-series data into a single algorithm inevitably degrades the model's accuracy. To solve this, a dual-stage feature extraction strategy is systematically deployed within the preprocessing pipeline. This bifurcation optimizes the input matrices specifically for the distinct mathematical requirements of the Extreme Gradient Boosting (XGBoost) and Long Short-Term Memory (LSTM) models.

### *Static Feature Extraction*

Engineered explicitly for the XGBoost module, static features represent the aggregate, holistic statistical profile of a network connection. These features do not account for the chronological order of packet arrival; rather, they mathematically summarize the overall composition and volume of the flow. During this extraction phase, the system computes over eighty distinct network flow characteristics.

Critical extracted features include the total flow duration, the mathematical variance in forward and backward packet lengths, the precise ratio of payload bytes to header bytes, the standard deviation of packet inter-arrival times, and the absolute count of active Transmission Control Protocol (TCP) flags (such as SYN, ACK, PSH, and URG). These structural characteristics act as highly effective, low-latency indicators of volumetric attacks. For instance, a brute-force authentication attempt against a university portal will generate a high volume of exceptionally short, uniform flows. Conversely, a massive, rapid data exfiltration event—often the final stage of a ransomware infection before the encryption payload is deployed—will radically alter the payload-to-header ratio, generating a significant statistical outlier in the backward packet length variance. By extracting these static features, the XGBoost model is provided with a high-dimensional structural map of every connection.

### *Sequential Feature Extraction*

In stark contrast, sequential features are engineered specifically for the LSTM module to capture the chronological progression and behavioral cadence of a device's network activity. Instead of mathematically summarizing an entire connection into a single row of tabular data, the sequential extraction system isolates an ordered sequence of flow vectors grouped by unique device identifiers (specifically, Media Access Control [MAC] and Internet Protocol [IP] address pairings).

To achieve this, the system implements a sliding time-window algorithm. A fixed window of size $T$ (representing a specific number of time steps or consecutive packets) slides across the continuous stream of network traffic with a defined stride, $S$. This operation groups the chronological metadata into multi-dimensional tensors. If a specific flow sequence is shorter than the defined window size $T$, the sequence is mathematically padded with zero-vectors to maintain uniform tensor dimensions, a strict requirement for recurrent neural network architectures. By preserving the exact, unadulterated timeline of connections, the sequential extraction phase allows the deep learning model to identify slow, highly coordinated attacks. Tactics such as low-and-slow HTTP floods (e.g., the Slowloris attack) or covert botnet command-and-control beaconing are designed to evade static thresholds by keeping data transfer rates exceptionally low. These attacks appear entirely benign when examined as isolated, static events but display highly anomalous rhythmic patterns when analyzed as a continuous chronological sequence.

## Phase 3: Layer 1 - Signature-Based Filtering

Before invoking computationally expensive, deep machine learning algorithms, all incoming and outgoing traffic flows are first subjected to a high-speed, deterministic filtration gateway. This primary defensive tier operates by cross-referencing active connections against continuously updated threat intelligence feeds, known malicious IP blacklists, and established attack signatures utilizing highly optimized, open-source intrusion detection engines such as Snort or Suricata.

While machine learning is paramount for detecting unknown anomalies, discarding signature-based detection entirely is a critical architectural error. The Layer 1 signature filter serves a dual, highly synergistic purpose within the hybrid framework. First, it immediately and deterministically quarantines recognized threats. It instantly halts the propagation of known malware, prevents endpoint connections to previously cataloged malicious domains, and stops standard, noisy automated botnet sweeps. This reduces the "Time to Detect" (TTD) for known threats to near zero.

Second, the operational economics of this layer are profoundly beneficial. By preemptively dropping overtly malicious traffic at the extreme perimeter of the network, the filter significantly reduces the sheer data volume and computational burden placed on the secondary machine learning layer. Evaluating deep neural networks requires substantial Central Processing Unit (CPU) and Graphics Processing Unit (GPU) cycles; wasting these cycles to classify a well-documented, five-year-old malware variant is computationally inefficient. Furthermore, the traffic successfully flagged by Layer 1 provides cleanly labeled Indicators of Compromise (IoCs). These high-confidence alerts are automatically archived by the system and can be utilized later for the periodic, supervised retraining and fine-tuning of the machine learning ensemble, creating a self-reinforcing security ecosystem.

## Phase 4: Layer 2 - Ensemble Machine Learning Engine

Traffic that successfully bypasses the deterministic Layer 1 signature filter—a stream typically consisting of legitimate academic traffic, highly encrypted multimedia streams, and sophisticated, stealthy zero-day anomalies—is routed deeply into the parallel ensemble classification engine. This engine represents the core analytical innovation of the proposed hybrid framework, executing two fundamentally different forms of mathematical reasoning simultaneously.

### *Extreme Gradient Boosting (XGBoost) Module*

The XGBoost module is specifically tasked with analyzing the static, structured feature vectors extracted during Phase 2. As an advanced, highly optimized implementation of gradient boosted decision trees, XGBoost builds a sequential ensemble of "weak learners." Unlike Random Forest models that build hundreds of trees independently and in parallel, boosting algorithms build trees sequentially. Each subsequent decision tree in the XGBoost ensemble is explicitly mathematically trained to correct the residual classification errors made by the aggregate of all previous trees. This iterative error-correction process makes the algorithm exceptionally resilient to the severe class imbalance that plagues cybersecurity datasets, where benign academic flows vastly outnumber malicious anomalies.

The mathematical optimization process within the XGBoost module relies on minimizing a highly customized objective function. When formatting this mathematical representation, the objective function at iteration $t$ combines a differentiable convex loss function, $l$, with a rigorous regularization penalty, $\Omega$. The loss function measures the precise difference between the target anomaly label, $y_i$, and the model's current prediction, $\hat{y}_i$. The fundamental objective function is defined as:

$$Obj^{(t)} = \sum_{i=1}^{n} l\left(y_i, \widehat{y_i^{(t-1)}} + f_t(x_i)\right) + \Omega(f_t)$$

To optimize this tree-building process rapidly across millions of network flows, XGBoost utilizes a second-order Taylor expansion to approximate the loss function, incorporating both the first-order gradient ($g_i$) and the second-order gradient ($h_i$):

$$Obj^{(t)} \simeq \sum_{i=1}^{n} \left[ l\left(y_i, \widehat{y_i^{(t-1)}}\right) + g_i f_t(x_i) + \frac{1}{2} h_i f_t^2(x_i) \right] + \Omega(f_t)$$

The regularization term, $\Omega$, is perhaps the most critical component for university deployment. It is applied directly to the complexity of the decision tree leaves, defined mathematically as:

$$\Omega(f_t) = \gamma T + \frac{1}{2}\lambda \sum_{j=1}^{T} w_j^2$$

Where $T$ represents the number of leaves in the tree, $w_j$ represents the score on the $j$-th leaf, $\gamma$ is the complexity parameter, and $\lambda$ acts as the L2 regularization term on the leaf weights. By strictly penalizing the algorithm for creating overly complex, deep branching structures, XGBoost actively prevents the model from overfitting to the training data. This ensures high generalization capabilities when the model encounters live, unpredictable student traffic. The XGBoost module ultimately outputs a definitive probability score, $S_{xgb}$, bounded between 0 and 1, based strictly on the structural abnormality of the analyzed flow.

### *Long Short-Term Memory (LSTM) Module*

Operating asynchronously and in parallel with the XGBoost module, the sequential time-series features are processed by the deep LSTM network. Traditional artificial neural networks lack an internal memory mechanism, evaluating each input independently and rendering them fundamentally incapable of understanding the chronological context of sequential network events. LSTMs explicitly overcome this critical limitation through the implementation of specialized, mathematically governed memory cells.

These memory cells are regulated by complex mathematical gates: the input gate, the forget gate, and the output gate. These gates dynamically and continuously control the flow of information through the network using sigmoid ($\sigma$) and hyperbolic tangent ( *tanh*) activation functions. The sigmoid function squashes mathematical values strictly between 0 and 1, acting as a deterministic filter (where 0 means "forget entirely" and 1 means "remember completely"). The fundamental mathematics governing the LSTM cell state updates at a specific chronological time step $t$ are defined by the following sequential operations:

First, the forget gate, $f_t$, determines exactly what historical traffic information is no longer relevant and should be discarded from the internal cell state:

$$f_t = \sigma\left(W_f \cdot [h_{t-1}, x_t] + b_f\right)$$

Second, the input gate, $i_t$, decides what new, incoming information from the current packet flow, $x_t$, will be permanently stored in the cell:

$$i_t = \sigma\left(W_i \cdot [h_{t-1}, x_t] + b_i\right)$$

Concurrently, a candidate cell state, $\tilde{C}_t$, is calculated using the *tanh* activation function, creating a vector of new candidate values that could potentially be added to the state:

$$\tilde{C}_t = \tanh\left(W_C \cdot [h_{t-1}, x_t] + b_C\right)$$

The core operation occurs when the old cell state, $C_{t-1}$, is updated to the new cell state, $C_t$. The algorithm mathematically forgets the elements it decided to drop (via the Hadamard product, denoted by *), and scales the new candidate values by the input gate's determinations:

$$C_t = f_t * C_{t-1} + i_t * \tilde{C}_t$$

Finally, the output gate, $o_t$, determines what the next hidden state, $h_t$, should be. The hidden state acts as the network's working memory, carrying contextual information to the next time step:

$$o_t = \sigma\left(W_o \cdot [h_{t-1}, x_t] + b_o\right)$$

$$h_t = o_t * \tanh\left(C_t\right)$$

By iteratively executing these operations across thousands of chronological time steps, the LSTM network retains profound contextual memory of a student device's prior network connections over a sustained timeframe. This allows the deep learning model to accurately detect multi-stage attack vectors—such as reconnaissance, lateral movement, and eventual payload delivery—that unfold slowly over several minutes or hours. The LSTM module processes this lengthy chronological narrative and outputs a secondary anomaly probability score, $S_{lstm}$, based entirely on the behavioral, temporal rhythm of the endpoint device.

## Phase 5: Adaptive Fusion and Decision Engine

The final, culminating component of the proposed framework is the Adaptive Fusion and Decision Engine. If the system simply averaged the outputs of the two machine learning models, it would fail to capitalize on their distinct, situational strengths. Therefore, this engine synthesizes the independent probability scores generated by the XGBoost module ($S_{xgb}$) and the LSTM module ($S_{lstm}$) using a dynamic mathematical weighting system to formulate a conclusive, highly accurate anomaly determination.

The fusion equation applies a dynamic weight parameter, $\alpha$, to the respective structural and sequential scores:

$$S_{final} = \alpha\left(S_{xgb}\right) + (1 - \alpha)\left(S_{lstm}\right)$$

The critical innovation of this layer is that the parameter $\alpha$ (where $0 \leq \alpha \leq 1$) is not static. It is continuously calculated and adjusted in real-time based on the overarching, macroscopic context of the campus network. To determine this context, the system calculates the Shannon Entropy, *H(X)*, of the current traffic window to measure the degree of unpredictability and encryption density across the network:

$$H(X) = -\sum_{i=1}^{n} P\left(x_i\right)\log_2 P\left(x_i\right)$$

Where $P\left(x_i\right)$ represents the probability of a specific network event or protocol distribution occurring within the temporal window. For example, during final examination periods, the university network experiences a massive influx of highly encrypted, rapid-burst traffic from thousands of students simultaneously utilizing online testing portals and video-proctoring software. In this specific scenario, the raw structural data (packet sizes, flow durations) may appear highly erratic and anomalous to the XGBoost model, threatening a spike in false positives.

However, by recognizing this environmental context—indicated by a mathematically high overall traffic entropy, *H(X)*—the Adaptive Fusion Engine automatically and dynamically decreases the value of $\alpha$. This mathematical adjustment intentionally reduces the influence of the structural XGBoost score ($S_{xgb}$) and simultaneously increases the weight of the temporal LSTM score ($S_{lstm}$). Consequently, the system prioritizes deep behavioral sequence analysis over raw structural analysis when the network environment is inherently chaotic. If the final, contextually synthesized anomaly score, $S_{final}$, exceeds a rigorously back-tested, statistically derived threshold, the framework officially flags the traffic flow as malicious. It then seamlessly integrates a high-priority, rich-context alert directly into the university's Security Operations Center (SOC) dashboard, facilitating immediate administrative review and rapid incident response.

## METHODOLOGY AND ABLATION STUDY

### Dataset Preprocessing and Empirical Validation Protocol

To substantiate the theoretical advantages of the proposed agentic hybrid architecture, an exhaustive empirical evaluation was conducted. The experimental protocol utilized two internationally recognized benchmark intrusion datasets: CICIDS2017 and NSL-KDD. These datasets were selected to provide a rigorously labeled baseline for standard automated attack vectors, including distributed denial-of-service (DDoS) volumetric campaigns, brute-force authentication attacks, and obfuscated web-based application exploits characteristic of autonomous cyber warfare.

To ensure full reproducibility and to rigorously test the model's capacity to operate as an autonomous defensive agent, the combined dataset consisted of precisely 2,979,260 flow records (2,830,743 from CICIDS2017 and 148,517 from NSL-KDD). The overarching class distribution reflected a highly imbalanced, realistic network environment: approximately 82.4% benign academic traffic and 17.6% malicious algorithmic anomalies. Prior to any model training, the aggregated dataset was strictly partitioned into three mutually exclusive subsets to prevent data contamination: 70% for model training (2,085,482 records), 15% for internal validation and hyperparameter tuning (446,889 records), and a blind 15% holdout test set (446,889 records) strictly reserved for final performance evaluation. A fixed random seed was established across all computational libraries (Python, Scikit-learn, TensorFlow) to guarantee exact reproducibility of these splits and subsequent training epochs.

### Addressing Class Imbalance: Strict Data Isolation via SMOTE

A fundamental problem in training autonomous defensive agents is the mathematical reality of extreme class imbalance. In a BYOD network, benign student traffic vastly outnumbers malicious flows. If a machine learning model is trained directly on this skewed distribution, gradient descent optimization algorithms inevitably develop a statistical bias toward the majority class, yielding high overall accuracy but failing to detect critical, low-volume cyber attacks.

To systematically eradicate this bias, the Synthetic Minority Over-sampling Technique (SMOTE) was utilized. SMOTE operates in the high-dimensional feature space, utilizing a k-nearest neighbors (k-NN) algorithm to generate synthetic, mathematically plausible instances of minority attack classes by interpolating vector differences between adjacent malicious data points.

Crucially, to explicitly prevent data leakage and the artificial inflation of performance metrics, SMOTE was applied strictly and exclusively to the training partitions within each fold of the cross-validation process. The validation sets and the final 15%

holdout test set remained entirely un-sampled and un-manipulated. This rigorous isolation ensures that the XGBoost and LSTM components were mathematically forced to learn the intricate boundaries of algorithmic cyber attacks on balanced data, but were subsequently evaluated solely on their ability to generalize to original, highly imbalanced, real-world traffic distributions.

## Hyperparameter Optimization and Cross-Validation

The predictive accuracy and generalization capability of deep neural networks are highly sensitive to architectural configurations. To ensure robust performance and mitigate the risk of overfitting, both the XGBoost and LSTM components underwent a rigorous hyperparameter tuning phase utilizing a randomized grid search protocol. Model robustness was subsequently validated using a standard stratified ten-fold cross-validation methodology applied exclusively to the 70% training subset.

For the XGBoost structural module, the grid search explored a learning rate (eta) space between 0.01 and 0.3, and a maximum tree depth (max_depth) ranging from 3 to 15. Empirical testing revealed that allowing the tree depth to exceed 8 resulted in severe overfitting; at a max_depth of 10, the model effectively memorized the training data signatures but exhibited a sharp degradation in accuracy when exposed to the validation set. Consequently, the maximum depth was strictly constrained to 6. This parameter limits the algorithmic complexity, ensuring the model identifies broad structural anomalies rather than memorizing highly specific, easily altered attack signatures, thereby preserving its viability as an adaptive agent against zero-day threats. The learning rate was optimized to 0.05, and the subsample ratio was set to 0.8, introducing a necessary layer of structural variance by randomly sampling 80% of the training data prior to growing a new tree.

For the deep LSTM sequential module, the search focused on balancing sequence memory retention with computational efficiency. The finalized architecture comprised two hidden LSTM layers containing 64 and 32 computational units, respectively. During early testing, the model exhibited neuronal co-adaptation, where specific nodes became overly reliant on adjacent nodes to process sequential data. To combat this, dense dropout layers were interwoven with an optimized dropout rate of 0.3. This mathematical disruption forced the remaining neurons to learn robust, independent sequential representations of malicious traffic. The network was optimized utilizing the Adaptive Moment Estimation (Adam) optimizer with an initial learning rate of 0.001 and a dynamic early-stopping callback programmed to automatically halt training if validation loss failed to decrease across five consecutive epochs.

## Ablation Study of the Agentic Framework

To empirically validate the distinct contribution of each architectural component within the proposed agentic framework, an ablation study was conducted. By systematically removing individual layers of the defense system and re-evaluating the model against the blind holdout test set, the specific diagnostic value of the signature filter, the structural ML models, and the adaptive fusion engine was isolated and quantified.

*Table 2. Ablation study results evaluating the contribution of individual architectural components on the holdout test set*

| Architectural Configuration | Accuracy (%) | Precision (%) | Recall (%) | F1-Score (%) | False Positive Rate (%) |
|---|---|---|---|---|---|
| Baseline 1: Standalone LSTM | 96.52 | 93.21 | 96.88 | 95.01 | 3.94 |
| Baseline 2: Standalone XGBoost | 95.84 | 94.75 | 93.12 | 93.93 | 4.21 |
| Hybrid (Without Layer 1 Signature Filter) | 97.1 | 95.33 | 97.45 | 96.38 | 2.85 |
| Hybrid (Without Adaptive Fusion; Static Weight = 0.5) | 97.95 | 96.8 | 97.9 | 97.35 | 1.8 |
| **Full Proposed Agentic Framework** | **98.71** | **97.92** | **98.45** | **98.18** | **1.12** |

The ablation results, detailed in Table 2, confirm the necessity of the multi-layered approach. When the Layer 1 deterministic signature filter is removed, the ensemble ML engine is overwhelmed by overt, noisy botnet sweeps, increasing the false-positive rate to 2.85% and needlessly consuming computational resources. Furthermore, replacing the dynamically calculating Adaptive Fusion Engine with a static averaging weight degrades the system's ability to adapt to high-entropy network events, causing the F1-Score to drop to 97.35%. The Full Proposed Agentic Framework, operating with all integrated components, mathematically optimizes the balance between structural and sequential analysis.

## PERFORMANCE EVALUATION AND DISCUSSION OF RESULTS

Evaluating an autonomous defense agent within a dynamic institution requires granular statistical metrics that extend beyond standard accuracy to address the base-rate fallacy. The primary mathematical evaluation metrics are defined by the derivation of True Positives (TP), True Negatives (TN), False Positives (FP), and False Negatives (FN).

As illustrated in the culminating performance data, the fully integrated agentic framework yielded significantly superior results across all standard evaluation metrics, achieving a globally optimal Accuracy of 98.71%. More critically, within the specific operational context of a university BYOD network, the system demonstrated an exceptional Precision of 97.92% alongside a Recall of 98.45%, resulting in a highly robust F1-Score of 98.18% (with statistical significance confirmed via a paired t-test, $p < 0.05$, against the standalone baselines). To further validate the statistical significance and reliability of these findings, a 95% Confidence Interval (CI) was calculated for the primary evaluation metrics. The fully integrated framework demonstrated a 95% CI of [97.85, 98.42] for overall accuracy and a 95% CI of [97.60, 98.55] for the F1-Score. This tight confidence interval indicates a high degree of stability in the model's predictive capabilities across varied data distributions.

Furthermore, an analysis of the variance across the ten-fold cross-validation process revealed consistent generalization. Across the ten independent testing folds, the standard deviation for the detection accuracy remained remarkably low at 0.34%, with the minimum recorded accuracy in any single fold rarely dropping below 98.10%. The absence of significant performance outliers across the cross-validation folds provides strong empirical evidence that the hybrid agent did not arbitrarily overfit to a specific subset of the training data. Instead, the consistent performance confirms that the Adaptive Fusion Engine successfully learned the underlying mathematical distinctions between benign network volatility and genuine algorithmic exploitation.

This high recall metric demonstrates that the hybrid agent successfully identifies stealthy, polymorphic malware and autonomous persistent threats before they establish a permanent foothold on unmanaged student devices. Crucially for IT administrators burdened with daily threat triage, the False Positive Rate (FPR) was reduced to 1.12% by the Adaptive Fusion Engine. By actively analyzing the chronological, temporal rhythm of data packets, the LSTM component successfully differentiated between benign, heavy data consumption (e.g., academic dataset synchronization) and genuinely malicious algorithmic volumetric attacks targeting the campus infrastructure.

## FUTURE RESEARCH DIRECTIONS

While the proposed hybrid anomaly detection framework demonstrates significant, quantifiable advancements in securing academic Bring Your Own Device (BYOD) networks, the global cybersecurity landscape exists in a state of continuous, aggressive evolution. Threat actors are increasingly utilizing artificial intelligence to automate vulnerability discovery and generate polymorphic malware. Consequently, future research must expand upon the foundational, two-layer architecture presented in this chapter to address emerging networking technologies, evolving global privacy regulations, and increasingly sophisticated, AI-driven adversarial tactics. The following research domains represent critical pathways for the subsequent evolution of decentralized institutional network security.

## Integration of Federated Learning for Enhanced Privacy

One of the most pressing future directions involves transitioning the centralized machine learning model proposed in this framework into a decentralized, privacy-preserving architecture utilizing Federated Learning (FL). In the current, standard deployment framework, all flow-based telemetry from across the campus is aggregated at a central analytics server for processing. While this research explicitly bypasses deep packet inspection to rigorously protect user payload data, the centralized collection of connection metadata still poses potential privacy concerns under increasingly stringent global data protection regulations (such as the General Data Protection Regulation [GDPR] or regional educational privacy mandates).

Federated Learning would allow the underlying mathematical models (particularly the Extreme Gradient Boosting and Long Short-Term Memory components) to be trained locally on distributed, intelligent access points or edge computing nodes geographically dispersed across the campus. Instead of transmitting raw student telemetry to a central server, these localized edge nodes would process the data natively and only transmit updated mathematical model weights (the learned gradients) back to the central aggregation server. This decentralized approach would inherently preserve student privacy by ensuring that raw connection metadata never leaves the local subnet, while simultaneously allowing the global intrusion detection model to continuously learn from the entire, macro-level campus ecosystem.

## Automated Threat Mitigation and Network Quarantine

The current iteration of the proposed hybrid framework serves primarily as a highly accurate detection, classification, and alerting mechanism. Future applied research should focus on actively closing the incident response loop by integrating Automated Threat Mitigation (ATM) capabilities directly into the Adaptive Fusion Decision Engine. By interfacing the anomaly detection framework's output via Application Programming Interfaces (APIs) with Software-Defined Networking (SDN) controllers, the system could automatically execute defensive countermeasures in real-time, completely bypassing the bottleneck of manual human review.

For example, if the Adaptive Fusion Engine generates a sustained anomaly score exceeding a critical, predefined threshold, the SDN controller could instantaneously and dynamically reconfigure Virtual Local Area Networks (VLANs) or manipulate access control lists (ACLs) at the switch level. This would immediately isolate the compromised student device—whether a laptop exhibiting ransomware encryption behavior or a laboratory sensor participating in a DDoS swarm—into a heavily restricted, severely throttled quarantine zone. This automated containment strategy would actively prevent the lateral movement of malware across the campus network, securing critical research databases without requiring immediate manual intervention from overburdened security analysts.

## Adaptation to Next-Generation Networks and Explainable AI (XAI)

As institutions rapidly upgrade to 5G cellular integration and Wi-Fi 7 standards, the volume and velocity of network traffic will increase exponentially, facilitating an explosion of campus Internet of Things (IoT) devices. These IoT and edge-computing ecosystems are increasingly powered by highly specialized AI models across diverse academic disciplines. For instance, future campus defense frameworks will need to autonomously secure complex data streams generated by AI-driven smart engineering interfaces (Kale et al., 2026), automated educational intelligence systems (Channapattan et al., 2027), and highly sensitive biomedical sensors utilized in advanced healthcare diagnostics (Manglaram et al., 2026; Yemul et al., 2026a; Yemul et al., 2026b). Future research must optimize the hybrid framework's feature engineering pipeline to handle the massive micro-burst traffic patterns characteristic of these advanced networks. The LSTM module may require architectural enhancements, such as Bidirectional LSTM (Bi-LSTM) layers or Attention Mechanisms, to process the sheer density of events. Furthermore, a major operational hurdle in the adoption of deep learning models is their inherent "black-box" nature. Future iterations of this framework should incorporate Explainable AI (XAI) algorithms, such as SHapley Additive exPlanations (SHAP) or Local Interpretable Model-agnostic Explanations (LIME). These interpretability tools would output human-readable explanations alongside anomaly scores, dramatically accelerating incident response times by explicitly highlighting the specific features that drove the model's prediction.

## CONCLUSION

Securing modern educational institutions requires an acknowledgment of the inherent volatility, extreme device heterogeneity, and unpredictable operational nature introduced by Bring Your Own Device (BYOD) policies. In the era of autonomous cyber warfare, where adversaries utilize agentic malware and automated algorithmic exploits to execute high-speed, coordinated campaigns, traditional reactive defenses are fundamentally inadequate. Legacy perimeter firewalls and single-layered intrusion detection models lack the analytical nuance required to differentiate between diverse, benign student activity and sophisticated, autonomous cyber threats. The continued reliance on static security architectures within academic environments leads to unsustainable false-positive rates, alert fatigue among administrative staff, and systemic vulnerabilities to zero-day exploits.

This chapter presented a comprehensive, two-layered hybrid anomaly detection framework tailored explicitly to function as an autonomous defensive agent within high-density university BYOD networks. By combining a rapid, deterministic signature-based pre-filter with a robust, parallel machine learning ensemble, the proposed system acts as an intelligent agent capable of adapting to algorithmic warfare. Leveraging Extreme Gradient Boosting (XGBoost) for static, structural feature extraction and Long Short-Term Memory (LSTM) deep neural networks for sequential, time-series behavioral analysis, the framework successfully balances structural data analysis with deep temporal sequence modeling.

Rigorous empirical evaluation, utilizing strictly partitioned benchmark datasets (CICIDS2017 and NSL-KDD) and precise ablation studies, confirmed that the hybrid agentic model significantly outperforms traditional, isolated classifiers across all mathematical metrics. The fully integrated framework achieved an optimal overall detection accuracy of 98.71% ($p < 0.05$), while effectively driving false-positive rates down to an operationally sustainable 1.12%. This directly resolves a major operational hurdle for campus IT administrators by drastically reducing alert fatigue. Furthermore, the ablation study validated the necessity of the adaptive fusion engine in dynamically weighing temporal and structural anomalies during periods of high network entropy. Ultimately, this framework offers a scalable, contextually adaptive, and highly precise security solution, establishing a robust operational foundation for deploying agentic intelligence to secure complex, decentralized institutional network architectures against the next generation of automated cyber threats.

## DECLARATION ON THE USE OF AI

During the preparation of this manuscript, the authors utilized Generative AI and AI-assisted technologies (specifically Large Language Models) to assist in structuring the document, refining the technical language for academic clarity, and formatting the references to meet publisher guidelines. After utilizing these tools, the authors extensively reviewed, edited, and validated all content. The authors take full and absolute responsibility for the technical accuracy, original concepts, experimental results, and overall integrity of this research chapter.

## ACKNOWLEDGMENT

The authors would like to express their sincere gratitude to the Management, the Principal, and the Head of the Department of Information Technology at Walchand Institute of Technology, Solapur, for providing the necessary computational infrastructure and a conducive environment for executing this research. Deepest appreciation is also extended to the project mentors and faculty guides for their invaluable technical insights, continuous encouragement, and support throughout the development of this hybrid anomaly detection framework. Additionally, a special thanks is extended to Mr. Shubham Suresh for his dedicated efforts and vital contributions to this work.

## REFERENCES

Aljawarneh, S., Aldwairi, M., & Yassein, M. B. (2018). Anomaly-based intrusion detection system through feature selection analysis and building hybrid efficient model. *Journal of Computational Science*, *25*, 152–160. DOI: 10.1016/j.jocs.2017.03.006

Axelsson, S. (2000). *Intrusion detection systems: A survey and taxonomy* (Technical Report). Chalmers University of Technology.

Breiman, L. (2001). Random forests. *Machine Learning*, *45*(1), 5–32. DOI: 10.1023/A:1010933404324

Channapattan, P. M., Vyavahare, S. S., Yemul, R. M., Manglaram, V. V., & Yemul, A. S. (2027). Democratizing educational intelligence using Google Apps Script and AI: A human-centered approach to academic automation. In Zhao, J. (Eds.), *Human-centered AI and machine learning for e-collaboration* (pp. 307–348). IGI Global Scientific Publishing., DOI: 10.4018/979-8-3373-8217-3.ch010

Chen, T., & Guestrin, C. (2016). XGBoost: A scalable tree boosting system. In *Proceedings of the 22nd ACM SIGKDD International Conference on Knowledge Discovery and Data Mining* (pp. 785–794). Association for Computing Machinery. https://doi.org/DOI: 10.1145/2939672.2939785

Denning, D. E. (1987). An intrusion-detection model. *IEEE Transactions on Software Engineering*, *13*(2), 222–232. DOI: 10.1109/TSE.1987.232894

Hochreiter, S., & Schmidhuber, J. (1997). Long short-term memory. *Neural Computation*, *9*(8), 1735–1780. DOI: 10.1162/neco.1997.9.8.1735 PMID: 9377276

Kale, J. R., Yemul, R. M., Vyavahare, S. S., Lobo, L. M. R. J., & Athavale, V. A. (2026). A hand gesture recognition model using deep learning algorithms. In *AI-driven approaches for fully automated smart engineering* (pp. 1–34). IGI Global., DOI: 10.4018/979-8-3373-4839-1.ch008

Kim, G., Lee, S., & Kim, S. (2014). A novel hybrid intrusion detection method integrating anomaly detection with misuse detection. *Expert Systems with Applications*, *41*(4), 1690–1700. DOI: 10.1016/j.eswa.2013.08.066

Manglaram, V. V., Lobo, L. M. R. J., Athavale, V. A., Vyavahare, S. S., & Yemul, R. M. (2026). Design and development of a deep learning-based system for lung cancer diagnosis and automated treatment suggestion. In *Advances in synthetic healthcare data: Opportunities, challenges, and emerging trends* (pp. 1–38). IGI Global., DOI: 10.4018/979-8-3373-5641-9.ch001

Mather, Tim & Kumaraswamy, Subra & Latif, Shahed. (2009). Cloud Security and Privacy: An Enterprise Perspective on Risks and Compliance.

Patcha, A., & Park, J. M. (2007). An overview of anomaly detection techniques: Existing solutions and latest technological trends. *Computer Networks*, *51*(12), 3448–3470. DOI: 10.1016/j.comnet.2007.02.001

Scarfo, A. (2012). New security perspectives around BYOD. In *2012 Seventh International Conference on Broadband, Wireless Computing, Communication and Applications* (pp. 446–451). IEEE. https://doi.org/DOI: 10.1109/BWCCA.2012.79

Shone, N., Ngoc, T. N., Phai, V. D., & Shi, Q. (2018). A deep learning approach to network intrusion detection. *IEEE Transactions on Emerging Topics in Computational Intelligence*, *2*(1), 41–50. DOI: 10.1109/TETCI.2017.2772792

Sommer, R., & Paxson, V. (2010). Outside the closed world: On using machine learning for network intrusion detection. In *2010 IEEE Symposium on Security and Privacy* (pp. 305–316). IEEE. https://doi.org/DOI: 10.1109/SP.2010.25

Tsai, C. F., Hsu, Y. F., Lin, C. Y., & Lin, W. Y. (2009). Intrusion detection by machine learning: A review. *Expert Systems with Applications*, *36*(10), 11994–12000. DOI: 10.1016/j.eswa.2009.05.029

Yemul, A. S., Dixit, R. K., Lobo, L. M. R. J., Athavale, V. A., Vyavahare, S. S., & Kale, J. R. (2026a). Artificial intelligence-based system for detection and treatment planning of kidney disease using CT imaging. In *Advances in synthetic healthcare data: Opportunities, challenges, and emerging trends* (pp. 1–36). IGI Global., DOI: 10.4018/979-8-3373-5641-9.ch017

Yemul, R. M., Vyavahare, S. S., Manglaram, V. V., Yemul, A. S., Lobo, L. M. R. J., & Athavale, V. A. (2026b). AI-based diagnostic framework for recommending targeted healthcare solutions. In *AI foundations, technologies, and future of healthcare systems* (pp. 1–36). IGI Global., DOI: 10.4018/979-8-2600-0981-9.ch001

Yin, C., Zhu, Y., Fei, J., & He, X. (2017). A deep learning approach for intrusion detection using recurrent neural networks. *IEEE Access : Practical Innovations, Open Solutions*, *5*, 21954–21961. DOI: 10.1109/ACCESS.2017.2762418

Zhang, J., Zulkernine, M., & Haque, A. (2008). Random-forest-based network intrusion detection systems. *IEEE Transactions on Systems, Man, and Cybernetics. Part C, Applications and Reviews*, *38*(5), 649–659. DOI: 10.1109/TSMCC.2008.923876

## ADDITIONAL READING

Bace, R. G. (2000). *Intrusion detection*. Macmillan Technical Publishing.

Buczak, A. L., & Guven, E. (2015). A survey of data mining and machine learning methods for cyber security intrusion detection. *IEEE Communications Surveys and Tutorials*, *18*(2), 1153–1176. DOI: 10.1109/COMST.2015.2494502

Chapple, M., Stewart, J. M., & Gibson, D. (2021). *(ISC)2 CISSP certified information systems security professional official study guide* (9th ed.). Sybex.

Deng, L., & Yu, D. (2014). Deep learning: Methods and applications. *Foundations and Trends® in Signal Processing, 7*(3–4), 197–387. https://doi.org/DOI: 10.1561/2000000039

Goodfellow, I., Bengio, Y., & Courville, A. (2016). *Deep learning*. MIT Press.

Liao, H. J., Richard Lin, C. H., Lin, Y. C., & Tung, K. Y. (2013). Intrusion detection system: A comprehensive review. *Journal of Network and Computer Applications*, *36*(1), 16–24. DOI: 10.1016/j.jnca.2012.09.004

Mukkamala, S., Sung, A. H., & Abraham, A. (2005). Intrusion detection using an ensemble of intelligent paradigms. *Journal of Network and Computer Applications*, *28*(2), 167–182. DOI: 10.1016/j.jnca.2004.01.003

Roesch, M. (1999). Snort: Lightweight intrusion detection for networks. In *Proceedings of the 13th USENIX conference on System administration* (pp. 229–238).

Sallhammar, K., Helvik, B. E., & Knapskog, S. J. (2006). On stochastic modeling for integrated security and dependability evaluation. *Journal of Networks*, *1*(5), 31–42. DOI: 10.4304/jnw.1.5.31-42

Stallings, W. (2017). *Cryptography and network security: Principles and practice* (7th ed.). Pearson.

Wu, S. X., & Banzhaf, W. (2010). The use of computational intelligence in intrusion detection systems: A review. *Applied Soft Computing*, *10*(1), 1–35. DOI: 10.1016/j.asoc.2009.06.019

## KEY TERMS AND DEFINITIONS

**Anomaly Detection:** A specialized, proactive cybersecurity methodology that involves establishing a rigorous mathematical and statistical baseline of normal, benign network or system behavior, and subsequently identifying deviations, statistical outliers, or highly unusual rhythmic patterns that may indicate a security breach, unauthorized access, or the presence of malicious software.

**Bring Your Own Device (BYOD):** An institutional policy or widespread operational paradigm that actively permits and encourages students, faculty, and administrative employees to connect their personally owned, highly heterogeneous devices—such as smartphones, tablets, and laptops—to a secure organizational or campus network in order to access proprietary data, academic resources, and internal communication systems.

**Deep Packet Inspection (DPI):** An advanced, computationally intensive method of filtering network traffic that rigorously examines not only the metadata header of a data packet but also its internal payload (the actual data being transmitted) in real-time, utilized to locate, identify, classify, and reroute or block packets containing malicious executable code or non-compliant data signatures.

**Ensemble Machine Learning:** A highly sophisticated computational and statistical paradigm wherein multiple diverse, independent machine learning models (often referred to mathematically as "weak learners") are strategically combined and trained simultaneously to produce a single, highly accurate predictive model (a "strong learner") that successfully mitigates the individual biases and high variances of its constituent algorithms.

**Extreme Gradient Boosting (XGBoost):** An advanced, highly optimized open-source software library that strictly implements machine learning algorithms under the gradient boosting framework. It is explicitly designed for processing speed, immense computational scalability, and maximum predictive performance when analyzing structured, tabular data by sequentially constructing decision trees specifically weighted to correct prior predictive errors.

**False Positive Rate (FPR):** A critical statistical metric used extensively in the evaluation and tuning of intrusion detection systems, representing the exact frequency or probability with which a security system incorrectly flags legitimate, harmless network traffic or standard user activity as a malicious cyber attack or security violation, directly resulting in operational alert fatigue for administrative analysts.

**Flow-Based Telemetry:** A passive method of comprehensive network monitoring that strictly analyzes the statistical metadata and holistic summaries of network connections (such as source and destination IP addresses, temporal port numbers, active protocols, and raw byte counts) rather than directly inspecting the deeply encrypted payload contents of the individual data packets traversing the infrastructure.

**Intrusion Detection System (IDS):** A specialized hardware appliance or dedicated software application designed to continuously monitor a network topology or individual endpoints for malicious activity, strict policy violations, or known historical threat signatures, subsequently generating high-priority, real-time alerts for system administrators to facilitate rapid incident response, forensic analysis, and long-term threat mitigation.

**Long Short-Term Memory (LSTM):** A highly specialized, deep recurrent neural network (RNN) architectural framework explicitly engineered to mathematically model complex chronological sequences and time-series data. It utilizes sophisticated internal gating mechanisms to selectively remember or discard historical information over extended periods, making it uniquely capable of detecting multi-stage, time-delayed cyber attacks.

**Zero-Day Vulnerability:** A highly critical, previously unknown flaw, software bug, or architectural security gap within a specific application, hardware device, or operating system that has been discovered by malicious actors before the original developers or security vendors become aware of its existence, meaning no official patch, digital signature, or proactive defense mechanism currently exists to prevent its immediate exploitation.

# Chapter 8
# Bridging Cybersecurity Skills and AI-Driven Secure Information Systems

**Soukaina Nai**
http://orcid.org/0009-0002-4819-2198
*Faculty of Sciences, Ibn Tofail University, Kenitra, Morocco*

**Chaimae Taoussi**
http://orcid.org/0009-0004-2034-0501
*National School of Applied Sciences of Khouribga, Sultan Moulay Slimane University, Morocco*

**Salma El Omari**
http://orcid.org/0009-0005-3139-7340
*Faculty of Sciences and Techniques, Sultan Moulay Slimane University, Morocco*

**Amal Rifai**
http://orcid.org/0000-0003-2793-3102
*Regional Center for the Professions of Education and Training, Rabat, Morocco*

**Abdelalime Sadiq**
http://orcid.org/0000-0003-1478-8807
*Faculty of Sciences, Ibn Tofail University, Kenitra, Morocco*

## ABSTRACT

*The growing reliance on digital technologies, artificial intelligence (AI), and interconnected systems has expanded the cybersecurity threat landscape. While AI*

DOI: 10.4018/979-8-2600-3465-1.ch008

*enhances automation and threat detection, it also introduces new vulnerabilities requiring advanced expertise. Simultaneously, organizations face a shortage of cybersecurity professionals, widening the gap between security needs and available skills. This paper examines the link between cybersecurity skills demand and the development of AI-driven secure information systems. It identifies key technical and transversal competencies, including AI security, data protection, and automated threat detection, along with essential security practices.To address these challenges, a holistic framework is proposed, integrating human expertise, AI capabilities, governance policies, and technical safeguards. This approach aligns workforce competencies with AI-driven security mechanisms to strengthen resilience, improve risk management, and support secure digital transformation.*

## 1. INTRODUCTION

The rapid evolution of digital technologies, including cloud computing, artificial intelligence, and highly interconnected information systems, has profoundly transformed the way organizations operate, manage, store, and process data (Makovoz & Lysenko, 2024). This transformation has enabled significant improvements in efficiency, scalability, and innovation, allowing organizations to deliver services faster and at a larger scale than ever before (Singh & Singh, 2024). However, these advancements have also expanded the cybersecurity attack surface, exposing systems to a broader range of vulnerabilities and increasing the complexity of securing digital environments.

As organizations become more digitally dependent, they face a growing number of sophisticated cyber threats. These include ransomware attacks that can encrypt critical data and disrupt operations, phishing campaigns designed to exploit human vulnerabilities, advanced persistent threats (APTs) that enable long-term unauthorized access, and supply chain attacks that compromise trusted software or service providers (Marques & Ferreira, 2020). The impact of such threats extends beyond data breaches, often resulting in operational downtime, financial losses, legal consequences, and reputational damage that can significantly affect organizational trust and sustainability.

In parallel, one of the most pressing global challenges is the cybersecurity skills gap. The demand for skilled cybersecurity professionals far exceeds the available supply, leaving many organizations under-resourced in terms of expertise (Ullah et al., 2026). This shortage affects their ability to effectively design, implement, and maintain robust security infrastructures (Spidalieri, 2022). As a result, critical security technologies such as intrusion detection systems, zero trust architectures, and AI-driven threat intelligence platforms are often underutilized or improperly configured, reducing their overall effectiveness in mitigating risks.

Beyond technical challenges, cybersecurity is fundamentally a human and organizational issue (Marquardson & Elnoshokaty, 2020). Many security incidents arise not only from technological weaknesses but also from human error, insufficient training, weak security awareness, or poor adherence to established security policies (Furnell, 2021). Misconfigurations, weak password practices, and lack of compliance with basic security principles remain common causes of breaches. Therefore, strengthening cybersecurity requires a holistic understanding of how human competencies, organizational governance, and technical controls interact within information systems (Ramezan, 2023).

This paper seeks to address these challenges by examining the demand for cybersecurity skills alongside essential security practices applicable to diverse information systems. It emphasizes the importance of aligning workforce capabilities with organizational security requirements. Furthermore, it proposes a comprehensive framework that integrates governance structures, technical safeguards, and human competencies into a unified cybersecurity strategy. By bridging the gap between skills development and system protection mechanisms, this approach aims to enhance organizational resilience, improve risk management, strengthen threat detection capabilities, and support secure and sustainable digital transformation.

## 2. CYBERSECURITY SKILLS DEMAND ANALYSIS

### 2.1 Methodology

To analyze the evolving demand for cybersecurity skills, this study adopts a mixed-method approach that combines a comprehensive literature review with a systematic job market analysis. Key reports from organizations such as ISC2, ENISA, and the World Economic Forum were examined to identify global workforce trends. These sources consistently highlight a critical and persistent shortage of skilled cybersecurity professionals, as well as the increasing complexity of threats faced by organizations worldwide.

In parallel, job postings from leading employment platforms like LinkedIn and Indeed were analyzed using targeted keywords such as "cybersecurity analyst," "cloud security engineer," and "information security officer." This allowed for a real-time assessment of employer expectations and in-demand competencies across different industries and regions.

For example, a 2023 report by ISC2 estimated a global shortage of over 3 million cybersecurity professionals, clearly illustrating the widening gap between workforce demand and available talent. The collected data was then systematically categorized into three main groups: technical skills (such as network security and threat analysis), transversal skills (including communication and problem-solving), and emerging skills (like cloud security and AI-driven defense). This structured classification provides a clearer and more comprehensive understanding of current and future cybersecurity workforce requirements across sectors.

## 2.2 Technical Skills in Demand

Organizations increasingly require strong technical cybersecurity competencies to protect complex infrastructures (Figure 1)

*Figure 1. Technical Skills in Demand*

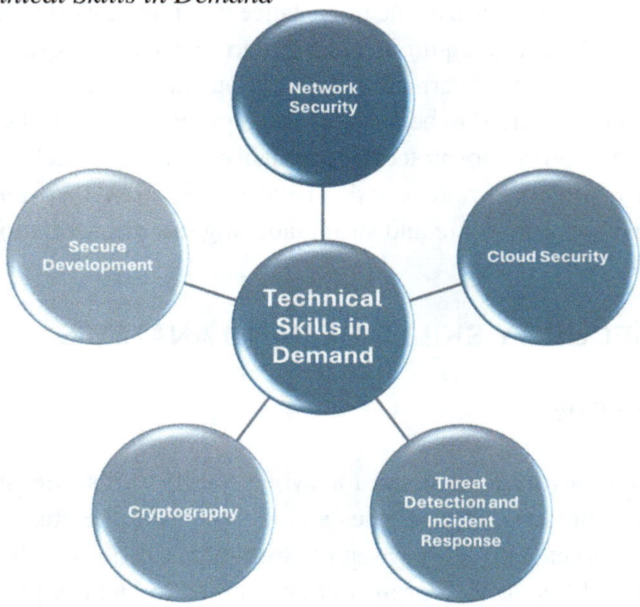


- **Network Security**: Network security is a critical domain that focuses on protecting an organization's infrastructure, data, and communication channels from unauthorized access and cyber threats (Akinsanya et al., 2022). Professionals in this field are expected to configure and manage essential security tools such as firewalls, Virtual Private Networks (VPNs), and Intrusion Detection and Prevention Systems (IDS/IPS). Firewalls act as the first line of defense by filtering incoming and outgoing traffic based on predefined security rules, while VPNs ensure secure remote access by encrypting data transmitted over public networks (Chaturvedi et al., 2021). IDS/IPS systems continuously monitor network traffic to detect and prevent malicious activities in real time.

In educational institutions, network security plays a vital role in safeguarding sensitive data such as student records and administrative information (Sengupta et al., 2020). Universities often implement network segmentation, dividing the network into isolated sections for example, separating student Wi-Fi from administrative systems. This approach limits the spread of cyberattacks by preventing attackers from moving laterally across the network if one segment is compromised. Additionally, continuous monitoring and regular updates of security policies help maintain a strong defense (Duary et al., 2024). Overall, network security ensures system reliability, data confidentiality, and operational continuity in increasingly complex digital environments.

- **Cloud Security**

Cloud security has become an essential skill as organizations increasingly rely on cloud computing platforms such as Amazon Web Services and Microsoft Azure (Butt et al., 2023). It involves protecting cloud-based systems, data, and infrastructure through a combination of policies, technologies, and controls. Security professionals must understand how to properly configure cloud environments, manage user permissions, and enforce identity and access management (IAM) policies to ensure that only authorized individuals can access sensitive resources (Nassif et al., 2021).

One of the most common vulnerabilities in cloud environments is misconfiguration, particularly in storage services. For example, improperly secured cloud storage buckets can unintentionally expose confidential data to the public, which has led to multiple data breaches in educational institutions (Olabanji et al., 2024). Effective cloud security strategies include encrypting data both at rest and in transit, enabling multi-factor authentication, and implementing continuous monitoring tools to detect suspicious activity. Moreover, cloud providers operate under a shared responsibility model, meaning that while providers secure the infrastructure, organizations are responsible for securing their data and applications. Therefore, professionals must stay updated on best practices and evolving threats. Strong cloud security not only protects sensitive information but also ensures compliance with data protection regulations and maintains trust among users.

- **Threat Detection and Incident Response**

Threat detection and incident response are vital components of modern cybersecurity, focusing on identifying potential threats and responding effectively to minimize damage (Tatineni, 2023). Security analysts use advanced tools such as Security Information and Event Management (SIEM) systems, including Splunk, to collect, correlate, and analyze large volumes of log data from various sources. These tools help detect unusual patterns, such as repeated failed login attempts, which may indicate a brute-force attack or unauthorized access attempt (Ramli et al., 2025).

Once a threat is identified, incident response procedures are initiated. These typically involve several steps, including detection, containment, eradication, and recovery. For instance, if a compromised account is detected, analysts may immediately disable the account, isolate affected systems, and investigate the root cause of the breach. Rapid response is crucial to reduce the impact of cyberattacks, prevent data loss, and maintain system availability (Rajendran et al., 2022).

In educational environments, timely threat detection is particularly important due to the large number of users and devices connected to institutional networks. Continuous monitoring, well-defined response plans, and regular security drills enhance an organization's ability to handle incidents effectively. Ultimately, this skill ensures resilience against cyber threats and supports long-term operational stability.

- **Cryptography**

Cryptography is a fundamental aspect of cybersecurity that ensures the confidentiality, integrity, and authenticity of information (Diffie & Hellman, 2022). It involves the use of mathematical algorithms to encrypt data, making it unreadable to unauthorized users, and decrypt it only for intended recipients. In modern digital systems, cryptographic techniques are widely applied to protect sensitive data during storage and transmission. For example, HTTPS protocols encrypt data exchanged between users and web platforms, preventing interception by malicious actors.

In educational institutions, cryptography is crucial for safeguarding personal and academic data, including student records, examination results, and financial information (Jain, 2021). Databases are often encrypted to protect stored data, while secure communication channels ensure that information shared between users and systems remains private. Additionally, cryptographic hashing is used to store passwords securely, preventing them from being easily compromised in case of a breach.

Beyond basic encryption, advanced cryptographic methods such as digital signatures and certificates are used to verify the authenticity of users and systems. This helps prevent impersonation and ensures trust in digital interactions (Dartois et al., 2024). By implementing strong cryptographic practices, organizations can significantly reduce the risk of data breaches and maintain the security and integrity of their information systems.

- **Secure Development (DevSecOps)**

Secure development, commonly known as DevSecOps, emphasizes integrating security practices throughout the entire software development lifecycle (Khan et al., 2022). Unlike traditional approaches where security is addressed after development, DevSecOps ensures that security is considered from the initial design phase through deployment and maintenance. This proactive approach helps identify and mitigate vulnerabilities early, reducing the cost and impact of potential security flaws.

Developers working within a DevSecOps framework use automated tools to scan code for vulnerabilities, perform security testing, and enforce secure coding standards. For example, when developing Learning Management Systems (LMS) used in universities, integrating vulnerability scanning tools into the development pipeline can detect issues such as SQL injection or cross-site scripting (XSS) before the software is deployed. This prevents attackers from exploiting weaknesses in the system (Otieno et al., 2023).

DevSecOps also promotes collaboration between development, security, and operations teams, fostering a culture of shared responsibility for security. Continuous integration and continuous deployment (CI/CD) pipelines are enhanced with security checks, ensuring that every update maintains a high level of protection. By embedding security into development processes, organizations can build robust, resilient, and trustworthy applications that meet modern cybersecurity challenges (Casola et al., 2024)

## 2.3 Transversal and Soft Skills

Beyond technical expertise, cybersecurity professionals must possess transversal skills that enable effective risk management and communication (Figure 2).

*Figure 2. Transversal and Soft Skills*

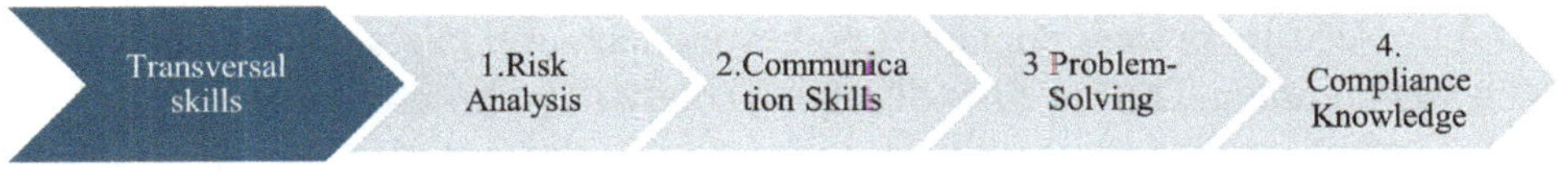


- **Risk Analysis**

Risk analysis is a fundamental cybersecurity skill that involves identifying, evaluating, and prioritizing potential threats to an organization's systems and data.

Professionals in this area assess both the likelihood of an attack and its potential impact, allowing organizations to allocate resources effectively. The goal is not to eliminate all risks an impossible task but to manage them in a way that minimizes damage and ensures operational continuity (Afsharnia, 2023).

A common framework used in risk analysis includes identifying assets (such as databases or networks), recognizing vulnerabilities, and determining possible threats that could exploit those weaknesses. For example, ransomware attacks have become one of the most significant risks for institutions, particularly in education. An IT team may classify ransomware as a high-impact, high-probability threat due to its ability to encrypt critical data and disrupt services.

Based on this assessment, organizations prioritize mitigation strategies such as implementing regular data backups, maintaining offline backup copies, and developing disaster recovery plans. Risk analysis also involves continuous monitoring and reassessment, as threats evolve over time. In universities, where large volumes of sensitive data are stored, this process is essential for protecting both academic and administrative operations (Muammar et al., 2023).

Ultimately, effective risk analysis enables informed decision-making, ensuring that security investments are aligned with the most critical threats. It also supports long-term resilience by preparing organizations to respond proactively rather than reactively to cyber incidents (Kiran et al., 2022).

- **Communication Skills**

Communication skills are essential for cybersecurity professionals, as they must bridge the gap between technical complexity and organizational decision-making (Bulganina et al., 2021). Security experts often work with non-technical stakeholders such as managers, administrators, or policymakers who may not fully understand cyber risks. Therefore, the ability to explain threats, vulnerabilities, and solutions in clear and accessible language is crucial.

For instance, when proposing the implementation of multi-factor authentication (MFA), a security professional must go beyond technical explanations. They need to clearly communicate the risks of relying solely on passwords, such as susceptibility to phishing or brute-force attacks, and demonstrate how MFA significantly reduces these risks (Hettiarachchi et al., 2023). By presenting real-world examples and potential consequences such as data breaches or financial losses professionals can make a compelling case for investment in security measures.

Effective communication also involves tailoring messages to different audiences. Technical teams may require detailed explanations, while executives need concise summaries that focus on business impact and return on investment. Visual aids, reports, and risk dashboards are often used to support these discussions.

In educational institutions, where budget constraints and competing priorities are common, strong communication skills are particularly important. Security professionals must justify expenditures and promote a culture of cybersecurity awareness among staff and students (Ujwary-Gil & Godlewska-Dzioboń, 2022). Ultimately, clear communication ensures that security initiatives are understood, supported, and successfully implemented across the organization.

- **Problem-Solving**

Problem-solving is a critical skill in cybersecurity, especially during active security incidents where time-sensitive decisions must be made (Nguyen & Vo, 2026). Cyber threats are often unpredictable, and professionals must quickly analyze situations, identify root causes, and implement effective solutions under pressure. This requires a combination of technical knowledge, analytical thinking, and the ability to remain calm in high-stress situations.

For example, during a phishing attack, attackers may trick users into revealing login credentials, leading to compromised accounts. Once such an incident is detected, cybersecurity professionals must act immediately. The first step is typically to contain the threat by disabling affected accounts and preventing further unauthorized access. Next, they investigate the scope of the attack, identify how many users were impacted, and determine whether sensitive data was accessed (Vu et al., 2024).

At the same time, communication with affected users is essential. They must be informed about the incident, advised to reset their passwords, and educated on how to recognize similar threats in the future. Problem-solving also involves implementing preventive measures, such as enhancing email filtering systems or conducting awareness training to reduce the likelihood of future attacks (Chaw & Tang, 2024).

In complex environments like universities, where thousands of users interact with digital systems daily, rapid and effective problem-solving is crucial. It minimizes damage, restores normal operations quickly, and strengthens the institution's overall security posture against future threats.

- **Compliance Knowledge**

Compliance knowledge refers to understanding and applying laws, regulations, and standards (Al-Rubaye & AL-TA'LI, 2023). Organizations must ensure that their data handling practices align with legal requirements to avoid penalties and maintain trust. Two important examples include the General Data Protection Regulation and Law 09-08, which govern how personal data is collected, processed, and stored. Cybersecurity professionals play a key role in ensuring compliance by implementing appropriate technical and organizational measures. For instance, institutions must establish strict access controls to ensure that only authorized individuals can access sensitive data. They are also required to maintain audit logs that track who accessed data and when, providing accountability and traceability in case of an incident. In educational institutions, compliance is particularly important because they handle large volumes of personal data, including student records, financial information, and research data. Failure to comply with regulations can result in legal consequences, financial penalties, and reputational damage. Moreover, compliance is not a one-time effort but an ongoing process (Oluoha et al., 2023). Organizations must regularly review their policies, conduct audits, and update their security practices to reflect changes in regulations and emerging threats. By maintaining strong compliance knowledge, cybersecurity professionals help ensure that institutions operate within legal frameworks while protecting the privacy and rights of individuals.

These competencies ensure that technical measures are effectively implemented and aligned with organizational goals.

## 2.4 Emerging Skills and Trends

The cybersecurity landscape is evolving rapidly, leading to new skill requirements (Figure 3):

*Figure 3. Emerging Skills and Trends*

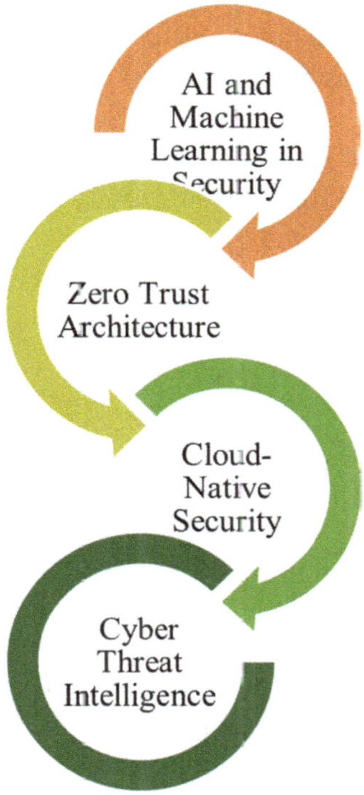


- **AI and Machine Learning in Security**

Artificial Intelligence (AI) and Machine Learning (ML) are transforming cybersecurity by enabling faster and more accurate detection of threats within large and complex datasets. Traditional security systems rely on predefined rules, which can struggle to identify new or evolving attacks (Tyagi et al., 2024). In contrast, ML models can learn patterns of normal behavior and automatically detect anomalies that may indicate malicious activity. This makes AI particularly effective in environments with high volumes of data, such as universities. For example, institutions can use AI-based systems to monitor student and staff login behavior. If a user suddenly logs in from an unusual location, at an abnormal time, or attempts 2ultiple rapid logins, the system can flag this as suspicious. Such anomalies may indicate compromised credentials or unauthorized access attempts. AI tools can then trigger automated responses, such as temporarily locking accounts or requiring additional verification steps.

Additionally, AI enhances threat detection by analyzing vast amounts of network traffic, emails, and system logs in real time. It can identify phishing attempts, malware patterns, and insider threats more efficiently than manual analysis (Schmitt, 2023). However, these systems require careful training and continuous updates to remain effective.

Despite its advantages, AI in cybersecurity also presents challenges, including false positives and the risk of adversarial attacks targeting AI models. Nevertheless, when properly implemented, AI and ML significantly strengthen an organization's ability to detect, prevent, and respond to cyber threats in a proactive and scalable manner.

- **Zero Trust Architecture**

Zero Trust Architecture is a modern security approach based on the principle "never trust, always verify." Unlike traditional models that assume users inside a network are trustworthy, Zero Trust requires continuous verification of every user, device, and application attempting to access resources. This approach is particularly relevant in today's environment, where remote work and cloud services have blurred traditional network boundaries (Chaturvedi et al., 2024). In practice, Zero Trust involves multiple layers of security controls. One key component is multi-factor authentication (MFA), which requires users to provide additional verification beyond a password, such as a code sent to a mobile device. Another important element is device validation, ensuring that only secure and compliant devices can access organizational systems. For example, a university may allow remote access to its systems only if the user's device has updated security patches and antivirus protection. Access is also granted based on the principle of least privilege, meaning users only have access to the resources necessary for their roles. Continuous monitoring ensures that access requests are evaluated in real time, and suspicious behavior can trigger immediate restrictions (Arora, 2025). By implementing Zero Trust Architecture, institutions can significantly reduce the risk of unauthorized access and data breaches. It provides a more resilient security framework that adapts to modern digital environments, protecting sensitive data even when users operate outside traditional network perimeters.

- **Cloud-Native Security**

Cloud-native security focuses on protecting applications that are built and deployed in cloud environments using modern technologies such as containers, microservices, and orchestration platforms. Unlike traditional applications, cloud-native systems are highly dynamic and distributed, requiring specialized security approaches. One widely used platform in this domain is Kubernetes, which automates the deployment and management of containerized applications (Arif et al., 2025). While cloud-native technologies offer scalability and flexibility, they also introduce new security challenges. Misconfigurations are among the most common risks. For instance, improperly configured Kubernetes clusters can expose applications, APIs, or sensitive data to unauthorized access. This can occur if access controls are too permissive or if security settings are not properly enforced.

To address these challenges, organizations implement security practices such as container image scanning, runtime protection, and network segmentation within clusters. Security must be integrated throughout the development and deployment lifecycle, aligning with DevSecOps principles. Automated tools are often used to detect vulnerabilities in container images before deployment and to monitor application behavior during runtime. In educational institutions adopting cloud-based systems, cloud-native security ensures that digital services remain protected while maintaining performance and scalability (Soni & Padhya, 2024). By securing containers, orchestration systems, and underlying infrastructure, organizations can safely leverage the benefits of cloud-native technologies without exposing themselves to unnecessary risks.

- **Cyber Threat Intelligence**

Cyber threat intelligence (CTI) involves the collection, analysis, and interpretation of information about current and potential cyber threats. It helps organizations understand attacker behavior, identify emerging risks, and make informed security decisions. Unlike reactive approaches, CTI enables a proactive defense strategy by anticipating threats before they occur. Analysts gather intelligence from various sources, including security reports, dark web monitoring, vulnerability databases, and past incident data (Möller, 2023). By analyzing this information, they can identify patterns and trends in cyberattacks. For example, tracking the rise of ransomware attacks allows institutions to strengthen their defenses by improving backup strategies, updating security controls, and training users to recognize phishing attempts. In universities, where diverse users and systems create a complex security environment, threat intelligence is particularly valuable. It helps IT teams stay informed about threats targeting the education sector and adapt their defenses accordingly. For instance, if a new phishing campaign targeting students is identified, the institution can quickly issue warnings and implement email filtering rules (Saeed et al., 2023).

Cyber threat intelligence is often integrated with security tools such as SIEM systems, enabling real-time threat detection and response. It also supports strategic planning by helping organizations prioritize risks based on current threat landscapes.

Overall, CTI enhances an organization's ability to anticipate, prevent, and respond effectively to cyber threats.

These emerging skills reflect a shift toward proactive, intelligent, and adaptive cybersecurity strategies.

## 2.5 Cybersecurity Skills Gap

Despite increasing demand, organizations face a significant shortage of qualified cybersecurity professionals. This gap is caused by several factors (Figure 4):

*Figure 4. Cybersecurity Skills Gap*

- **Rapid Technological Evolution**

One of the most significant challenges in cybersecurity today is the rapid pace of technological evolution. As digital transformation accelerates, new technologies such as artificial intelligence, cloud computing, and automation continuously reshape the threat landscape (Voronkova et al., 2023). Fields like Artificial Intelligence and Cloud Computing are not only driving innovation but also introducing new vulnerabilities that cybersecurity professionals must understand and mitigate. For example, AI is increasingly used by organizations to enhance threat detection, but it is also exploited by attackers to automate phishing campaigns or develop more sophisticated malware. This creates a constant cycle where defenders must adapt just as quickly as attackers. Similarly, the widespread adoption of cloud platforms has shifted security responsibilities. Misconfigured cloud environments, insecure APIs, and weak access controls have become common entry points for cyberattacks.

As a result, cybersecurity professionals are required to continuously update their knowledge and skills. Traditional education alone is no longer sufficient, as what is learned today may become outdated within a few years. Professionals must engage in lifelong learning through certifications, online courses, and practical experience. For instance, a security analyst trained primarily in on-premise systems may struggle to secure cloud-native applications without additional training.

In educational institutions, this rapid evolution presents a challenge in curriculum design. Universities must frequently revise their programs to include emerging topics such as AI-driven security, DevSecOps, and zero trust models (Si et al., 2023). However, keeping pace with industry developments is difficult due to limited resources and slow academic updates.

Ultimately, the fast-changing nature of technology requires adaptability, curiosity, and continuous learning. Without these, both individuals and institutions risk falling behind, leaving systems vulnerable to increasingly advanced cyber threats.

- **Mismatch Between Education and Industry Needs**

A major issue in cybersecurity workforce development is the mismatch between academic education and industry requirements. While universities provide theoretical foundations in areas such as networking, cryptography, and information systems, many graduates lack the practical skills needed to perform effectively in real-world environments. This gap becomes evident when employers seek candidates with hands-on experience using industry-standard tools and technologies (Rahman et al., 2024).

For example, security operations often rely on tools like Splunk for log analysis or Wireshark for traffic inspection. However, many students graduate without ever having used these tools in a practical setting. As a result, they may understand theoretical concepts such as intrusion detection but struggle to apply them in real scenarios. This creates challenges for employers, who must invest additional time and resources in training new hires.

Another example is incident response. While students may learn about the steps involved in handling cyber incidents, they often lack experience dealing with live simulations or real attacks. This limits their ability to respond effectively under pressure. Similarly, knowledge of frameworks and standards is often taught without practical implementation, reducing its real-world relevance.

The root of this mismatch lies in several factors, including outdated curricula, limited collaboration between academia and industry, and insufficient access to practical training environments. Universities may not always have the resources to provide up-to-date labs or licensed tools, and academic programs may not evolve quickly enough to reflect current industry practices.

To address this gap, stronger partnerships between universities and industry are essential. Internships, cooperative education programs, and hands-on projects can help students gain practical experience. Additionally, integrating real-world case studies and simulation-based learning into curricula can better prepare graduates for the demands of the cybersecurity workforce. Bridging this gap is critical for developing a skilled and job-ready cybersecurity workforce.

- **Limited Training Opportunities**

Limited Training Opportunities is another key challenge in developing cybersecurity skills. While theoretical knowledge is important, cybersecurity is a highly practical field that requires hands-on experience to master. However, many students and professionals face barriers when trying to access realistic training environments, tools, and simulations. One major limitation is the lack of access to cybersecurity labs. Setting up a secure and functional lab environment requires specialized infrastructure, software licenses, and technical expertise. Many educational institutions, particularly in developing regions, may not have the financial or technical resources to provide such facilities. As a result, students may only learn concepts in theory without the opportunity to apply them in practice (Carulli et al., 2024). For example, learning how to detect and respond to cyberattacks requires exposure to simulated environments where attacks can be safely executed and analyzed. Without such simulations, students cannot fully understand how threats behave or how to respond effectively. Platforms like TryHackMe and Hack The Box attempt to address this issue by offering virtual labs and challenges. However, access to advanced features or structured learning paths may require paid subscriptions, which can be a barrier for some learners. Additionally, opportunities for internships or real-world experience may be limited, especially in regions with fewer cybersecurity-focused organizations. This further restricts students' ability to gain practical exposure. To overcome these challenges, institutions and governments must invest in accessible training solutions, such as virtual labs, open-source tools, and partnerships with industry. Encouraging self-learning through online platforms and competitions can also help bridge the gap. Ultimately, expanding access to hands-on training is essential for building competent cybersecurity professionals who are prepared to world threats. In this context, many institutions invest heavily in advanced security technologies such as Security Information and Event Management (SIEM) systems, including platforms like Splunk, with the expectation of strengthening their cybersecurity posture. These systems are designed to collect, analyze, and correlate large volumes of log data from across networks, enabling real-time detection of suspicious activities. However, the effectiveness of such tools depends largely on the expertise of the personnel managing them.

## 2.6 Implications for Secure Information Systems

The cybersecurity skills gap directly impacts the security and resilience of information systems. Without skilled professionals:

- **Security tools may be misconfigured, leaving vulnerabilities open**

Security tools are designed to protect systems, but when they are misconfigured, they can unintentionally create serious vulnerabilities. Misconfiguration occurs when security settings are incorrectly applied, left incomplete, or remain at insecure default values. This problem is particularly common with complex tools such as firewalls, intrusion detection systems, and SIEM platforms like Splunk, which require careful customization and continuous tuning (Serac, 2023). For example, a firewall may be configured with overly permissive rules that allow unauthorized traffic to pass through. An organization might unintentionally leave certain ports open for testing purposes and forget to close them, giving attackers an easy entry point. In cloud environments, misconfigurations are even more dangerous. A well-known example involves publicly accessible cloud storage buckets where sensitive data such as student records or internal documents is exposed due to incorrect access permissions. These incidents often occur not because of sophisticated attacks, but because of simple configuration errors. Another example involves SIEM systems that are not properly integrated with all relevant data sources. If logs from critical servers or applications are missing, the system cannot detect suspicious activity in those areas. Similarly, poorly configured alert thresholds may either generate too many false positives or fail to trigger alerts for genuine threats (George et al., 2024). The root cause of these issues is often a lack of expertise or insufficient training. Security tools are powerful but complex, and without proper knowledge, organizations may not use them effectively. Regular audits, automated configuration checks, and adherence to best practices are essential to minimize these risks. Ultimately, misconfigured tools can transform security defenses into weak points, exposing organizations to preventable cyberattacks.

- **Threats may go undetected or unaddressed, increasing risk exposure**

One of the most dangerous consequences of weak cybersecurity practices is the failure to detect or respond to threats in a timely manner. Modern cyberattacks are increasingly sophisticated and designed to remain hidden for long periods. Attackers often use stealth techniques, such as encrypting their communications or mimicking legitimate user behavior, making detection more difficult (Abbadi, 2025). For example, an attacker who gains access to a university network through stolen credentials may quietly monitor systems, collect sensitive data, and move laterally across the network without triggering obvious alarms. If monitoring systems are not properly configured or if alerts are not carefully analyzed, this activity can go unnoticed for weeks or even months. During this time, the attacker may access research data, financial records, or personal information. Even when security tools like Splunk generate alerts, these warnings may be ignored due to alert fatigue or lack of skilled personnel. For instance, repeated failed login attempts might indicate a brute-force attack, but if such alerts are frequent and not prioritized, they may be dismissed as harmless. Similarly, unusual data transfers to external servers could signal data exfiltration, yet go uninvestigated.

A real-world pattern seen in many breaches is that early warning signs are present but not acted upon. This failure to respond allows attackers to strengthen their foothold, escalate privileges, and expand the scope of the attack. In educational institutions with large and diverse networks, this challenge is even greater due to the high volume of users and devices. Continuous monitoring, skilled analysis, and clear response procedures are essential to reduce risk exposure. Without them, undetected threats can cause significant damage, including data breaches, financial loss, and reputational harm.

- **Incident response may be delayed, amplifying damage**

Delayed incident response amplifies the impact of cyberattacks, allowing attackers to escalate privileges, compromise additional systems, or steal sensitive data. For example, phishing incidents at universities can spread quickly if not addressed, and ransomware can encrypt multiple servers, disrupting operations and increasing recovery costs. Causes include unclear procedures, inadequate training, or poor communication (Kuforiji, 2025). Misconfigured firewalls and cloud storage, such as unsecured AWS or Azure buckets, further expose sensitive data, creating legal and reputational risks. Effective incident response requires clear protocols, automation, skilled personnel, and regular simulations to minimize downtime, protect data, ensure compliance, and maintain trust during cyber incidents.

To address these challenges, organizations must:

## Invest in Continuous Training and Certification Programs

To effectively address the growing cybersecurity skills gap, organizations must invest in continuous training and certification programs for their staff. The cybersecurity landscape is constantly evolving due to emerging threats, new technologies, and increasingly sophisticated attack methods. Without regular skill updates, even experienced professionals may struggle to keep pace, reducing the effectiveness of security measures (Yertas, 2024).

Continuous training programs can include internal workshops, online courses, and hands-on lab exercises that allow personnel to practice real-world scenarios. For example, a university IT department might provide staff with access to platforms like TryHackMe or Hack The Box, where they can safely simulate attacks, analyze vulnerabilities, and improve response techniques.

Certification programs, such as Certified Information Systems Security Professional (CISSP) or Certified Ethical Hacker (CEH), offer structured learning and globally recognized validation of expertise. By encouraging employees to obtain these certifications, organizations ensure that staff are trained in best practices and current industry standards.

Investing in ongoing education not only enhances technical skills but also helps build a culture of security awareness. Employees become more capable of identifying threats, responding effectively to incidents, and proactively mitigating risks. Over time, these programs strengthen the organization's overall security posture, reducing vulnerabilities and improving resilience against cyberattacks.

## Integrate Cybersecurity into Academic Curricula

Integrating cybersecurity into academic curricula is essential to prepare future professionals for industry demands. Many graduates enter the workforce with strong theoretical knowledge but limited practical experience, making it difficult for them to meet real-world security requirements (Stephen et al., 2025). By embedding cybersecurity education into university programs, students gain exposure to both foundational concepts and hands-on skills.

For example, a computer science program might include modules on network security, cloud security, and incident response, supplemented by lab exercises where students configure firewalls, analyze traffic with tools like Wireshark, or detect simulated threats using SIEM platforms. Capstone projects and internships further provide real-world experience, bridging the gap between classroom learning and industry needs.

Academic integration also promotes awareness of regulatory compliance, ethical considerations, and emerging technologies such as AI-driven security tools.

Graduates with practical experience and industry-relevant skills are more likely to succeed in security roles and contribute immediately to organizational defenses.

By fostering partnerships between universities and cybersecurity companies, curricula can be continuously updated to reflect evolving threats and technologies. This proactive approach ensures that the next generation of professionals is equipped to address complex security challenges and supports long-term workforce development in the field.

## Align Workforce Development with Security Needs

Aligning workforce development with organizational security needs ensures that employees acquire the skills required to address the most pressing threats. A misalignment can result in unprepared staff, underutilized resources, and increased risk exposure. Workforce planning should begin with an assessment of current threats, organizational priorities, and gaps in existing skill sets (Judijanto et al., 2025).

For instance, if a university is increasingly adopting cloud services, developing expertise in cloud security, DevSecOps, and identity access management becomes critical. Similarly, if the institution faces frequent phishing attacks, staff must be trained in incident response, threat detection, and user awareness. Tailored programs can combine workshops, certifications, and practical exercises to address these needs.

Aligning development with real security needs also improves efficiency. Employees focus on skills that directly impact organizational resilience rather than generic training. For example, a security team responsible for managing student data can prioritize training in encryption, access control, and regulatory compliance such as GDPR or Law 09-08, ensuring both security and legal adherence.

This alignment fosters proactive security practices. Trained personnel are better equipped to anticipate threats, implement effective controls, and respond swiftly during incidents. Over time, organizations benefit from a workforce capable of supporting evolving security strategies, reducing vulnerability, and sustaining operational continuity. By linking skill development to concrete security requirements, institutions ensure that investments in training and recruitment deliver tangible protection and measurable value.

Ultimately, bridging the cybersecurity skills gap is essential to building secure, resilient, and adaptive information systems, capable of withstanding modern cyber threats.

# 3. CYBERSECURITY STATISTICS FROM THE PAST FIVE YEARS (2019–2025)

## 3.1 Malware & Ransomware Activity

Malware and ransomware are among the most damaging cyber threats, targeting systems, stealing data, and demanding ransom payments. Evolving tools and polymorphic variants increase sophistication, while sectors like education and healthcare remain vulnerable. Detection tools help, but high attack volumes and skill shortages often outpace defenses, heightening risk globally (Table 1).

*Table 1. Malware & Ransomware Activity*

| Statistic / Trend | Explanation | Example |
|---|---|---|
| Millions of malware events yearly | Malware detections across networks and endpoints continue to rise as attackers automate and diversify payloads. | A university network detects daily malware attempts through endpoint logs. |
| Ransomware variants | New ransomware families and versions increase the complexity of defense | A school district hit by a variant that both encrypts data and exfiltrates sensitive files. |
| Double-extortion ransomware | Attackers both encrypt and threaten leakage of data. | Hospital systems forced offline until ransom paid to prevent public leakage. |
| Polymorphic malware growth | Malware that changes signature to evade traditional antivirus. | Banking trojans that regularly modify code to avoid detection engines. |

## 3.2 Data Breaches & Information Exfiltration

Data breaches, where sensitive information is accessed or disclosed without authorization, have surged in frequency and impact. Causes include phishing, insider threats, and misconfigurations. Cloud adoption introduces new risks, while discovery delays amplify damage. Breaches expose personal and financial data, incur high costs, and can trigger legal penalties (Table 2) .

*Table 2. Data Breaches*

| Statistic / Trend | Explanation | Example |
|---|---|---|
| Billion records breached annually | The total number of personal or proprietary records exposed across incidents. | A cloud storage misconfiguration exposes millions of student records. |
| Raise Frequency of breaches | Yearly counts of reported incidents continue climbing. | A mid-size business reports multiple quarterly breaches due to phishing. |
| Long breach residence time | Average time attackers remain undetected before discovery. | Attackers in a university network go unnoticed for 90+ days. |
| Regulatory fines increase | Penalties for failing to protect data under data protection laws. | A company fined under GDPR for improper access controls. |

## 3.3 Phishing & Social Engineering Attacks

Phishing and social engineering exploit human behavior to steal credentials or install malware. Attackers mimic trusted institutions, use spear phishing, and automate campaigns. Often the entry point for ransomware or data breaches, these attacks persist despite training, email filters, and multi-factor authentication, remaining a leading driver of cybersecurity incidents (Table 3).

*Table 3. Phishing & Social Engineering Attacks*

| Statistic / Trend | Explanation | Example |
|---|---|---|
| Millions of phishing sites detected quarterly | The number of active phishing pages targeting users. | Email claiming to be university IT requests account "verification." |
| ↑ Spear phishing incidents | Targeted phishing designed for specific individuals or organizations. | A faculty member receives fake HR payroll link, compromising credentials. |
| Social engineering success rate | Percentage of attempts resulting in fraudulent access. | Help-desk impersonation leads to reset of an admin password. |
| Automation in campaigns | Attackers using bots to scale email and message distribution. | Thousands of fake SMS messages sent to students with malware links. |

## 3.4 Cloud & IoT Exploits

Cloud and IoT environments face growing attacks due to misconfigurations, weak device security, and limited monitoring. Over the past five years, cloud misconfigurations have caused data exposures, while IoT devices are exploited for botnets and DDoS attacks. Understanding these trends guides organizations in prioritizing targeted security controls (Table 4).

*Table 4. Cloud & IoT Exploits*

| Statistic / Trend | Explanation | Example |
|---|---|---|
| Cloud misconfigurations detected | Percentage of cloud assets incorrectly configured. | S3 bucket exposing academic records due to open ACL. |
| IoT botnet growth | Increase in IoT devices conscripted for DDoS attacks. | Smart cameras hijacked and used in a large botnet attack. |
| Weak default credentials in IoT | Many devices shipped with insecure logins. | Campus sensors breached due to unchanged factory passwords. |
| API attack increases | Automated abuse of cloud APIs for data exfiltration. | Cloud API key leaked, leading to unauthorized data pulls. |

## 3.5 Economic & Financial Impact of Cybercrime

Cybercrime costs extend beyond theft or ransom to downtime, recovery, fines, and reputational damage. Over five years, global losses have grown rapidly, with ransomware alone causing billions in payouts. Organizations spend heavily on response and security, while intangible impacts like trust erosion and market effects amplify long-term financial consequences (Table 5).

*Table 5. Cybercrime costs*

| Statistic / Trend | Explanation | Example |
|---|---|---|
| Raise of annual cybercrime economic cost | Total annual losses from cybercrime worldwide. | Company reports $10M+ loss from breach recovery. |
| Ransomware payout volume | Aggregate amount paid by victims to attackers. | A municipality pays ransom to restore critical systems. |
| Average breach cost (global) | Average financial impact per incident. | Healthcare provider incurs multi-million-dollar breach expenses. |
| Downtime & productivity loss | Estimated operational impact of systems outages. | University systems offline for days after attack, costing academic hours. |

# 4. NEW CYBERSECURITY STRATEGIES AND SOLUTIONS

## 4.1 Proactive Risk Management and Cyber Threat Intelligence

Over the past five years, organizations have shifted from reactive cybersecurity to proactive risk management, emphasizing continuous monitoring, threat modeling, and scenario planning. Cyber Threat Intelligence (CTI) enables early detection of phishing, malware, and attack patterns, allowing analysts to preemptively block threats. Automation, integrated with SIEM systems, accelerates detection and response by flagging anomalies and executing containment actions. Regular risk assessments and vulnerability management prioritize remediation based on impact. By combining CTI, automation, and proactive measures, organizations reduce attack likelihood, improve decision-making, optimize resource allocation, and respond more effectively to incidents compared to reactive approaches.

## 4.2 Zero Trust Architecture (ZTA)

Traditional network security assumes internal networks are safe, but remote work, cloud services, and advanced attacks have invalidated this. Zero Trust Architecture (ZTA) enforces continuous verification of users, devices, and applications. Key principles include least privilege access, micro-segmentation, and continuous monitoring. For example, universities use multi-factor authentication, device compliance checks, and behavioral analytics to limit lateral movement. ZTA isolates network segments, revokes suspicious access, and integrates real-time threat intelligence, reducing risks from compromised credentials and insider threats. By eliminating implicit trust, Zero Trust strengthens organizational security and ensures adaptive, dynamic protection across all network resources.

## 4.3 AI and Machine Learning in Cybersecurity

Artificial Intelligence (AI) and Machine Learning (ML) enhance cybersecurity by analyzing large datasets, detecting anomalies, predicting attacks, and automating responses. For example, AI can flag unusual login patterns or compromised credentials in university accounts, while ML correlates signals across platforms to detect multi-stage malware or phishing campaigns. Predictive analytics prioritize high-risk systems, enabling proactive defenses. AI also supports automated threat hunting across endpoints, networks, and cloud environments. While human expertise remains essential to interpret alerts and implement mitigation, combining AI/ML with skilled analysts accelerates detection, improves response times, and reduces successful breaches across organizations.

## 4.4 Cloud-Native Security and DevSecOps

Cloud-native security protects dynamic cloud and microservices environments throughout the application lifecycle, from development to runtime. Traditional perimeter defenses are insufficient for distributed workloads. DevSecOps integrates security into development pipelines, using automated tools for code analysis, dependency checks, and container scanning. For example, universities deploying Learning Management Systems can detect insecure APIs, hard-coded credentials, or misconfigured containers early. By embedding security into development and operations, organizations shift from reactive to preventive models, minimizing exploitable vulnerabilities. This approach improves breach detection, reduces impact, and ensures compliance, enabling proactive, continuous protection across cloud-native applications and workloads.

### 4.5 Cyber Resilience and Incident Response Planning

Modern cybersecurity emphasizes **cyber resilience** the ability to maintain operations and recover quickly after incidents. Incident response planning, including predefined workflows, rapid communication, and simulations, prepares organizations for attacks. For example, universities may simulate ransomware to test server isolation, stakeholder communication, and backup restoration. Automation enables immediate containment, while recovery strategies minimize downtime. Cross-department coordination among IT, legal, communications, and executives strengthens response. Organizations investing in resilience experience faster recovery, lower financial losses, and higher stakeholder confidence. By combining preparation, simulation, and adaptive responses, cyber resilience transforms inevitable attacks into manageable events, reducing operational and reputational impact.

## 5. CHALLENGES AND FUTURE PROSPECTS

### 5.1 Skills Shortage and Workforce Gaps

Organizations face a global shortage of cybersecurity professionals, leaving critical roles unfilled. Many existing staff lack hands-on experience with modern security tools, cloud environments, or threat intelligence platforms. Bridging this gap requires targeted training, certifications, and educational programs to develop practical expertise, ensuring teams can detect, respond to, and mitigate sophisticated cyber threats effectively.

### 5.2 Rapidly Evolving Threats

Cyber threats are increasingly sophisticated, including APTs, AI-powered malware, and multi-stage ransomware. Emerging technologies like cloud computing, IoT, and remote work platforms expand attack surfaces. Threat actors exploit misconfigurations and human error, challenging traditional defenses. Organizations must adopt continuous monitoring, adaptive security, and intelligence-driven approaches to stay ahead of attackers and reduce operational risk.

## 5.3 Regulatory Complexity and Compliance

Organizations must navigate complex global and sector-specific regulations, such as GDPR and HIPAA. Compliance requires robust policies, monitoring, and audit mechanisms. Failure to comply can result in financial penalties, reputational damage, and operational disruption. Implementing governance frameworks, enforcing data access controls, and maintaining consistent reporting are essential to meet evolving regulatory requirements without compromising security or business agility.

## 5.4 Integration of Security Across the Enterprise

Embedding security throughout organizations is difficult due to siloed teams, inconsistent policies, and fragmented monitoring. Integrating cybersecurity into development, cloud deployments, IoT, and operational technology is crucial. Practices like DevSecOps, centralized visibility, and automated controls ensure threats are detected early. Without holistic integration, even advanced tools may fail, leaving gaps in defense and delaying incident response.

# CONCLUSION

Cybersecurity has become a strategic priority as digital technologies, cloud computing, IoT, and artificial intelligence (AI) expand the attack surface. While AI enhances automation and decision-making, it also introduces new vulnerabilities. Recent trends show a rise in ransomware, data breaches, and social engineering attacks, exposing weaknesses in both technical systems and human practices. At the same time, the cybersecurity skills gap limits organizations' ability to secure complex, AI-driven environments. To address these challenges, organizations are adopting advanced strategies such as proactive risk management, Cyber Threat Intelligence (CTI), Zero Trust Architecture, AI-driven threat detection, and security-by-design approaches. These emphasize continuous monitoring, automation, and adaptive defense. However, challenges remain, including regulatory complexity, integration issues, and evolving attack techniques. AI and automation offer strong potential, but bridging the skills gap through education and upskilling is essential to build resilient and secure digital ecosystems.

## Future Prospects

- **AI and Automation in Cyber Defense**

AI and automation enhance threat detection and response by analyzing large datasets in real time. Predictive analytics identify attack patterns, while automated actions reduce human error and response time. These technologies empower smaller teams to manage complex environments, streamline operations, and anticipate threats, making defenses more proactive and adaptive against advanced cyberattacks.

- **Expansion of Zero Trust and Resilience Frameworks**

Zero Trust Architecture enforces continuous verification of users and devices, reducing lateral movement risks. Resilience frameworks focus on maintaining operations and recovering quickly from attacks. Combining least-privilege access, segmentation, monitoring, and disaster recovery enhances proactive defense, minimizes exposure, and ensures business continuity in complex, evolving cyber environments.

- **Skills Development and Education**

Upskilling and education are critical to closing the cybersecurity talent gap. Academic programs, hands-on labs, certifications, and industry partnerships equip professionals with practical expertise in threat detection, cloud security, and incident response. Continuous training ensures teams remain prepared for evolving threats, strengthening organizational defense and fostering a resilient cybersecurity workforce.

- **Threat Intelligence Collaboration**

Sharing threat intelligence across sectors and governments improves situational awareness and speeds response. Collaborative platforms, real-time feeds, and ISAC participation allow organizations to anticipate attacks, prioritize defenses, and mitigate threats proactively. Coordinated intelligence reduces duplicate efforts, strengthens collective security, and supports a more resilient global cybersecurity ecosystem.

## REFERENCES


Abbadi, D. (2025). Digital Gaps and Cyber Risks: Strategies to Ensure Equal Opportunities and Digital Education Security. *International Journal of Information & Digital Security*, *3*(2), 19–32. DOI: 10.54878/ba2nbk39

Afsharnia, F. (2023). Risk and reliability analysis in the era of digital transformation. In *Advances in reliability, failure and risk analysis* (pp. 269–284). Springer Nature Singapore. DOI: 10.1007/978-981-19-9909-3_12

Akinsanya, M. O., Adeusi, O. C., & Ajanaku, K. B. (2022). A detailed review of contemporary cyber/network security approaches and emerging challenges. *Communication in Physical Sciences*, *8*(4), 721–732.

Al-Rubaye, M. H. A., & A'Ll, A. L.-T. (2023). The Impact of Digital Knowledge Management on Tax Compliance Efficiency: An Empirical Study of the General Tax Authority. *Tikrit Journal of Administrative and Economic Sciences*, *19*(62), 434–455. DOI: 10.25130/tjaes.19.62.2.24

Arif, T., Jo, B., & Park, J. H. (2025). A comprehensive survey of privacy-enhancing and trust-centric cloud-native security techniques against cyber threats. *Sensors (Basel)*, *25*(8), 2350. DOI: 10.3390/s25082350 PMID: 40285041

Arora, A. (2025). Zero Trust Architecture: Revolutionizing Cybersecurity for Modern Digital Environments. *Available at SSRN* 5268151. DOI: 10.2139/ssrn.5268151

Bulganina, S. V., Prokhorova, M. P., Lebedeva, T. E., Shkunova, A. A., & Mikhailov, M. S. (2021). Digital skills as a response to the challenges of the modern society. *Revista Turismo Estudos e Práticas-RTEP/GEPLAT/UERN*, (01), 1-7.

Butt, U. A., Amin, R., Mehmood, M., Aldabbas, H., Alharbi, M. T., & Albaqami, N. (2023). Cloud security threats and solutions: A survey. *Wireless Personal Communications*, *128*(1), 387–413. DOI: 10.1007/s11277-022-09960-z

Carulli, M., Rossoni, M., Spadoni, E., Dozio, N., Giussani, R., Ferrise, F., & Bordegoni, M. (2024). A case study on digital training: Benefits and unexplored opportunities. *Journal of Computing and Information Science in Engineering*, *24*(5), 1–10. DOI: 10.1115/1.4064797

Casola, V., De Benedictis, A., Mazzocca, C., & Orbinato, V. (2024). Secure software development and testing: A model-based methodology. *Computers & Security*, *137*, 103639. DOI: 10.1016/j.cose.2023.103639

Chaturvedi, I., Pawar, P. M., Muthalagu, R., & Tamizharasan, P. S. (2024). Zero trust security architecture for digital privacy in healthcare. In *Information Technology Security: Modern Trends and Challenges* (pp. 1–23). Springer Nature Singapore. DOI: 10.1007/978-981-97-0407-1_1

Chaturvedi, M., Sharma, S., & Ahmed, G. (2021, March). Study of baseline cyber security for various application domains. []. IOP Publishing.]. *IOP Conference Series. Materials Science and Engineering*, *1099*(1), 012051. DOI: 10.1088/1757-899X/1099/1/012051

Chaw, L. Y., & Tang, C. M. (2024). Exploring the relationship between digital competence proficiency and student learning performance. *European Journal of Education*, *59*(1), e12593. DOI: 10.1111/ejed.12593

Dartois, P., Leroux, A., Robert, D., & Wesolowski, B. (2024, April). SQISignHD: new dimensions in cryptography. In *Annual International Conference on the Theory and Applications of Cryptographic Techniques* (pp. 3-32). Cham: Springer Nature Switzerland.

Diffie, W., & Hellman, M. E. (2022). New directions in cryptography. In *Democratizing cryptography: the work of Whitfield Diffie and Martin Hellman* (pp. 365-390). DOI: 10.1145/3549993.3550007

Duary, S., Choudhury, P., Mishra, S., Sharma, V., Rao, D. D., & Aderemi, A. P. (2024, February). Cybersecurity threats detection in intelligent networks using predictive analytics approaches. In *2024 4th International Conference on Innovative Practices in Technology and Management (ICIPTM)* (pp. 1-5). Ieee. DOI: 10.1109/ICIPTM59628.2024.10563348

Furnell, S. (2021). The cybersecurity workforce and skills. *Computers & Security*, *100*, 102080. DOI: 10.1016/j.cose.2020.102080

George, A. S., Baskar, T., & Srikaanth, P. B. (2024). Cyber threats to critical infrastructure: Assessing vulnerabilities across key sectors. *Partners Universal International Innovation Journal*, *2*(1), 51–75.

Hettiarachchi, N. L., Subramaniam, T. S., Palpanadan, S. T., & Al-Fattal, A. (2023). Infusing communication skills into financial accounting curriculum: A perspective from the digital era. *International Journal of Information and Education Technology (IJIET)*, *13*(4), 664–672. DOI: 10.18178/ijiet.2023.13.4.1851

Jain, V. (2021). A review on different types of cryptography techniques. *ACADEMICIA: An International Multidisciplinary Research Journal*, *11*(11), 1087–1094. DOI: 10.5958/2249-7137.2021.02568.4

Judijanto, L., Hendriana, T. I., & Muhammad, A. F. (2025). Strategic human capital planning in the asian digital economy: Aligning workforce development with business objectives. *INTERNATIONAL JOURNAL OF FINANCIAL ECONOMICS, 1*(8), 344–360.

Khan, R. A., Khan, S. U., Khan, H. U., & Ilyas, M. (2022). Systematic literature review on security risks and its practices in secure software development. *ieee. IEEE Access : Practical Innovations, Open Solutions, 10*, 5456–5481. DOI: 10.1109/ACCESS.2022.3140181

Kiran, B. R., Kopperi, H., & Venkata Mohan, S. (2022). Micro/nano-plastics occurrence, identification, risk analysis and mitigation: Challenges and perspectives. *Reviews in Environmental Science and Biotechnology, 21*(1), 169–203. DOI: 10.1007/s11157-021-09609-6 PMID: 35103051

Kuforiji, J. (2025). Digital Forensics and Incident Response (DFIR) Automation: Leveraging AI to Accelerate Breach Investigation, Evidence Collection, and Cyberattack Mitigation. *Journal of Data Analysis and Critical Management, 1*(04), 1–19. DOI: 10.64235/tsvfvz27

Makovoz, O., & Lysenko, S. (2024). Evolution of digital transformations in IT companies. *London Journal of Social Sciences*, (8), 1–7. DOI: 10.31039/ljss.2024.8.202

Marquardson, J., & Elnoshokaty, A. (2020). Skills, certifications, or degrees: What companies demand for entry-level cybersecurity jobs. *Information Systems Education Journal, 18*(1), 22–28. DOI: 10.62273/TDSH7421

Marques, I. C., & Ferreira, J. J. (2020). Digital transformation in the area of health: Systematic review of 45 years of evolution. *Health Technology (Hong Kong), 10*(3), 575–586.

Möller, D. P. (2023). Threats and threat intelligence. In *Guide to cybersecurity in digital transformation: Trends, methods, technologies, applications and best practices* (pp. 71–129). Springer Nature Switzerland. DOI: 10.1007/978-3-031-26845-8_2

Muammar, S., Shehada, D., & Mansoor, W. (2023). Digital risk assessment framework for individuals: Analysis and recommendations. *IEEE Access : Practical Innovations, Open Solutions, 11*, 85561–85570. DOI: 10.1109/ACCESS.2023.3293062

Nassif, A. B., Talib, M. A., Nasir, Q., Albadani, H., & Dakalbab, F. M. (2021). Machine learning for cloud security: A systematic review. *IEEE Access : Practical Innovations, Open Solutions, 9*, 20717–20735. DOI: 10.1109/ACCESS.2021.3054129

Nguyen, P. N. T., & Vo, D. V. (2026). Exploring digital competence and its relationship with problem-solving self-efficacy in undergraduate students. *Asian Education and Development Studies*, *15*(1), 73–88. DOI: 10.1108/AEDS-12-2024-0299

Olabanji, S. O., Marquis, Y., Adigwe, C. S., Ajayi, S. A., Oladoyinbo, T. O., & Olaniyi, O. O. (2024). AI-driven cloud security: Examining the impact of user behavior analysis on threat detection. *Asian Journal of Research in Computer Science*, *17*(3), 57–74. DOI: 10.9734/ajrcos/2024/v17i3424

Oluoha, O. M., Odeshina, A. B. I. S. O. L. A., Reis, O. L. U. W. A. T. O. S. I. N., Okpeke, F. R. I. D. A. Y., Attipoe, V. E. R. L. I. N. D. A., & Orieno, O. (2023). A privacy-first framework for data protection and compliance assurance in digital ecosystems. *Iconic Research and Engineering Journals*, *7*(4), 620–646.

Otieno, M., Odera, D., & Ounza, J. E. (2023). Theory and practice in secure software development lifecycle: A comprehensive survey. *World Journal of Advanced Research and Reviews, 18*(3), 053-078.

Rahman, M. M., Alam, G. M., Aziz, N. A. B. A., Bashir, K., & Kader, R. (2024). Whether mismatch finds match in the digitalized era: A comparison of five types of graduates to align business education and banking jobs. *Industry and Higher Education*, *38*(6), 547–561. DOI: 10.1177/09504222241249900

Rajendran, S., Valarmathi, A., & Kumar, M. S. (2022). Threat detection and incident response in cloud security. In *Privacy and Security Challenges in Cloud Computing* (pp. 207–227). CRC Press. DOI: 10.1201/9781003219880-11

Ramezan, C. A. (2023). Examining the cyber skills gap: An analysis of cybersecurity positions by sub-field. *Journal of Information Systems Education*, *34*(1), 94–105.

Ramli, A., Darus, M. Y., Mohd Yussoff, Y., & Azni, B. (2025). Integrated cybersecurity framework for enhanced threat detection and incident response in the digital era. [MJoC]. *Malaysian Journal of Computing*, *10*(1), 2099–2116. DOI: 10.24191/mjoc.v10i1.4520

Saeed, S., Suayyid, S. A., Al-Ghamdi, M. S., Al-Muhaisen, H., & Almuhaideb, A. M. (2023). A systematic literature review on cyber threat intelligence for organizational cybersecurity resilience. *Sensors (Basel)*, *23*(16), 7273. DOI: 10.3390/s23167273 PMID: 37631808

Schmitt, M. (2023). Securing the digital world: Protecting smart infrastructures and digital industries with artificial intelligence (AI)-enabled malware and intrusion detection. *Journal of Industrial Information Integration*, *36*, 100520. DOI: 10.1016/j.jii.2023.100520

Sengupta, S., Chowdhary, A., Sabur, A., Alshamrani, A., Huang, D., & Kambhampati, S. (2020). A survey of moving target defenses for network security. *IEEE Communications Surveys and Tutorials*, *22*(3), 1909–1941. DOI: 10.1109/COMST.2020.2982955

Serac, C. A. (2023). Digital transformation vulnerabilities: Assessing the risks and strengthening cyber security. *Ann Univ ORADEA*, *32*(1), 771–781. DOI: 10.47535/1991AUOES32(1)059

Si, S., Hall, J., Suddaby, R., Ahlstrom, D., & Wei, J. (2023). Technology, entrepreneurship, innovation and social change in digital economics. *Technovation*, *119*, 102484. DOI: 10.1016/j.technovation.2022.102484

Singh, A. J., & Singh, A. P. (2024). Evolution of Information Technology: A Comprehensive Review. *Asian Journal of Current Research*, *9*(4), 78–90. DOI: 10.56557/ajocr/2024/v9i48892

Soni, B., & Padhya, M. (2024, October). Enhancing Cloud-Native Security Through 4C Architecture: A Comprehensive Analysis. In *International Conference on Information Security, Privacy and Digital Forensics* (pp. 525-546). Singapore: Springer Nature Singapore.

Spidalieri, F. (2022). Meeting the growing demand for cybersecurity skills and talent in Europe. In *European cybersecurity in context a policy-oriented comparative analysis. European Liberal Forum* (pp. 9-19).

Stephen, O. B., Olatoye, G. O., Oluwabukola, J. A., Olaniyi, O. P., & Kolash, B. J. (2025). Exploring the Integration of Digital Literacy and Cyber Security Education for Ethical and Safe Digital Citizenship in Schools. *BIMA JOURNAL OF SCIENCE AND TECHNOLOGY GOMBE*, *9*(3B), 183–188.

Tatineni, S. (2023). AI-infused threat detection and incident response in cloud security. [IJSR]. *International Journal of Science and Research (Raipur, India)*, *12*(11), 998–1004. DOI: 10.21275/SR231113063646

Tyagi, A. K., Kumari, S., & Richa. (2024). Artificial Intelligence-Based Cyber Security and Digital Forensics: A Review. *Artificial Intelligence-Enabled Digital Twin for Smart Manufacturing*, 391-419.

Ujwary-Gil, A., & Godlewska-Dzioboń, B. (2022). The two-mode network approach to digital skills and tasks among technology park employees. *Entrepreneurial Business and Economics Review*, *10*(2), 187–204. DOI: 10.15678/EBER.2022.100211

Ullah, F., Ye, X., Fatima, U., Wu, Y., Akhtar, Z., & Ahmad, H. (2026). What skills do cybersecurity professionals need? *Information and Computer Security*, •••, 1–19. DOI: 10.1108/ICS-01-2025-0027

Voronkova, V., Nikitenko, V., Oleksenko, R., Andriukaitiene, R., Kharchenko, J., & Kliuienko, E. (2023). Digital technology evolution of the industrial revolution from 4g to 5g in the context of the challenges of digital globalization. *TEM Journal.*, *12*(2), 732–742. DOI: 10.18421/TEM122-17

Vu, H. T. T., Tan, C. C., Tran, H. T., & Thuyen, T. D. (2024). Exploratory Study of Factors Affecting Problem-Solving Competence among School Administrators in Vietnam during the Digital Era. *Journal of Education and e-learning Research*, *11*(4), 676–687. DOI: 10.20448/jeelr.v11i4.6093

Yertas, M. (2024). The role of training and continuous development in improving employee productivity and its impact on company financial performance. *Atestasi: Jurnal Ilmiah Akuntansi*, *7*(2), 1362–1379. DOI: 10.57178/atestasi.v7i2.1047 [illegible] H., [illegible] Fauzi, D., [illegible] & [illegible] [illegible] [illegible] professionals' model [illegible] [illegible] [illegible] [illegible] [illegible] [illegible]/S[illegible]2025[illegible]

[illegible]kova, V., Nikonova, V., Orlovskaya, K., [illegible]kulova, Z., Khamchenko, E., Khudenko, [illegible] (2023). Digital technology evolution of the industrial revolution: [illegible] [illegible] technological challenges, [illegible] [illegible] [illegible] (7), [illegible] DOI: 10.16[illegible]

[illegible] P., [illegible] C., [illegible] H., [illegible] & [illegible] (20[illegible]). [illegible] Study [illegible] Solving [illegible] [illegible] [illegible] [illegible] [illegible] during the [illegible] Pandemic. [illegible] [illegible] [illegible], [illegible] DOI: [illegible]

[illegible] (20[illegible]). The role of training and [illegible] [illegible] development in improving [illegible] productivity and its impact on [illegible] [illegible] [illegible] [illegible] [illegible] of [illegible] [illegible], [illegible] (2), [illegible] DOI: [illegible]

Chapter 9

# Intelligent Cybersecurity for Smart Education: Securing AI-Driven Learning Environments

**Soukaina Nai**
http://orcid.org/0009-0002-4819-2198
*Faculty of Sciences, University Ibn Tofail, Kenitra, Morocco*

**Chaimae Taoussi**
http://orcid.org/0009-0004-2034-0501
*National School of Applied Sciences of Khouribga, Sultan Moulay Slimane University, Morocco*

**Bahaa Eddine Elbaghazaoui**
http://orcid.org/0000-0002-3206-5162
*National School of Applied Sciences, Sultan Moulay Slimane University, Beni Mellal, Morocco*

**Amal Rifai**
http://orcid.org/0000-0003-2793-3102
*Regional Center for the Professions of Education and Training, Morocco*

**Salma El Omari**
http://orcid.org/0009-0005-3139-7340
*Faculty of Sciences and Techniques, Sultan Moulay Slimane University, Morocco*

**Abdelalime Sadiq**
http://orcid.org/0000-0003-1478-8807
*Faculty of Science, Ibn Tofail University, Kenitra, Morocco*

## ABSTRACT

*The rapid digital transformation of education has accelerated the adoption of artificial intelligence (AI), cloud computing, and smart learning platforms, enabling personalized and adaptive learning experiences. However, this evolution has also increased exposure to cybersecurity threats, making educational institutions prime targets due to the sensitivity and volume of data they handle. This chapter examines key cybersecurity challenges in AI-driven educational environments, including threats such as phishing, ransomware, and data breaches, as well as vulnerabilities*

DOI: 10.4018/979-8-2600-3465-1.ch009

*related to human behavior and system weaknesses. It proposes a comprehensive approach combining governance, technical safeguards, and user awareness. The chapter also highlights the role of machine learning in enhancing threat detection, predictive security, and automated responses, emphasizing the need for proactive and adaptive cybersecurity strategies.*

## 1. INTRODUCTION

The rapid evolution of digital technologies has profoundly transformed the educational landscape, giving rise to what is commonly referred to as smart education (Badshah et al., 2023). The integration of artificial intelligence (AI), cloud computing, learning management systems, and data-driven platforms has enabled more personalized, adaptive, and accessible learning experiences (Adel, 2024). These innovations support intelligent tutoring systems (Nai et al., 2025), real-time analytics, and automated decision-making processes that enhance both teaching effectiveness and learner engagement (Nai et al., 2026).

However, this increasing reliance on interconnected digital infrastructures also exposes educational institutions to a growing spectrum of cybersecurity risks. Universities, schools, and online learning platforms manage vast amounts of sensitive data, including personal information, academic records, and research outputs. As a result, they have become attractive targets for cybercriminals seeking to exploit vulnerabilities for financial gain, espionage, or disruption of services (Akrami et al., 2024).

Unlike traditional sectors, the educational environment is inherently open and heterogeneous, involving multiple stakeholders with varying levels of digital literacy (Quraishi et al., 2024). This openness, combined with the widespread use of personal devices and remote access technologies, significantly expands the attack surface and complicates the implementation of robust security measures . Moreover, the integration of AI introduces new challenges, such as data integrity, model manipulation, and algorithmic vulnerabilities (Stanojević, 2025).

In this context, cybersecurity is no longer a purely technical concern but a strategic imperative for ensuring the resilience and trustworthiness of smart education systems (Mızrak, 2023). This chapter aims to explore the key cybersecurity challenges facing AI-driven learning environments, analyze potential threats and vulnerabilities, and propose intelligent, adaptive solutions to protect modern educational ecosystems.

## 2. CYBERSECURITY IN SMART EDUCATION

Cybersecurity in smart education is shaped by a combination of technical, human, and organizational factors. The growing reliance on AI-driven platforms and interconnected systems amplifies both opportunities and risks. This section provides a deeper analysis of key challenges, supported by real-world examples.

### 2.1 Sensitivity and Diversity of Educational Data

Educational institutions manage highly sensitive and diverse datasets, including personally identifiable information (PII), academic records, behavioral learning data, and research outputs. In AI-driven environments, these data are also used to train models for personalization, making them even more valuable targets.

A notable example is the Blackbaud ransomware attack (Mızrak, 2023), which impacted multiple universities worldwide. Attackers accessed donor information, student records, and institutional data, highlighting how third-party service providers can become entry points for large-scale breaches. Similarly, research institutions have been targeted to steal intellectual property, particularly in fields such as biotechnology and artificial intelligence (Adeyemo et al., 2025).

These incidents demonstrate that data confidentiality and integrity are critical not only for privacy but also for protecting institutional reputation and innovation.

### 2.2 Openness and Heterogeneity of Educational Environments

Smart education ecosystems are inherently open, supporting remote learning, Bring Your Own Device (BYOD) policies, and access from various geographic locations. While this flexibility enhances learning accessibility, it significantly increases the attack surface.

During the COVID-19 pandemic, platforms like Zoom experienced security issues such as "Zoombombing," where unauthorized users disrupted online classes (Siddiqui & Ahmad, 2023). This exposed weaknesses in access control and session management.

Additionally, universities often allow students and staff to connect personal devices to institutional networks. These devices may lack proper security configurations, making them potential entry points for attackers. The diversity of users ranging from tech-savvy researchers to less experienced students further complicate the enforcement of consistent cybersecurity practices (Ling & Stringhini, 2024).

## 2.3 Integration of Emerging Technologies

The adoption of cloud computing, AI-based learning systems, and collaborative tools introduces new layers of complexity and vulnerability (Bogatinov et al., 2025). Educational institutions increasingly rely on third-party platforms such as Google Classroom and Microsoft Teams for content delivery and communication.

While these platforms offer scalability and efficiency, misconfigurations or weak access controls can expose sensitive data. For example, improperly configured cloud storage buckets have led to unintended public access to student data in several institutions.

Moreover, AI systems themselves can be targeted through adversarial attacks or data poisoning, where malicious data is introduced to manipulate learning outcomes. This raises new concerns about the reliability and trustworthiness of AI-driven educational tools (Serafimova et al., 2025).

## 2.4 Human Factors and Risky Behaviors

Human error remains one of the most significant contributors to cybersecurity incidents (Khadka & Ullah, 2025). In educational contexts, users often prioritize convenience over security, leading to risky behaviors such as password reuse, clicking on suspicious links, or sharing credentials.

A common real-world scenario involves phishing attacks targeting university email systems. Attackers impersonate administrative staff or IT services to trick students into revealing login credentials. Once compromised, these accounts can be used to send further phishing emails or access sensitive systems (Hakimi et al., 2024).

For instance, several universities have reported large-scale phishing campaigns where attackers gained access to student portals and financial information. These incidents highlight the importance of continuous awareness and training programs tailored to the educational community.

## 2.5 Strategic and Institutional Implications

Cybersecurity in education is not merely a technical issue but a strategic priority that affects institutional resilience and trust (Durst et al., 2024). A successful cyberattack can disrupt academic activities, delay research projects, and damage the institution's reputation.

A prominent example is the University of California San Francisco ransomware attack, where the university paid a ransom to recover critical research data. This incident underscores the high stakes involved, especially when research continuity is threatened (Neprash et al., 2022).

Furthermore, educational institutions must comply with data protection regulations, which vary by region. Failure to do so can result in legal penalties and loss of stakeholder confidence. As a result, institutions are increasingly investing in cybersecurity governance, risk management frameworks, and incident response strategies.

## 3. CYBER THREATS AND VULNERABILITIES IN AI-DRIVEN EDUCATIONAL ENVIRONMENTS

As educational institutions increasingly adopt AI-powered platforms and smart learning systems, the exposure to cyber threats grows. Understanding the main threats and vulnerabilities is essential for designing effective protection strategies. This section examines the types of cyberattacks, human-related risks, and technological weaknesses specific to the education sector, with real-world examples.

### 3.1 Common Cyber Threats

Educational institutions face a variety of cyber threats, often targeting sensitive data or disrupting academic operations:

#### 1. Phishing Attacks

Phishing is a social engineering technique in which attackers attempt to deceive individuals into divulging sensitive information such as usernames, passwords, or personal details. In educational institutions, phishing is particularly dangerous because of the large number of users, including students, faculty, administrative staff, and researchers, all of whom have access to different levels of data (Mamman, 2024).

Methods Used: Attackers typically send fraudulent emails or messages that appear legitimate. These messages may mimic official university communications, IT alerts, scholarship announcements, or learning management system notifications (Ayeni et al., 2024). Links in these emails often lead to fake login pages designed to steal credentials. Some phishing emails may contain malicious attachments that install malware or keyloggers when opened (Manoharan et al., 2025).

University of Cambridge Case (2021): In this incident, attackers sent phishing emails targeting faculty and staff, pretending to be official internal communications. Several users entered their login credentials on the fake portal, which allowed attackers to access internal email accounts and potentially sensitive academic information. While the attack was contained, it highlighted the vulnerability of academic communications, where trust between colleagues can be exploited.

Impact:

- Successful phishing attacks can lead to:
- Unauthorized access to student records, research data, and staff emails
- Leakage of sensitive personal or financial information
- Disruption of academic operations if internal systems are compromised

Prevention Measures:
Institutions can reduce phishing risks by:

- Implementing multi-factor authentication (MFA) for all accounts
- Conducting regular cybersecurity awareness training
- Using email filtering tools to detect and block suspicious messages
- Encouraging users to report phishing attempts immediately
- Phishing remains one of the most common and effective attack vectors in education because it exploits human trust and behavior rather than relying solely on technical vulnerabilities.

## 2. Ransomware

Ransomware is a type of malicious software (malware) that encrypts an institution's files or systems, making them inaccessible until a ransom is paid to the attacker, usually in cryptocurrency (Butt et al., 2023a). Educational institutions are increasingly targeted because they store large volumes of sensitive data including student records, research outputs, and financial information and often have complex IT infrastructures with varying levels of security (Jaya & Razak, 2022).

### *How Ransomware Works*

Attackers usually gain access through phishing emails, malicious downloads, or exploiting software vulnerabilities. Once inside the network, ransomware spreads, encrypting files on local machines and network servers. Victims are then presented with a ransom demand, often accompanied by threats of data deletion or public release.

### *University of Utah Case (2020)*

In this incident, attackers deployed ransomware that encrypted critical university data, temporarily blocking access to student records, payroll information, and ongoing research files. The disruption affected both administrative operations and academic activities, forcing the university to shut down parts of its IT network to contain the spread. The case illustrated how ransomware can paralyze an educational institution, impacting students, faculty, and research continuity.

Impact:

Ransomware attacks in education can result in:

- o Operational disruption (inability to access LMS, email, or research files)
- o Financial loss due to ransom payments or system recovery costs
- o Data loss or leakage, especially if backups are unavailable or compromised
- o Damage to institutional reputation and trust among stakeholders

Prevention and Mitigation Measures:

- o Implement regular, isolated backups of critical data
- o Keep all systems and software updated to prevent exploitation of known vulnerabilities
- o Deploy endpoint protection and intrusion detection systems
- o Educate staff and students to recognize suspicious emails and links
- o Develop and test an incident response plan specifically for ransomware scenarios

Ransomware attacks are particularly damaging in educational contexts because even short downtime can disrupt learning, research, and administrative operations, highlighting the need for proactive security strategies.

## 3. Malware and Spyware

Malware (malicious software) and spyware are types of cyber threats designed to infiltrate systems, steal information, or monitor user activities without consent (Qabalin et al., 2022). Educational networks are increasingly targeted because they manage sensitive student and faculty data, including personal information, academic records, financial details, and ongoing research (Maniriho et al., 2024).

### *How Malware and Spyware Operate*

Attackers often distribute malware through infected software downloads, malicious email attachments, or compromised websites. Spyware, in particular, can silently monitor user activity, logging keystrokes, browsing behavior, or credentials. In AI-driven learning environments, spyware may even track students' learning behaviors or access sensitive training datasets (Maniriho et al., 2024).

### *Open-Source Repository Threats*

Many educational institutions rely on open-source software for teaching, research, or LMS integration. Occasionally, these repositories have been compromised with trojans or backdoors that infect any system that installs or interacts with the software. For example, researchers have reported infected open-source packages on Python and Java repositories used in university labs, leading to unauthorized access to connected lab systems or academic databases.

Impact:

Malware and spyware can result in:

- o Exfiltration of sensitive data, including PII and research information
- o Unauthorized access to institutional systems or networks
- o Degraded system performance or network slowdowns
- o Compromise of AI-driven platforms, potentially manipulating adaptive learning outputs

Prevention Measures:

- o Use endpoint protection software with real-time scanning
- o Restrict installation of unverified software on institutional systems
- o Keep software repositories and applications updated
- o Educate students and staff about safe download and installation practices
- o Monitor network traffic for unusual behavior indicative of spyware or malware

Malware and spyware attacks highlight that even trusted software or open platforms can become threats in an educational environment. Protecting both user devices and institutional networks is essential to maintaining data confidentiality, system integrity, and learning continuity.

## 4. Distributed Denial-of-Service (DDoS) Attacks

A Distributed Denial-of-Service (DDoS) attack is a cyberattack in which multiple compromised systems (often part of a botnet) flood a target server, network, or online service with excessive traffic (Berqia et al., 2025). The goal is to overwhelm resources, causing system slowdowns or complete downtime, which prevents legitimate users from accessing services (Afraji et al., 2025).

- **Why Educational Institutions Are Vulnerable:**

Educational platforms such as Learning Management Systems (LMS), video conferencing tools, and student portals are heavily used, especially during peak periods like exam weeks or remote learning sessions. These platforms often lack the robust traffic-handling capacity of large commercial services, making them susceptible to DDoS attacks.

- **Real-World Examples:**

During the COVID-19 pandemic, several universities experienced DDoS attacks on their LMS platforms:

- o University of Cambridge (2020) faced temporary LMS slowdowns during remote assessments due to coordinated traffic floods.
- o Several U.S. universities reported outages of Blackboard and Canvas platforms, disrupting thousands of students' online classes.
  - **Impact:**
- o Disruption of learning activities: Students and faculty cannot access course materials or submit assignments.
- o Operational losses: Administrative tasks relying on online portals are delayed.
- o Reputational damage: Students and stakeholders lose trust in the reliability of digital services.
- o Potential secondary risks: During downtime, some users may resort to insecure alternatives (e.g., personal cloud storage), creating additional vulnerabilities.
  - **Prevention and Mitigation Measures:**
- o Implement network traffic monitoring to detect unusual spikes in real-time.
- o Use DDoS mitigation services such as cloud-based scrubbing or content delivery networks (CDNs) to absorb malicious traffic.
- o Load balancing and redundancy in server architecture to distribute traffic.
- o Prepare incident response plans for rapid recovery of services during attacks.
- o Educate IT staff to differentiate between legitimate traffic surges and attack traffic.

DDoS attacks illustrate that service availability is as critical as data confidentiality and integrity in smart education. Institutions must proactively strengthen infrastructure resilience to ensure uninterrupted access to online learning environments.

## 5. Insider Threats

Insider threats occur when individuals within an organization students, faculty, administrative staff, or IT personnel intentionally or unintentionally compromise the security of systems or data (Gelman et al., 2024). In educational institutions, insiders often have legitimate access to sensitive resources, which makes it difficult to detect misuse or accidental data leaks.

- **Types of Insider Threats:**

    1. Malicious insiders: Individuals who deliberately exploit their access for personal gain, sabotage, or espionage. For example, a staff member could steal research data to sell to competitors.
    2. Negligent insiders: Individuals who unintentionally cause security breaches through careless actions, such as sending confidential student information to the wrong email address, misconfiguring cloud storage, or using weak passwords.

- **Real-World Examples:**
    - Penn State University (2019): A former IT contractor improperly accessed student records, illustrating how insiders with elevated privileges can exploit sensitive information.
    - Harvard University (2020): Accidental data exposure occurred when administrative staff shared a spreadsheet containing student grades with unauthorized recipients.
- **Impact of Insider Threats:**
    - Data leakage: Personal information, research data, or financial records may be exposed.
    - Reputational damage: Stakeholders lose trust in the institution's ability to protect sensitive data.
    - Operational disruption: Insider actions may corrupt databases or disrupt services, causing downtime and additional costs.
    - Difficulty in detection: Since insiders often have legitimate access, traditional perimeter defenses are ineffective at preventing these threats.
- **Prevention and Mitigation Measures:**
    - Implement role-based access control (RBAC) to limit data access to only what is necessary.
    - Use continuous monitoring and behavioral analytics to detect unusual activities by authorized users.
    - Conduct regular cybersecurity training, emphasizing safe handling of data and awareness of social engineering tactics.
    - Establish incident reporting mechanisms and enforce strict disciplinary actions for deliberate misuse.
    - Perform audit trails and logging to maintain visibility into user actions on critical systems.

Insider threats highlight that cybersecurity in education is not only about defending against external attackers but also managing trust, access, and behavior internally. A combination of technical controls, monitoring, and user education is essential to reduce these risks.

To provide a clear overview of the cybersecurity landscape in educational environments, Table 1 summarizes the main threats, real-world examples, their potential impacts, and recommended mitigation strategies. This structured representation highlights both the technical and human dimensions of cybersecurity challenges faced by AI-driven learning systems.

*Table 1. Key Cybersecurity Threats in AI-Driven Educational Environments*

| Threat Type | Description | Real-World Example | Impact on Education | Mitigation Strategies |
|---|---|---|---|---|
| **Phishing** (Onwudebelu et al., 2026) | Fraudulent emails or messages trick users into revealing credentials or personal info | University of Cambridge (2021): attackers accessed internal email systems via phishing | Unauthorized access to emails, student records, research data; loss of trust | Multi-factor authentication (MFA), user training, email filtering, reporting mechanisms |
| **Ransomware** (Maghanaki et al., 2026) | Malicious software encrypts files, demanding ransom for release | University of Utah (2020): student records and research files blocked temporarily | Operational disruption, data loss, financial costs, reputation damage | Regular backups, patch management, endpoint protection, incident response plans |
| **Malware & Spyware** (Ahmed et al., 2026) | Software that steals data or monitors activities without consent | Compromised open-source repositories used in university labs | Exfiltration of sensitive data, compromised AI systems, reduced system performance | Endpoint protection, controlled software installation, updates, network monitoring |
| **DDoS (Distributed Denial-of-Service)** (Eufrazio Martins Júnior et al., 2026) | Flooding servers or networks with traffic to block access | Multiple universities during COVID-19: LMS outages due to traffic floods | Disruption of classes, delayed administrative tasks, potential secondary security risks | Network traffic monitoring, DDoS mitigation services, load balancing, incident response |
| **Insider Threats** (Saleem et al., 2026) | Malicious or careless insiders misuse access privileges | Penn State University (2019): IT contractor accessed student records improperly | Data leakage, operational disruption, reputational damage | Role-based access control, behavioral monitoring, training, audit logs, reporting mechanisms |

## 3.2 Human-Related Vulnerabilities

Human factors remain one of the largest contributors to cybersecurity risks in education (Vásquez-Méndez et al., 2026):

- Weak Passwords and Credential Reuse: Students and staff often use easily guessable passwords or repeat them across multiple platforms. This practice was a contributing factor in the Georgia Tech student portal breach.
- Lack of Cybersecurity Awareness: Many users are unaware of best practices, making them susceptible to phishing, social engineering, and malware attacks.
- Negligent Sharing: Students or staff may unintentionally share sensitive files on cloud platforms or via email, exposing the institution to data leaks.

## 3.3 Technical Vulnerabilities

Educational infrastructures present unique technical challenges due to their openness and heterogeneity:

- Unpatched Systems (Castro-Ortiz & Martínez-López, 2026): Institutions often operate multiple legacy systems that are not regularly updated, leaving known vulnerabilities exploitable by attackers.
- Misconfigured Cloud Services (Anas et al., 2026): Cloud-based LMS or collaboration tools, if misconfigured, may expose sensitive student data to the public. For example, several universities experienced accidental exposure of student records due to unsecured cloud storage buckets.
- AI Model Vulnerabilities (Arikan et al., 2026): In AI-driven learning environments, models can be attacked through adversarial inputs or data poisoning, which can compromise personalization and decision-making in adaptive learning systems.
- Network Security Gaps (Nazir et al., 2026): Inadequate firewall configurations, outdated intrusion detection systems, and unsecured Wi-Fi networks increase the likelihood of unauthorized access.

Table 2 presents the key technical vulnerabilities commonly found in AI-driven educational environments, highlighting their potential impacts and real-world examples. It also outlines practical mitigation strategies to strengthen system security and protect sensitive educational data.

*Table 2. Key technical vulnerabilities commonly found in AI-driven educational environments*

| Vulnerability | Description | Real-World Example | Impact on Education | Mitigation Strategies |
|---|---|---|---|---|
| **Unpatched Systems** | Legacy or outdated systems that are not regularly updated, leaving known vulnerabilities exploitable | Universities running old versions of LMS software that were exploited by ransomware attacks | Increased risk of malware, ransomware, and unauthorized access, disruption of learning and administrative operations | Implement regular patch management, automated updates, vulnerability scanning, and software lifecycle management |
| **Misconfigured Cloud Services** | Incorrectly configured cloud-based LMS or collaboration tools exposing sensitive data | Multiple universities accidentally exposed student records through unsecured cloud storage buckets | Data breaches, privacy violations, potential regulatory penalties, loss of trust | Apply strict access control, configure cloud services securely, use cloud monitoring tools, encrypt sensitive data |
| **AI Model Vulnerabilities** | AI systems targeted through adversarial inputs or data poisoning that affect model decisions | Research labs where adaptive learning algorithms were fed manipulated data affecting grading or recommendation systems | Compromised adaptive learning, inaccurate personalization, potential bias in automated grading | Validate training datasets, implement anomaly detection, perform regular model audits, use robust AI algorithms resistant to adversarial attacks |
| **Network Security Gaps** | Weaknesses in network defenses, including outdated firewalls, IDS, or unsecured Wi-Fi | Universities with open Wi-Fi networks leading to unauthorized access to internal systems | Unauthorized access, data exfiltration, disruption of LMS or research systems | Update firewalls and IDS, secure Wi-Fi networks with strong encryption, implement network segmentation, continuous monitoring |

## 3.4 Emerging Threats in AI-Driven Education

As AI becomes more central to educational technologies, new classes of threats emerge (Puri & Rathor, 2026):

- Algorithm Manipulation: Malicious actors could manipulate AI models to favor certain outcomes, affecting automated grading or adaptive learning recommendations.

- Data Poisoning: Introducing corrupted data into AI training datasets can degrade model performance, potentially harming learners' educational experience.
- Privacy Attacks: AI models may inadvertently expose sensitive information from training data, such as student performance or personal identifiers, through model inversion or reconstruction attacks.

Table 3 highlights the key AI-related vulnerabilities in smart educational environments, illustrating how attacks on algorithms and data can compromise learning outcomes and student privacy. It also presents mitigation strategies to ensure the integrity, fairness, and confidentiality of AI-driven educational systems.

*Table 3. AI-Specific Vulnerabilities in Smart Educational Environments*

| AI Vulnerability | Description | Real-World Example | Impact on Education | Mitigation Strategies |
|---|---|---|---|---|
| **Algorithm Manipulation** | Malicious actors manipulate AI models to favor certain outcomes | Automated grading system in a university manipulated to alter scores in favor of certain students | Biased grading, unfair learning outcomes, loss of trust in AI-driven systems | Implement model integrity checks, monitor outputs for anomalies, use secure model versioning and access controls |
| **Data Poisoning** | Introducing corrupted or malicious data into AI training datasets to degrade model performance | Adaptive learning platforms fed with manipulated learning data affecting recommendation accuracy | Reduced personalization, inaccurate learning recommendations, potential negative impact on student performance | Validate training data, use anomaly detection, maintain clean and controlled datasets, implement robust training pipelines |
| **Privacy Attacks** | AI models may unintentionally leak sensitive information via model inversion or reconstruction attacks | Research on student performance datasets where models inadvertently exposed individual scores | Breach of student privacy, regulatory non-compliance, reputational damage | Use differential privacy techniques, limit model exposure, apply secure aggregation methods, audit AI models regularly |

# 4. STRATEGIES AND SOLUTIONS FOR CYBERSECURITY IN SMART EDUCATION

Protecting AI-driven educational environments requires a multilayered and proactive approach that combines technical safeguards, organizational policies, human-centric measures, and intelligent systems. This section outlines effective strategies and solutions, illustrated with real-world applications in academic settings.

## 4.1 Governance and Policy Frameworks

Establishing robust governance is the first step in securing educational institutions:

### 1. Security Policies and Protocols

Security policies and protocols are the foundation of institutional cybersecurity, providing clear rules for how data, systems, and user access should be managed (Adamu et al., 2026). These policies define:

- Access control rules: Who can access which systems and data, and under what conditions. For example, only authorized staff can access student grades or research data.
- Data handling procedures: How sensitive information (e.g., student personal data, research outputs) is collected, stored, transmitted, and deleted.
- Incident response protocols: Step-by-step procedures for detecting, reporting, and responding to cybersecurity incidents, such as ransomware attacks or data breaches.
- Acceptable use policies: Guidelines on how faculty, students, and staff may use institutional IT resources responsibly.

Real-world example: Harvard University IT Security Policy mandates that all student records be encrypted in storage, and that all administrative accounts use multi-factor authentication (MFA) to prevent unauthorized access. This ensures that even if credentials are compromised, sensitive data remains protected.

Impact:

- Establishes a baseline for consistent cybersecurity practices
- Reduces the likelihood of accidental or malicious data breaches
- Supports accountability among users

## 2. Compliance with Regulations

Educational institutions operate in a landscape regulated by national and international privacy and security laws (Gunasekaran, 2026). Compliance ensures that institutions legally and ethically handle sensitive data. Key regulations include:

- GDPR (General Data Protection Regulation) in Europe: Governs the processing of personal data, requiring explicit consent, secure storage, and breach notification.
- FERPA (Family Educational Rights and Privacy Act) in the US: Protects student education records and grants students rights to access and control their records.
- Morocco's Law 09-08: Governs the protection of personal data processed by institutions and mandates secure handling and consent.

Impact:

- Avoids legal penalties and fines
- Enhances trust among students, faculty, and stakeholders
- Provides a structured framework for data governance and cybersecurity planning

## 3. Risk Management

Risk management is a proactive approach to identify, evaluate, and mitigate cybersecurity threats before they cause harm (Razavi et al., 2026). Key activities include:

- Cybersecurity audits: Assess current security posture, identify vulnerabilities, and evaluate policy compliance.
- Risk assessments: Determine which threats are most likely and which would have the highest impact, helping prioritize resources.
- Resource allocation: Direct investments in security technologies, personnel, and training based on assessed risks.

Example:

A university may conduct a risk assessment of its cloud LMS, identifying misconfigured access controls as a high-risk vulnerability. It can then prioritize patching, staff training, and monitoring to reduce exposure.

Impact:

- Ensures efficient allocation of cybersecurity resources
- Minimizes the likelihood and severity of attacks
- Provides a framework for continuous improvement and security resilience

## 4.2 Technical Measures

Technical defenses form the backbone of smart education cybersecurity (Talu, 2025):

- Encryption: Data at rest and in transit should be encrypted using industry standards (e.g., AES-256, TLS 1.3). Cloud-based LMS like Canvas LMS apply encryption to secure sensitive student information.
- Multi-Factor Authentication (MFA): MFA mitigates risks from stolen credentials. Many universities now require MFA for student and staff portals.
- Firewalls and Intrusion Detection/Prevention Systems (IDS/IPS): These tools monitor and block unauthorized access, protecting networks and learning platforms.
- Regular Software Updates and Patch Management: Keeping LMS, collaboration tools, and servers updated prevents exploitation of known vulnerabilities.
- Backup and Disaster Recovery: Periodic backups ensure continuity of learning and research in the event of ransomware or system failure. The University of California San Francisco ransomware incident demonstrated the importance of maintaining secure, tested backups.

## 4.3 Human-Centric Measures and Awareness

Humans often represent the weakest link in cybersecurity (Josephson, 2026). Institutions should focus on:

- Cybersecurity Training: Educating students, teachers, and staff on phishing, password hygiene, and safe online practices reduces risk exposure.
- Simulated Attacks: Conducting phishing simulations increases awareness and helps measure user readiness. For instance, several universities in the UK and US implement quarterly phishing drills to identify vulnerable accounts.
- Access Management: Limiting privileges based on roles ensures that users only access the resources necessary for their tasks.

## 4.4 Intelligent and AI-Based Security Solutions

AI can enhance cybersecurity through predictive and adaptive approaches (Alqudhaibi et al., 2026):

- Anomaly Detection: Machine learning models can analyze network traffic and user behavior to identify suspicious activity in real-time. Tools like Darktrace for Education have been adopted by multiple universities to detect early signs of breaches.
- Automated Threat Response: AI-powered systems can automatically isolate compromised accounts or devices, reducing response time and minimizing damage.
- Adaptive Security for LMS and AI Platforms: Intelligent systems can adjust security measures dynamically based on user behavior, device type, or location, improving protection without disrupting learning.

## 4.5 Cloud Security Best Practices

With cloud adoption central to smart education (Sarraf & Pal, 2026), institutions should:

- Configure Access Controls Carefully: Ensure correct permissions to avoid data exposure, as seen in incidents where misconfigured cloud buckets leaked student records.
- Monitor Cloud Environments Continuously: Use AI-based monitoring to detect suspicious activity across multiple cloud services.
- Data Segmentation: Separate sensitive data from less critical data to reduce the impact of potential breaches.

## 4.6 Integrated Security Approach

A holistic strategy combining governance, technical measures, human awareness, and AI-based intelligence is essential (Pallaw et al., 2026). Educational institutions adopting this approach report:

- Reduced incident response times
- Improved detection of phishing and malware attacks
- Enhanced trust among students, staff, and external partners

## 5. PROPOSED INTEGRATED CYBERSECURITY STRATEGY FOR SMART EDUCATION

The complexity of AI-driven educational environments calls for a holistic, multi-layered cybersecurity strategy. The proposed strategy combines four key dimensions: Governance, Technical Controls, Human-Centric Measures, and AI-Driven Security Intelligence, with continuous monitoring and adaptive response.

### 5.1 Governance and Policy Layer

**Objective:** Establish clear rules, compliance, and risk management to guide all cybersecurity initiatives (Figure 1).

Key Actions:

- Develop comprehensive security policies covering data handling, access control, and incident response.
- Ensure regulatory compliance (e.g., GDPR, FERPA, Law 09-08).
- Conduct regular risk assessments to prioritize threats.
- Assign a dedicated cybersecurity team responsible for monitoring, auditing, and enforcing policies.

*Figure 1. Governance as a continuous cycle*

## 5.2 Technical Security Layer

**Objective:** Protect data, systems, and networks using layered defense mechanisms (Figure 2).

Key Measures:

- Multi-Factor Authentication (MFA) for all portals.
- End-to-end encryption for data in transit and at rest.
- Firewalls, IDS/IPS, and VPNs to secure networks.
- Regular patching and configuration of all software and cloud services.
- Cloud segmentation and backup redundancy.

*Figure 2. Layered security model*

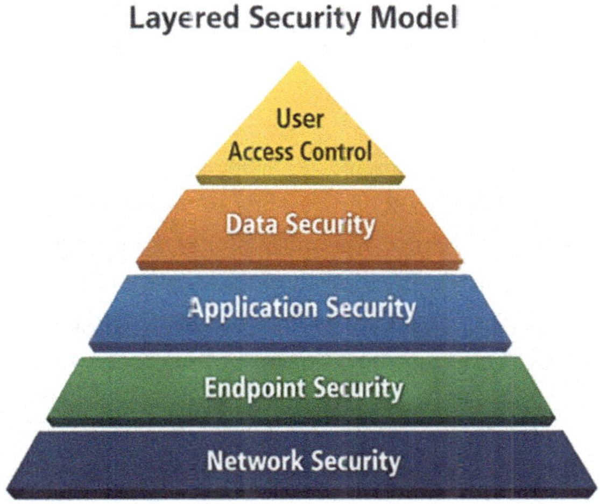


## 5.3 Human-Centric Security Layer

**Objective:** Reduce risks arising from user behavior and human error (Figure 3).
Key Measures:

- Continuous cybersecurity awareness programs and phishing simulations.
- Role-based access control to minimize unnecessary privileges.
- Integration of cybersecurity education into the curriculum for students and staff.
- Reporting mechanisms for suspicious activities.

*Figure 3. Human-centric security process*

## 5.4 AI-Driven Security Intelligence Layer

**Objective:** Leverage AI to monitor, detect, and respond to threats in real time (Figure 4).

Key Measures:

- Behavioral analytics to detect anomalies in user activity.
- Predictive threat intelligence for ransomware, phishing, or insider attacks.
- Adaptive access control based on device, location, and risk score.
- Automated incident response to isolate compromised systems.
- AI monitoring of AI: using meta-learning to detect attacks on adaptive learning algorithms.

*Figure 4. AI-Driven security intelligence*

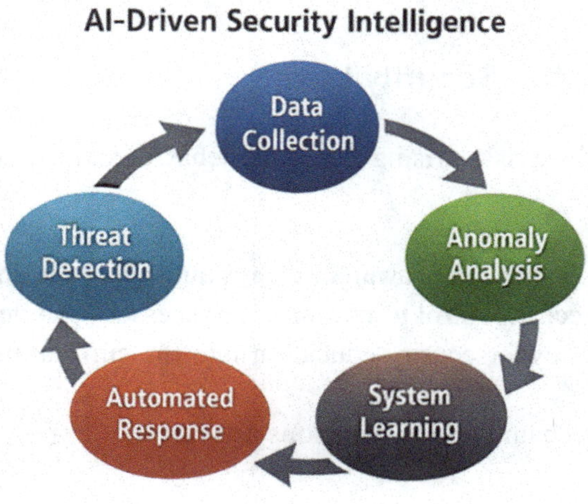


## 5.5 Integrated Strategy Overview

The proposed strategy integrates all four layers into a cohesive framework. Continuous monitoring, feedback, and AI-driven adaptation ensure that the system evolves alongside emerging threats.

Benefits of the Proposed Strategy:

- Proactive detection and prevention of cyberattacks.

- Reduced reliance on reactive measures.
- Increased trust and safety for students, staff, and stakeholders.
- Resilient AI-driven learning systems capable of adapting to emerging threats.

*Figure 5. Integrated cybersecurity Framework*

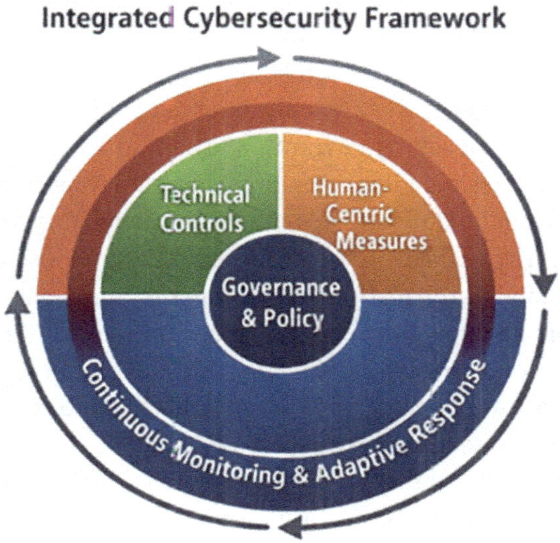


## 6. CHALLENGES AND FUTURE DIRECTIONS IN CYBERSECURITY FOR SMART EDUCATION

Despite the availability of technical solutions and governance frameworks, educational institutions face persistent challenges in securing AI-driven learning environments (Alhazmi, 2026). Rapid technological evolution, complex infrastructures, and human factors make cybersecurity a moving target. This section examines current challenges, emerging threats, and future directions for building resilient and adaptive educational systems.

### 6.1 Current Challenges

1. Resource Constraints (Lakhal et al., 2025): Many educational institutions, particularly K-12 schools and smaller universities, face significant limitations in IT budgets, staffing, and technical expertise. These constraints hinder their

ability to implement advanced cybersecurity measures, including up-to-date firewalls, intrusion detection systems, and AI-driven monitoring tools. Limited resources also reduce the frequency and scope of security audits, vulnerability assessments, and staff training programs. Consequently, these institutions remain more vulnerable to cyberattacks, data breaches, and system disruptions. Addressing resource gaps through strategic investment, shared services, or government support is essential to strengthen cybersecurity resilience and protect sensitive student, faculty, and institutional data.

2. Complex and Legacy Systems (Bhise & Rangisetti, 2026): Universities often operate a mix of legacy software, on-premises applications, and modern cloud platforms to support teaching, research, and administration. This heterogeneous IT environment creates challenges in implementing consistent security policies, patch management, and monitoring. Legacy systems may lack vendor support or modern security features, leaving vulnerabilities exposed. Integrating these systems with cloud-based platforms increases the complexity of access controls, data protection, and network security. Attackers can exploit these gaps to gain unauthorized access or disrupt services. Addressing these risks requires systematic modernization, secure integration practices, and continuous monitoring to ensure robust protection across all systems.
3. Human Factor Vulnerabilities (Schelble et al., 2024): Despite cybersecurity training programs, students, faculty, and staff remain highly susceptible to threats such as phishing, social engineering, weak or reused passwords, and accidental exposure of sensitive data. Human error continues to be one of the leading causes of security breaches in educational institutions. Ensuring long-term awareness and adherence to best practices is particularly challenging due to turnover, varying technical skills, and evolving threat landscapes. Continuous education, simulated phishing exercises, and behavior-based reinforcement are critical to cultivating a security-conscious culture that minimizes human-related risks and strengthens overall cybersecurity resilience within smart educational environments
4. Evolving Threat Landscape (Abdullah et al., 2024): Cyberattacks in educational environments are becoming increasingly sophisticated, with attackers targeting AI-driven systems, cloud platforms, and critical infrastructure. Threats such as adversarial AI attacks can manipulate adaptive learning algorithms, compromising personalized education and decision-making. Ransomware-as-a-service enables attackers to deploy highly effective ransomware without deep technical expertise, increasing the frequency and impact of attacks. Supply chain vulnerabilities in third-party educational software or cloud services further expand the attack surface. These evolving threats expose institutions to data breaches, operational disruptions, and reputational damage. Proactive monitoring, threat

intelligence, and AI-resilient security measures are essential to reduce exposure and enhance institutional cybersecurity.

5. Regulatory Compliance (Salako et al., 2024): Ensuring compliance with local and international regulations, such as GDPR, FERPA, and Morocco's Law 09-08, presents significant challenges for educational institutions, especially those operating across multiple jurisdictions. Differences in legal requirements, data handling standards, and reporting obligations create complexity in policy implementation and enforcement. Non-compliance can result in substantial financial penalties, legal liabilities, and reputational damage. Maintaining consistent practices across on-premises systems, cloud platforms, and AI-driven learning tools requires coordinated governance, regular audits, staff training, and robust data protection measures. Proactive compliance strategies are essential to safeguard sensitive student and institutional data while ensuring legal and ethical operations.

## 6.2 Emerging Trends and Solutions

1. Zero Trust Architectures (Gambo & Almulhem, 2026)

Traditional perimeter-based security models, which rely on firewalls and network boundaries to protect institutional resources, are increasingly inadequate in modern educational environments. The rise of cloud-based Learning Management Systems (LMS), remote learning, mobile devices, and AI-driven platforms means that sensitive data and services are often accessed from outside the traditional network perimeter. Zero Trust (ZT) architectures address these challenges by operating under the principle of "never trust, always verify," where every user, device, and service is continuously authenticated and authorized before accessing any resource (Syrotynskyi et al., 2024). In practice, ZT models incorporate multi-factor authentication, device health checks, contextual access policies, and micro-segmentation to reduce lateral movement of potential attackers within the network. Several universities have begun piloting Zero Trust frameworks to secure remote learning platforms, research databases, and administrative systems. For example, implementing continuous verification for student and faculty logins helps prevent credential-based attacks and unauthorized access. Beyond security, Zero Trust enhances visibility and monitoring, allowing IT teams to quickly detect anomalies and respond to threats in real time Paul et al., 2024). For AI-driven learning environments, this approach ensures that both human and system interactions are continually validated, reducing the risk of data breaches, insider threats, and AI manipulation. Overall, Zero Trust represents a proactive and adaptive approach to modern educational cybersecurity, aligning with the evolving demands of digital campuses

2. Insufficiency of Perimeter-Based Security Cloud Services

As educational institutions increasingly adopt cloud services, remote learning platforms, and AI-driven systems, traditional perimeter-based security models have become insufficient (Capili, 2024). These legacy approaches assume that internal networks and users can be implicitly trusted, leaving institutions vulnerable to insider threats, compromised credentials, and lateral movement by attackers. To address these risks, many universities are transitioning to a Zero Trust (ZT) security model, which operates on the principle of "never trust, always verify.". In a Zero Trust framework, every user, device, and service must be continuously authenticated and authorized before accessing any system or resource, regardless of their location. Selon (Ojha & Vaish, 2025) This includes multi-factor authentication, device compliance checks, contextual access policies, and micro-segmentation of networks to limit the spread of potential breaches. By verifying access continuously, ZT reduces the reliance on perimeter defenses and minimizes vulnerabilities associated with remote or hybrid learning environments. Several universities have begun piloting Zero Trust architectures to protect sensitive academic data, learning management systems, and administrative platforms (Intazar et al., 2024). This approach not only strengthens access control but also enhances monitoring and threat detection, allowing IT teams to respond proactively to unusual activity. In AI-driven learning contexts, Zero Trust helps ensure that both users and automated systems interact securely, preserving data integrity, privacy, and the reliability of adaptive learning outcomes (Paya & Gómez, 2024).

3. AI-Resilient Learning Systems

As educational institutions increasingly integrate artificial intelligence into adaptive learning platforms, the integrity and reliability of these systems have become critical (Yazmyradov, 2024). AI models personalize learning by analyzing student behavior, performance, and preferences, delivering tailored content and recommendations (Admass et al., 2024). However, these models are vulnerable to adversarial attacks, data poisoning, and algorithm manipulation, which can compromise the accuracy of personalized learning, grading systems, and recommendation engines (Ajayi et al., 2025). Such attacks may be intentional, as in malicious manipulation, or accidental, through corrupted datasets. Developing AI-resilient learning systems is essential to safeguard the quality and fairness of adaptive education. Resilient models incorporate robust training techniques, anomaly detection, and data validation protocols that reduce susceptibility to adversarial inputs or corrupted datasets (Villegas-Ch & García-Ortiz, 2023). For example, universities can implement controlled testing environments where AI models are stress-tested against simulated attacks, ensuring that decision-making remains accurate even under malicious conditions. Additionally, techniques such as differential privacy and secure model aggregation help prevent inadvertent leakage of sensitive student data. AI-resilient systems not only protect data integrity and privacy but also enhance student trust in digital learning platforms (Hanbal et al., 2024). By designing models that withstand manipulation, educational institutions can ensure that personalized learning remains fair, reliable, and secure, even in increasingly complex and adversarial digital environments.

4. Adaptive Learning Platforms

In modern educational environments, adaptive learning platforms increasingly rely on artificial intelligence to personalize instruction, assess student performance, and provide targeted recommendations (Shayea et al., 2025). However, these AI models are vulnerable to adversarial attacks, data poisoning, and other manipulations, which can compromise the integrity and reliability of learning outcomes (Alvi, 2025). Adversarial attacks involve subtly altering input data to mislead the AI, while data poisoning introduces corrupted or biased data during model training, potentially skewing recommendations or automated assessments (Syed, 2025). Such vulnerabilities can undermine trust in AI-driven education and negatively affect students' learning experiences. Developing AI-resilient learning systems is therefore essential. Resilient models employ robust training methods that detect and mitigate malicious inputs, ensuring that predictions and recommendations remain accurate even under attack (Rahman et al., 2023). Techniques such as anomaly detection, adversarial training, and secure data pipelines are critical to maintaining system integrity. Additionally, privacy-preserving methods like differential privacy prevent leakage of sensitive student information while safeguarding model functionality (Olutimehin et al., 2025). Institutions can also implement continuous monitoring and validation of AI models, performing stress tests with simulated attacks to evaluate resilience (Gupta & Dasgupta, 2022). By prioritizing AI robustness, universities ensure that adaptive learning systems remain trustworthy, fair, and effective, protecting both student outcomes and institutional reputation in increasingly complex digital learning environments (Al-Khassawneh, 2023).

5. Behavioral Analytics and Predictive Security

As educational institutions adopt AI-driven platforms and remote learning technologies, the volume and complexity of digital interactions increase, creating new security challenges (Olabanji et al., 2024). Traditional reactive security measures are often insufficient to detect subtle or emerging threats in real time (Subrahmanyam,

2025). Behavioral analytics and predictive security address this gap by leveraging AI-powered monitoring tools to continuously analyze user and system behavior, identifying patterns that deviate from established norms (Danish, 2024). Such tools can detect unusual login times, abnormal file access, unexpected network traffic, or irregular interactions with AI-driven learning systems (Wu et al., 2024). By identifying these anomalies, institutions can predict potential threats before they fully materialize, enabling proactive intervention. For example, a sudden spike in failed login attempts across multiple student accounts may indicate a credential-stuffing attack, prompting IT staff to enforce additional verification or temporarily restrict access (Adeniran et al., 2024). Similarly, predictive models can flag AI input manipulation attempts or unauthorized data exfiltration, safeguarding sensitive academic and personal information (Nagamalla & Sanapala, 2023). Behavioral analytics also enhances insider threat detection, identifying both malicious and unintentional risky actions by staff or students. By combining real-time monitoring, predictive modeling, and automated alerts, educational institutions can create an adaptive cybersecurity posture that not only mitigates threats but also ensures continuity, integrity, and trust in AI-driven learning environments (Jack & Nawaz, 2025).

6. Cloud Security Enhancements

With the rapid adoption of cloud-based Learning Management Systems (LMS), collaboration tools, and AI-driven platforms, educational institutions are increasingly dependent on third-party cloud services (Akinade et al., 2025). While these solutions provide scalability, flexibility, and accessibility, they also introduce new security challenges (Devi & Jain, 2024). Misconfigured cloud storage, weak access controls, and insufficient monitoring can expose sensitive student data, research information, and administrative records to unauthorized access (Mostafa et al., 2023). Consequently, enhancing cloud security is critical for protecting institutional assets and ensuring compliance with privacy regulations. Secure cloud configurations form the first layer of defense, including proper identity and access management (IAM), encryption of data at rest and in transit, and role-based access controls. Continuous monitoring allows institutions to track user activities, detect anomalies, and respond to potential threats in real time (Butt et al., 2023b). Automated threat response systems, such as AI-driven alerts and policy enforcement, can mitigate risks before significant damage occurs, minimizing the impact of attacks or misconfigurations. Real-world incidents highlight the risks: several universities have accidentally exposed student records through unsecured cloud storage buckets, emphasizing the need for proactive security measures (Yeboah-Ofori et al., 2023). By implementing comprehensive cloud security practices, institutions can protect sensitive data, maintain service availability, and foster trust among students, faculty, and stakeholders (Achar, 2022).

Cloud security enhancements are thus essential for resilient, secure, and compliant AI-driven educational environments (Arunkumar, 2023).

7. Integration of Cybersecurity into Curricula

In modern educational environments, human behavior remains one of the most significant factors contributing to cybersecurity risks (Arunkumar, 2023). Despite technical defenses, students, faculty, and staff can inadvertently cause breaches through phishing, weak passwords, or unsafe use of digital tools. To address this, integrating cybersecurity education directly into curricula is essential for cultivating a security-conscious culture across institutions (Kuforiji, 2025). This approach involves teaching students about cyber hygiene, digital ethics, privacy protection, and safe AI practices, helping them understand both the technical and ethical implications of their online activities (Tian, 2025). By incorporating these topics into courses across disciplines not just IT or computer science students gain a practical understanding of secure digital practices in everyday academic and professional settings (Grover et al., 2023. For example, lessons can include recognizing phishing attempts, responsibly handling personal and institutional data, or evaluating the security of AI-driven platforms. Beyond students, faculty and staff should receive regular training to reinforce awareness of institutional policies, secure system usage, and incident reporting procedures (Azzeh et al., 2022). Embedding cybersecurity education into the academic experience reduces human-related risks, strengthens institutional resilience, and prepares students to navigate an increasingly digital world safely and responsibly. Ultimately, this proactive strategy ensures that technology adoption is paired with informed, security-aware users, enhancing the overall security posture of AI-driven educational environments.

## 6.3 Strategic and Institutional Perspectives

Cybersecurity in education is no longer a purely technical concern but a strategic priority:

- It safeguards sensitive research and academic data.
- It ensures continuity of teaching and learning in remote or hybrid environments.
- It builds trust among students, staff, and external stakeholders.
- It supports the ethical and responsible use of AI technologies in education.

By adopting a proactive, adaptive, and intelligence-driven approach, institutions can transform cybersecurity from a reactive necessity into a strategic enabler for innovation and resilience in AI-driven education.

## 7. CONCLUSION AND PERSPECTIVES

The rapid integration of digital technologies and artificial intelligence into education has significantly transformed learning environments, making them more adaptive, accessible, and data-driven. However, this transformation has also introduced a wide range of cybersecurity challenges, exposing educational institutions to threats such as phishing, ransomware, malware, insider misuse, and AI-specific attacks. As demonstrated throughout this chapter, the complexity of smart education ecosystems requires a comprehensive understanding of both traditional and emerging vulnerabilities.

To address these challenges, this chapter emphasized the importance of a holistic cybersecurity approach that combines governance frameworks, technical safeguards, human awareness, and AI-driven security solutions. The proposed multi-layered strategy highlights that cybersecurity is not only a technical necessity but also a strategic pillar for ensuring the confidentiality, integrity, and availability of educational systems. Moreover, the integration of intelligent security mechanisms enables institutions to move from reactive defense to proactive and adaptive protection.

### Perspectives

Looking forward, several research and practical directions emerge:

- Development of AI-resilient educational systems: Future work should focus on designing robust AI models capable of resisting adversarial attacks and ensuring fairness and transparency in learning processes.
- Adoption of Zero Trust architectures: Educational institutions are expected to increasingly adopt Zero Trust principles to secure distributed and remote learning environments.
- Integration of cybersecurity into educational curricula: Promoting cybersecurity awareness among students and educators will foster a culture of security by design.
- Advanced predictive security models: Leveraging machine learning for early threat detection and risk prediction will enhance institutional resilience.
- Standardization and regulatory evolution: The development of frameworks specifically tailored to smart education will support better governance and compliance.

In conclusion, ensuring cybersecurity in AI-driven education is essential for maintaining trust, protecting sensitive data, and enabling sustainable digital transformation. Institutions that invest in intelligent, adaptive, and user-centered cybersecurity strategies will be better positioned to face future challenges and fully harness the potential of smart education systems.

## REFERENCES


Abdullah, S. M., Cheruvu, A., Kanchi, S., Chung, T., Gao, P., Jadliwala, M., & Viswanath, B. (2024, May). An analysis of recent advances in deepfake image detection in an evolving threat landscape. In *2024 IEEE Symposium on Security and Privacy (SP)* (pp. 91-109). IEEE. DOI: 10.1109/SP54263.2024.00194

Achar, S. (2022). Cloud computing security for multi-cloud service providers: Controls and techniques in our modern threat landscape. *International Journal of Computer and Systems Engineering*, *16*(9), 379–384.

Adamu, S. U., Ahmad, M. A., & Ibrahim, M. (2026). A systematic literature review on the adoption and effectiveness of cybersecurity frameworks in higher education institutions. *Information and Computer Security*, •••, 1–16. DOI: 10.1108/ICS-10-2025-0403

Adel, A. (2024). The convergence of intelligent tutoring, robotics, and IoT in smart education for the transition from industry 4.0 to 5.0. *Smart Cities*, *7*(1), 325–369. DOI: 10.3390/smartcities7010014

Adeniran, I. A., Efunniyi, C. P., Osundare, O. S., & Abhulimen, A. O. (2024). Enhancing security and risk management with predictive analytics: A proactive approach. *International Journal of Management & Entrepreneurship Research*, *6*(8), 32–40.

Adeyemo, D., Muhammad, I., Alagbe, J., & Ifelola, A. (2025). Global Cybersecurity Challenges for Students Using Online Learning in Higher Education. Available at *SSRN* 5361434. DOI: 10.2139/ssrn.5361434

Admass, W. S., Munaye, Y. Y., & Diro, A. A. (2024). Cyber security: State of the art, challenges and future directions. *Cyber Security and Applications*, *2*, 100031. DOI: 10.1016/j.csa.2023.100031

Afraji, D. M. A. A., Lloret, J., & Peñalver, L. (2025). Deep learning-driven defense strategies for mitigating DDoS attacks in cloud computing environments. *Cyber Security and Applications*, *3*, 100085. DOI: 10.1016/j.csa.2025.100085

Ahmed, A., Mostafa, R., Qutqut, M. H., & Ragab, N. (2026). A Systematic Literature Review on Machine Learning for Intrusion Detection Systems.

Ajayi, O. O., Alozie, C. E., & Abieba, O. A. (2025). Enhancing cybersecurity in energy infrastructure: Strategies for safeguarding critical systems in the digital age. *Trends in Renewable Energy*, *11*(2), 201–212. DOI: 10.17737/tre.2025.11.2.00192

Akinade, A. O., Adepoju, P. A., Ige, A. B., & Afolabi, A. I. (2025). Cloud security challenges and solutions: A review of current best practices. *Int J Multidiscip Res Growth Eval*, *6*(1), 26–35. DOI: 10.54660/.IJMRGE.2025.6.1.26-35

Akrami, K., Akrami, M., Akrami, F., Ahrari, M., Hakimi, M., & Fazil, A. W. (2024). Investigating the adverse effects of social media and cybercrime in higher education: A case study of an online university. Studies in Media. *The Journal of Communication*, *2*(1), 22–33.

Al-Khassawneh, Y. A. (2023). A review of artificial intelligence in security and privacy: Research advances, applications, opportunities, and challenges. *Indonesian Journal of Science and Technology*, *8*(1), 79–96. DOI: 10.17509/ijost.v8i1.52709

Alhazmi, A. K. (2026). Data Privacy and Security in AI-Driven Education Systems. In Revolutionizing Secure Learning in the Age of AI (pp. 263-294). IGI Global Scientific Publishing.

Alqudhaibi, A., Albarrak, M., Aloseel, A., Munshi, A., Alsharif, T., Jagtap, S., & Salonitis, K. (2026). Proactive cybersecurity in industry 4.0: A survey of cybersecurity threat prediction approaches in manufacturing systems. *International Journal of Information Security*, *25*(1), 14. DOI: 10.1007/s10207-025-01188-9

Alvi, S. (2025).Adversarial attacks on AI security systems: Investigating the vulnerability of AI-powered security solutions. In *Handbook of AI-Driven Threat Detection and Prevention* (pp. 165–176). CRC Press.

Anas, A. J. K., Syed, A. R., Tanveer, M. A., Chaudhry, M. A., & Paraddy, S. S. V. (2026). Cloud Computing Security Challenges and Emerging Solutions. Journal of Scientific Research and Technology, 96-100.

Arikan, K. E., Doğan, S. M., Yilmaz, E. N., & Gönen, S. (2026). From code to security: Machine learning approaches in android vulnerability detection. *International Journal of Information Security*, *25*(1), 17. DOI: 10.1007/s10207-025-01190-1

Arunkumar, J. R. (2023). Study Analysis of Cloud Security Challenges and Issues in Cloud Computing Technologies. Journal of Science. *Computing and Engineering Research*, *6*(8), 6–10.

Ayeni, R. K., Adebiyi, A. A., Okesola, J. O., & Igbekele, E. (2024, April). Phishing attacks and detection techniques: A systematic review. In 2024 international conference on science, engineering and business for driving sustainable development goals (SEB4SDG) (pp. 1-17). IEEE.

Azzeh, M., Altamimi, A. M., Albashayreh, M., & Al-Oudat, M. A. (2022). Adopting the Cybersecurity Concepts into Curriculum The Potential Effects on Students Cybersecurity Knowledge. arXiv preprint arXiv:2209.10407.

Badshah, A., Ghani, A., Daud, A., Jalal, A., Bilal, M., & Crowcroft, J. (2023). Towards smart education through internet of things: A survey. *ACM Computing Surveys*, *56*(2), 1–33. DOI: 10.1145/3610401

Berqia, A., Ismaili, O., Chahbi, M., & Bouijij, H. (2025, April). Advanced DDoS Detection in Online Learning Environments. In 2025 13th International Symposium on Digital Forensics and Security (ISDFS) (pp. 1-5). IEEE. DOI: 10.1109/ISDFS65363.2025.11012095

Bhise, C. A., & Rangisetti, A. K. (2026). Edge computational resources and security aware serverless application deployment. *Cluster Computing*, *29*(1), 58. DOI: 10.1007/s10586-025-05851-7

Bogatinov, D., Nevena, S., Iliev, A., Karovska Andonovska, B., & Petrovski, A. (2025). Integration of Emerging Technologies in Cybersecurity Education. Journal of peace, conflict and security studies, 1(1), 133-146.

Butt, U., Dauda, Y., & Shaheer, B. (2023a). Ransomware attack on the educational sector. In *AI, Blockchain and Self-Sovereign Identity in Higher Education* (pp. 279–313). Springer Nature Switzerland. DOI: 10.1007/978-3-031-33627-0_11

Butt, U. A., Amin, R., Mehmood, M., Aldabbas, H., Alharbi, M. T., & Albaqami, N. (2023b). Cloud security threats and solutions: A survey. *Wireless Personal Communications*, *128*(1), 387–413. DOI: 10.1007/s11277-022-09960-z

Capili, M. (2024). Simulation-Based Evaluation of Perimeter-Based and Zero Trust Security Implementation on Internet of Things (Doctoral dissertation, The George Washington University).

Castro-Ortiz, J. C., & Martínez-López, F. J. (2026). Cybersecurity in educational platforms: Threats, challenges, and best practices. *Campus Virtuales*, *15*(1), 191–213. DOI: 10.54988/cv.2026.1.1700

Danish, M. (2024). Enhancing cyber security through predictive analytics: Real-time threat detection and response. arXiv preprint arXiv:2407.10864.

Devi, T. A., & Jain, A. (2024, May). Enhancing cloud security with deep learning-based intrusion detection in cloud computing environments. In 2024 2nd International Conference on Advancement in Computation & Computer Technologies (InCACCT) (pp. 541-546). IEEE. DOI: 10.1109/InCACCT61598.2024.10551040

Durst, S., Hinteregger, C., & Zieba, M. (2024). The effect of environmental turbulence on cyber security risk management and organizational resilience. *Computers & Security*, *137*, 103591. DOI: 10.1016/j.cose.2023.103591

Eufrazio Martins Júnior, G., Guimaraes Marques, T., Souza da Silva, W., & Celestino, J.Junior. (2026). Edge-Oriented DoS/DDoS Intrusion Detection and Supervision Platform. *Security and Privacy*, *9*(2), e70193. DOI: 10.1002/spy2.70193

Gambo, M. L., & Almulhem, A. (2026). Zero Trust Architecture: A systematic literature review. *Journal of Network and Systems Management*, *34*(1), 25. DOI: 10.1007/s10922-025-09998-x

Gelman, H., Hastings, J. D., Kenley, D., & Loiacono, E. (2024, December). Toward an insider threat education platform: A theoretical literature review. In 2024 International Conference on Computer and Applications (ICCA) (pp. 01-06). IEEE. DOI: 10.1109/ICCA62237.2024.10928083

Grover, S., Broll, B., & Babb, D. (2023, March). Cybersecurity education in the age of ai: Integrating ai learning into cybersecurity high school curricula. In *Proceedings of the 54th ACM Technical Symposium on Computer Science Education* V. 1 (pp. 980-986). DOI: 10.1145/3545945.3569750

Gunasekaran, R. M. N. (2026). AI-Driven Data Governance: Ensuring Compliance in Big Data Ecosystems. International Journal of AI, BigData, Computational and Management Studies, 262-275.

Gupta, K. D., & Dasgupta, D. (2022). Adversarial attacks and defenses for deployed AI models. *IT Professional*, *24*(4), 37–41. DOI: 10.1109/MITP.2022.3180330

Habbal, A., Ali, M. K., & Abuzaraida, M. A. (2024). Artificial Intelligence Trust, risk and security management (AI trism): Frameworks, applications, challenges and future research directions. *Expert Systems with Applications*, *240*, 122442. DOI: 10.1016/j.eswa.2023.122442

Hakimi, M., Quchi, M. M., & Fazil, A. W. (2024). Human factors in cybersecurity: an in depth analysis of user centric studies. Jurnal Ilmiah Multidisiplin Indonesia (JIM-ID), 3(01), 20-33.

Intazar, M., Zohra, T., Ansari, N. M., Iqbal, R., & Gul, H. (2024). Beyond Perimeter Defenses: Implementing Zero-Trust Security Models for Cloud Computing in the Era of Advanced Cyber Threats. Global Research Journal of Natural Science and Technology, 2(3).

Jack, W., & Nawaz, D. (2025). Next-Gen Cybersecurity: Integrating Artificial Intelligence with Behavioral Analytics for Threat Prediction.

Jaya, M. I., & Razak, M. F. A. (2022). Dynamic ransomware detection for windows platform using machine learning classifiers. JOIV: International Journal on Informatics Visualization, 6(2-2), 469-474.

Josephson, C. (2026). When Humans Become False Positives: Measurement Geometry, Cognitive Load, and False Alarms in Human-Centred Cybersecurity. Cognitive Load, and False Alarms in Human-Centred Cybersecurity (January 01, 2026).

Khadka, K., & Ullah, A. B. (2025). Human factors in cybersecurity: an interdisciplinary review and framework proposal: K. Khadka, AB Ullah. *International Journal of Information Security*, *24*(3), 119. DOI: 10.1007/s10207-025-01032-0

Kuforiji, J. (2025). The importance of integrating security education into university curricula and professional certifications. International Journal of Technology. *Management and Humanities*, *11*(03), 1–10.

Lakhal, H., Zegrari, M., & Bahnasse, A. (2025). Next-Generation Smart Grid Cybersecurity: A Systematic Review of OT Cyber Threats, AI-Driven Defense, Cyber Deception Techniques, and Emerging Security Strategies. *IEEE Access : Practical Innovations, Open Solutions*, *13*, 181519–181552. DOI: 10.1109/ACCESS.2025.3623834

Ling, C., & Stringhini, G. (2024, September). " It was jerks on the Internet being jerks on the Internet": Understanding Zoombombing Through the Eyes of Its Victims. In *Proceedings of the 2024 European Symposium on Usable Security* (pp. 261-276). DOI: 10.1145/3688459.3688466

Maghanaki, M., Keramati, S., Chen, F. F., & Shahin, M. (2026). Systematic Evaluation of Machine Learning and Deep Learning Models for IoT Malware Detection Across Ransomware, Rootkit, Spyware, Trojan, Botnet, Worm, Virus, and Keylogger. *Sensors (Basel)*, *26*(6), 1750. DOI: 10.3390/s26061750 PMID: 41901920

MAMMAN. J. O. (2024). Mitigating The Impact Of Phishing Attacks On The E-learning Infrastructure. Scientific and Practical Cyber Security Journal (SPCSJ) 8 (3): 21–34 ISSN 2587-4667 Scientific Cyber Security Association (SCSA).

Maniriho, P., Mahmood, A. N., & Chowdhury, M. J. M. (2024). A survey of recent advances in deep learning models for detecting malware in desktop and mobile platforms. *ACM Computing Surveys*, *56*(6), 1–41. DOI: 10.1145/3638240

Maniriho, P., Mahmood, A. N., & Chowdhury, M. J. M. (2024). A survey of recent advances in deep learning models for detecting malware in desktop and mobile platforms. *ACM Computing Surveys*, *56*(6), 1–41. DOI: 10.1145/3638240

Manoharan, A., Sriskantharajah, A., Herath, H. M. K. K. M. B., Guruge, L. G. P. K., & Yasakethu, S. L. P. (2025). MetaHuman based phishing attacks in the metaverse realm: Awareness for cyber security education. *Education and Information Technologies*, *30*(9), 12939–12965. DOI: 10.1007/s10639-025-13326-w

Mızrak, F. (2023). Integrating cybersecurity risk management into strategic management: A comprehensive literature review. *Research Journal of Business and Management*, *10*(3), 98–108. DOI: 10.17261/Pressacademia.2023.1807

Mostafa, A. M., Ezz, M., Elbashir, M. K., Alruily, M., Hamouda, E., Alsarhani, M., & Said, W. (2023). Strengthening cloud security: An innovative multi-factor multi-layer authentication framework for cloud user authentication. *Applied Sciences (Basel, Switzerland)*, *13*(19), 10871. DOI: 10.3390/app131910871

Nagamalla, V., & Sanapala, R. K. (2023). Integrating Predictive Big Data Analytics with Behavioral Machine Learning Models for Proactive Threat Intelligence in Industrial IoT Cybersecurity. *International Journal of Wireless & Ad Hoc Communication*, *7*(2), 08–24. DOI: 10.54216/IJWAC.070201

Nai, S., El Moudden, T., Rifai, A., & Sadiq, A. (2026). Design and Evaluation of a Personalized AI Tutoring System Using ChatGPT. In Generative AI Applications and Intelligent Systems: From Chatbots to Cybersecurity (pp. 137-160). IGI Global Scientific Publishing.

Nai, S., Rifai, A., Sadiq, A., & Elbaghazaoui, B. E. (2025). An in-depth analysis of a tutoring solution by digital technology. *International Journal of Electrical & Computer Engineering (2088-8708)*, *15*(4).

Nazir, R., Laghari, A. A., Dahri, F. H., Shoulin, Y., Alhakeem, Z. M., Hakim, H., & Mughal, Z. A. (2026). A review on machine learning techniques for network security. *Journal of Cyber Security Technology*, *10*(1), 1–45. DOI: 10.1080/23742917.2025.2480730

Neprash, H. T., McGlave, C. C., Cross, D. A., Virnig, B. A., Puskarich, M. A., Huling, J. D., Rozenshtein, A. Z., & Nikpay, S. S. (2022, December). Trends in ransomware attacks on US hospitals, clinics, and other health care delivery organizations, 2016-2021. *JAMA Health Forum*, *3*(12), e224873. DOI: 10.1001/jamahealthforum.2022.4873 PMID: 36580326

Ojha, N., & Vaish, A. (2025). Why perimeter security is no longer enough: Observations and open challenges. In *Zero-Trust Learning* (pp. 305–328). Apple Academic Press. DOI: 10.1201/9781779643575-15

Olabanji, S. O., Marquis, Y., Adigwe, C. S., Ajayi, S. A., Oladoyinbo, T. O., & Olaniyi, O. O. (2024). AI-driven cloud security: Examining the impact of user behavior analysis on threat detection. *Asian Journal of Research in Computer Science, 17*(3), 57–74. DOI: 10.9734/ajrcos/2024/v17i3424

Olutimehin, A. T., Ajayi, A. J., Metibemu, O. C., Balogun, A. Y., Oladoyinbo, T. O., & Olaniyi, O. O. (2025). Adversarial threats to AI-driven systems: Exploring the attack surface of machine learning models and countermeasures. Available at *SSRN* 5137026.

Onwudebelu, U., Ugah, J. O., Ezeh, S. E., & Olugbemi, O. (2026). Securing Online Platforms: Hybrid Machine Learning Approaches for URL Phishing Detections. *Journal of International Communication, 5*(1), 24–46.

Pallaw, V. K., Singh, S. K., Singh, A. K., Saxena, S., & Mishra, D. (2026). Securing AI-Integrated Learning Platform: Cyber Threats in the Age of Digital Education. Cybernetic Shield, 39-51.

Paul, E. M., Mmaduekwe, U., Kessie, J. D., & Dolapo, M.Ebuka Mmaduekwe PaulEbuka Mmaduekwe PaulJoseph Darko KessieMukhtar Dolapo Salawudeen. (2024). Zero trust architecture and AI: A synergistic approach to next-generation cybersecurity frameworks. *International Journal of Science and Research Archive, 13*(2), 4159–4169. DOI: 10.30574/ijsra.2024.13.2.2583

Paya, A., & Gómez, A. (2024). Securesdp: A novel software-defined perimeter implementation for enhanced network security and scalability. *International Journal of Information Security, 23*(4), 2793–2808. DOI: 10.1007/s10207-024-00863-7

Puri, S., & Rathor, D. S. (2026). AI-Driven Cybersecurity: Emerging Threats and Defensive Strategies with Focus on College Youth in Delhi. *International Journal of Cultural Inheritance & Social Sciences ISSN: 2632-7597, 8*(15), 1-13.

Qabalin, M. K., Naser, M., & Alkasassbeh, M. (2022). Android spyware detection using machine learning: a novel dataset. sensors, 22(15), 5765.

Quraishi, T., Ulusi, H., Muhid, A., Hakimi, M., & Olusi, M. R. (2024). Empowering students through digital literacy: A case study of successful integration in a higher education curriculum. Journal of Digital Learning and Distance Education, 2(9), 667-681.

Stanojević, A. (2025). Algorithmic governance and social vulnerability: A value analysis of equality and trust. In Public governance and emerging technologies: Values, trust, and regulatory compliance (pp. 335–354). Springer Nature Switzerland.

Rahman, M. M., Arshi, A. S., Hasan, M. M., Mishu, S. F., Shahriar, H., & Wu, F. (2023, June). Security risk and attacks in ai: A survey of security and privacy. In 2023 IEEE 47th Annual Computers, Software, and Applications Conference (COMPSAC) (pp. 1834-1839). IEEE. DOI: 10.1109/COMPSAC57700.2023.00284

Razavi, H., Franco, M. F., Ouaissa, M., Ouaissa, M., & Srivastava, G. (Eds.). (2026). *AI-driven Cyber Risk Management*. CRC Press. DOI: 10.1201/9788743808077

Salako, A. O., Fabuyi, J. A., Aideyan, N. T., Selesi-Aina, O., Dapo-Oyewole, D. L., & Olaniyi, O. O. (2024). Advancing information governance in AI-driven cloud ecosystem: Strategies for enhancing data security and meeting regulatory compliance. *Asian Journal of Research in Computer Science*, *17*(12), 66–88. DOI: 10.9734/ajrcos/2024/v17i12530

Saleem, M. A., Aslam, M. S., Chishti, A. F., & Qureshi, M. A. (2026). ANOM-ALERT: INSIDER THREAT MONITORING SUITE. *Spectrum of Engineering Sciences*, *4*(1), 677–687.

Sarraf, G., & Pal, V. (2026). Autonomous Threat Detection and Response in Cloud Security: A Comprehensive Survey of AI-Driven Strategies. arXiv preprint arXiv:2601.03303.

Schelble, B. G., Lopez, J., Textor, C., Zhang, R., McNeese, N. J., Pak, R., & Freeman, G. (2024). Towards ethical AI: Empirically investigating dimensions of AI ethics, trust repair, and performance in human-AI teaming. *Human Factors*, *66*(4), 1037–1055. DOI: 10.1177/00187208221116952 PMID: 35938319

Serafimova, N., Petrovski, A., Iliev, A., & Karovska, B. (2025). Itegration of Emerging Technologies in Cybersecurity Education. *Journal of Peace, Conflict, and Security Studies*, *1*(1), 11.

Shayea, G. G., Zabil, M. H. M., Habeeb, M. A., Khaleel, Y. L., & Albahri, A. S. (2025). Strategies for protection against adversarial attacks in AI models: An in-depth review. *Journal of Intelligent Systems*, *34*(1), 20240277. DOI: 10.1515/jisys-2024-0277

Siddiqui, K., & Ahmad, S. (2023). Zoombombing: causes and preventions. In E3S Web of Conferences (Vol. 371, p. 05026). EDP Sciences. DOI: 10.1051/e3sconf/202337105026

Subrahmanyam, S. (2025). Behavioral Analysis for Threat Detection. In Handbook of AI-Driven Threat Detection and Prevention (pp. 95-115). CRC Press. DOI: 10.1201/9781003521020-6

Syed, S. A. (2025). Adversarial AI and cybersecurity: Defending against AI-powered cyber threats. *Iconic Research and Engineering Journals*, *8*(9), 1030–1041.

Syrotynskyi, R., Tyshyk, I., Kochan, O., Sokolov, V., & Skladannyi, P. (2024). Methodology of network infrastructure analysis as part of migration to zero-trust architecture. *Cyber Security and Data Protection*, *2024*(3800), 97–105.

Talu, M. (2025). Insights in Cybersecurity of a Smart Campus--A Review. Journal of Cybersecurity Education, Research and Practice, 2025(1).

Tian, J. (2025). Integrating artificial intelligence into the cybersecurity curriculum in higher education: A systematic literature review. *Education Sciences*, *15*(11), 1540. DOI: 10.3390/educsci15111540

Vásquez-Méndez, P. B., Arce Cuesta, D. C., & Zambrano-Martinez, J. L. (2026). The Human Factor: Assessing Ransomware Vulnerability in Developing Nations' Governments. *Information (Basel)*, *17*(2), 211. DOI: 10.3390/info17020211

Villegas-Ch, W., & García-Ortiz, J. (2023). Toward a comprehensive framework for ensuring security and privacy in artificial intelligence. *Electronics (Basel)*, *12*(18), 3786. DOI: 10.3390/electronics12183786

Wu, Z., Feng, E., & Zhang, Z. (2024). Temporal-Contextual Behavioral Analytics for Proactive Cloud Security Threat Detection. Academia Nexus Journal, 3(2).

Yazmyradov, S. (2024). A comprehensive review of AI security: Threats, challenges, and mitigation strategies. The International Journal of Internet. *Broadcasting and Communication*, *16*(4), 375–384.

Yeboah-Ofori, A., Darvishi, I., & Opeyemi, A. S. (2023, August). Enhancement of big data security in cloud computing using RSA algorithm. In 2023 10th International conference on future Internet of Things and Cloud (FICloud) (pp. 312-319). IEEE. DOI: 10.1109/FiCloud58648.2023.00053

# Compilation of References


Abbadi, D. (2025). Digital Gaps and Cyber Risks: Strategies to Ensure Equal Opportunities and Digital Education Security. *International Journal of Information & Digital Security*, *3*(2), 19–32. DOI: 10.54878/ba2nbk39

Abdullah, S. M., Cheruvu, A., Kanchi, S., Chung, T., Gao, P., Jadliwala, M., & Viswanath, B. (2024, May). An analysis of recent advances in deepfake image detection in an evolving threat landscape. In *2024 IEEE Symposium on Security and Privacy (SP)* (pp. 91-109). IEEE. DOI: 10.1109/SP54263.2024.00194

Abu-Nimeh, S., Nappa, D., Wang, X., & Nair, S. (2007). A comparison of machine learning techniques for phishing detection. *Proceedings of the Anti-Phishing Working Groups 2nd Annual eCrime Researchers Summit*, 60–69. DOI: 10.1145/1299015.1299021

Achar, S. (2022). Cloud computing security for multi-cloud service providers: Controls and techniques in our modern threat landscape. *International Journal of Computer and Systems Engineering*, *16*(9), 379–384.

Adamu, S. U., Ahmad, M. A., & Ibrahim, M. (2026). A systematic literature review on the adoption and effectiveness of cybersecurity frameworks in higher education institutions. *Information and Computer Security*, •••, 1–16. DOI: 10.1108/ICS-10-2025-0403

Adel, A. (2024). The convergence of intelligent tutoring, robotics, and IoT in smart education for the transition from industry 4.0 to 5.0. *Smart Cities*, *7*(1), 325–369. DOI: 10.3390/smartcities7010014

Adeniran, I. A., Efunniyi, C. P., Osundare, O. S., & Abhulimen, A. O. (2024). Enhancing security and risk management with predictive analytics: A proactive approach. *International Journal of Management & Entrepreneurship Research*, *6*(8), 32–40.

Adeyemo, D., Muhammad, I., Alagbe, J., & Ifelola, A. (2025). Global Cybersecurity Challenges for Students Using Online Learning in Higher Education. Available at *SSRN* 5361434. DOI: 10.2139/ssrn.5361434

Admass, W. S., Munaye, Y. Y., & Diro, A. A. (2024). Cyber security: State of the art, challenges and future directions. *Cyber Security and Applications*, *2*, 100031. DOI: 10.1016/j.csa.2023.100031

Afraji, D. M. A. A., Lloret, J., & Peñalver, L. (2025). Deep learning-driven defense strategies for mitigating DDoS attacks in cloud computing environments. *Cyber Security and Applications*, *3*, 100085. DOI: 10.1016/j.csa.2025.100085

Afsharnia, F. (2023). Risk and reliability analysis in the era of digital transformation. In *Advances in reliability, failure and risk analysis* (pp. 269–284). Springer Nature Singapore. DOI: 10.1007/978-981-19-9909-3_12

Ahmad, I., Imran, M., Qayyum, A., Ramzan, M. S., & Alassafi, M. O. (2023). An optimized hybrid deep intrusion detection model (HD-IDM) for enhancing network security. *Mathematics*, *11*(21), 4501. DOI: 10.3390/math11214501

Ahmad, J., Latif, S., Khan, I. U., Alshehri, M. S., Khan, M. S., Alasbali, N., & Jiang, W. (2025). An interpretable deep learning framework for intrusion detection in industrial Internet of Things. *Internet of Things : Engineering Cyber Physical Human Systems*, *33*, 101681. DOI: 10.1016/j.iot.2025.101681

Ahmed, A., Mostafa, R., Qutqut, M. H., & Ragab, N. (2026). A Systematic Literature Review on Machine Learning for Intrusion Detection Systems.

Ajayi, O. O., Alozie, C. E., & Abieba, O. A. (2025). Enhancing cybersecurity in energy infrastructure: Strategies for safeguarding critical systems in the digital age. *Trends in Renewable Energy*, *11*(2), 201–212. DOI: 10.17737/tre.2025.11.2.00192

Akhtar, M. S., & Feng, T. (2022). Detection of malware by deep learning as CNN-LSTM machine learning techniques in real time. *Symmetry*, *14*(11), 2308. DOI: 10.3390/sym14112308

Akinade, A. O., Adepoju, P. A., Ige, A. B., & Afolabi, A. I. (2025). Cloud security challenges and solutions: A review of current best practices. *Int J Multidiscip Res Growth Eval*, *6*(1), 26–35. DOI: 10.54660/.IJMRGE.2025.6.1.26-35

Akinsanya, M. O., Adeusi, O. C., & Ajanaku, K. B. (2022). A detailed review of contemporary cyber/network security approaches and emerging challenges. *Communication in Physical Sciences*, *8*(4), 721–732.

Akrami, K., Akrami, M., Akrami, F., Ahrari, M., Hakimi, M., & Fazil, A. W. (2024). Investigating the adverse effects of social media and cybercrime in higher education: A case study of an online university. Studies in Media. *The Journal of Communication*, *2*(1), 22–33.

Al Sawafi, Y., Touzene, A., & Hedjam, R. (2023). Hybrid deep learning-based intrusion detection system for RPL IoT networks. *Journal of Sensor and Actuator Networks*, *12*(2), 21. DOI: 10.3390/jsan12020021

Aldaej, A., Ahanger, T. A., & Ullah, I. (2023). Deep learning-inspired IoT-IDS mechanism for edge computing environments. *Sensors (Basel)*, *23*(24), 9869. DOI: 10.3390/s23249869 PMID: 38139716

Aldakheel, E. A., Zakariah, M., Gashgari, G. A., Almarshad, F. A., & Alzahrani, A. I. A. (2023). A Deep Learning-Based Innovative Technique for Phishing Detection in Modern Security with Uniform Resource Locators. *Sensors (Basel)*, *23*(9), 4403. DOI: 10.3390/s23094403 PMID: 37177607

Alharthi, A., Alaryani, M., & Kaddoura, S. (2025). A comparative study of machine learning and deep learning models in binary and multiclass classification for intrusion detection systems. *Array (New York, N.Y.)*, *26*, 100406. DOI: 10.1016/j.array.2025.100406

Alhazmi, A. K. (2026). Data Privacy and Security in AI-Driven Education Systems. In Revolutionizing Secure Learning in the Age of AI (pp. 263-294). IGI Global Scientific Publishing.

Ali, A., Li, J., Chen, H., Bhatti, U. A., & Khan, A. (2023). Real-time spammers detection based on metadata features with machine learning. *Intelligent Automation & Soft Computing*, *38*(3), 241–258. DOI: 10.32604/iasc.2023.041645

Ali, M. L., Thakur, K., Schmeelk, S., Debello, J., & Dragos, D. (2025). Deep learning vs. machine learning for intrusion detection in computer networks: A comparative study. *Applied Sciences (Basel, Switzerland)*, *15*(4), 1903. DOI: 10.3390/app15041903

Ali, S., Wang, J., Leung, V. C. M., Bashir, F., Bhatti, U. A., Wadho, S. A., & Humayun, M. (2025). CLDM-MMNNs: Cross-layer defense mechanisms through multi-modal neural networks fusion for end-to-end cybersecurity—Issues, challenges, and future directions. *Information Fusion*, *122*, 103222. DOI: 10.1016/j.inffus.2025.103222

Aljawarneh, S., Aldwairi, M., & Yassein, M. B. (2018). Anomaly-based intrusion detection system through feature selection analysis and building hybrid efficient model. *Journal of Computational Science*, *25*, 152–160. DOI: 10.1016/j.jocs.2017.03.006

Al-Khassawneh, Y. A. (2023). A review of artificial intelligence in security and privacy: Research advances, applications, opportunities, and challenges. *Indonesian Journal of Science and Technology*, *8*(1), 79–96. DOI: 10.17509/ijost.v8i1.52709

Almheiri, S. J., Shah, A. A., Abbas, S., Ahmad, M., & Khan, M. A. (2025). Smart sustainable cyber security: Modelling an interpretable and transparent threat detection with explainable artificial intelligence. *Discover Sustainability*, *6*(1), 442. DOI: 10.1007/s43621-025-01280-z

Alqudhaibi, A., Albarrak, M., Aloseel, A., Munshi, A., Alsharif, T., Jagtap, S., & Salonitis, K. (2026). Proactive cybersecurity in industry 4.0: A survey of cybersecurity threat prediction approaches in manufacturing systems. *International Journal of Information Security*, *25*(1), 14. DOI: 10.1007/s10207-025-01188-9

Al-Rubaye, M. H. A., & A'Ll, A. L.-T. (2023). The Impact of Digital Knowledge Management on Tax Compliance Efficiency: An Empirical Study of the General Tax Authority. *Tikrit Journal of Administrative and Economic Sciences*, *19*(62), 434–455. DOI: 10.25130/tjaes.19.62.2.24

Al-Sarem, M., Saeed, F., Al-Mekhlafi, Z. G., Mohammed, B. A., Al-Hadhrami, T., Alshammari, M. T., Alreshidi, A., & Alshammari, T. S. (2021). An optimized stacking ensemble model for phishing websites detection. *Electronics (Basel)*, *10*(11), 1285. DOI: 10.3390/electronics10111285

Alsubaei, F. S. (2025). Smart deep learning model for enhanced IoT intrusion detection. *Scientific Reports*, *15*(1), 20577. DOI: 10.1038/s41598-025-06363-5 PMID: 40596059

Alvi, S. (2025).Adversarial attacks on AI security systems: Investigating the vulnerability of AI-powered security solutions. In *Handbook of AI-Driven Threat Detection and Prevention* (pp. 165–176). CRC Press.

Amoo, O. O., Atadoga, A., Osasona, F., Abrahams, T. O., Ayinla, B. S., & Farayola, O. A. (2024). GDPR's impact on cybersecurity: A review focusing on USA and European practices. *International Journal of Science and Research Archive*, *11*(1), 1338–1347. DOI: 10.30574/ijsra.2024.11.1.0220

Anas, A. J. K., Syed, A. R., Tanveer, M. A., Chaudhry, M. A., & Paraddy, S. S. V. (2026). Cloud Computing Security Challenges and Emerging Solutions. Journal of Scientific Research and Technology, 96-100.

Anderson, H. S., & Roth, P. (2018). EMBER: An open dataset for training static PE malware machine learning models. arXiv preprint arXiv:1804.04637. https://arxiv.org/abs/1804.04637

Antonakakis, M., Perdisci, R., Nadji, Y., Vasiloglou, N., Abu-Nimeh, S., Lee, W., & Dagon, D. (2012). From throw-away traffic to bots: Detecting the rise of DGA-based malware. In *Proceedings of the 21st USENIX Security Symposium* (pp. 491–506). USENIX Association., https://www.usenix.org/conference/usenixsecurity12/technical-sessions/presentation/antonakakis

Arif, M., Kim, W., & Qureshi, S. (2022). Interference characterization in cellular-assisted vehicular communications with jamming. *IEEE Access : Practical Innovations, Open Solutions*, *10*, 42469–42480. DOI: 10.1109/ACCESS.2022.3168709

Arif, T., Jo, B., & Park, J. H. (2025). A comprehensive survey of privacy-enhancing and trust-centric cloud-native security techniques against cyber threats. *Sensors (Basel)*, *25*(8), 2350. DOI: 10.3390/s25082350 PMID: 40285041

Arikan, K. E., Doğan, S. M., Yilmaz, E. N., & Gönen, S. (2026). From code to security: Machine learning approaches in android vulnerability detection. *International Journal of Information Security*, *25*(1), 17. DOI: 10.1007/s10207-025-01190-1

Arora, A. (2025). Zero Trust Architecture: Revolutionizing Cybersecurity for Modern Digital Environments. *Available at SSRN* 5268151. DOI: 10.2139/ssrn.5268151

Arunkumar, J. R. (2023). Study Analysis of Cloud Security Challenges and Issues in Cloud Computing Technologies. Journal of Science. *Computing and Engineering Research*, *6*(8), 6–10.

Aslam, N., Khan, I. U., Mirza, S., AlOwayed, A., Anis, F. M., Aljuaid, R. M., & Baageel, R. (2022). Interpretable machine learning models for malicious domains detection using explainable artificial intelligence (XAI). *Sustainability (Basel)*, *14*(12), 7375. DOI: 10.3390/su14127375

Aslan, O., & Yilmaz, A. A. (2021). A new malware classification framework based on deep learning algorithms. *IEEE Access : Practical Innovations, Open Solutions*, *9*, 87936–87951. https://ieeexplore.ieee.org/document/9455368. DOI: 10.1109/ACCESS.2021.3089586

Assiri, A., & Almagwashi, H. (2018, April). IoT security and privacy issues. In 2018 1st International Conference on Computer Applications & Information Security (ICCAIS) (pp. 1-5). IEEE. DOI: 10.1109/CAIS.2018.8442002

Aung, Z., Rahman, M., & Islam, S. (2025). Generative AI for cybersecurity in IoT: Opportunities and challenges. *arXiv*. https://arxiv.org/abs/2502.08886

Axelsson, S. (2000). *Intrusion detection systems: A survey and taxonomy* (Technical Report). Chalmers University of Technology.

Axon, L., Fletcher, K., Scott, A. S., Stolz, M., Hannigan, R., Kaafarani, A. E., Goldsmith, M., & Creese, S. (2022). Emerging cybersecurity capability gaps in the industrial internet of things: Overview and research agenda. *Digital Threats : Research and Practice*, *3*(4), 1–27. DOI: 10.1145/3503920

Ayeni, R. K., Adebiyi, A. A., Okesola, J. O., & Igbekele, E. (2024, April). Phishing attacks and detection techniques: A systematic review. In 2024 international conference on science, engineering and business for driving sustainable development goals (SEB4SDG) (pp. 1-17). IEEE.

Azzeh, M., Altamimi, A. M., Albashayreh, M., & Al-Oudat, M. A. (2022). Adopting the Cybersecurity Concepts into Curriculum The Potential Effects on Students Cybersecurity Knowledge. arXiv preprint arXiv:2209.10407.

Badshah, A., Ghani, A., Daud, A., Jalal, A., Bilal, M., & Crowcroft, J. (2023). Towards smart education through internet of things: A survey. *ACM Computing Surveys*, *56*(2), 1–33. DOI: 10.1145/3610401

Bagdasaryan, E., Veit, A., Hua, Y., Estrin, D., & Shmatikov, V. (2020). "How to backdoor federated learning." In *International conference on artificial intelligence and statistics*, pp. 2938-2948. PMLR.

Bailetti, T., Craigen, D., Hudson, D., Levesque, R., McKeen, S., & Walsh, D. A. (2013). Developing an innovation engine to make Canada a global leader in cybersecurity. *Technology Innovation Management Review*, *3*(8), 5–14. Advance online publication. DOI: 10.22215/timreview/711

Bai, Y., Xing, G., Wu, H., Rao, Z., Ma, C., Wang, S., Liu, X., Zhou, Y., Tang, J., Huang, K., & Kang, J. (2024). Backdoor attack and defense on deep learning: A survey. *IEEE Transactions on Computational Social Systems*, *12*(1), 404–434. DOI: 10.1109/TCSS.2024.3482723

Basnet, M., & Hasan Ali, M. (2020). Deep learning-based intrusion detection system for electric vehicle charging station. *Proceedings of SPIES 2020*, Bangkok, 408–413. DOI: 10.1109/SPIES48661.2020.9243152

Basnet, M., & Hasan Ali, M. (2021). Exploring cybersecurity issues in 5G-enabled electric vehicle charging stations with deep learning. *IET Generation, Transmission & Distribution*, *15*(21), 3435–3449. DOI: 10.1049/gtd2.12275

Basnet, M., & Hasan Ali, M. (2022). WCGAN-based cyber-attacks detection system in the EV charging infrastructure. *Proceedings of SPIES 2022*, Beijing, 1761–1766. DOI: 10.1109/SPIES55999.2022.10082342

Basnet, M., & Hasan Ali, M. (2023). Deep-learning-powered cyber-attacks mitigation strategy in the EV charging infrastructure. *Proceedings of IEEE PESGM 2023*, Orlando, FL, 1–5. DOI: 10.1109/PESGM52003.2023.10252470

Basnet, R. B., Sung, A. H., & Liu, Q. (2011). Rule-based phishing attack detection. In *Proceedings of the 2011 International Conference on Security and Management (SAM)* (pp. 624–630). CSREA Press.

Bell, C. (2006). Surveillance strategies and populations at risk: Biopolitical governance in Canada's national security policy. *Security Dialogue*, *37*(2), 147–165. DOI: 10.1177/0967010606066168

Berqia, A., Ismaili, O., Chahbi, M., & Bouijij, H. (2025, April). Advanced DDoS Detection in Online Learning Environments. In 2025 13th International Symposium on Digital Forensics and Security (ISDFS) (pp. 1-5). IEEE. DOI: 10.1109/ISDFS65363.2025.11012095

Bhise, C. A., & Rangisetti, A. K. (2026). Edge computational resources and security aware serverless application deployment. *Cluster Computing*, *29*(1), 58. DOI: 10.1007/s10586-025-05851-7

Bogatinov, D., Nevena, S., Iliev, A., Karovska Andonovska, B., & Petrovski, A. (2025). Integration of Emerging Technologies in Cybersecurity Education. Journal of peace, conflict and security studies, 1(1), 133-146.

Breiman, L. (2001). Random forests. *Machine Learning*, *45*(1), 5–32. DOI: 10.1023/A:1010933404324

Brogan, J., Baskaran, I., & Ramachandran, N. (2018). Authenticating health activity data using distributed ledger technologies. *Computational and Structural Biotechnology Journal*, *16*, 257–266. DOI: 10.1016/j.csbj.2018.06.004 PMID: 30101004

Buczak, A. L., & Guven, E. (2015). A survey of data mining and machine learning methods for cyber security intrusion detection. *IEEE Communications Surveys and Tutorials*, *18*(2), 1153–1176. DOI: 10.1109/COMST.2015.2494502

Bulganina, S. V., Prokhorova, M. P., Lebedeva, T. E., Shkunova, A. A., & Mikhailov, M. S. (2021). Digital skills as a response to the challenges of the modern society. *Revista Turismo Estudos e Práticas-RTEP/GEPLAT/UERN*, (01), 1-7.

Butt, U. A., Amin, R., Mehmood, M., Aldabbas, H., Alharbi, M. T., & Albaqami, N. (2023). Cloud security threats and solutions: A survey. *Wireless Personal Communications*, *128*(1), 387–413. DOI: 10.1007/s11277-022-09960-z

Butt, U., Dauda, Y., & Shaheer, B. (2023a). Ransomware attack on the educational sector. In *AI, Blockchain and Self-Sovereign Identity in Higher Education* (pp. 279–313). Springer Nature Switzerland. DOI: 10.1007/978-3-031-33627-0_11

Cagnazzo, M., Hertlein, M., Holz, T., & Pohlmann, N. (2018, April). Threat modeling for mobile health systems. In *2018 IEEE Wireless Communications and Networking Conference Workshops (WCNCW)* (pp. 314-319). IEEE. DOI: 10.1109/WCNCW.2018.8369033

Calik Bayazit, E., Koray Sahingoz, O., & Dogan, B. (2023). Deep learning based malware detection for Android systems: A comparative analysis. *Tehnički Vjesnik (Strojarski Fakultet)*, *30*(3), 787–796. DOI: 10.17559/TV-20220907113227

Cano-Quiveu, G., Ruiz-de-Clavijo-Vazquez, P., Bellido, M. J., Juan-Chico, J., & Viejo-Cortes, J. (2023). IRIS: An embedded secure boot for IoT devices. *Internet of Things : Engineering Cyber Physical Human Systems*, *23*, 100874. DOI: 10.1016/j.iot.2023.100874

Cao, J., & Zhang, S. (2016, December). Research and design of RFID-based equipment incident management system for industry 4.0. In *2016 4th International Conference on Electrical & Electronics Engineering and Computer Science (ICEEECS 2016)* (pp. 889-894). Atlantis Press. DOI: 10.2991/iceeecs-16.2016.172

Capili, M. (2024). Simulation-Based Evaluation of Perimeter-Based and Zero Trust Security Implementation on Internet of Things (Doctoral dissertation, The George Washington University).

Carulli, M., Rossoni, M., Spadoni, E., Dozio, N., Giussani, R., Ferrise, F., & Bordegoni, M. (2024). A case study on digital training: Benefits and unexplored opportunities. *Journal of Computing and Information Science in Engineering*, *24*(5), 1–10. DOI: 10.1115/1.4064797

Casola, V., De Benedictis, A., Mazzocca, C., & Orbinato, V. (2024). Secure software development and testing: A model-based methodology. *Computers & Security*, *137*, 103639. DOI: 10.1016/j.cose.2023.103639

Castro-Ortiz, J. C., & Martínez-López, F. J. (2026). Cybersecurity in educational platforms: Threats, challenges, and best practices. *Campus Virtuales*, *15*(1), 191–213. DOI: 10.54988/cv.2026.1.1700

Catak, F. O., Yazı, A. F., Elezaj, O., & Ahmed, J. (2020). Deep learning based sequential model for malware analysis using Windows exe API calls. *PeerJ. Computer Science*, *6*, e285. DOI: 10.7717/peerj-cs.285 PMID: 33816936

Catuogno, L., & Galdi, C. (2023). Secure Firmware Update: Challenges and Solutions. *Cryptography*, *7*(2), 30. DOI: 10.3390/cryptography7020030

Chaganti, R., Ravi, V., & Pham, T. D. (2022). Deep learning based cross architecture internet of things malware detection and classification. *Computers & Security*, *120*, 102779. https://www.sciencedirect.com/science/article/pii/S0167404822001742. DOI: 10.1016/j.cose.2022.102779

Chanal, P. M., & Kakkasageri, M. S. (2020). Security and privacy in IoT: A survey. *Wireless Personal Communications*, *115*(2), 1667–1693. DOI: 10.1007/s11277-020-07649-9

Channapattan, P. M., Vyavahare, S. S., Yemul, R. M., Manglaram, V. V., & Yemul, A. S. (2027). Democratizing educational intelligence using Google Apps Script and AI: A human-centered approach to academic automation. In Zhao, J. (Eds.), *Human-centered AI and machine learning for e-collaboration* (pp. 307–348). IGI Global Scientific Publishing., DOI: 10.4018/979-8-3373-8217-3.ch010

Chaturvedi, I., Pawar, P. M., Muthalagu, R., & Tamizharasan, P. S. (2024). Zero trust security architecture for digital privacy in healthcare. In *Information Technology Security: Modern Trends and Challenges* (pp. 1–23). Springer Nature Singapore. DOI: 10.1007/978-981-97-0407-1_1

Chaturvedi, M., Sharma, S., & Ahmed, G. (2021, March). Study of baseline cyber security for various application domains. [). IOP Publishing.]. *IOP Conference Series. Materials Science and Engineering*, *1099*(1), 012051. DOI: 10.1088/1757-899X/1099/1/012051

Chaw, L. Y., & Tang, C. M. (2024). Exploring the relationship between digital competence proficiency and student learning performance. *European Journal of Education*, *59*(1), e12593. DOI: 10.1111/ejed.12593

Chawla, N. V. (2005). Data mining for imbalanced datasets: An overview. In Maimon, O., & Rokach, L. (Eds.), *Data mining and knowledge discovery handbook* (pp. 853–867). Springer., DOI: 10.1007/0-387-25465-X_40

Chen, X., Liu, C., Li, B., Lu, K., & Song, D. (2017). "Targeted backdoor attacks on deep learning systems using data poisoning." arXiv preprint arXiv:1712.05526

Chen, C. C., Shu, D., Ravishankar, H., Li, X., Agarwal, Y., & Cranor, L. F. (2024, May). Is a Trustmark and QR code enough? The effect of IoT security and privacy label information complexity on consumer comprehension and behavior. In *Proceedings of the 2024 CHI Conference on Human Factors in Computing Systems* (pp. 1-32). DOI: 10.1145/3613904.3642011

Chen, T., & Guestrin, C. (2016). XGBoost: A scalable tree boosting system. In *Proceedings of the 22nd ACM SIGKDD International Conference on Knowledge Discovery and Data Mining* (pp. 785–794). Association for Computing Machinery. https://doi.org/DOI: 10.1145/2939672.2939785

Chen, X., Li, M., Sun, Y., & Tian, Z. (2025). Invisible trigger image: A dynamic neural backdoor attack based on hidden features. *Neurocomputing*, *639*, 130296. DOI: 10.1016/j.neucom.2025.130296

Choudhary, Y., Umamaheswari, B., & Kumawat, V. (2021). A study of threats, vulnerabilities and countermeasures: An iot perspective. *Humanities (Washington)*, *8*(4), 39–45. DOI: 10.34293/sijash.v8i4.3583

Cirani, S., Picone, M., Gonizzi, P., Veltri, L., & Ferrari, G. (2014). Iot-oas: An oauth-based authorization service architecture for secure services in iot scenarios. *IEEE Sensors Journal*, *15*(2), 1224–1234. DOI: 10.1109/JSEN.2014.2361406

Cortes, C., & Vapnik, V. (1995). Support-vector networks. *Machine Learning*, *20*(3), 273–297. DOI: 10.1023/A:1022627411411

Danish, M. (2024). Enhancing cyber security through predictive analytics: Real-time threat detection and response. arXiv preprint arXiv:2407.10864.

Dartois, P., Leroux, A., Robert, D., & Wesolowski, B. (2024, April). SQISignHD: new dimensions in cryptography. In *Annual International Conference on the Theory and Applications of Cryptographic Techniques* (pp. 3-32). Cham: Springer Nature Switzerland.

Datta, P., & Sharma, B. (2017, July). A survey on IoT architectures, protocols, security and smart city-based applications. In *2017 8th International conference on computing, communication and networking technologies (ICCCNT)* (pp. 1-5). IEEE. DOI: 10.1109/ICCCNT.2017.8203943

Denning, D. E. (1987). An intrusion-detection model. *IEEE Transactions on Software Engineering*, *13*(2), 222–232. DOI: 10.1109/TSE.1987.232894

Devi, T. A., & Jain, A. (2024, May). Enhancing cloud security with deep learning-based intrusion detection in cloud computing environments. In 2024 2nd International Conference on Advancement in Computation & Computer Technologies (InCACCT) (pp. 541-546). IEEE. DOI: 10.1109/InCACCT61598.2024.10551040

Dhamija, R., Tygar, J. D., & Hearst, M. (2006). Why phishing works. *Proceedings of the SIGCHI Conference on Human Factors in Computing Systems*, 581–590. DOI: 10.1145/1124772.1124861

Diffie, W., & Hellman, M. E. (2022). New directions in cryptography. In *Democratizing cryptography: the work of Whitfield Diffie and Martin Hellman* (pp. 365-390). DOI: 10.1145/3549993.3550007

Ding, W., Abdel-Basset, M., & Mohamed, R. (2023). DeepAK-IoT: An effective deep learning model for cyberattack detection in IoT networks. *Information Sciences*, *634*, 157–171. DOI: 10.1016/j.ins.2023.03.052

Downs, J. S., Holbrook, M. B., & Cranor, L. F. (2006). Decision strategies and susceptibility to phishing. *Proceedings of the Symposium on Usable Privacy and Security*, 79–90. DOI: 10.1145/1143120.1143131

Dua, D., & Graff, C. (2019). *UCI machine learning repository. University of California*. School of Information and Computer Sciences., http://archive.ics.uci.edu/ml

Duary, S., Choudhury, P., Mishra, S., Sharma, V., Rao, D. D., & Aderemi, A. P. (2024, February). Cybersecurity threats detection in intelligent networks using predictive analytics approaches. In *2024 4th International Conference on Innovative Practices in Technology and Management (ICIPTM)* (pp. 1-5). Ieee. DOI: 10.1109/ICIPTM59628.2024.10563348

Dupuis, M., & Ebenezer, M. (2018, September). Help wanted: Consumer privacy behavior and smart home internet of things (iot) devices. In *Proceedings of the 19th annual SIG conference on information technology education* (pp. 117-122).DOI: 10.1145/3241815.3241869

Durst, S., Hinteregger, C., & Zieba, M. (2024). The effect of environmental turbulence on cyber security risk management and organizational resilience. *Computers & Security*, *137*, 103591. DOI: 10.1016/j.cose.2023.103591

Edupuganti, S., Tenneti, N. S. S., Iqbal, M. M., & Rajaram, G. (2023). An IoT implemented dynamic air pollution monitoring system. *EAI Endorsed Transactions on Internet of Things*, *9*(4), 1–6. DOI: 10.4108/eetiot.v9i4.4316

Eggers, S. (2021). A novel approach for analyzing the nuclear supply chain cyberattack surface. *Nuclear Engineering and Technology*, *53*(3), 879–887. DOI: 10.1016/j.net.2020.08.021

ElKashlan, M., Aslan, H., Elsayed, M. S., Jurcut, A. D., & Azer, M. A. (2023a). Intrusion detection for electric vehicle charging systems (EVCS). *Algorithms*, *16*(2), 75. DOI: 10.3390/a16020075

ElKashlan, M., Elsayed, M. S., Jurcut, A. D., & Azer, M. (2023b). A machine learning-based intrusion detection system for IoT electric vehicle charging stations. *Electronics (Basel)*, *12*(4), 1044. DOI: 10.3390/electronics12041044

Emami-Naeini, P., Dixon, H., Agarwal, Y., & Cranor, L. F. (2019, May). Exploring how privacy and security factor into IoT device purchase behavior. In *Proceedings of the 2019 CHI Conference on Human Factors in Computing Systems* (pp. 1-12). DOI: 10.1145/3290605.3300764

Enam, M. M. R., Joarder, M. M. I., Taimun, M. T. Y., & Sharan, S. M. I. (2025). Framework for Smart SCADA Systems: Integrating Cloud Computing, IIoT, and Cybersecurity for Enhanced Industrial Automation. *Saudi J Eng Technol, 10*(4), 152–158. DOI: 10.36348/sjet.2025.v10i04.005

Eufrazio Martins Júnior, G., Guimaraes Marques, T., Souza da Silva, W., & Celestino, J.Junior. (2026). Edge-Oriented DoS/DDoS Intrusion Detection and Supervision Platform. *Security and Privacy, 9*(2), e70193. DOI: 10.1002/spy2.70193

Fagan, M., Megas, K. N., Scarfone, K. A., & Smith, M. (2025). *Foundational cybersecurity activities for IoT device manufacturers (NIST IR 8259 Revision 1, Initial public draft)*. National Institute of Standards and Technology., DOI: 10.6028/NIST.IR.8259r1.ipd

Fahrurozi, M., Tarigan, S. A., Tanjung, M. A., & Mutijarsa, K. (2020, October). The use of ISO/IEC 27005: 2018 for strengthening information security management (a case study at data and information Center of Ministry of Defence). In *2020 12th International Conference on Information Technology and Electrical Engineering (ICITEE)* (pp. 86-91). IEEE.DOI: 10.1109/ICITEE49829.2020.9271748

Ferrag, M. A., Friha, O., Hamouda, D., Maglaras, L., & Janicke, H. (2022). Edge-IIoTset: A new comprehensive realistic cyber security dataset of IoT and IIoT applications. *IEEE Access : Practical Innovations, Open Solutions, 10*, 40281–40306. DOI: 10.1109/ACCESS.2022.3165809

Ferrag, M. A., Maglaras, L. A., Janicke, H., Jiang, J., & Shu, L. (2017). Authentication protocols for internet of things: A comprehensive survey. *Security and Communication Networks, 2017*(1), 6562953. DOI: 10.1155/2017/6562953

Figueira, P. T., Bravo, C. L., & José, L. R. L. Improving information security risk analysis by including threat-occurrence predictive models, *Computers & Security, Volume 88*,2020,101609,ISSN 0167-4048, DOI: 10.1016/j.cose.2019.101609

Florea, B. C., & Taralunga, D. D. (2020). Blockchain IoT for smart electric vehicles battery management. *Sustainability (Basel), 12*(10), 3984. DOI: 10.3390/su12103984

Friedman, J. H. (2001). Greedy function approximation: A gradient boosting machine. *Annals of Statistics, 29*(5), 1189–1232. DOI: 10.1214/aos/1013203451

Furnell, S. (2021). The cybersecurity workforce and skills. *Computers & Security, 100*, 102080. DOI: 10.1016/j.cose.2020.102080

Gadde, H. (2023). AI-Driven Anomaly Detection in NoSQL Databases for Enhanced Security. *International Journal of Machine Learning Research in Cybersecurity and Artificial Intelligence, 14*(1), 497–522.

Gadde, H. (2023). Leveraging AI for Scalable Query Processing in Big Data Environments. *International Journal of Advanced Engineering Technologies and Innovations, 1*(02), 435–465.

Gaitan, E. (2022). *Developing and sharing threat intelligence: Strategies for small and medium-sized businesses* (Doctoral dissertation, Capella University).

Gambo, M. L., & Almulhem, A. (2026). Zero Trust Architecture: A systematic literature review. *Journal of Network and Systems Management, 34*(1), 25. DOI: 10.1007/s10922-025-09998-x

Gao, Y., Doan, B. G., Zhang, Z., Ma, S., Zhang, J., Fu, A., Nepal, S., & Kim, H. (2020). "Backdoor attacks and countermeasures on deep learning: A comprehensive review." arXiv preprint arXiv:2007.10760

Gao, Y., Xu, C., Wang, D., Chen, S., Ranasinghe, D. C., & Nepal, S. (2019). "Strip: A defence against trojan attacks on deep neural networks." In *Proceedings of the 35th annual computer security applications conference*, pp. 113-125. DOI: 10.1145/3359789.3359790

Garera, S., Provos, N., Chew, M., & Rubin, A. D. (2007). A framework for detection and measurement of phishing attacks. *Proceedings of the 2007 ACM Workshop on Recurring Malcode*, 1–8. DOI: 10.1145/1314389.1314391

Garg, S., Aujla, G. S., Kaur, K., & Syed, H. A. S. (Eds.). (2022). *Intelligent cyber-physical systems for autonomous transportation*. Springer. DOI: 10.1007/978-3-030-92054-8

Geater, J., Hirsch, F., Richter, D., Robkin, M., & Zahavi, R. (2022). Iot security maturity model digital twin profile. Tech. rep., Digital Twin Consortium (June 2022).

Gelman, H., Hastings, J. D., Kenley, D., & Loiacono, E. (2024, December). Toward an insider threat education platform: A theoretical literature review. In 2024 International Conference on Computer and Applications (ICCA) (pp. 01-06). IEEE. DOI: 10.1109/ICCA62237.2024.10928083

George, A. S., Baskar, T., & Srikaanth, P. B. (2024). Cyber threats to critical infrastructure: Assessing vulnerabilities across key sectors. *Partners Universal International Innovation Journal*, *2*(1), 51–75.

Girdhar, M., Hong, J., You, Y., Song, T. J., & Govindarasu, M. (2023). Cyber-attack event analysis for EV charging stations. *Proceedings of IEEE PESGM 2023*, Orlando, FL, 1–5. DOI: 10.1109/PESGM52003.2023.10252504

Goldblum, M., Tsipras, D., Xie, C., Chen, X., Schwarzschild, A., Song, D., Mądry, A., Li, B., & Goldstein, T. (2022). Dataset security for machine learning: Data poisoning, backdoor attacks, and defenses. *IEEE Transactions on Pattern Analysis and Machine Intelligence*, *45*(2), 1563–1580. DOI: 10.1109/TPAMI.2022.3162397 PMID: 35333711

Gou, W., Zhang, H., & Zhang, R. (2023). Multi-classification and tree-based hybrid network for the intrusion detection system in the Internet of Vehicles. *Sensors (Basel)*, *23*(21), 8788. DOI: 10.3390/s23218788 PMID: 37960485

Grover, S., Broll, B., & Babb, D. (2023, March). Cybersecurity education in the age of ai: Integrating ai learning into cybersecurity high school curricula. In *Proceedings of the 54th ACM Technical Symposium on Computer Science Education* V. 1 (pp. 980-986). DOI: 10.1145/3545945.3569750

Gu, T., Dolan-Gavitt, B., & Garg, S. (2017). "Badnets: Identifying vulnerabilities in the machine learning model supply chain." arXiv preprint arXiv:1708.06733

Gunasekaran, R. M. N. (2026). AI-Driven Data Governance: Ensuring Compliance in Big Data Ecosystems. International Journal of AI, BigData, Computational and Management Studies, 262-275.

Gupta, K. D., & Dasgupta, D. (2022). Adversarial attacks and defenses for deployed AI models. *IT Professional*, *24*(4), 37–41. DOI: 10.1109/MITP.2022.3180330

Habbal, A., Ali, M. K., & Abuzaraida, M. A. (2024). Artificial Intelligence Trust, risk and security management (AI trism): Frameworks, applications, challenges and future research directions. *Expert Systems with Applications*, *240*, 122442. DOI: 10.1016/j.eswa.2023.122442

Hadnagy, C. (2010). *Social engineering: The art of human hacking*. John Wiley & Sons.

Hakimi, M., Quchi, M. M., & Fazil, A. W. (2024). Human factors in cybersecurity: an in depth analysis of user centric studies. Jurnal Ilmiah Multidisiplin Indonesia (JIM-ID), 3(01), 20-33.

Hamdare, S., Kaiwartya, O., Aljaidi, M., Jugran, M., Cao, Y., Kumar, S., Mahmud, M., Brown, D., & Lloret, J. (2023). Cybersecurity risk analysis of electric vehicles charging stations. *Sensors (Basel), 23*(15), 6716. DOI: 10.3390/s23156716 PMID: 37571500

Han, M., Huang, M., Zhang, Y., & Bhatti, U. A. (2018). An architecture of secure health information storage system based on blockchain technology. In *International conference on cloud computing and security* (pp. 578–588). DOI: 10.1007/978-3-030-00009-7_52

Hannousse, A., & Yahiouche, S. (2021). Towards benchmark datasets for machine learning based website phishing detection: An experimental study. *Engineering Applications of Artificial Intelligence, 104*, 104347. DOI: 10.1016/j.engappai.2021.104347

Han, X., Xu, G., Zhou, Y., Yang, X., Li, J., & Zhang, T. (2022). "Physical backdoor attacks to lane detection systems in autonomous driving." In *Proceedings of the 30th ACM International Conference on Multimedia*, pp. 2957-2968. DOI: 10.1145/3503161.3548171

Harris, C. R., Millman, K. J., van der Walt, S. J., Gommers, R., Virtanen, P., Cournapeau, D., Wieser, E., Taylor, J., Berg, S., Smith, N. J., Kern, R., Picus, M., Hoyer, S., van Kerkwijk, M. H., Brett, M., Haldane, A., del Río, J. F., Wiebe, M., Peterson, P., & Oliphant, T. E. (2020). Array programming with NumPy. *Nature, 585*(7825), 357–362. DOI: 10.1038/s41586-020-2649-2 PMID: 32939066

Hartmann, K., & Steup, C. (2020). "Hacking the AI-the next generation of hijacked systems." In 2020 12th International Conference on Cyber Conflict (CyCon), vol. 1300, pp. 327-349. IEEE. DOI: 10.23919/CyCon49761.2020.9131724

Hashemi, M., Forte, D., & Ganji, F. (2025). GuardianMPC: Backdoor-Resilient Neural Network Computation. *IEEE Access : Practical Innovations, Open Solutions, 13*, 11029–11048. DOI: 10.1109/ACCESS.2025.3528304

Hettiarachchi, N. L., Subramaniam, T. S., Palpanadan, S. T., & Al-Fattal, A. (2023). Infusing communication skills into financial accounting curriculum: A perspective from the digital era. *International Journal of Information and Education Technology (IJIET), 13*(4), 664–672. DOI: 10.18178/ijiet.2023.13.4.1851

Hochreiter, S., & Schmidhuber, J. (1997). Long short-term memory. *Neural Computation, 9*(8), 1735–1780. DOI: 10.1162/neco.1997.9.8.1735 PMID: 9377276

Hosseini, S., Nezhad, A. E., & Seilani, H. (2021). Android malware classification using convolutional neural network and LSTM. *Journal of Computer Virology and Hacking Techniques, 17*(4), 307–318. DOI: 10.1007/s11416-021-00385-z

Hu, C., & Hu, Y.-H. F. (2020). "Data poisoning on deep learning models." In *2020 International Conference on Computational Science and Computational Intelligence (CSCI)*, pp. 628-632. IEEE. DOI: 10.1109/CSCI51800.2020.00111

Hwang, Y. H. (2015, April). Iot security & privacy: threats and challenges. In *Proceedings of the 1st ACM workshop on IoT privacy, trust, and security* (pp. 1-1). DOI: 10.1145/2732209.2732216

Ikram, I., & Huma, Z. (2024). *An explainable AI approach to intrusion detection using interpretable machine learning models*. Euro Vantage Journal of Artificial Intelligence.

Intazar, M., Zohra, T., Ansari, N. M., Iqbal, R., & Gul, H. (2024). Beyond Perimeter Defenses: Implementing Zero-Trust Security Models for Cloud Computing in the Era of Advanced Cyber Threats. Global Research Journal of Natural Science and Technology, 2(3).

Iqbal, S., Kiah, M. L. M., Dhaghighi, B., Hussain, M., Khan, S., Khan, M. K., & Choo, K. K. R. (2016). On cloud security attacks: A taxonomy and intrusion detection and prevention as a service. *Journal of Network and Computer Applications*, *74*, 98–120. DOI: 10.1016/j.jnca.2016.08.016

Islam, S., Badsha, S., Sengupta, S., Khalil, I., & Atiquzzaman, M. (2023). An intelligent privacy preservation scheme for EV charging infrastructure. *IEEE Transactions on Industrial Informatics*, *19*(2), 1238–1247. DOI: 10.1109/TII.2022.3203707

Jack, W., & Nawaz, D. (2025). Next-Gen Cybersecurity: Integrating Artificial Intelligence with Behavioral Analytics for Threat Prediction.

Jain, A. K., & Gupta, B. B. (2017). Phishing detection: Analysis of visual similarity based approaches. *Security and Communication Networks*, *5421046*, 1–20. Advance online publication. DOI: 10.1155/2017/5421046

Jain, S. (2025). Advancing cybersecurity with artificial intelligence and machine learning: Architectures, algorithms, and future directions in threat detection and mitigation. *World Journal of Advanced Engineering Technology and Sciences*, *14*(1), 273–290. DOI: 10.30574/wjaets.2025.14.1.0022

Jain, V. (2021). A review on different types of cryptography techniques. *ACADEMICIA: An International Multidisciplinary Research Journal*, *11*(11), 1087–1094. DOI: 10.5958/2249-7137.2021.02568.4

Jaspers, E. D., & Pearson, E. (2022). Consumers' acceptance of domestic Internet-of-Things: The role of trust and privacy concerns. *Journal of Business Research*, *142*, 255–265. DOI: 10.1016/j.jbusres.2021.12.043

Jaya, M. I., & Razak, M. F. A. (2022). Dynamic ransomware detection for windows platform using machine learning classifiers. JOIV: International Journal on Informatics Visualization, 6(2-2), 469-474.

Josephson, C. (2026). When Humans Become False Positives: Measurement Geometry, Cognitive Load, and False Alarms in Human-Centred Cybersecurity. Cognitive Load, and False Alarms in Human-Centred Cybersecurity (January 01, 2026).

Judijanto, L., Hendriana, T. I., & Muhammad, A. F. (2025). Strategic human capital planning in the asian digital economy: Aligning workforce development with business objectives. *INTERNATIONAL JOURNAL OF FINANCIAL ECONOMICS*, *1*(8), 344–360.

Juma, M., Monem, A. A., & Shaalan, K. (2020). Hybrid end-to-end VPN security approach for smart IoT objects. *Journal of Network and Computer Applications*, *158*, 102598. DOI: 10.1016/j.jnca.2020.102598

Kaksonen, R., Halunen, K., Laakso, M., & Röning, J. (2024, February). Automating IoT Security Standard Testing by Common Security Tools. In *Proceedings of the 10th International Conference on Information Systems Security and Privacy*. SCITEPRESS Science and Technology Publications. DOI: 10.5220/0012345900003648

Kale, J. R., Yemul, R. M., Vyavahare, S. S., Lobo, L. M. R. J., & Athavale, V. A. (2026). A hand gesture recognition model using deep learning algorithms. In *AI-driven approaches for fully automated smart engineering* (pp. 1–34). IGI Global., DOI: 10.4018/979-8-3373-4839-1.ch008

Karat, G., Kannimoola, J. M., Nair, N., Vazhayil, A., G, S. V., & Poornachandran, P. (2024). CNN-LSTM hybrid model for enhanced malware analysis and detection. *Procedia Computer Science*, *233*, 492–503. https://www.sciencedirect.com/science/article/pii/S1877050924005982. DOI: 10.1016/j.procs.2024.03.239

Kashef, M., Visvizi, A., & Troisi, O. (2021). Smart city as a smart service system: Human-computer interaction and smart city surveillance systems. *Computers in Human Behavior*, *124*, 106923. DOI: 10.1016/j.chb.2021.106923

Khacha, A., Saadouni, R., Harbi, Y., & Aliouat, Z. (2022). Hybrid deep learning-based intrusion detection system for industrial Internet of Things. *Proceedings of ISIA 2022, M'sila*, Algeria. DOI: 10.1109/ISIA55826.2022.9993487

Khadka, K., & Ullah, A. B. (2025). Human factors in cybersecurity: an interdisciplinary review and framework proposal: K. Khadka, AB Ullah. *International Journal of Information Security*, *24*(3), 119. DOI: 10.1007/s10207-025-01032-0

Khan, M. J. (2023). Zero trust architecture: Redefining network security paradigms in the digital age. *World Journal of Advanced Research and Reviews, 19*(3), 105–116. DOI: 10.30574/wjarr.2023.19.3.1785

Khan, R. A., Khan, S. U., Khan, H. U., & Ilyas, M. (2022). Systematic literature review on security risks and its practices in secure software development. *ieee. IEEE Access : Practical Innovations, Open Solutions, 10*, 5456–5481. DOI: 10.1109/ACCESS.2022.3140181

Khan, S. U., Akram, M., & Usman, M. (2022). URL-based phishing detection using ensemble learning. *Proceedings of the IEEE International Conference on Cyber Security and Resilience*, 118–125. DOI: 10.1109/CSR54599.2022.9850326

Kilichev, D., & Kim, W. (2023). Hyperparameter optimization for 1D-CNN-based network intrusion detection using GA and PSO. *Mathematics, 11*(17), 3724. DOI: 10.3390/math11173724

Kilichev, D., Turimov, D., & Kim, W. (2024). Next-generation intrusion detection for IoT EVCS: Integrating CNN, LSTM, and GRU models. *Mathematics, 12*(4), 571. DOI: 10.3390/math12040571

Kim, G., Lee, S., & Kim, S. (2014). A novel hybrid intrusion detection method integrating anomaly detection with misuse detection. *Expert Systems with Applications, 41*(4), 1690–1700. DOI: 10.1016/j.eswa.2013.08.066

Kim, H., & Kim, M. (2024). Malware detection and classification system based on CNN-BiLSTM. *Electronics (Basel), 13*(13), 1–14. https://www.mdpi.com/2079-9292/13/13/2539. DOI: 10.3390/electronics13132539

Kiran, B. R., Kopperi, H., & Venkata Mohan, S. (2022). Micro/nano-plastics occurrence, identification, risk analysis and mitigation: Challenges and perspectives. *Reviews in Environmental Science and Biotechnology, 21*(1), 169–203. DOI: 10.1007/s11157-021-09609-6 PMID: 35103051

Kolosnjaji, B., Zarras, A., Webster, G., & Eckert, C. (2016). Deep learning for classification of malware system call sequences. In AI 2016. Advances in Artificial Intelligence., , LNCS 9992.DOI: 10.1007/978-3-319-50127-7_11

Koppula, M., & LM, L. J. (2023). LNKDSEA: Machine learning based IoT/IIoT attack detection method. *Proceedings of ICAECIS 2023*, Bengaluru, India, 655–662. DOI: 10.1109/ICAECIS58353.2023.10170095

Koren, O., Koren, M., & Peretz, O. A procedure for anomaly detection and analysis, Engineering Applications of Artificial Intelligence, Volume 117, Part A,2023,105503, ISSN 0952-1976. DOI: 10.1016/j.engappai.2022.105503

Kousar, H., Fatima, S., Ahmed, S. I., Sajithra, S., Kushwaha, S., & Balaji, N. A. (2023, September). AI based security for internet of transportation systems. In 2023 4th International Conference on Smart Electronics and Communication (ICOSEC) (pp. 701-708). IEEE.

Kshetri, N. (2010). *The global cybercrime industry: Economic, institutional and strategic perspectives*. Springer., DOI: 10.1007/978-3-642-11522-6

Kuforiji, J. (2025). Digital Forensics and Incident Response (DFIR) Automation: Leveraging AI to Accelerate Breach Investigation, Evidence Collection, and Cyberattack Mitigation. *Journal of Data Analysis and Critical Management*, *1*(04), 1–19. DOI: 10.64235/tsvfvz27

Kuforiji, J. (2025). The importance of integrating security education into university curricula and professional certifications. International Journal of Technology. *Management and Humanities*, *11*(03), 1–10.

Kumar, J. S., & Patel, D. R. (2014). A survey on internet of things: Security and privacy issues. *International Journal of Computer Applications*, *90*(11). Advance online publication. DOI: 10.5120/15764-4454

Kurte, S., Sharma, P., & Singh, R. (2025). Supporting decentralized IoT applications under resource constraints. *Internet of Things : Engineering Cyber Physical Human Systems*, *30*, 101496. Advance online publication. DOI: 10.1016/j.iot.2025.101496

Lakhal, H., Zegrari, M., & Bahnasse, A. (2025). Next-Generation Smart Grid Cybersecurity: A Systematic Review of OT Cyber Threats, AI-Driven Defense, Cyber Deception Techniques, and Emerging Security Strategies. *IEEE Access : Practical Innovations, Open Solutions*, *13*, 181519–181552. DOI: 10.1109/ACCESS.2025.3623834

Le, H., Pham, Q., Sahoo, D., & Hoi, S. C. (2018). URLNet: Learning a URL representation with deep learning for malicious URL detection. *arXiv preprint arXiv:1802.03162*. /arXiv.1802.03162DOI: 10.48550

Lee, H. C., Liu, H. Y., Lin, T. C., & Lee, C. Y. (2023). A customized energy management system for distributed PV, energy storage units, and charging stations. *Sensors (Basel)*, *23*(11), 5286. DOI: 10.3390/s23115286 PMID: 37300014

Li, C., Chen, X., Wang, D., Wen, S., Ahmed, M. E., Camtepe, S., & Xiang, Y. (2021). Backdoor attack on machine learning based android malware detectors. *IEEE Transactions on Dependable and Secure Computing*, *19*(5), 3357–3370. DOI: 10.1109/TDSC.2021.3094824

Lilhore, U. K., Manoharan, P., Simaiya, S., Alroobaea, R., Alsafyani, M., Baqasah, A. M., Dalal, S., Sharma, A., & Raahemifar, K. (2023). HIDM: Hybrid intrusion detection model for Industry 4.0 networks using an optimized CNN-LSTM with transfer learning. *Sensors (Basel)*, *23*(18), 7856. DOI: 10.3390/s23187856 PMID: 37765912

Lim, C., & Maglio, P. P. (2018). Clarifying the Concept of Smart Service System. In: Maglio, P.P., Kieliszewski, C.A., Spohrer, J.C., Lyons, K., Patrício, L., Sawatani, Y. (eds) *Handbook of Service Science, Volume II*. Service Science: Research and Innovations in the Service Economy. Springer, Cham. DOI: 10.1007/978-3-319-98512-1_16

Ling, C., & Stringhini, G. (2024, September). " It was jerks on the Internet being jerks on the Internet": Understanding Zoombombing Through the Eyes of Its Victims. In *Proceedings of the 2024 European Symposium on Usable Security* (pp. 261-276). DOI: 10.1145/3688459.3688466

Li, Y., Jiang, Y., Li, Z., & Xia, S.-T. (2022). Backdoor learning: A survey. *IEEE Transactions on Neural Networks and Learning Systems*, *35*(1), 5–22. DOI: 10.1109/TNNLS.2022.3182979 PMID: 35731760

Maghanaki, M., Keramati, S., Chen, F. F., & Shahin, M. (2026). Systematic Evaluation of Machine Learning and Deep Learning Models for IoT Malware Detection Across Ransomware, Rootkit, Spyware, Trojan, Botnet, Worm, Virus, and Keylogger. *Sensors (Basel)*, *26*(6), 1750. DOI: 10.3390/s26061750 PMID: 41901920

Ma, J., Saul, L. K., Savage, S., & Voelker, G. M. (2011). Learning to detect malicious URLs. ACM Transactions on Intelligent Systems and Technology, 2(3). *ACM Transactions on Intelligent Systems and Technology*, *30*(3), 1–24. DOI: 10.1145/1961189.1961202

Makovoz, O., & Lysenko, S. (2024). Evolution of digital transformations in IT companies. *London Journal of Social Sciences*, (8), 1–7. DOI: 10.31039/ljss.2024.8.202

MAMMAN. J. O. (2024). Mitigating The Impact Of Phishing Attacks On The E-learning Infrastructure. Scientific and Practical Cyber Security Journal (SPCSJ) 8 (3): 21–34 ISSN 2587-4667 Scientific Cyber Security Association (SCSA).

Manglaram, V. V., Lobo, L. M. R. J., Athavale, V. A., Vyavahare, S. S., & Yemul, R. M. (2026). Design and development of a deep learning-based system for lung cancer diagnosis and automated treatment suggestion. In *Advances in synthetic healthcare data: Opportunities, challenges, and emerging trends* (pp. 1–38). IGI Global., DOI: 10.4018/979-8-3373-5641-9.ch001

Maniath, S., . . .. (2017). Deep learning LSTM based ransomware detection. In Recent Developments in Control, Automation & Power Engineering (RDCAPE) (pp. 442–446). https://ieeexplore.ieee.org/document/8358312

Maniriho, P., Mahmood, A. N., & Chowdhury, M. J. M. (2024). A survey of recent advances in deep learning models for detecting malware in desktop and mobile platforms. *ACM Computing Surveys*, *56*(6), 1–41. DOI: 10.1145/3638240

Manoharan, A., Sriskantharajah, A., Herath, H. M. K. K. M. B., Guruge, L. G. P. K., & Yasakethu, S. L. P. (2025). MetaHuman based phishing attacks in the metaverse realm: Awareness for cyber security education. *Education and Information Technologies*, *30*(9), 12939–12965. DOI: 10.1007/s10639-025-13326-w

Marquardson, J., & Elnoshokaty, A. (2020). Skills, certifications, or degrees: What companies demand for entry-level cybersecurity jobs. *Information Systems Education Journal*, *18*(1), 22–28. DOI: 10.62273/TDSH7421

Marques, I. C., & Ferreira, J. J. (2020). Digital transformation in the area of health: Systematic review of 45 years of evolution. *Health Technology (Hong Kong)*, *10*(3), 575–586.

Mather, Tim & Kumaraswamy, Subra & Latif, Shahed. (2009). Cloud Security and Privacy: An Enterprise Perspective on Risks and Compliance.

Maulana, R. J., & Kusuma, G. P. (2020). Malware classification based on system call sequences using deep learning. *Advances in Science, Technology and Engineering Systems Journal*, *5*(4), 207–216. https://www.academia.edu/download/94248244/ASTESJ_050426.pdf. DOI: 10.25046/aj050426

McGrath, D. K., & Gupta, M. (2008). Behind phishing: An examination of phisher modi operandi. In *Proceedings of the 1st USENIX Workshop on Large-Scale Exploits and Emergent Threats* (pp. 1–8). USENIX Association., https://www.usenix.org/conference/leet-08/behind-phishing-examination-phisher-modi-operandi

McKinney, W. (2010). Data structures for statistical computing in python. *Proceedings of the 9th Python in Science Conference*, 445, 51–56. DOI: 10.25080/Majora-92bf1922-00a

Mehra, T. (2025). *Building a Resilient Backup Infrastructure: Combining Data Redundancy*. Encryption, and RBAC for Maximum Protection., DOI: 10.55041/IJSREM41975

Mell, P., & Grance, T. (2011). *The NIST definition of cloud computing*., DOI: 10.6028/NIST.SP.800-145

Miao, Y., Xie, R., Li, X., Liu, Z., Choo, K.-K. R., & Deng, R. H. (2024). Efficient and secure federated learning against backdoor attacks. *IEEE Transactions on Dependable and Secure Computing*, *21*(5), 4619–4636. DOI: 10.1109/TDSC.2024.3354736

Mızrak, F. (2023). Integrating cybersecurity risk management into strategic management: A comprehensive literature review. *Research Journal of Business and Management*, *10*(3), 98–108. DOI: 10.17261/Pressacademia.2023.1807

Mohale, V. Z., & Obagbuwa, I. C. (2025). Evaluating machine learning-based intrusion detection systems with explainable AI: Enhancing transparency and interpretability. *Frontiers of Computer Science*, *7*, 1520741. DOI: 10.3389/fcomp.2025.1520741

Mohammad, R. M., Thabtah, F., & McCluskey, L. (2014). Predicting phishing websites based on self-structuring neural network. *Neural Computing & Applications*, *25*(2), 443–458. DOI: 10.1007/s00521-013-1490-z

Möller, D. P. (2023). Threats and threat intelligence. In *Guide to cybersecurity in digital transformation: Trends, methods, technologies, applications and best practices* (pp. 71–129). Springer Nature Switzerland. DOI: 10.1007/978-3-031-26845-8_2

Mostafa, A. M., Ezz, M., Elbashir, M. K., Alruily, M., Hamouda, E., Alsarhani, M., & Said, W. (2023). Strengthening cloud security: An innovative multi-factor multi-layer authentication framework for cloud user authentication. *Applied Sciences (Basel, Switzerland)*, *13*(19), 10871. DOI: 10.3390/app131910871

Muammar, S., Shehada, D., & Mansoor, W. (2023). Digital risk assessment framework for individuals: Analysis and recommendations. *IEEE Access : Practical Innovations, Open Solutions*, *11*, 85561–85570. DOI: 10.1109/ACCESS.2023.3293062

Mughal, A. A. (2019). Cybersecurity hygiene in the era of internet of things (IoT): Best practices and challenges. *Applied Research in Artificial Intelligence and Cloud Computing*, *2*(1), 1–31.

Nagamalla, V., & Sanapala, R. K. (2023). Integrating Predictive Big Data Analytics with Behavioral Machine Learning Models for Proactive Threat Intelligence in Industrial IoT Cybersecurity. *International Journal of Wireless & Ad Hoc Communication*, *7*(2), 08–24. DOI: 10.54216/IJWAC.070201

Nai, S., El Moudden, T., Rifai, A., & Sadiq, A. (2026). Design and Evaluation of a Personalized AI Tutoring System Using ChatGPT. In Generative AI Applications and Intelligent Systems: From Chatbots to Cybersecurity (pp. 137-160). IGI Global Scientific Publishing.

Nai, S., Rifai, A., Sadiq, A., & Elbaghazaoui, B. E. (2025). An in-depth analysis of a tutoring solution by digital technology. *International Journal of Electrical & Computer Engineering (2088-8708), 15*(4).

Nassif, A. B., Talib, M. A., Nasir, Q., Albadani, H., & Dakalbab, F. M. (2021). Machine learning for cloud security: A systematic review. *IEEE Access : Practical Innovations, Open Solutions, 9*, 20717–20735. DOI: 10.1109/ACCESS.2021.3054129

Nazir, R., Laghari, A. A., Dahri, F. H., Shoulin, Y., Alhakeem, Z. M., Hakim, H., & Mughal, Z. A. (2026). A review on machine learning techniques for network security. *Journal of Cyber Security Technology, 10*(1), 1–45. DOI: 10.1080/23742917.2025.2480730

Neprash, H. T., McGlave, C. C., Cross, D. A., Virnig, B. A., Puskarich, M. A., Huling, J. D., Rozenshtein, A. Z., & Nikpay, S. S. (2022, December). Trends in ransomware attacks on US hospitals, clinics, and other health care delivery organizations, 2016-2021. *JAMA Health Forum, 3*(12), e224873. DOI: 10.1001/jamahealthforum.2022.4873 PMID: 36580326

Nguyen, K. T., Laurent, M., & Oualha, N. (2015). Survey on secure communication protocols for the Internet of Things. *Ad Hoc Networks, 32*, 17–31. DOI: 10.1016/j.adhoc.2015.01.006

Nguyen, P. N. T., & Vo, D. V. (2026). Exploring digital competence and its relationship with problem-solving self-efficacy in undergraduate students. *Asian Education and Development Studies, 15*(1), 73–88. DOI: 10.1108/AEDS-12-2024-0299

Nguyen, T. A., & Tran, A. (2020). Input-aware dynamic backdoor attack. *Advances in Neural Information Processing Systems, 33*, 3454–3464.

Nie, P., Huang, S., Zheng, C., & Gu, M. (2025). "Backdoor Attacks with Hybrid Triggers: A Dual-Feature Injection Approach for Code Summarization Models." In 2025 25th International Conference on Software Quality, Reliability and Security (QRS), pp. 679-690. IEEE. DOI: 10.1109/QRS65678.2025.00072

Ogenyi, O. M. (2025). Explainable artificial intelligence for adaptive cybersecurity in IoT environments. *Frontiers in Internet of Things, 4*, 1658273. Advance online publication. DOI: 10.3389/friot.2025.1658273

Ojha, N., & Vaish, A. (2025). Why perimeter security is no longer enough: Observations and open challenges. In *Zero-Trust Learning* (pp. 305–328). Apple Academic Press. DOI: 10.1201/9781779643575-15

Olabanji, S. O., Marquis, Y., Adigwe, C. S., Ajayi, S. A., Oladoyinbo, T. O., & Olaniyi, O. O. (2024). AI-driven cloud security: Examining the impact of user behavior analysis on threat detection. *Asian Journal of Research in Computer Science*, *17*(3), 57–74. DOI: 10.9734/ajrcos/2024/v17i3424

Olanrewaju-George, B., & Pranggono, B. (2025). Federated learning-based intrusion detection system for the internet of things using unsupervised and supervised deep learning models. *Cyber Security and Applications*, *3*, 100068. DOI: 10.1016/j.csa.2024.100068

Oluoha, O. M., Odeshina, A. B. I. S. O. L. A., Reis, O. L. U. W. A. T. O. S. I. N., Okpeke, F. R. I. D. A. Y., Attipoe, V. E. R. L. I. N. D. A., & Orieno, O. (2023). A privacy-first framework for data protection and compliance assurance in digital ecosystems. *Iconic Research and Engineering Journals*, *7*(4), 620–646.

Olutimehin, A. T., Ajayi, A. J., Metibemu, O. C., Balogun, A. Y., Oladoyinbo, T. O., & Olaniyi, O. O. (2025). Adversarial threats to AI-driven systems: Exploring the attack surface of machine learning models and countermeasures. Available at *SSRN* 5137026.

Onwudebelu, U., Ugah, J. O., Ezeh, S. E., & Olugbemi, O. (2026). Securing Online Platforms: Hybrid Machine Learning Approaches for URL Phishing Detections. *Journal of International Communication*, *5*(1), 24–46.

Otieno, M., Odera, D., & Ounza, J. E. (2023). Theory and practice in secure software development lifecycle: A comprehensive survey. *World Journal of Advanced Research and Reviews, 18*(3), 053-078.

Pallaw, V. K., Singh, S. K., Singh, A. K., Saxena, S., & Mishra, D. (2026). Securing AI-Integrated Learning Platform: Cyber Threats in the Age of Digital Education. Cybernetic Shield, 39-51.

Patcha, A., & Park, J. M. (2007). An overview of anomaly detection techniques: Existing solutions and latest technological trends. *Computer Networks*, *51*(12), 3448–3470. DOI: 10.1016/j.comnet.2007.02.001

Paul, E. M., Mmaduekwe, U., Kessie, J. D., & Dolapo, M.Ebuka Mmaduekwe PaulEbuka Mmaduekwe PaulJoseph Darko KessieMukhtar Dolapo Salawudeen. (2024). Zero trust architecture and AI: A synergistic approach to next-generation cybersecurity frameworks. *International Journal of Science and Research Archive*, *13*(2), 4159–4169. DOI: 10.30574/ijsra.2024.13.2.2583

Paya, A., & Gómez, A. (2024). Securesdp: A novel software-defined perimeter implementation for enhanced network security and scalability. *International Journal of Information Security*, *23*(4), 2793–2808. DOI: 10.1007/s10207-024-00863-7

Pedregosa, F., Varoquaux, G., Gramfort, A., Michel, V., Thirion, B., Grisel, O., Blondel, M., Prettenhofer, P., Weiss, R., Dubourg, V., Vanderplas, J., Passos, A., Cournapeau, D., Brucher, M., Perrot, M., & Duchesnay, E. (2011). Scikit-learn: Machine learning in Python. *Journal of Machine Learning Research*, *12*, 2825–2830. http://jmlr.org/papers/v12/pedregosa11a.html

Phillips, M. (2018). International data-sharing norms: From the OECD to the General Data Protection Regulation (GDPR). *Human Genetics*, *137*(8), 575–582. DOI: 10.1007/s00439-018-1919-7 PMID: 30069638

Prakash, P., Kumar, M., Kompella, R. R., & Gupta, M. (2010). PhishNet: Predictive blacklisting to detect phishing attacks. 2010. *Proceedings - IEEE INFOCOM*, *1–5*, 1–5. Advance online publication. DOI: 10.1109/INFCOM.2010.5462216

Prasad, H., Prasad, U., & Paul, P. (2025). Explainable AI for cybersecurity: Implementing interpretable models for real-time threat detection. In *2025 International Conference on ….* IEEE. DOI: 10.1109/ICCoSD66074.2025.11348330

Prity, F. S., Islam, M. S., Fahim, E. H., & Hossain, M. M.. (2024). *Machine learning-based cyber threat detection: An approach to malware detection and security with explainable AI insights. Human-Intelligent Systems Integration*. Springer.

Puat, H. A. M., & Abd Rahman, N. A. (2020, December). IoMT: a review of pacemaker vulnerabilities and security strategy. In *Journal of Physics: Conference Series (*Vol. 1712, No. 1, p. 012009). IOP Publishing. DOI: 10.1088/1742-6596/1712/1/012009

Puri, S., & Rathor, D. S. (2026). AI-Driven Cybersecurity: Emerging Threats and Defensive Strategies with Focus on College Youth in Delhi. *International Journal of Cultural Inheritance & Social Sciences ISSN: 2632-7597, 8*(15), 1-13.

Qabalin, M. K., Naser, M., & Alkasassbeh, M. (2022). Android spyware detection using machine learning: a novel dataset. sensors, 22(15), 5765.

Qiqieh, I., Alzubi, O., Alzubi, J., Sreedhar, K. C., & Al-Zoubi, A. M. (2025). An intelligent cyber threat detection: A swarm-optimized machine learning approach. *Alexandria Engineering Journal*, *115*, 553–563. DOI: 10.1016/j.aej.2024.12.039

Quraishi, T., Ulusi, H., Muhid, A., Hakimi, M., & Olusi, M. R. (2024). Empowering students through digital literacy: A case study of successful integration in a higher education curriculum. Journal of Digital Learning and Distance Education, 2(9), 667-681.

Rahman, M. M., Arshi, A. S., Hasan, M. M., Mishu, S. F., Shahriar, H., & Wu, F. (2023, June). Security risk and attacks in ai: A survey of security and privacy. In 2023 IEEE 47th Annual Computers, Software, and Applications Conference (COMPSAC) (pp. 1834-1839). IEEE. DOI: 10.1109/COMPSAC57700.2023.00284

Rahman, M. M., Alam, G. M., Aziz, N. A. B. A., Bashir, K., & Kader, R. (2024). Whether mismatch finds match in the digitalized era: A comparison of five types of graduates to align business education and banking jobs. *Industry and Higher Education*, *38*(6), 547–561. DOI: 10.1177/09504222241249900

Rajendran, S., Valarmathi, A., & Kumar, M. S. (2022). Threat detection and incident response in cloud security. In *Privacy and Security Challenges in Cloud Computing* (pp. 207–227). CRC Press. DOI: 10.1201/9781003219880-11

Raman, R., Dhivya, K., Sapra, P., Gurpur, S., Maniraj, S. P., & Murugan, S. (2023, December). IoT-driven Smart Packaging for Pharmaceuticals: Ensuring Product Integrity and Patient Safety. In 2023 *International Conference on Artificial Intelligence for Innovations in Healthcare Industries (ICAIIHI)* (Vol. 1, pp. 1-6). IEEE. DOI: 10.1109/ICAIIHI57871.2023.10489420

Ramezan, C. A. (2023). Examining the cyber skills gap: An analysis of cybersecurity positions by sub-field. *Journal of Information Systems Education*, *34*(1), 94–105.

Ramli, A., Darus, M. Y., Mohd Yussoff, Y., & Azni, B. (2025). Integrated cybersecurity framework for enhanced threat detection and incident response in the digital era. [MJoC]. *Malaysian Journal of Computing*, *10*(1), 2099–2116. DOI: 10.24191/mjoc.v10i1.4520

Rao, R. S., & Pais, A. R. (2019). Detection of phishing websites using an efficient feature-based machine learning framework. *Neural Computing & Applications*, *31*(8), 3851–3873. DOI: 10.1007/s00521-017-3305-0

Rashid, M. M., Khan, S. U., Eusufzai, F., Redwan, M. A., Sabuj, S. R., & Elsharief, M. (2023). A federated learning-based approach for improving intrusion detection in industrial Internet of Things networks. *Network : Computation in Neural Systems*, *3*(1), 158–179. DOI: 10.3390/network3010008

Ravi, V., Pham, T. D., & Alazab, M. (2023). Attention-based multidimensional deep learning approach for cross-architecture IoMT malware detection and classification in healthcare cyber-physical systems. *IEEE Transactions on Computational Social Systems*, *10*(4), 1597–1606. https://ieeexplore.ieee.org/document/9863062. DOI: 10.1109/TCSS.2022.3198123

Rayes, A., & Salam, S. (2022). Internet of things security and privacy. In *Internet of Things From Hype to Reality: The Road to Digitization* (pp. 213–246). Springer International Publishing., DOI: 10.1007/978-3-030-90158-5_8

Razavi, H., Franco, M. F., Ouaissa, M., Ouaissa, M., & Srivastava, G. (Eds.). (2026). *AI-driven Cyber Risk Management*. CRC Press. DOI: 10.1201/9788743808077

Rimal, B. P., Kong, C., Poudel, B., Wang, Y., & Shahi, P. (2022). Smart electric vehicle charging in the era of Internet of Vehicles, emerging trends, and open issues. *Energies*, *15*(5), 1908. DOI: 10.3390/en15051908

Sadeghi, A. R. (2008, January). Trusted computing—special aspects and challenges. In *International Conference on Current Trends in Theory and Practice of Computer Science* (pp. 98-117). Berlin, Heidelberg: Springer Berlin Heidelberg. DOI: 10.1007/978-3-540-77566-9_9

Saeed, S., Suayyid, S. A., Al-Ghamdi, M. S., Al-Muhaisen, H., & Almuhaideb, A. M. (2023). A systematic literature review on cyber threat intelligence for organizational cybersecurity resilience. *Sensors (Basel)*, *23*(16), 7273. DOI: 10.3390/s23167273 PMID: 37631808

Sahingoz, O. K., Buber, E., Demir, O., & Diri, B. (2019). Machine learning based phishing detection from URLs. *Expert Systems with Applications*, *117*, 345–357. DOI: 10.1016/j.eswa.2018.09.029

Salako, A. O., Fabuyi, J. A., Aideyan, N. T., Selesi-Aina, O., Dapo-Oyewole, D. L., & Olaniyi, O. O. (2024). Advancing information governance in AI-driven cloud ecosystem: Strategies for enhancing data security and meeting regulatory compliance. *Asian Journal of Research in Computer Science*, *17*(12), 66–88. DOI: 10.9734/ajrcos/2024/v17i12530

Saleem, M. A., Aslam, M. S., Chishti, A. F., & Qureshi, M. A. (2026). ANOM-ALERT: INSIDER THREAT MONITORING SUITE. *Spectrum of Engineering Sciences*, *4*(1), 677–687.

Salem, A., Wen, R., Backes, M., Ma, S., & Zhang, Y. (2022). "Dynamic Backdoor Attacks Against Machine Learning Models." In Proceedings of the 2022 IEEE 7th European Symposium on Security andPrivacy (EuroS&P), pp. 703–718. IEEE. DOI: 10.1109/EuroSP53844.2022.00049

Salih, K. M. M., & Ibrahim, N. B. (2023). Enhancing IoT forensics through deep learning: Investigating cyber-attacks and analyzing big data for improved security measures. *Proceedings of IBDAP 2023*, Bangkok, Thailand, 1–8. DOI: 10.1109/IBDAP58581.2023.10271950

Sankar, K. M., Booba, B., Rangaswamy, C., Pramila, P. V., Kar, S. R., Kumar, A., & Sudhakar, M. (2023, February). IoT-based Weather, Soil, Earthquake, Air pollution Monitoring System. In *2023 3rd International Conference on Innovative Practices in Technology and Management (ICIPTM)* (pp. 1-6). IEEE.DOI: 10.1109/ICIPTM57143.2023.10118160

Sarieddine, K., Sayed, M. A., Assi, C., Atallah, R., Torabi, S., Khoury, J., Pour, M. S., & Bou-Harb, E. (2023). EV charging infrastructure discovery to contextualize its deployment security. *IEEE Transactions on Network and Service Management, 21*(1), 1287–1301. DOI: 10.1109/TNSM.2023.3318406

Sarraf, G., & Pal, V. (2026). Autonomous Threat Detection and Response in Cloud Security: A Comprehensive Survey of AI-Driven Strategies. arXiv preprint arXiv:2601.03303.

Savaglio, C., Fortino, G., Gravina, R., & Russo, W. (2018a). A Methodology for Integrating Internet of Things Platforms. In: *2018 IEEE International Conference on Cloud Engineering. IC2E,* pp. 317–322. DOI: 10.1109/IC2E.2018.00062

Sayegh, H. R., Dong, W., & Al-madani, A. M. (2024). Enhanced intrusion detection with LSTM-based model, feature selection, and SMOTE for imbalanced data. *Applied Sciences (Basel, Switzerland), 14*(2), 479. DOI: 10.3390/app14020479

Scarfo, A. (2012). New security perspectives around BYOD. In *2012 Seventh International Conference on Broadband, Wireless Computing, Communication and Applications* (pp. 446–451). IEEE. https://doi.org/DOI: 10.1109/BWCCA.2012.79

Schelble, B. G., Lopez, J., Textor, C., Zhang, R., McNeese, N. J., Pak, R., & Freeman, G. (2024). Towards ethical AI: Empirically investigating dimensions of AI ethics, trust repair, and performance in human-AI teaming. *Human Factors, 66*(4), 1037–1055. DOI: 10.1177/00187208221116952 PMID: 35938319

Schmitt, M. (2023). Securing the digital world: Protecting smart infrastructures and digital industries with artificial intelligence (AI)-enabled malware and intrusion detection. *Journal of Industrial Information Integration, 36*, 100520. DOI: 10.1016/j.jii.2023.100520

Seet, P. S., Jones, J., Klarin, A., & Suseno, Y. (2021). *IoT and the Future Workforce: Potential Implications.* Australian Council of Learned Academies.

Sengupta, S., Chowdhary, A., Sabur, A., Alshamrani, A., Huang, D., & Kambhampati, S. (2020). A survey of moving target defenses for network security. *IEEE Communications Surveys and Tutorials, 22*(3), 1909–1941. DOI: 10.1109/COMST.2020.2982955

Serac, C. A. (2023). Digital transformation vulnerabilities: Assessing the risks and strengthening cyber security. *Ann Univ ORADEA*, *32*(1), 771–781. DOI: 10.47535/1991AUOES32(1)059

Serafimova, N., Petrovski, A., Iliev, A., & Karovska, B. (2025). Itegration of Emerging Technologies in Cybersecurity Education. *Journal of Peace, Conflict, and Security Studies*, *1*(1), 11.

Shah, S. B. (2025). Machine Learning for Cyber Threat Detection and Prevention in Critical Infrastructure. *J. Glob Res. Electron. Commun.*, *2*(2), 1–7.

Shaik, Y. (2024). Securing Firmware updates: Addressing security challenges in UEFI capsule update mechanisms.

Sharafaldin, I., Lashkari, A. H., & Ghorbani, A. A. (2019). Developing realistic distributed denial of service (DDoS) attack dataset and taxonomy. *Proceedings of ICCST 2019*. IEEE. DOI: 10.1109/CCST.2019.8888419

Sharma, N., & Nihalani, N. (2025). DCNN-BIGRU: A proficient hybrid classifier for reliable intrusion detection and prevention. International Journal of Industrial Engineering: Theory. *Applications and Practice*, *32*(1). Advance online publication. DOI: 10.23055/ijietap.2025.32.1.10159

Shayea, G. G., Zabil, M. H. M., Habeeb, M. A., Khaleel, Y. L., & Albahri, A. S. (2025). Strategies for protection against adversarial attacks in AI models: An in-depth review. *Journal of Intelligent Systems*, *34*(1), 20240277. DOI: 10.1515/jisys-2024-0277

Sheng, S., Wardman, B., Warner, G., Cranor, L. F., Hong, J., & Zhang, C. (2009, July 16–17). An empirical analysis of phishing blacklists [Paper presentation]. *6th Annual Conference on Email and Anti-Spam (CEAS)*, Mountain View, CA, United States. DOI: 10.1184/R1/6469805

Shokri, R. (2020). "Bypassing backdoor detection algorithms in deep learning." In 2020 IEEE European Symposium on Security and Privacy (EuroS&P), pp. 175-183. IEEE.

Shone, N., Ngoc, T. N., Phai, V. D., & Shi, Q. (2018). A deep learning approach to network intrusion detection. *IEEE Transactions on Emerging Topics in Computational Intelligence*, *2*(1), 41–50 DOI: 10.1109/TETCI.2017.2772792

Siddiqui, K., & Ahmad, S. (2023). Zoombombing: causes and preventions. In E3S Web of Conferences (Vol. 371, p. 05026). EDP Sciences. DOI: 10.1051/e3sconf/202337105026

Singh, A. J., & Singh, A. P. (2024). Evolution of Information Technology: A Comprehensive Review. *Asian Journal of Current Research, 9*(4), 78–90. DOI: 10.56557/ajocr/2024/v9i48892

Si, S., Hall, J., Suddaby, R., Ahlstrom, D., & Wei, J. (2023). Technology, entrepreneurship, innovation and social change in digital economics. *Technovation, 119*, 102484. DOI: 10.1016/j.technovation.2022.102484

Skarga-Bandurova, I., Kotsiuba, I., & Velasco, E. R. (2021). Cyber Hygiene Maturity Assessment Framework for Smart Grid Scenarios. *Frontiers of Computer Science, 3*, 614337. DOI: 10.3389/fcomp.2021.614337

Sobahi, N., & Bamabad, A. (2024). Cyber-attacks Risk Analysis of a Connected Pulse Oximeter Device: A Threat Modeling Using STRIDE and DREAD Models. *International Journal for Scientific Research, 3*(5), 280–315. DOI: 10.59992/IJSR.2024.v3n5p10

Sommer, R., & Paxson, V. (2010). Outside the closed world: On using machine learning for network intrusion detection. In *2010 IEEE Symposium on Security and Privacy* (pp. 305–316). IEEE. https://doi.org/DOI: 10.1109/SP.2010.25

Soni, B., & Padhya, M. (2024, October). Enhancing Cloud-Native Security Through 4C Architecture: A Comprehensive Analysis. In *International Conference on Information Security, Privacy and Digital Forensics* (pp. 525-546). Singapore: Springer Nature Singapore.

Spidalieri, F. (2022). Meeting the growing demand for cybersecurity skills and talent in Europe. In *European cybersecurity in context a policy-oriented comparative analysis. European Liberal Forum* (pp. 9-19).

Stanojević, A. (2025). Algorithmic governance and social vulnerability: A value analysis of equality and trust. In Public governance and emerging technologies: Values, trust, and regulatory compliance (pp. 335–354). Springer Nature Switzerland.

Stephen, O. B., Olatoye, G. O., Oluwabukola, J. A., Olaniyi, O. P., & Kolash, B. J. (2025). Exploring the Integration of Digital Literacy and Cyber Security Education for Ethical and Safe Digital Citizenship in Schools. *BIMA JOURNAL OF SCIENCE AND TECHNOLOGY GOMBE, 9*(3B), 183–188.

Subrahmanyam, S. (2025). Behavioral Analysis for Threat Detection. In Handbook of AI-Driven Threat Detection and Prevention (pp. 95-115). CRC Press. DOI: 10.1201/9781003521020-6

Sun, R., Wang, Q., & Guo, L. (2022, July). Research towards key issues of api security. In *China Cyber Security Annual Conference* (pp. 179-192). Singapore: Springer Nature Singapore.DOI: 10.1007/978-981-16-9229-1_11

Syed, F. M., & ES, F. (2021). Role of IAM in Data Loss Prevention (DLP) Strategies for Pharmaceutical Security Operations. *Revista de Inteligencia Artificial en Medicina*, *12*(1), 407–4.

Syed, S. A. (2025). Adversarial AI and cybersecurity: Defending against AI-powered cyber threats. *Iconic Research and Engineering Journals*, *8*(9), 1030–1041.

Syrotynskyi, R., Tyshyk, I., Kochan, O., Sokolov, V., & Skladannyi, P. (2024). Methodology of network infrastructure analysis as part of migration to zero-trust architecture. *Cyber Security and Data Protection*, *2024*(3800), 97–105.

Talakola, S. (2025). Security challenges in autonomous systems: A zero-trust approach. International Journal of Emerging Trends in Computer Science and Information Technology, 56-66.

Talu, M. (2025). Insights in Cybersecurity of a Smart Campus--A Review. Journal of Cybersecurity Education, Research and Practice, 2025(1).

Tan, W. C., & Sidhu, M. S. (2022). Review of RFID and IoT integration in supply chain management. *Operations Research Perspectives*, *9*, 100229. DOI: 10.1016/j.orp.2022.100229

Tareq, I., Elbagoury, B. M., El-Regaily, S., & El-Horbaty, E. S. M. (2022). Analysis of ToN-IoT, UNW-NB15, and Edge-IIoT datasets using DL in cybersecurity for IoT. *Applied Sciences (Basel, Switzerland)*, *12*(19), 9572. DOI: 10.3390/app12199572

Tatineni, S. (2023). AI-infused threat detection and incident response in cloud security. [IJSR]. *International Journal of Science and Research (Raipur, India)*, *12*(11), 998–1004. DOI: 10.21275/SR231113063646

Taylor, R., Johnson, P., & Lee, K. (2025). A framework for testing and monitoring IoT cybersecurity. *arXiv*. https://arxiv.org/abs/2502.12837

Thakur, P., Kansal, V., & Rishiwal, V. (2024). Hybrid deep learning approach based on LSTM and CNN for malware detection. *Wireless Personal Communications*, *136*(3), 1879–1901. DOI: 10.1007/s11277-024-11366-y

Tian, J. (2025). Integrating artificial intelligence into the cybersecurity curriculum in higher education: A systematic literature review. *Education Sciences*, *15*(11), 1540. DOI: 10.3390/educsci15111540

Tomar, K., Bisht, K., Joshi, K., & Katarya, R. (2023). Cyber attack detection in IoT using deep learning techniques. *Proceedings of ISCON 2023*, Mathura, India. DOI: 10.1109/ISCON57294.2023.10111990

Trillo, J. R., González-López, F., Morente-Molinera, J. A., Magán-Carrión, R., & García-Sánchez, P. (2025). Evaluation of explainable, interpretable and non-interpretable algorithms for cyber threat detection. *Electronics (Basel)*, *14*(15), 3073. DOI: 10.3390/electronics14153073

Tsai, C. F., Hsu, Y. F., Lin, C. Y., & Lin, W. Y. (2009). Intrusion detection by machine learning: A review. *Expert Systems with Applications*, *36*(10), 11994–12000. DOI: 10.1016/j.eswa.2009.05.029

Turcu, C. O., & Turcu, C. E. (2018). Industrial Internet of Things as a challenge for higher education. *International Journal of Advanced Computer Science and Applications*, *9*(11), 55–60. DOI: 10.14569/IJACSA.2018.091108

Tyagi, A. K., Kumari, S., & Richa. (2024). Artificial Intelligence-Based Cyber Security and Digital Forensics: A Review. *Artificial Intelligence-Enabled Digital Twin for Smart Manufacturing*, 391-419.

Ujwary-Gil, A., & Godlewska-Dziobon, B. (2022). The two-mode network approach to digital skills and tasks among technology park employees. *Entrepreneurial Business and Economics Review*, *10*(2), 187–204. DOI: 10.15678/EBER.2022.100211

Ukidve, A., Mantha, S. S., & Reddy, D. N. (2022). Analyzing Mapping of ISO 27001: 2013 Controls for Alignment with Enterprise Risks Management. *Asian Journal of Organic & Medicinal Chemistry*, *7*(2), 123–129.

Ullah, F., Ye, X., Fatima, U., Wu, Y., Akhtar, Z., & Ahmad, H. (2026). What skills do cybersecurity professionals need? *Information and Computer Security*, •••, 1–19. DOI: 10.1108/ICS-01-2025-0027

Ullah, S., Boulila, W., Koubâa, A., & Ahmad, J. (2023). MAGRU-IDS: A multi-head attention-based gated recurrent unit for intrusion detection in IIoT networks. *IEEE Access : Practical Innovations, Open Solutions*, *11*, 114590–114601. DOI: 10.1109/ACCESS.2023.3324657

Vardakis, G., Hatzivasilis, G., Koutsaki, E., & Papadakis, N. (2024). Review of Smart-Home Security Using the Internet of Things. *Electronics (Basel)*, *13*(16), 3343. DOI: 10.3390/electronics13163343

Vásquez-Méndez, P. B., Arce Cuesta, D. C., & Zambrano-Martinez, J. L. (2026). The Human Factor: Assessing Ransomware Vulnerability in Developing Nations' Governments. *Information (Basel)*, *17*(2), 211. DOI: 10.3390/info17020211

Veeramachaneni, V. (2025). Edge Computing: Architecture, Applications, and Future Challenges in a Decentralized Era. *Recent Trends in Computer Graphics and Multimedia Technology*, *7*(1), 8–23. DOI: 10.5281/zenodo.14166793

Verma, R., & Hossain, N. (2014). Semantic feature selection for text with application to phishing email detection. In Lee, H. S., & Han, D. G. (Eds.), *Information security and cryptology – ICISC 2013* (pp. 455–468). Springer., DOI: 10.1007/978-3-319-12160-4_27

Villegas-Ch, W., & García-Ortiz, J. (2023). Toward a comprehensive framework for ensuring security and privacy in artificial intelligence. *Electronics (Basel)*, *12*(18), 3786. DOI: 10.3390/electronics12183786

Voronkova, V., Nikitenko, V., Oleksenko, R., Andriukaitiene, R., Kharchenko, J., & Kliuienko, E. (2023). Digital technology evolution of the industrial revolution from 4g to 5g in the context of the challenges of digital globalization. *TEM Journal.*, *12*(2), 732–742. DOI: 10.18421/TEM122-17

Vu, H. T. T., Tan, C. C., Tran, H. T., & Thuyen, T. D. (2024). Exploratory Study of Factors Affecting Problem-Solving Competence among School Administrators in Vietnam during the Digital Era. *Journal of Education and e-learning Research*, *11*(4), 676–687. DOI: 10.20448/jeelr.v11i4.6093

Wang, J.-J., & Mu, S. Security issues and countermeasures in cloud computing. In *Proceedings of the 2011 IEEE International Conference on Grey Systems and Intelligent Services* (GSIS), Nanjing, China, 15–18 September 2011; pp. 843–846. DOI: 10.1109/GSIS.2011.6043978

Wang, L., Li, J., Bhatti, U. A., & Liu, Y. (2019). Anomaly detection in wireless sensor networks based on KNN. In *International conference on artificial intelligence and security* (pp. 632–643). DOI: 10.1007/978-3-030-24271-8_56

Wang, L., Li, J., Cheng, J., Bhatti, U. A., & Dai, Q. (2018). DOS attacks intrusion detection algorithm based on support vector machine. In *International conference on cloud computing and security* (pp. 286–297). DOI: 10.1007/978-3-030-00018-9_26

Wang, W., & Yongchareon, S. (2020). Security-as-a-service: A literature review. *International Journal of Web Information Systems*, *16*(5), 493–517. DOI: 10.1108/IJWIS-06-2020-0031

Wang, Z., Wang, R., & Jing, L. (2025). Attention-imperceptible backdoor attacks on vision transformers. *Proceedings of the AAAI Conference on Artificial Intelligence*, *39*(8), 8241–8249. DOI: 10.1609/aaai.v39i8.32889

Wan, Z., Swaminathan, K., Chen, P.-Y., Chandramoorthy, N., & Raychowdhury, A. (2022). "Analyzing and improving resilience and robustness of autonomous systems." In *Proceedings of the 41st IEEE/ACM International Conference on Computer-Aided Design*, pp. 1-9. DOI: 10.1145/3508352.3561111

Wenger, E., Passananti, J., Bhagoji, A. N., Yao, Y., Zheng, H., & Zhao, B. Y. (2021). "Backdoor attacks against deep learning systems in the physical world." In *Proceedings of the IEEE/CVF conference on computer vision and pattern recognition*, pp. 6206-6215. DOI: 10.1109/CVPR46437.2021.00614

Wright, R. T., & Marett, K. (2010). The influence of experiential and dispositional factors in phishing: An empirical investigation of the deceived. *Journal of Management Information Systems*, *27*(1), 273–303. DOI: 10.2753/MIS0742-1222270111

Wu, Z., Feng, E., & Zhang, Z. (2024). Temporal-Contextual Behavioral Analytics for Proactive Cloud Security Threat Detection. Academia Nexus Journal, 3(2).

Xiao, G., Guo, J., Xu, L. D., & Gong, Z. (2014). User interoperability with heterogeneous IoT devices through transformation. *IEEE Transactions on Industrial Informatics*, *10*(2), 1486–1496. DOI: 10.1109/TII.2014.2306772

Xiao, X., Zhang, S., Mercaldo, F., Hu, G., & Sangaiah, A. K. (2019). Android malware detection based on system call sequences and LSTM. *Multimedia Tools and Applications*, *78*(4), 3979–3999. DOI: 10.1007/s11042-017-5104-0

Xu, B., Bhatti, U. A., Tang, H., Yan, J., Wu, S., Sarhan, N., Awwad, E. M., & Sethumadhavan, S. M. (2024a). Towards explainability for AI-based edge wireless signal automatic modulation classification. *Journal of Cloud Computing (Heidelberg, Germany)*, *13*(1), 10. DOI: 10.1186/s13677-024-00590-3

Xu, B., Luo, C., Tang, H., Bhatti, U. A., & Wang, X. (2024b). Advancing transparency in AI-based automatic modulation classification. In *2024 IEEE/CIC International Conference on Communications in China (ICCC)*. DOI: 10.1109/ICCC62479.2024.10682007

Xu, W., Jiang, Y., Zhang, X., Liang, Z., Yang, Y., Bi, L., Xu, H., Yang, Q., & Huang, Y. (2025). "Backdoor Detection Method for Vision Transformer Model Based on Attention Map Analysis." In *2025 IEEE/CIC International Conference on Communications in China (ICCC)*, pp. 1-6. IEEE. DOI: 10.1109/ICCC65529.2025.11148748

Yazmyradov, S. (2024). A comprehensive review of AI security: Threats, challenges, and mitigation strategies. The International Journal of Internet. *Broadcasting and Communication*, *16*(4), 375–384.

Yeboah-Ofori, A., Darvishi, I., & Opeyemi, A. S. (2023, August). Enhancement of big data security in cloud computing using RSA algorithm. In 2023 10th International conference on future Internet of Things and Cloud (FICloud) (pp. 312-319). IEEE. DOI: 10.1109/FiCloud58648.2023.00053

Yemul, R. M., Vyavahare, S. S., Manglaram, V. V., Yemul, A. S., Lobo, L. M. R. J., & Athavale, V. A. (2026b). AI-based diagnostic framework for recommending targeted healthcare solutions. In *AI foundations, technologies, and future of healthcare systems* (pp. 1–36). IGI Global., DOI: 10.4018/979-8-2600-0981-9.ch001

Yertas, M. (2024). The role of training and continuous development in improving employee productivity and its impact on company financial performance. *Atestasi: Jurnal Ilmiah Akuntansi*, *7*(2), 1362–1379. DOI: 10.57178/atestasi.v7i2.1047

Yin, C., Zhu, Y., Fei, J., & He, X. (2017). A deep learning approach for intrusion detection using recurrent neural networks. *IEEE Access : Practical Innovations, Open Solutions*, *5*, 21954–21961. DOI: 10.1109/ACCESS.2017.2762418

Younis, Y. A., Kifayat, K., & Merabti, M. (2014). An access control model for cloud computing. *Journal of Information Security and Applications*, *19*(1), 45–60. DOI: 10.1016/j.jisa.2014.04.003

Yousseef, A., Lin, Y.-Z., Satam, S., Latibari, B. S., Pacheco, J., Salehi, S., Hariri, S., & Satam, P. (2025). Autonomous Vehicle Security: Hybrid Threat Modeling Approach. *IEEE Open Journal of Vehicular Technology*, *6*, 1774–1795. DOI: 10.1109/OJVT.2025.3580538

Yu, Y., Wang, Y., Yang, W., Lu, S., Tan, Y.-P., & Kot, A. C. (2023). "Backdoor attacks against deep image compression via adaptive frequency trigger." In *Proceedings of the IEEE/CVF Conference on Computer Vision and Pattern Recognition*, pp. 12250-12259. DOI: 10.1109/CVPR52729.2023.01179

Zeinali, M., Erdogan, N., Bayram, I. S., & Thompson, J. S. (2023). Impact of communication system characteristics on electric vehicle grid integration. *Electricity*, *4*(4), 309–319. DOI: 10.3390/electricity4040018

Zemmouchi-Ghomari, L. (2025). Artificial intelligence in intelligent transportation systems. *Journal of Intelligent Manufacturing and Special Equipment*, *6*(1), 26–42. DOI: 10.1108/JIMSE-11-2024-0035

Zhang, B., Li, J., Ren, J., & Huang, G. (2021). Efficiency and effectiveness of web application vulnerability detection approaches: A review. *ACM Computing Surveys*, *54*(9), 1–35. DOI: 10.1145/3474553

Zhang, J., Zulkernine, M., & Haque, A. (2008). Random-forest-based network intrusion detection systems. *IEEE Transactions on Systems, Man, and Cybernetics. Part C, Applications and Reviews*, *38*(5), 649–659. DOI: 10.1109/TSMCC.2008.923876

Zhang, K., Wang, Y., Bhatti, U. A., Zhou, Y., & Jin, M. (2025). Enhanced ransomware attacks detection using feature selection, sensitivity analysis, and optimized hybrid model. *Journal of Big Data*, *12*(1), 245. DOI: 10.1186/s40537-025-01289-1

Zheng, X., Li, Y., Wang, J., & Chen, Z. (2025). Game-theoretic modeling and prediction of cyber-attacks in IoT environments. *Internet of Things : Engineering Cyber Physical Human Systems*, *30*, 101522. Advance online publication. DOI: 10.1016/j.iot.2025.101522

# About the Contributors

**Bahaa Eddine Elbaghazaoui** is a professor at ENSA Beni Mellal and a PhD holder in Computer Science and Artificial Intelligence. With extensive experience in software engineering, he specializes in full-stack development, microservices, AI integration, and cloud computing. As a project manager and trainer, he has led and contributed to innovative solutions in telecommunications, insurance, and government sectors. His research focuses on data profiling and predictive analytics, with numerous publications in high-impact journals. Passionate about technology and education, he actively mentors, reviews scientific work, and advances cutting-edge software solutions.

***

**Rahmath Nisha A** is a dedicated professional with comprehensive, hands-on experience in Human Resource Management (HRM), having successfully managed the entire employee life cycle—from recruitment and onboarding to performance management and employee engagement. She holds an MBA in Human Resource Management, where she was recognized as a Gold Medalist and awarded the title of Best Outgoing Student. Her academic journey began with a Bachelor's degree in Electronics and Communication Engineering, showcasing her diverse educational foundation. Currently serving as an Assistant Professor, she combines industry expertise with academic insight to mentor and inspire the next generation of HR professionals

**Subramani A K** is a distinguished academic with a PhD in Business Administration from Manonmaniam Sundaranar University, Tirunelveli, India. With 18 years of teaching experience, he has made significant contributions to the field of human resource management and organisational behaviour. He has an impressive publication record with 80 articles in international journals, including two papers in the ABDC-A category, eight in the ABDC-B category, three in the ABDC-C category, 33 in Scopus-indexed journals, and eight in Web of Science journals. He has served as a resource person for various training workshops on SPSS and AMOS software packages

**Poorva Agrawal** obtained her PhD degree in Computer Science and Engineering from Symbiosis International (Deemed University), Pune, India in 2020. She obtained her M.Tech degree in Computer Science and Engineering from SGSITS, Indore, India in 2012. She has been engaged in research and teaching for more than 14 years. At present she is working as Associate Professor in CE Department at MPSTME, Mumbai, NMIMS, MH, India. She has presented more than 60 papers in International/National Journals/ Conferences. Her research interests include Artificial Intelligence, Machine Learning, Data Science, Image Processing, and Computer Vision.

**Salma El Omari** received her Master's degree in Cloud Computing and High-Performance Computing from the National Higher School for Computer Science and Systems Analysis (ENSIAS), Morocco. She is currently a Ph.D. student at Sultan Moulay Slimane University, Faculty of Sciences and Techniques. Her research interests include artificial intelligence, intelligent recommender systems, and adaptive learning technologies. Her current work focuses on developing AI-driven approaches for personalized learning path recommendation in e-learning environments

**Yonis Gulzar** is an Associate Professor in the Department of Management Information Systems at King Faisal University, Saudi Arabia. His research focuses on artificial intelligence applications in healthcare and smart agriculture, with particular emphasis on computer vision, deep learning, and intelligent decision-support systems. He is actively involved in developing AI-driven solutions for sustainable agricultural systems and medical image analysis.

**Alakananda K** is an Assistant Professor in the Department of Computer Science and Engineering at Sahyadri College of Engineering and Management, Mangaluru, Karnataka, India. Her teaching and research interests include cybersecurity, artificial intelligence, machine learning, deep learning, data science, and software engineering. She has guided undergraduate research projects in emerging areas of computing and has contributed to academic research in cybersecurity and intelligent computing. Her work focuses on applying advanced computational techniques to address contemporary challenges in information security and data-driven systems.

**Jishnu K S** is currently working as an Assistant Professor at SRM Institute of Science and Technology, Chennai. He completed his B Tech. in Computer Science from KMCT College of Engineering, affiliated with the University of Calicut, and obtained his M.Tech. from Government Engineering College, Wayanad, under APJ Abdul Kalam Technological University. He earned his Ph.D. in Computer Science and Engineering from SRM Institute of Science and Technology. His research focuses on cybersecurity and deep learning applications, with a particular emphasis on phishing detection using NLP techniques and data science projects. He has published multiple research papers and actively participated in academic conferences.

**Keerthi Krishnan** is currently working as Associate Professor in the department of Computer Science and Engineering in Marian Engineering College, Trivandrum, Kerala. Her research interest includes, Artificial Intelligence, Text Mining, Information Retrieval, Deep learning etc.

**Monisha Devi M.** completed her undergraduate degree in Biomedical Engineering (B.Tech) and is currently pursuing a postgraduate degree in Management Studies. With a multidisciplinary academic background, she offers a unique perspective connecting technology, healthcare, and management. Actively engaged in research, she demonstrates a strong commitment to innovation and collaboration across disciplines Her core competencies include data science and data analysis She applies these skills to generate data-driven insights and develop intelligent solutions, particularly in biomedical and management domains.

**Nisha Madathil** received the Bachelor's degree in Information Technology from the University of Calicut, Kerala, India, and the M.Tech degree in Computer Science and Engineering from the University of Calicut, Kerala, India. She completed her PhD in Informatics and Computing from UAE University, Abu Dhabi, UAE, in 2024. She has 12 years of teaching experience and is currently working as visiting faculty at the College of IT, UAE University. Her research interests include privacy and security, with a focus on federated learning, multiparty computation, and advanced privacy and security techniques.

**Sathwik Krishna N** received the Bachelor of Engineering (B.E.) degree in Computer Science and Engineering from Sahyadri College of Engineering and Management, Mangaluru, Karnataka, India. His research interests include artificial intelligence, deep learning, cybersecurity, malware analysis, computer vision, and 3D model generation. He has worked on research involving deep learning-based malware detection using CNN and LSTM architectures, as well as AI-driven image processing and computer vision applications. He is passionate about developing intelligent systems that address real-world cybersecurity challenges and continues to explore advanced AI-based security solutions.

**Soukaina Nai** is an IT Engineer and a PhD at the Laboratory of Computer Science, Faculty of Sciences, Ibn Tofail University, Kenitra, Morocco. Her research interests include machine learning, integrated management systems, decision support systems, evolutionary algorithms, and intelligent educational systems. Her work focuses on leveraging artificial intelligence to enhance decision-making processes and develop adaptive and data-driven solutions in complex environments. She has authored and co-authored several scientific publications in national and international journals and conferences.

**Shiju Kumar P S** is currently serving as Assistant Professor, Department of Computer Technologies, School of Computing, Faculty of Engineering and Technology at SRM Institute of Science and Technology, Kattankulathur. He has been awarded his Ph.D. in Wireless Sensor Networks from Hindustan University, Chennai. An academician for over 14 years, he is an avid learner and researcher with expertise spanning Wireless Sensor Networks, Mobile Ad-hoc Networks, Internet of Things, Machine Learning, Deep Learning, Natural Language Processing and Computational Intelligence. He has authored numerous research papers in SCI, Scopus, and WoS indexed journals and presented his work at national and international conferences. His research contributions include work on energy-efficient routing, secure data collection, AI-driven systems, and deep learning models for environmental and healthcare applications. In addition to academic responsibilities, Dr. Shiju Kumar actively contributes to curriculum design as a Member of the Board of Studies for APJ Abdul Kalam Technological University, Kerala.

**Virupakshappa Patil** is a Professor in the Department of Computer Science and Engineering at Sharnbasva University, Kalaburagi, with over 14 years of professional experience. He earned his Ph.D. in 2019 from Visvesvaraya Technological University, specializing in the computer-based analysis of MRI brain tumor images. His research interests include Digital Image Processing, Biomedical Image Processing, Pattern Recognition, and Computer Vision. Dr. Patil has published 41 international journal papers and 21 conference papers, many of which are indexed in SCI and Scopus. He is also the author of five books covering topics such as Machine Learning, Artificial Intelligence, and Deep Learning for crop disease detection.

**Amal Rifai** is a Professor of Computer Science at the Centre régional des métiers de l'éducation et de la formation (RCPET), Rabat, Morocco. She is also head of the research team in Computer Environment Engineering for Human

Learning. Her research interests include artificial intelligence, machine learning, digital systems and technology, evolutionary algorithms, and educational systems. She has published extensively in numerous journals. She can be contacted at email: rifaiamal10@gmail.com.

**Archana Nair S** is an accomplished academician serving as Assistant Professor and Head of the Department of Computer Applications at Don Bosco College, KR Puram, Bengaluru, with over 20 years of teaching experience. She specializes in computer science education with a strong focus on emerging technologies and practical learning approaches. Her research interests include Deep Learning and Convolutional Neural Networks (CNNs), where she explores innovative applications of AI to solve real-world problems. As an academic leader, she has actively contributed to organizing expert lectures, faculty development programs, and student-centered initiatives that enhance technical competence and industry readiness, reflecting her commitment to excellence in teaching, research, and institutional development.

**Abdelalim Sadiq** is a Professor of Higher Education of Computer Science, at Ibn Tofail University in Kinetra, and head of the Computer Science Research Laboratory, his research interests are Artificial Intelligence, Machine Learning, Digital Systems and Technology, Evolutionary Algorithms. He has published numerous articles in a wide range of journals.

**Chaimae Taoussi** is a PhD in Computer Science and Data Science from the National School of Applied Sciences of Khouribga, Sultan Moulay Slimane University, Morocco. Her research focuses on the analysis of medical data and the prediction of pathologies using artificial intelligence and Big Data techniques, aiming to improve diagnostic accuracy and support clinical decision-making. Her work integrates advanced data analytics, machine learning, and deep learning approaches applied to healthcare systems. Her research interests include artificial intelligence, data science, big data analytics, machine learning, deep learning, and healthcare informatics, and she is actively engaged in developing intelligent data-driven solutions for medical applications.

**Shubham Vyavahare** is a Technical Assistant in the Department of Information Technology at Walchand Institute of Technology (WIT), Solapur, where he combines a strong foundation in computer applications with an ongoing pursuit of an advanced academic degree. His technical expertise spans Artificial Intelligence, Cloud Computing, DevOps Engineering, and academic automation using Google Apps Script. An active contributor to the global academic community, he maintains a robust scholarly footprint with multiple published IGI Global book chapters, Scopus-indexed research, international-national conference presentations, and dedicated service as a peer reviewer. Beyond his academic and professional endeavors, he is deeply committed to spiritual and community service, actively coordinating major religious festivals, managing activities at the Jain Temple, and leading the publication of religious literature.

**Mahesh Yemul** holds an M.B.A. from Sinhgad Business School, Solapur University. He has worked as a Sale and Support Executive at Sinewave Computer Services Pvt Ltd. His professional experience includes four years of handling E-TDS and ITR returns, along with leading software product launching programs and relationship management.

**Rajani Yemul** holds a B.E. and an M.Tech. in Computer Science & Engineering from Punyashlok Ahilyadevi Holkar Solapur University, India, and is currently a qualified Ph.D. candidate. Her primary areas of research include Artificial Intelligence, Machine Learning, Computer Networks, and System Software. She presently serves as an Assistant Professor in the Department of Information Technology at the Walchand Institute of Technology, Solapur, India. A recent recipient of the "Best Professor Award," she has published her research extensively in reputed international journals and conferences.

# Index

## A



## B



## C



## D



## E



## F



## G



## H